SOLDIERS
OF THE KING

*This book is dedicated to those
Upper Canadians of 1812 who loyally
served their country and suffered
in its defence.
It is also dedicated to my wife, Carol,
who has never pressed the question of why
it has taken longer to write this book
than it did to fight the war.*

SOLDIERS
OF THE KING

THE UPPER
CANADIAN MILITIA
1812 ~ 1815

A Reference Guide

WILLIAM GRAY

A BOSTON MILLS PRESS BOOK

Canadian Cataloguing in Publication Data

Gray, W. M. (William Melville), 1953-
Soldiers of the King: the Upper Canadian Militia 1812-1815

ISBN 1-55046-142-7

1. Upper Canada. Militia. 2. Upper Canada. Militia - Registers.
3. Canada - History - War of 1812 - Campaigns.* I. Title.

FC442.G73 1995   971.03 '4   C95-931050-9   E359.85.G73 1995

Design and typography by Daniel Crack,
Kinetics Design & Illustration
Printed in Canada

First published in 1995 by
The Boston Mills Press
132 Main Street
Erin, Ontario
N0B 1T0
519-833-2407 fax 519-833-2195

An affiliate of
Stoddart Publishing Co. Limited
34 Lesmill Road
North York, Ontario
M3B 2T6

The publisher gratefully acknowledges the support of the Canada Council,
Ontario Arts Council and Ontario Publishing Centre in the development of
writing and publishing in Canada.

Stoddart Books are available for bulk purchase for sales promotions,
premiums, fundraising and seminars. For details, contact:

Special Sales Department
Stoddart Publishing Co. Limited
34 Lesmill Road
North York, Ontario M3B 2T6
Tel. 1-416-445-3333
Fax 1-416-445-5967

CONTENTS

PREFACE 7

A GENERAL GUIDE 11

INTRODUCTION 17
    UPPER CANADA 17
    AN OVERVIEW OF THE WAR, 1812–1815 19
    THE MILITIA ACT 25
    THE SEDENTARY MILITIA 32
    PAROLES 39
    DISAFFECTION 41
    CONCLUSION 43

I   THE MILITIA GENERAL STAFF 47

II   THE MILITIA LIST 51

III   THE FLANK COMPANIES 85

IV   THE VOLUNTEER CORPS 1812–1813 157

V   THE PROVINCIAL CORPS 179

VI   THE INCORPORATED CORPS 187

VII   THE MILITIA VOLUNTEERS 1813–1815 243

VIII   CASUALTIES 249

    BIBLIOGRAPHIC NOTE 285

PREFACE

THIS is not a history of the War of 1812. It is a reference guide to the militia of Upper Canada from 1812 to 1815 with a general introduction to the war in this province. A proposed companion volume, *The Upper Canadians' War of 1812,* will encompass in much greater detail the story of the war from the perspective of the Upper Canadians.

For a general history of the conflict, one can do no better than to turn to J. Mackay Hitsman's *The Incredible War of 1812* (Toronto: University of Toronto Press, 1965). Hitsman's account, published 30 years ago, has yet to be surpassed. It offers an incisive and balanced view of the war and of wartime occurrences in this province, and quite naturally is preoccupied with the men who bore the brunt of the action, the regular forces of the Crown.

However, there is another story that deserves more study, that of the militia of Upper Canada. It is one that has never been adequately told; it is a complex tale with many conflicting plots and a largely unknown cast of characters. It is impossible, given the paucity of information that has survived, to offer a definitive account, but it is possible to present some underlying factors that cast new light on the situation. One way of exploring the conflict is through the militia's participation.

A basic truth that must be accepted is that the postwar interpretations of the war and its times reflected postwar realities. The ongoing constitutional wrangling that dominated Upper Canada for decades following the war, and that culminated in the

Rebellion of 1837, coloured the thinking of observers and participants. In the next generation the story was skewed, the role the regular forces was downplayed, and a disproportionate amount of attention was given to the militia and its valiant successes in throwing out the foreign "banditti" with the help of a handful of regular troops.

Historians started to seriously question this so-called militia myth at the turn of the century, and it has now become popular in some circles to interpret the events of those days in simple terms of disaffection, or at best the passive neutrality of the inhabitants.

There is a wealth of information in the surviving records of the adjutant general of militia's files that brings a new if incomplete picture of the situation in this province during those tumultuous days. It is a picture at odds with the commonly accepted facts about the local situation. Drawing on returns, muster lists and other contemporary documents, a more complete account of the nature and extent of the participation of the people of Upper Canada in the war is revealed.

In 1819 Nathaniel Coffin, the adjutant general of militia, called on the commanding officers to make returns of those who were eligible to apply for the Prince Regent's bounty; to apply for waste lands in recognition for their services to the Crown during the war. The nominal list that was eventually assembled included the men who had served with the Incorporated Militia Battalion and were regularly discharged, the men who had served with the flank companies in 1812, the men who had been called out on actual service who were enrolled in other volunteer corps. For reasons that are not clear, this composite nominal list did not include returns from Glengarry, Hastings or Kent counties.

In the 1870s there was a move to recognize the men who had served in the militia during conflict. The clerks were instructed to determine who was entitled to receive the bounty of the Dominion government and discovered the nominal return of men who were entitled to apply for the Prince Regent's bounty, which had been offered half a century earlier. This list was incomplete and misleading, as it excluded all those who had served but were ineligible to apply for a grant of land.

To compound this misconception, historians have often turned to a return that indicates that 1,800 men were enrolled in the flank companies. However, if this return does in fact refer to the flank companies, it would reflect only the peacetime enrolment. The companies that were formed in the spring of 1812 were typically only made up of 25 to 35 rank and file and were only filled up to the regulated numbers in early July 1812, after war had been declared. The number of rank and file who served in the flank companies was over 4,000.

In examining accounts of the war in Upper Canada it must be borne in mind that all the official written reports were composed by British military authorities for a specific audience: their superiors, either in Lower Canada or at the Horse Guards in London. They dealt primarily with the regular forces and they reflected the concerns of the local commanding officer. No officer commanding during the conflict was happy with the level of regular support he received or the number of troops that each had at his disposal in the upper province (let alone the lower), and the one constant refrain was the absolute and vital need for more men for the successful prosecution of the war.

The officers identified in dispatches and the corps singled out were quite understandably the regulars, the men and units whose reputations and careers were dependent on their being drawn to the attention of the authorities at home. The officers of the militia and the men of the various corps were either overlooked or in some cases added as an afterthought, since they were not part of the establishment.

The militia was seen as both a boon and an obstacle by the officers commanding. They wanted more men, but they wanted men who would be subject to the discipline that they felt necessary to the successful management of the war effort. The Upper Canadian militia did not, in general, provide what they wanted. There was a peculiar mind set, endorsed wholeheartedly by successive commanders, that the Upper Canadian males enrolled in the militia should act and perform as regularly enlisted men in the forces. As late as 1812 official thinking was that no more than a third of the men were safe to arm.

In this volume I attempt to present a brief guide to the militia corps that were active during the war and a nominal list of the commissioned officers, and the men who volunteered to serve in corps outside of their legislated responsibilities as members of the sedentary militia. I must emphasize that this guide is to be seen as an aid and not a definitive account of their service. Readers who have information to add to or correct that presented in this volume are encouraged to write to me so that a more complete and accurate guide can be produced at a later date.

The names of the officers and volunteers are generally recorded as found in the nominal rolls assembled after the war. Very few French Canadians were literate, and only about three out of five of the rest of the population could sign their names; as a result there are a number of highly original phonetic variations. French Canadians suffered particularly in this regard.

I am indebted to Carl Benn, Don Graves and especially Stuart Sutherland for their support and assistance. They are not responsible for the book's contents, for factual errors and omissions, or the interpretation presented in this volume.

A GENERAL GUIDE

THERE is no index to this work. It has been organized by subject and many cross-references have been included, where known.

An act of the provincial legislature, *The Militia Act* defined the legal responsibilities of the male population for the defence of the province. Provision was made for its enforcement and allowed for penalties for non-compliance. Revisions and supplementary laws were passed to meet changing circumstances, during the war, on an annual basis.

Colonels, lieutenant colonels, majors (known collectively as field officers), captains, lieutenants, ensigns and adjutants (the regimental officers) of the militia were commissioned by the Crown to hold and exercise the responsibilities of their respective ranks. Date of commission determined seniority among officers of the same rank within a regiment. A typical militia regiment, composed of all eligible men between 16 and 60 living within a defined geographic boundary, was divided into ten companies, each company commanded by a captain. The captain was assisted by one or two subaltern officers (a lieutenant and/or an ensign) and two or three sergeants. Sergeants and corporals (where appointed) were non-commissioned officers and held their appointments at the pleasure of the officer commanding the regiment. Drummers and fifers attached to a company were noted in nominal or numerical reports, called returns, but again did not hold commissions. The regiment (sometimes referred to as the battalion; there was no distinction made in the militia or the regulars) was designated by the name of the county within which it was based; if there was one regiment it was the 1st; if two, the 1st and 2nd, and so on.

Each regiment would be commanded by a colonel or a lieutenant colonel, who would be assisted by a major. These field officers (who alone were mounted) would command the regimental officers, who could number up to 30, if each of the ten companies had a full complement of commissioned officers, that is, a captain, a lieutenant, and an ensign. If a company was mounted, it was referred to as a troop of horse, or troop of dragoons, and the ensign was called a cornet.

This provincial organization was known as the sedentary militia. Militiamen who were called out and either volunteered or were drafted to serve for a defined (and relatively short period, generally no more than a month) were described as "embodied militia." Militiamen who were embodied for a longer period but who were governed by the provisions of the local militia act were designated "incorporated." Men who were recruited for service within the province but under the provisions of the articles of war, that is, British regulations, were in a sense "provincial regulars."

All men known to have held commissions, or known to have been recommended and to have acted, are entered in *The Militia List*. The list is arranged by county division. The counties are organized in the traditional fashion, reading from east to west. There is a list of the districts and counties on the back flap of the dust jacket that may be used as a ready reference. The commissioned men enumerated in each of the regimental divisions are listed alphabetically, and note is made if they are known to be found elsewhere in this guide.

Section I, *The Militia General Staff,* outlines the organization of the staff and names the principal men responsible for the various branches of the militia department by district.

In 1812, companies of volunteers from each regimental division were authorized, and denominated *Flank Companies*. These companies were all "reduced," or disbanded, in the spring of 1813. The nominal rolls of the flank companies are arranged by county and, where known, by company.

There were a number of other *Volunteer Corps* that were organized in 1812 across the province. These units were joined in

1813 by *Provincial Corps,* who were enlisted as "provincial regulars;" *Incorporated Corps*, militia units enlisted under the provisions of the Militia Act of 1813; and additional companies of *Militia Volunteers.*

In each of these principal sections of this guide — *The Militia List, The Flank Companies, The Volunteer Corps 1812–1813, The Provincial Corps, The Incorporated Corps,* and *The Militia Volunteers 1813–1815* — there is a brief outline of the corps included, and note is made of many other known references in other sections. A Military General Service Medal (GSM) was issued in 1848 for those who were present at Chrysler's Farm and at Detroit. Medals were only issued to those who applied.

The final section, *Casualties,* is a nominal list of some 575 militiamen who were killed, died of disease, were wounded, or made prisoners of war and removed to the United States. No note is made of those who were captured and paroled. This section has been intentionally called a preliminary list and as such must be relied upon with greater caution.

REFERENCE INDEX TO MILITIA

The province was divided into eight districts, and each district into counties. The incorporated and provincial corps were recruited across the province. Flank companies, volunteer companies and troops were generally raised within the different sedentary regimental boundaries.

INCORPORATED CORPS

	Section	Page
Incorporated Provincial Light Dragoons	VI	197
Incorporated Provincial Artillery Company	VI	201
Battalion of Incorporated Militia	VI	202

PROVINCIAL CORPS

	Section	Page
Provincial Light Dragoons Niagara (Captain Merritt's)	V	182
Royal Provincial Artillery Drivers	V	183
Corps of Artificers (The Coloured Company)	V	185

THE SEDENTARY REGIMENTS AND
VOLUNTEER COMPANIES AND TROOPS

Eastern District

	Section	Page
1st Glengarry		
Flank Companies	III	96
2nd Glengarry		
Flank Companies	III	98
1st Prescott		
1st Stormont		
Flank Companies	III	101
1st Dundas		
Flank Companies	III	104

Johnstown District

1st Grenville		
Flank Companies	III	105
Rifle Company	IV	106
2nd Grenville		
Flank Companies	III	107
Troop of Horse	IV	163
1st Leeds		
Flank Companies	III	108
Troop of Horse	IV	162
Rifle Company	IV	161
2nd Leeds		
Flank Companies	III	112
Rifle Company	IV	161

Midland District

1st Frontenac		
Flank Companies	III	114
Artillery Company	IV	171
1st Lennox		
Flank Companies	III	117
Troop of Horse	IV	164

	Section	Page
1st Addington		
Flank Companies	III	119
Troop of Horse	IV	165
1st Hastings		
Flank Companies	III	122
1st Prince Edward		
Flank Companies	III	123
Troop of Horse	IV	166

Newcastle District

1st Northumberland		
Flank Companies	III	125
1st Durham		
Flank Company	III	126

Home District

1st York		
Flank Company	III	127
Troop of Horse	IV	168
Rifle Company	IV	176
2nd York		
Flank Companies	III	128
3rd York		
Flank Companies	III	130

Niagara District

1st Lincoln		
Flank Companies	III	132
Troop of Horse	IV	160
Artillery Company	IV	172
2nd Lincoln		
Flank Companies	III	136
Troop of Horse	IV	160
Artillery Company	IV	174
3rd Lincoln		
Flank Companies	III	138
4th Lincoln		
Flank Companies	III	140
5th Lincoln		
Flank Companies	III	143

London District

	Section	Page
The Loyal London Volunteers	VII	244
1st Norfolk		
Flank Companies	III	145
2nd Norfolk		
Flank Companies	III	146
1st Oxford		
Flank Companies	III	148
Rifle Company	IV	178
1st Middlesex		
Flank Companies	III	149

Western District

The Western Rangers	VII	245
1st Essex		
Flank Companies	III	151
Marine Company	IV	159
Loyal Essex Volunteers, or Essex Rangers	VII	247
2nd Essex		
Flank Companies	III	153
Troop of Horse	IV	160
1st Kent		
Flank Company	III	155
Troop of Horse	IV	160
Loyal Kent Volunteers, or Kent Rangers	VII	245

INTRODUCTION

UPPER CANADA

PROVISION for the division of the Province of Quebec and the establishment of Upper Canada as a separate colony was made by an act of the Imperial Parliament in 1791. The area had been governed as a part of Quebec, and initially had been administered as a part of the District of Montreal. As a result of the increase of population with the coming of the Loyalists, it had been subdivided in 1788 into four new districts: Lunenburg, Mecklenburg, Nassau and Hesse.

The districts were renamed and subdivided as the population grew, and in 1812 Upper Canada consisted of eight districts: the Eastern, Johnstown, Midland, Newcastle, Home, Niagara, London and Western. Each of these districts was made up of a number of counties, and the counties of townships. The boundaries of the districts and counties could and did change. Townships, as units of survey, were for the most part unchanging.

The counties were primarily used for the definition of electoral divisions or ridings, and for the organization of the sedentary militia.

The provincial legislature was a traditional bicameral body; it consisted of an elected assembly and an appointed legislative council. Suffrage was extended to virtually all freeholders (of either sex). There were 16 members elected to the assembly in the first parliament and 24 by 1812.

The principal local political organization was the district. Justices of the peace, or magistrates, were appointed by the lieutenant-governor in each district. The magistrates, meeting in the Court of Quarter Sessions, chaired by the clerk of the peace, formed the basis of local government. This court both tried legal cases and was responsible for the general administration of the community.

The principal officers of the district were the clerk of the peace, the treasurer, the sheriff and the district court judges — all appointed by the lieutenant-governor. There were numerous other positions appointed by the governor, and in many instances one man would hold many commissions.

It is thought that the population of Upper Canada in 1812 was about 75,000. This figure does not include the Native inhabitants, who may have numbered 3,500. A very significant element of the general population were recent immigrants from the United States, and in many districts they were a clear majority.

Most of the province was very thinly settled, and while there were pockets of wealth and settlers with flourishing farms and merchants with fine homes, it was still very much a frontier society. At the war's end there were approximately 2,000 men of all ranks enrolled in the militia and 1,710 properties assessed in the Eastern District. The properties assessed averaged 22 acres of land classified as arable, pasture or meadow, one or two horses, and three milk cows. There was one ox for every three assessed properties. There were 25 brick or stone houses, about 300 of squared timber and 365 of framed timber. The majority were shanties or simple log cabins.

A survey that was made of the resources of a part of Norfolk County early in 1814 illustrates something of the state of the people to the west of the Niagara Peninsula. It was an area with good agricultural potential and had been open to settlement for over 15 years. The typical farm consisted of 10 to 20 acres cleared and under cultivation, 2 or 3 milk cows, 1 or 2 horses or oxen, half a dozen sheep and a few hogs. Of one group of 26 farms supporting 150 people, there were 140 acres in wheat and 79 in rye; 32 horses, 21 oxen, 54 milk cows, 35 horned cattle, 66 hogs and 113 sheep. In total the inhabitants owned but 6 wagons and 11 sleighs.

The perpetual shortage of money (specie) was a major concern before the war, and during the war became much more acute. There were any number of different coins in circulation, but accounts were kept in pounds (£), shillings and pence: 12 pennies made one shilling and 20 shillings one pound. Unless otherwise noted, all monetary references in the text are quoted in Halifax or provincial currency, which was worth about 10 percent less than sterling.

Under normal conditions a farmer in Upper Canada could expect a yield of up to 20 to 25 bushels of wheat to the acre, or the equivalent of four or five barrels of flour. Millers using traditional practices could get about one barrel of flour (196 lbs was standard measure) from six bushels of wheat (Winchester measure, 60 lbs of wheat to the bushel). Prior to the war a new process had been introduced that significantly improved the yields; five bushels rather than six would make a barrel of superfine flour.

To help put the currency in perspective, a barrel of flour in 1812 sold for about 45 shillings, a bateau cost £15 to £17, and a day labourer could earn 3 to 5 shillings a day.

AN OVERVIEW OF THE WAR
~ 1812 ~

In October 1811 Major General Isaac Brock was appointed head of the military and civil establishments of Upper Canada. The lieutenant-governor, Francis Gore, had been granted a leave of absence and returned to England. His timely withdrawal from Upper Canada may have been a part of a plan to concentrate the civil and military authority to better prepare the province for war.

Brock toured the province extensively, concentrating his efforts on bringing the military works on land and the vessels that made up the Provincial Marine on the lakes into some sort of order and on courting the Native people. Most important, he was showing the flag to the local population, reassuring them that Upper Canada would not be abandoned in a general withdrawal to Montreal, but would be defended in the event of an American attack.

In the spring sitting of the legislature in 1812, he attempted to intiate a series of measures that would enhance his ability to defend the province, both from enemies without and from the all too numerous enemies within. He was largely successful, though not satisfied with what he considered the half-measures adopted by the assembly.

A principal feature of the new Militia Act called for the formation of unpaid volunteer companies called flank companies that were to be armed, accoutred, and partially trained. The "flankers" were to provide a body of loyal young men that could be called on in an emergency. In addition, other volunteer companies of horse, artillery and rifles were authorized.

Brock also turned his attention to the organization of the sedentary militia that spring. He ordered the division of the regiments in Glengarry, Grenville, the 1st York (divided into 1st and 3rd) and Norfolk, and he had a new regiment formed in Middlesex. He attempted to bring the militia list up-to-date, commissioning officers to fill vacancies across the province.

The United States declared war on Great Britain on June 18, 1812. Their principal objective in the first campaign was the occupation of Upper Canada and as much of Lower Canada down the St. Lawrence as possible. Active preparations for the war had commenced in late 1811.

A large army crossed the Detroit River in July and took Sandwich (Windsor). The initial response of the Upper Canadians satisfied the most sanguine hopes of the Americans and also met the worst apprehensions of the British. Over half the militia simply melted away, many returning to their homes. A significant minority joined the enemy. It appeared that the American claim, that the taking of Upper Canada would be merely a matter of marching, was realistic.

Brock issued a directive on the 9th of July that was the cause of a great deal of confusion and discontent. In it he laid out the regulations that were to govern the numbers of commissioned officers that could be mustered according to the size of the companies that were on actual service. For every company consisting of 30 rank and file, one captain and two subalterns would be entitled to receive pay and allowances; for every company consisting of more than 80 rank and file, one captain and three subalterns; for every 250 rank and file, one field officer, and so on. As a result, no field officer in Kent, Middlesex, Durham, Hastings, Prescott and the 2nd Essex would be eligible for pay if embodied with their county division, since all mustered fewer than 250 rank and file. In addition a great many battalion companies did not consist of 30 men and the commanding captain would thus not be eligible for pay when the sedentary companies were called out.

In a daring stroke in early July the British seized the American post at Michilimackinac, and Brock, in an even more audacious move, demanded and received the surrender of the American army at Detroit on the 16th of August. The Americans now turned their attentions to the Niagara Peninsula, where they launched another invasion on October 13. Once again they were defeated and their force captured, but not before Brock had been killed. He was succeeded by Major General Roger Hale Sheaffe. Another abortive attempt was made by the Americans at Fort Erie in late November before the campaigning season ended.

At the close of 1812 the Americans had twice been decisively repulsed on the Niagara frontier, had been dramatically defeated at Detroit, and had been effectually thrown out of the Northwest with the capitulation of Michilimackinac. It was the high point of the war for the Crown.

The role of the militia was considerable in these very significant affairs. At Detroit more than half of the men (other than the Native allies, whose role was without doubt a determining factor) were militiamen. On the Niagara, half to two thirds of the men on duty were from the militia; at York, all the men; and at Kingston, the majority. The Provincial Marine on both lakes was brought up to strength by local levies, and the posts securing the St. Lawrence were manned entirely by local forces. In all, about three of five of the men under arms supporting the Crown in Upper Canada throughout the first campaign were drawn from the local population.

~ 1813 ~

Although a great many men had turned out in 1812, in many instances they had proved of little use to the regular officers commanding. They did not entertain the same appreciation for discipline and subordination as the regulars. In addition, the severe shortage of all manner of supplies, from clothing to camp equipage, and the critical scarcity of money of any description with which to pay the men led to discontent.

Sheaffe tidied up many of the administrative loose ends from the previous year, authorizing appointments that had been irregularly made and organizing the militia general staff. He also decided against trying to get the legislature to renew the authorization of the flank companies for another year. Instead he wanted a troop of provincial light dragoons, a company of artillery drivers and a company of artificers raised that could be considered provincial regulars, distinct from the sedentary organization. This measure was intended to encourage men who had been serving through 1812 in the Niagara Troop, the Car Brigade, and the Coloured Company (the Corps of Artificers) to enlist in corps that would be subject to greater discipline, and that would, it was hoped, prove more dependable. He planned to replace the flankers with companies of infantry raised under the provisions of the Militia Act to serve for 18 months, or the duration of the war, whichever was shorter.

The general lot of the militia was greatly improved in early March when Sheaffe ordered that provisions be issued to the wives and children of all ranks while the men were actually on duty. At the same time he appointed a board of accounts to examine all claims against the government in an effort to bring some order to the haphazard settlement of pay matters, claims for damage, and purchases by the commissariat.

This year the Americans again took the offensive, and this time with success. They took York on April 27, occupying the town for a few days, and the British garrison retired to Kingston. A month later Fort George was taken by assault and the British withdrew from the whole Niagara front in the direction of the Head-of-the-Lake (Burlington). The American pursuit was repulsed in the night action at Stoney Creek on June 6, and suffered another setback when a detached force was forced to surrender at Beaver Dams on June 23.

The American forces then withdrew to Fort George, abandoning Fort Erie (which they blew up) and the intermediate strong points. The British, though numerically inferior, then began to push back into the district and settled into a seige of the American camp at Niagara. Many of the militia were captured and paroled in these actions, a number joined the enemy, and many more were paroled in an unorthodox fashion while not under arms when the Americans were in control of the townships.

In 1813 the situation had changed very dramatically. In the centre of the province, the early successes of the Americans at York and on the Niagara Frontier were effectively countered by the end of the year with the withdrawal of the Americans from Upper Canada and the successful storming of Fort Niagara. In the west, the Americans had destroyed the British squadron on Lake Erie in September and then the Right Division at Moraviantown in October. They occupied the Western District and were in a postion to threaten the London District. In the east, the major American campaign on the St. Lawrence in the late autumn had collapsed with defeats at Chateauguay and Chrysler's Farm.

~ 1814 ~

Well, what then of 1814? The British were obviously making a tangible effort to prosecute the war to a successful conclusion. It was evident to all but the most determined of the disaffected inhabitants that the upper province was not going to be simply abandoned in a general withdrawal to the key to the Canadas, Quebec.

The reinforcement of the regular troops, the quantities of supplies being moved laboriously up the lines, and most important, the steady stream of good news from Europe of the successes of the allied armies — all boded well for the future. The tremendous shipbuilding program and new fortifications at Kingston, the establishment of York as a defensible post, and the entrenchments and associated works at Burlington were a clear demonstration of the determination of the British to hold Upper Canada.

Fort Niagara was still firmly in the control of the Crown, and Fort George was in the process of being reestablished as a significant position with new works at Mississauga Point. And in addition, a new work was being thrown up on Queenston Heights, Fort Drummond, or Drummond Castle. In the early spring a strong detachment of troops was stationed at Long Point to reestablish a regular presence in the London District.

Most of the overtly treasonous locals had decamped by this time. The population in some districts had decreased by about a fifth over the previous two years. The temper of the townships must have shown a decided change with the removal of those who actively courted the change of authority.

It must be emphasized that there was a basic distrust of the military and its pretensions. Even the most loyal were yet free-born Britons governed by common law, and while they might be firm in their allegiance to the Crown, they were also firm in their commitment to the rights of property and due process. Arbitrary actions on the part of the military were unwelcome.

The new commanding officer and head of the civil administration, Lieutenant General Gordon Drummond, was determined to make more efficient use of the militia in the 1814 campaign than Sheaffe had been able to in 1813. An important element of his plan was to call out, or embody, very large numbers of men for a longer period of time than had been the case the previous year. He wanted to call out three fourteenths of the sedentary militia for one year, which would have resulted in a draft of slightly more than one fifth of the male population. The provincial legislature, which was on the whole amenable to the initiatives laid before it, balked, and would only agree to the conscription of one fourteenth. Drummond was unhappy because it had been estimated that 750 men (about the same number that the legislature agreed could be drafted) were required for bateau service alone.

Nevertheless hundreds were embodied from the 10th of June at Prescott, Kingston and York and on the lines at Niagara. Drummond thought that more than the stipulated fourteenth were required in the Home District. As a result, one third of the militia in the Home District was called out on June 10, and 179 of them were attached to the Incorporated Militia Battalion at York, where they drilled with the battalion. They were outfitted and accoutred, as far as possible, as regulars. As was common, 10 percent of those who were drafted and attached to the battalion deserted, but the men who were simply embodied to garrison the post proved much less inclined to desert. This may have had something to do with the discipline and "subordination" that was the hallmark of Lieutenant Colonel William Robinson, the officer commanding the Incorporated Battalion.

The remaining embodied militia were stationed at the garrison and commanded by Major William Allan of the 3rd York. More men were called out at the beginning of July to make up for the regulars and the incorporated militia who were hurriedly being pressed forward to the front in response to the new American invasion of July 3. On the 7th of July, 530 of all ranks from the 1st and 3rd York and 1st Durham sedentary militia were embodied at York. About 1,000 others from the 2nd York, 5th Lincoln, and London Districts assembled at Burlington. Over 775 of all ranks in the London District were embodied in July.

Major actions near Niagara Falls at Chippewa and Lundy's Lane in July were followed by the seige of Fort Erie before the American army withdrew to the United States at the end of October. The principal role of the regular forces in the eventual repulsion of the American army in 1814 cannot be overstated. At the same time the contribution of the militia to the successful frustration of their designs must be recognized. Many references to the militia in official reports clearly indicate that there were a great number in the field in 1814.

THE MILITIA ACT

Whereas a well regulated Militia is of the utmost importance to the defence of this Province...

The military obligations of Upper Canadians were detailed by acts of the local legislature. The Militia Act of 1793, the first law governing the militia in Upper Canada, was amended on a number of occasions, and in the winter of 1807, with a heightened threat of war with the United States, all the legislation governing the militia was revised. A new act consolidated the laws and was signed on March 16, 1808, by Lieutenant-Governor Francis Gore.

New supplementary acts were passed in February and August of 1812, February 1813, and February 1814. These "war" acts were designed to meet the exigencies of the times and were specifically drawn up to remain in force only for a stated period; generally until the end of the next ensuing sitting of the legislature. The basic law was still that of 1808.

The principal provisions of the 1808 act called for every male inhabitant from 16 to 60 years of age who was deemed capable of bearing arms to enrol in the company in which division he lived on the first training day that was called after his coming of age or after moving within the company limits.

Provision was made for Quakers, Mennonites and Tunkers, who, "from certain scruples of conscience decline bearing arms," to not serve. Each year they were required to register with the treasurer of their respective districts by December 1 and pay 20 shillings in peacetime, and £5 in time of war or insurrection if the militia of the district was called out. These sums were not token amounts and would have proved a significant burden to the average farmer. The penalty in peacetime would have been about a week's or more wages for a day labourer; in wartime, one month's wages.

The act also exempted, except in time of actual service, judges of the Court of King's Bench, the clergy, the members of the legislative and executive councils and their respective officers, the members of the House of Assembly and its respective officers, the civil officers of the province (attorney general, solicitor general, and so on), magistrates, sheriffs, coroners, half-pay officers, militia officers who had held a commission in any of the King's dominions and had not been cashiered, the surveyor general and his deputies, seafaring men actually employed in the line of their calling, physicians, surgeons, masters of public schools, ferrymen, and one miller to every grist mill. That was not to say that anyone who fell within this list of exempted men could not hold commissions, and the majority did in fact hold commissions in the sedentary militia.

Organization

A regiment was to consist of no more than ten companies and no fewer than eight; the county division was styled a battalion if there were five to eight companies. The companies were to be composed of no more than 50 privates and no less than 20. A colonel, lieutenant colonel and major were to be appointed for each regiment; a lieutenant colonel and major were to be appointed to a battalion. In counties where there were not sufficient men to form a battalion, independent companies were authorized and no field officers were to be commissioned. According to regulations, a battalion could muster as few as 100 rank and file and a regiment up to 500.

In February 1812, Brock's Militia Act allowed for companies to consist of up to 100 men. This was done to provide for flank companies to be established in each battalion. The flank companies were to be composed of not more than one third of the battalion strength. For example, if a battalion numbered 450 rank and file, then each of the two companies would have no more than 75 privates enrolled; if there were 300, then each flank company would consist of 50 rank and file. This provision was rescinded in 1813 and the maximum number of rank and file in a company was once again made 50.

Training

The officer commanding a regiment was to call out each regiment or battalion every year for annual training on the 4th of June (King George III's birthday) or on the following day, if the 4th fell on a Sunday. Failure to turn out resulted in a fine of 40 shillings for officers and 10 shillings for non-commissioned officers and privates. Captains were to call out their companies at least twice and no more than four times annually for inspection and exercise, having duly warned their companies six days in advance. Again the fines for neglect or disobedience of orders were 40 shillings for officers and 10 shillings for other ranks.

Limits of Service

The militia was to serve anywhere in the province in times of emergency. They could also be called on to serve on the Lakes. The militia could only be marched out of Upper Canada under certain carefully defined circumstances: if Lower Canada was invaded or in a state of insurrection, the Upper Canadian militia could be ordered to march to the lower province; or in time of war, they could be ordered to pursue an enemy who had invaded; or if it were clear that an invasion of the province was imminent, they could be ordered to attack and destroy magazines, depots, fortifications, vessels and so on across the border. If an officer refused, he was to be fined £50 and lose his commission, other ranks would be fined £20; and, in case of default, would be jailed for 6 to 12 months.

Periods of Service

It was specified that no militiaman would have to serve more than six months, and no man over the age of 50 would be embodied or called out on service unless the whole body of militia in that district was called out. Allowance was made for a militiaman to provide an able-bodied substitute if only a part of the militia was called out. If the entire body was called, no substitutes were allowed.

Commissioning of Officers

All officers were to be commissioned by the lieutenant-governor and were to rank with the regular officers in the province as the most junior of their respective ranks. In other words, a major of the militia whose commission was dated in 1800 would be considered the junior of a regular major whose commission was dated later. Under Simcoe's act, officers had to be landowners (with unencumbered title) within their militia limits of a set number of acres; colonels and lieutenant colonels had to be in possession of 400 acres, majors and captains 300 acres, and subaltern officers 200 acres. This consideration was dropped in 1808.

Subordination

Non-commissioned officers and privates who refused to obey lawful orders or abused their officers could be fined from 10 shillings to £5 at the discretion of the local magistrate. In the spring of 1812 this stipulation was changed to allow for regimental courts-martial.

Enforcement

Gore's act was to be enforced by the local magistrates with the significant exceptions of mutiny, desertion, desertion to the enemy, incitement to mutiny or desertion, and the use of traitorous or disrespectful language against any of the royal family or the person administering the province. In these cases the lieutenant-governor would order a general court-martial.

A general court-martial was to be assembled on order of the lieutenant-governor to the officer commanding the regiment. The court was to be composed of a president (who was to be a field officer) and 12 other commissioned officers of the militia. The judge advocate was to be appointed by the lieutenant-governor. There was no mention made in the act of regimental or garrison courts-martial; the primary burden for the enforcement of the act lay with the local justices of the peace.

The act provided for the death penalty in the case of defection to the enemy and in cases of mutiny or sedition, or any lesser punishment as awarded by a general court-martial. Flogging or whipping was a standard method of maintaining discipline in the regular forces, but in the militia it was specifically stated that no militiaman could be subject to corporal punishment. A stated scale of fines for various misdemeanors was laid out, and failure to pay resulted in confinement in the district jail.

Impressment of Carriages and Teams

Officers were permitted to apply to a magistrate for a warrant to impress carriages and horses. The owners were to receive 7 shillings 6 pence per day for every cart or carriage and pair of horses or oxen detained on public service. This provision was amended in 1812 to allow for a payment of 10 shillings if a driver with his team and cart were impressed. In 1813 this was increased to 12 shillings 6 pence for each carriage and team and a further 2 shillings 6 pence for a driver. The following year this was increased again to 20 shillings for a carriage, team and driver and 15 shillings without a driver. In addition, provision was made for the impressment of horses at 7 shillings 6 pence per day.

Brock's Act of February 1812

Significant changes were made by the legislature to the Militia Act in response to Brock's requests, though he was still not happy with the result. Nevertheless, a number of problems and weaknesses with the old act were addressed in an effort to make the militia of the province a more effectual force.

The potential for problems developing between regular and militia officers was reduced by making all militia colonels and lieutenant colonels subject to the commands of any lieutenant colonel of the line.

If any militiaman (commissioned officers excepted) was killed or died on active service, his widow and family would be eligible for an annuity of £5. If the militiaman was disabled and incapable of earning his livelihood, he would be eligible for an annuity of £9.

Incidents of insubordination were defined as the refusal to obey orders, quarrelling and the use of abusive language to an officer or non-commissioned officer, or general misbehaviour, and they would now be quickly dealt with. The commanding officer could order the miscreant taken into immediate custody and tried by a court-martial composed of three militia officers. This court could impose fines of 5 shillings to £5, or order the offender, if in default of payment, to be committed to the district jail for a period of three days to one month. If three officers were not available to form a court-martial within 12 hours, the offender was to be released from confinement and tried before the local justice of the peace.

In addition, it was stipulated that if anyone was deemed to interrupt or disturb a party of militia while on duty, the officer commanding was permitted to detain them and bring them before the nearest justice of the peace for trial. The offender could be fined from 10 shillings to £5, or sentenced to ten days to a month in the common jail.

The regulation that stated that the militia could not be called out on active service for more than six months was repealed. The new regulation called for one third of the detachment to be balloted and relieved by a new draft at the end of six months' service, the second third at the end of seven months, and the remainder at the end of eight months' service.

The act included a number of important articles designed to force the issue of loyalty to the Crown. All officers were required to take and to subscribe an oath of allegiance on or before June 4 in front of one or more of the district justices of the peace. All non-commissioned officers and privates could be called on to take the same oath. Anyone who refused or neglected to take the oath, and was convicted by the Court of Quarter Sessions in time of peace, or before a court-martial in time of war, was to be deemed an alien.

The oath included an unequivocable declaration of loyalty to King George III, and affirmed the obligation to defend "his Person, Crown and Dignity, and particularly his Dominions in North America." In addition, the subscriber swore to do his "utmost endeavour to disclose and make known to his Majesty, his heirs or successors all treasons and traitorous conspiracies and attempts." The subscriber swore the oath "without any equivocation, mental evasion, or secret reservation, and renouncing all pardons and dispensations from any person or power whatsoever to the contrary."

Fines and penalties that had previously been paid to the district treasurer were now to be forwarded to the receiver general of the province for the general use of the militia.

Brock's Act of August 1812

Brock wrote despairingly about the new assembly and its lack of will in responding to his measures that were designed to promote the war effort. However, it is clear in examining the revised act adopted at this session that a number of changes were adopted to strengthen its enforcement. Courts-martial that tried non-commissioned officers and privates who refused to obey orders or acted in a disrespectful manner could now impose fines of up to £20 in time of war, that is, four times what had been allowed in the act passed that spring.

Furthermore, in time of war or emergency, if an officer did not march when ordered to any part of the province, or absconded, he would be tried by court-martial or two or more justices and would be cashiered and subjected to a fine of £50. A non-commissioned officer or private would be fined £20 and, in case of default, both officers and other ranks could be jailed for 6 to 12 months.

Sheaffe's Act of February 1813

In the spring of 1813 Major General Sheaffe introduced a new act, the principal provision of which allowed for the raising of companies of incorporated militia to be formed into one or more regiments. The regulations authorizing the flank companies were not included in the new act and as a result they were disbanded.

The other principal measures that were introduced were concerned with the more effectual enforcement of penalties; they dealt with the mechanics of courts-martial, the collection of fines and of costs that were awarded.

Drummond's Act of February 1814

Sheaffe's scheme of raising volunteers to be enrolled in incorporated companies was not nearly as successful as had been hoped. General Drummond, the new head of the civil and military administration of the province, faced with the perennial shortage of men, was determined to make more effective use of the militia. He proposed that three fourteenths of all the militia should be conscripted for one years' service and attached to the incorporated corps. The legislature thought that this was entirely unrealistic and would only agree to the conscription of one fourteenth.

THE SEDENTARY MILITIA

The militia was organized by county. As townships were filled up and the population increased, the limits would be divided and a second regiment created, officers were commissioned, and the limits, or beats, of the individual companies established.

The companies that made up the regiments varied in size from 20 to over 50 rank and file. Many included drummers and fifers on their rolls: the 1st Lincoln, for instance, had purchased 12 suitably painted new drums in 1811. From numerous references it would appear that officers were uniformed, and again turning to the 1st Lincoln, a uniform complete with silver epaulettes had been purchased with regimental funds for the regimental sergeant major.

Regiments in closest proximity to the American border were supplied with a number of stands of arms of varying makes. An effort was made before the war to collect some of the arms that had been distributed and to concentrate British arms on the Niagara Peninsula and French arms at York.

At the annual training days on the King's Birthday, there was a rudimentary effort to perform simple manoeuvres on the field, general orders were read, and shooting contests were conducted, the winning shot often taking a hat as a prize. It was not unusual for the day to end in a general jollification and brawl.

Before the war, it was thought that only about a third of the militia was safe to arm. The majority of the men enrolled were relatively recent arrivals from the United States, who had no particular affection for the Crown, but who had a decided interest in good lands, at a good price, with minimal taxation. Many of these new Upper Canadians, only just establishing themselves on the new frontier, together with those who either sympathized with the Americans or sought to better their positions, gambled that the Americans would prevail, and fled to the United States or were expelled as aliens.

The composite militia returns for the war years makes this graphically clear.

Year	1812	1813	1814	1815
Colonels	14	12	13	12
Lieutenant Colonels	23	25	24	23
Majors	26	28	28	27
Captains	246	259	247	240
Lieutenants	255	268	252	246
Ensigns	244	264	246	240
Adjutants	23	27	25	23
Quarter Masters	24	25	22	22
Sergeants	745	752	727	725
Drummers	18	21	18	16
Rank and File	11,650	10,819	9,455	10,096

The totals for rank and file include all men from 16 to 60. The regimental returns sometimes included all Mennonites, Quakers and Tunkers, though they were not expected to bear arms. Note was also made that about 1,000 men of the return for 1814 were located in areas occupied or controlled by the enemy in the London and Western Districts.

The sedentary militia was called out at different times throughout the war. At general alarms they would congregate at Cornwall, Prescott, Gananoque, Kingston, York, Burlington, on the Niagara lines, at Long Point, Burford, Amherstburg, Sandwich and intermediate points. Drafts of the sedentary militia were embodied at the different posts throughout the war. This simply means that men were called out for a specific and limited period, generally a month at a time, to do garrison duty, man piquets, do fatigue duty and so on. For instance, at Kingston, some 400 to 700 men from the Midland and Newcastle Districts were constantly embodied in monthly drafts throughout the war.

Unless the entire regiment was called out, drafts of the different companies would be balloted and sent to do duty. Once they had served, they were not to be balloted again until every other man in the company had been called on. Provision was made for a balloted man to send a subsitute to serve in his stead.

There is no question that local circumstances dictated the willingness of men to turn out and to remain on duty. Desertion, not to the enemy, but back to the farm, was endemic in different areas at different times. Men apparently would turn out more readily if they thought that they were actually needed, and not simply being called from their occupations to work on roads or for the engineers department at one of the posts. In October 1813, Adjutant General Æneas Shaw was dismissed by the regular officer commanding the Centre Division because there were so few militia in the field. At the same time it was reported in a monthly state of the sick that there were over 1,300 militia on duty, but these evidently in other districts.

A cursory survey of the numbers of men who were mustered at different times throughout the war indicates that the population was not truly sedentary and that there was a great deal of movement between districts. About 600 different men served in the 3rd York at some time between 1812 and 1815, even though the reported strength of the regiment was reported to number no more than 400. By war's end the great majority of the men in the province who had not decamped for the United States must have served in some fashion, whether or not under duress, for at least a short time.

The following table illustrates the degree of participation of three regiments in the London District, broken down by month, for the war. The men did not necessarily serve for the entire period, but were on actual service during the period. Each number is also presented as a percentage of the total rank and file and non-commissioned officers as found in regimental returns for 1814. It must be noted that the percentages give only a general indication of the participation of the militia. The returns are often simple estimates, drawing on past returns, and vary considerably. Desertion was a major problem in 1812, became less prevalent in 1813, and in 1814 the company muster lists indicate that it was a minor problem.

MILITIA PARTICIPATION IN THE WAR

	1st Norfolk		2nd Norfolk		1st Middlesex	
1812						
June 30 to July 24	34	(17%)	45	(19%)	16	(10%)
July 25 to Aug. 24	74	(36%)	80	(34%)	16	(10%)
Aug. 25 to Sept. 24	64	(32%)	74	(31%)	10	(6%)
Sept. 25 to Oct. 24	32	(16%)	16	(7%)	10	(6%)
Oct. 25 to Nov. 24	64	(32%)	69	(29%)	84	(52%)
Nov. 25 to Dec. 24	54	(27%)	42	(18%)	64	(40%)
1813						
Dec. 25 to Jan. 24	25	(12%)	42	(18%)	64	(40%)
Jan. 25 to Feb. 24	34	(17%)	16	(7%)	15	(9%)
Feb. 25 to Mar. 24	30	(15%)	16	(7%)	15	(9%)
Mar. 25 to Apr. 24	12	(6%)	12	(5%)	15	(9%)
Apr. 25 to May 24	47	(23%)	50	(21%)	21	(13%)
May 25 to June 24	42	(21%)	50	(21%)	20	(12%)
June 25 to July 24	42	(21%)	21	(9%)	20	(12%)
July 25 to Aug. 24	42	(21%)	26	(11%)	20	(12%)
Aug. 25 to Sept. 24	34	(17%)	53	(22%)	21	(13%)
Sept. 25 to Oct. 24	148	(73%)	181	(75%)	22	(14%)
Oct. 25 to Nov. 24	181	(89%)	181	(75%)	44	(27%)
Nov. 25 to Dec. 24	181	(89%)	115	(48%)	22	(14%)
1814						
Dec. 25 to Jan. 24	27	(13%)	27	(11%)	22	(14%)
Jan. 25 to Feb. 24	22	(11%)	32	(13%)	54	(34%)
Feb. 25 to Mar. 24	22	(11%)	32	(13%)	22	(14%)
Mar. 25 to Apr. 24	22	(11%)	13	(13%)	22	(14%)
Apr. 25 to May 24	200	(96%)	171	(71%)	22	(14%)
May 25 to June 24	200	(96%)	171	(71%)	172	(106%)
June 25 to July 24	200	(96%)	171	(71%)	172	(106%)
July 25 to Aug. 24	47	(23%)	79	(33%)	44	(27%)
Aug. 25 to Sept. 24	39	(19%)	83	(35%)	64	(40%)
Sept. 25 to Oct. 24	39	(19%)	47	(20%)	45	(28%)
Oct. 25 to Nov. 24	205	(101%)	184	(77%)	58	(36%)
Nov. 25 to Dec. 24	27	(13%)	43	(18%)	34	(21%)

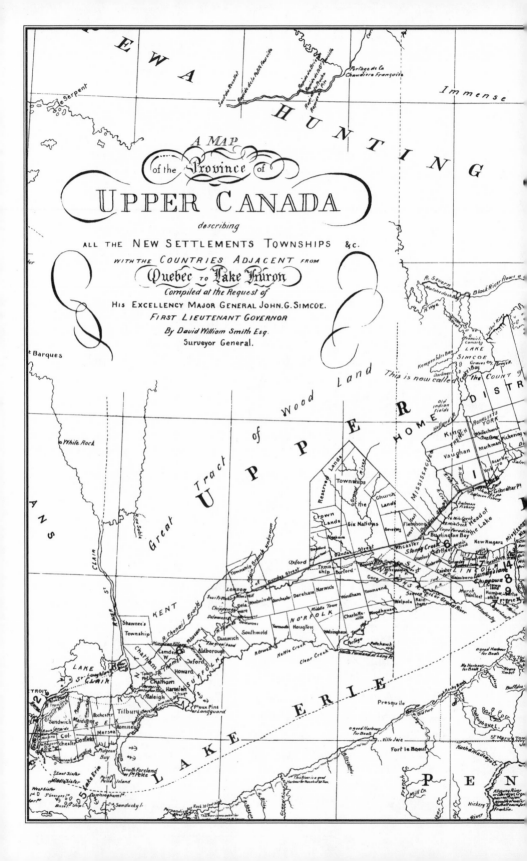

BRITISH VICTORIES.	DATES.	☀ R E F E R E N C E S ☀		DATES.		DATES.
1 MICHILLIMAKINAC.	17.7.12.	8 CHATEAUGUAY.	26.10.13.	15 MICHILLIMAKINAC.	4.8.14.	6 THE THAMES.	5.10.13.
2 DETROIT.	16.8.12.	9 CHRYSLER FARM.	11.11.13.	AMERICAN VICTORIES.	DATES.	7 FORT ERIE.	3.7.14.
3 QUEENSTON.	13.10.12.	10 FORT NIAGARA.	19.12.13.	1 YORK.	27.4.13.	8 CHIPPAWA.	5.7.14.
4 FRENCHTOWN.	22.1.13.	11 BLACK ROCK.	30.12.13.	2 FORT GEORGE.	27.5.13.	9 FORT ERIE.	15.8.14.
5 OGDENSBURG.	22.2.13.	12 LA COLLE.	30.3.14.	3 SACKETT'S HARBOUR.	29.5.13.	10 PLATTSBURG.	11.9.14.
6 STONEY CREEK.	6.6.13.	13 OSWEGO.	6.5.14.	4 FORT STEPHENSON.	2.8.13.		
7 BEAVER DAMS.	24.6.13.	14 LUNDY'S LANE.	25.7.14.	5 LAKE ERIE.	10.9.13.		

ROLL OF THE SEDENTARY MILITIA

EASTERN DISTRICT

1st Glengarry, Lieutenant Colonel Alexander McMillan
2nd Glengarry, Lieutenant Colonel Alexander McDonell
1st Prescott, Lieutenant Colonel Joseph Fortune
1st Stormont, Lieutenant Colonel Neil McLean
1st Dundas, Lieutenant Colonel Thomas Fraser

JOHNSTOWN DISTRICT

1st Grenville, Colonel William Fraser
2nd Grenville, Lieutenant Colonel Thomas Fraser
1st Leeds, Lieutenant Colonel Levius P. Sherwood
2nd Leeds, Colonel Joel Stone

MIDLAND DISTRICT

1st Frontenac, Colonel The Hon. Richard Cartwright
1st Lennox, Colonel Hazelton Spencer. Died February 6, 1813.
    Lieutenant Colonel Timothy Thompson
1st Addington, Colonel William Johnston
1st Hastings, Colonel John Ferguson
1st Prince Edward, Colonel Archibald McDonell

NEWCASTLE DISTRICT

1st Northumberland, Lieutenant Colonel John Peters
1st Durham, Lieutenant Colonel William W. Baldwin

HOME DISTRICT

1st York, Colonel William Graham. Died 1813. Major Samuel
    Wilmot
2nd York, Colonel Richard Beasley
3rd York, Lieutenant Colonel William Chewit

NIAGARA DISTRICT

1st Lincoln, Colonel The Hon. William Claus
2nd Lincoln, Lieutenant Colonel Thomas Clark Lieutenant
    Colonel Thomas Dickson (January 5, 1814) in absence
    of Clark.

3rd Lincoln, Lieutenant Colonel John Warren
4th Lincoln, Lieutenant Colonel Johnson Butler. Died
   December 1812. Major Jacob Ten Broeck. Resigned
   October 1814. Lieutenant Colonel Robert Nelles
5th Lincoln, Lieutenant Colonel Andrew Bradt

LONDON DISTRICT

1st Norfolk, Lieutenant Colonel Joseph Ryerson
2nd Norfolk, Lieutenant Colonel Robert Nichol
1st Oxford, Lieutenant Colonel Henry Bostwick
1st Middlesex, Colonel The Hon. Thomas Talbot

WESTERN DISTRICT

1st Essex, Colonel Matthew Elliott
2nd Essex, Lieutenant Colonel Jean Baptiste Baby
1st Kent, Colonel The Hon. James Baby

PAROLES

During the course of the war a large number of the militia were captured, or in several instances voluntarily surrendered and were paroled. Those men who were paroled were registered and gave their word that they would not take an active part in hostilities until they had been exchanged. A large number of men in the Western, London, Niagara, and Home Districts were paroled in 1813 when their townships were occupied by United States forces. As yet, no list of those who were legally paroled has been found.

There has been a great deal of confusion about the question of paroles and the protocol surrounding them. Books have been written based on exaggerated second-hand statements that bear no resemblance to surviving documentary evidence. A good example of this is found in a passage in E. G. Firth's *The Town of York, 1793–1815* (Toronto, 1962). She quotes Dr. William Beaumont's diary, wherein it is stated that nearly 1,700 militia and inhabitants had given themselves up to be paroled (between April 27 and April 30, 1813). This passage was taken from a book published in 1912.

Men did indeed seek parole after the fall of York, but the report of the inquiry held in early 1814 presents an entirely different picture. A total of some 264 non-commissioned officers and privates from the 1st Durham and the 1st and 3rd York surrendered on the 27th of April. In the course of the American occupation, a further 47 men from the 3rd York came in to surrender and obtain a parole. In a return from the following spring (1814), one man from Durham and another six from the 1st York were reported as having sought parole. All those who were determined to have either voluntarily surrendered, or as it was phrased, "put themselves in the position of being made prisoners," were subsequently ordered into the garrison for three months' service. Some men cleared their names, others, most probably in the 1st York, escaped further attention because the commanding officer, Colonel William Graham, died shortly after the capitulation.

The American forces and some disaffected Upper Canadians made a concerted effort to encourage all local men to "enrol," in some instances by threatening to burn the Loyalists' homes, and in others threatening to carry them off to prison in the United States. The American commander at Fort Erie, Lieutenant Colonel James Preston, published a proclamation following the British withdrawal from the Niagara frontier in May 1813 in which he invited the men living around Fort Erie to "enrol" with him. He went on to "solemnly [warn] those who may obstinately continue inimical, that they are bringing on themselves the most rigorous and disastrous consequences: as they will be pursued and treated with that spirit of retaliation which the treatment of American prisoners in the hands of the British so justly inspires." His unveiled allusion to the massacre of some Americans by the Natives at the River Raisin earlier that year would not have been lost on anyone.

The occupying force and Canadian renegades at Fort George worked as efficiently and paroled all and sundry. A remarkable number of men enumerated on the American parole list are not found on any militia rolls, which would tend to support the contemporary suggestion that the old and young were sought out, as well as the unarmed militia on farms.

Nevertheless, a good number did welcome the Americans and embraced the opportunity to remove themselves from the conflict. A significant element in the general population would have gladly welcomed a change in government.

In addition to the men who were paroled and simply left to mind their own business, a great many men, officers and other ranks, were seized by the Americans and imprisoned in the United States. During the campaign in 1814 on the Niagara frontier, this became especially prevalent as men were taken from their farms and sent to Greenbush, New York; Burlington, Vermont; and Pittsfield, Massachusetts; and many were not returned until mid-March 1815. Men seized in the London and Western Districts were sent to Frankfort, Kentucky.

DISAFFECTION

A good study of disaffection in the province during the war was published over 80 years ago. E. A. Cruikshank, the great historian of the war, read a paper on the subject to the Royal Society of Canada in 1912. The paper surveys the general evidence and concludes that a large minority of the general population, and in some districts a distinct majority, were lukewarm at best in their attachment to the Crown.

Given that so many of the inhabitants were very recent arrivals from the United States, the question should really be one of affection, rather than disaffection. The reason why so many recent settlers, in addition to those whom one would assume would be loyal, the United Empire Loyalists, actively participated and risked all to ensure the ultimate success of the Crown is the more interesting question.

According to the returns of Colonel Joel Stone's 2nd Leeds between July 1812 and late 1814, a total of 103 men had deserted to the enemy. İn 1811 this regiment was officially made up of 418 rank and file, which would indicate that approximately one in four of the county division had fled the country. The Johnstown District was not considered one of the more dependable.

Nearer the other end of the province, in Norfolk, Major Salmon, the officer commanding the 2nd Norfolk, stated that from June 1812 to June 1814, before the particularly vicious fighting that took place in the locality in the summer and autumn of that year, some 48 men had fled the country and joined the enemy (though not necessarily in arms). The regiment consisted of 230 of all ranks in 1814. It is interesting to note that only 14 of the 48 owned any land.

The question of disaffection cannot be seen in simple terms of the settler being for or against the government. An important factor in this issue is the question of pay. Upper Canada in 1812 was a predominately frontier society. Much of the province had been opened to settlement for less than 20 years, and was made up for the most part of small farms.

The pay of a private after the deduction for rations amounted to 6 pence. At the top of the scale, a lieutenant colonel (the highest-paid officer in the militia) received 17 shillings, or the equivalent of 34 days' pay of a private, from which his rations and a property tax of 10 percent were deducted. However, a farmer, if contracted to transport supplies for the commissariat, would receive 20 shillings a day for his labour and team, or the equivalent of 40 days' wages if he was serving in the local garrison, about a fifth more than the best-paid commissioned officer.

A day labourer during the war could earn from 5 to 10 shillings a day if he was a civilian working at the king's works, and the different army departments were constantly advertising for labour at the posts throughout the war. In addition to the crying need for general labour, there was a overwhelming need for all manner of foodstuffs, fodder, building materials and fuel to support the war effort. The farmer who was called out for prolonged service could not work his farm and could not support his family. In many districts, especially where the enemy were active, or where there were concentrations of Natives and troops, he could not protect his family and property from their foraging.

Even in the first year of the war, before the shortages and inflation that raised the price of all food and fuel, the Loyal and Patriotic Society made a special grant to a militiaman at York for the subsistence of his family, as he had no land. A wage earner could not support his family on 6 pence a day. The problem was exacerbated by an ongoing shortage of cash of any sort. Pay was often at least several months in arrears.

CONCLUSION

The war might be called "Madison's patent Nostrum." To our House of Assembly it has been a timely emetic; to our Country a gently sweating cathartic — one threw up 2 traitors, the other threw off some, and by way of appendix hung up some. A sedative shall be prescribed should further symptoms require it.

— The Upper Canada Almanac, 1815

There is a great deal of difficulty in determining exactly what role the militia played and the extent of the participation of the men. Many very different interpretations of the contribution of the militia to the war effort have been expressed. Unfortunately they seem to be couched in diametrically opposed terms. Needless to say, the truth lies somewhere in between.

The "militia myth" of the past century, that is, that the loyal population of Upper Canada with the help of a handful of regulars threw back the rapacious Yankees, was effectively put to rest decades ago. Today it is more popular to portray the militia as being completely ineffectual and, more to the point, either actively disloyal or at best indifferent. Both cases are overstated, but there is an element of truth in each.

The militia was not intended to be the primary line of defence. In the first campaigns they did play a very active and vital role across the province, but in the campaigns of 1813, with the increased number of regulars, the importance of their contribution in the field declined, especially in the areas east of York. To the west, however, the summer of 1814 witnessed the greatest activity of the militia during the conflict.

There were a great number of disaffected people living in the province. Many did desert to the enemy; about one in five in some districts fled or were expelled as aliens. Support for the Crown was not by any means universal or wholehearted. But the contribution of the loyal element, a large percentage of the population, was significant and proved vital to the ultimate success of the forces of the Crown.

The militia's most significant contribution to the war effort was not on the battlefield and does not appear in the official dispatches. The militia made up a great part of the different garrisons, so allowing the regular troops to act in the field. They also formed the bulk of the men who maintained the commissariat, constructed the roads, and laboured at the king's works. They built fortifications and blockhouses, cleared land around the fortified posts, and aided in the building of the Royal Navy's ships that sailed on the Great Lakes.

Without doubt, a key to the success of the British in repulsing the American invasion of this country was the support and to a marked degree the mere quiescence of the Native inhabitants in the west. Their goodwill was ensured and cemented by the provision to them of vast quantities of trade goods and foodstuffs transported from Montreal. Detachments of militia were regularly called upon to move these convoys of bateaux up the St. Lawrence and, after the control of the Lakes was lost in early 1813, overland by road and water to the northwest.

A number of different solutions were proposed to try to draw effectually on the local population to strengthen the forces in the field. The first was the raising of a fencible regiment, the Glengarry Light Infantry Fencibles, in February 1812. The other traditional avenue was the augmentation of the numbers enrolled in the Provincial Marine. Brock toyed with the idea of creating volunteer companies that would in effect be incorporated troops, but given the political temper of the times, he settled on short-period volunteer flank companies. Sheaffe made provision for incorporated troops of cavalry, artillery and infantry, and Drummond vainly attempted to conscript a third of the eligible population for a one-year term. Brock alone enjoyed a degree of success.

There is a natural preoccupation with the campaigns that were planned and fought by the regular forces, the battles on the Niagara frontier, the exchanges on the Lakes — the set-piece contests. These are the incidents and actions that figure in the histories of the conflict. However, we must take into account the minor plots of the story, and the simple fact that the whole province from Cornwall to Sandwich was vulnerable and was in fact periodically visited by the enemy. Most accounts of the war make note of the raids on the Lake Erie shores; few mention the similar, if more limited, vulnerability of the Lake Ontario shores when the American fleet enjoyed the ascendancy of the lake. In midsummer 1814, Colonel Baldwin of Durham wrote:

It seems that the enemy have been into Presquile Harbour here and burnt a vessel and a storehouse and threatened to come to Smith's Creek and burn up all the property belonging to Loyalists. Since we heard this Captain Smith and myself have thought proper to keep a guard in the night on the point at Smith's Creek, but we are in a very poor situation to defend ourselves having neither arms or ammunition. If you would be so good as to make a requisition to the President for 50 stand of arms and 1000 rounds of ball cartridge I have not the least doubt but that he would send them to us.

The uncertainty caused by the question of whether or not any settlement could and would be visited by the enemy or renegade Upper Canadians allied to them, and the threat of the resident disloyal element would surely have affected the willingness of the local population, however loyal to the Crown, to leave their homes and travel far afield in answer to a summons from Kingston or York.

Another important factor that must not be overlooked in examining the militia's participation is the question of pay. Colonel Hercules Scott of the regular army dismissed the Glengarry militia under his command at the River Raisin on February 26, 1814. The companies were now under strength, as most of the young men had all left the county, "in consequence of the great inducement held out to them to public employ at the different posts in the two provinces particularly at Kingston and Coteau de Lac." This was true across the province. Army pay of 6 pence a day was not enough to support a family with the bare necessities of life, and at that, pay was often in months and in some cases years in arrears. Men could not afford to serve for a prolonged period even if they were willing.

A good summary of the situation, written before the notable campaigns of 1814, was made in an address to the Prince Regent by the legislature at the spring session in 1814:

When it is considered, may it please Your Royal Highness, that the whole male population of Upper Canada able to bear arms does not exceed ten thousand men, and it is scattered over a frontier of at least eight hundred miles in extent, when it is considered that nearly one-half of these were embodied for the whole of the first, and a very considerable proportion for the greatest part of the last campaign, and that they composed the principal part of the force which successively captured the forces of Michilmackinac and the army of General Hull; which carried by assault the batteries of Ogdensburgh, which fought and gained the battles of Queenston, River Raison and Fort Meigs, and which repulsed the enemy under General Smith near Fort Erie; when it is known that in the disastrous affair near Fort George, on the twenty-seventh of May last, they were warmly engaged with the enemy, and actually suffered as severely as His Majesty's regular Forces, when it is known that the greatest part of the transportation and provisioning of the Forces in Upper Canada fell upon them, and that in such parts as have been visited by the enemy, their properties have been plundered and destroyed, and themselves as prisoners carried away, when it is known that the whole efforts of the enemy during the last two campaigns have been directed towards the ajudication of Upper Canada and that is yet unsubdued, we think, may it please Your Royal Highness, it will be admitted that the Militia of this Province have faithfully performed their duty; that their services have very largely contributed to the security of this portion of his Majesty's dominions, and that it was the duty of the representative of Our Sovereign to have laid before Your Royal Highness a faithful account of our services and our sufferings.

I

THE MILITIA
GENERAL STAFF

I N June 1812 the militia general staff consisted of the adjutant general, Major General Æneas Shaw; he was the Militia Department. Provision was not even made for a clerk until November 1812, four months after hostilities had commenced, when a single clerk was allowed.

The militia staff functions parallelled, on a very much smaller scale, those of the regular establishment, and evolved into three departments: the adjutant general's, the quarter master general's and the deputy paymaster's. Deputies or assistants were appointed in each of the principal districts to carry out the functions of the different departments. Major General Sir Roger Hale Sheaffe was responsible in spring of 1813 for reorganizing the establishment that was to remain in effect until the end of the war.

District paymasters were appointed in the Western, London, Niagara (Fort Erie and Fort George), Home (at York), Midland (at Kingston), and Eastern and Johnstown Districts (Prescott and Cornwall). The militia from Newcastle served in Kingston and York. They submitted their estimates to the deputy paymaster general, who was stationed at headquarters, which was not established in a fixed location.

INSPECTING FIELD OFFICERS

Inspecting field officers were regular officers who were attached to the militia with the local rank of lieutenant colonel.

Lieutenant Colonel Robert Lethbridge
Lieutenant Colonel Thomas Pearson
Lieutenant Colonel Cecil Bisshopp
Lieutenant Colonel John Murray
Lieutenant Colonel Christopher Hamilton
Lieutenant Colonel Augustus Warburton
Lieutenant Colonel Thomas Bligh St. George

PROVINCIAL AIDES DE CAMP

Lieutenant Colonel John McDonell (April 15, 1812),
    killed in action October 13, 1812.
Captain John Powell, 1st Lincoln (June 23, 1812)
James Givins, with the provincial rank of major
    (August 14, 1812).
Lieutenant Colonel Nathaniel Coffin (February 6, 1813)
Christopher A. Hagerman, with provincial rank of
    lieutenant colonel (December 13, 1813)
Captain Duncan Cameron (March 22, 1815)

ADJUTANT GENERAL

Major General Æneas Shaw (December 2, 1807),
    died February 6, 1814.
Lieutenant Colonel Colley Foster (March 1, 1814)
Lieutenant Colonel Nathaniel Coffin (March 25, 1815)

DEPUTY ADJUTANT GENERAL

Lieutenant Colonel Nathaniel Coffin (January 18, 1814)

ASSISTANT ADJUTANT GENERALS

Eastern and Johnstown Districts

Ensign Joseph Frobisher (May 21, 1813)
Ensign Archibald McDonell Sr. (April 16, 1814)

Midland District

Captain Patrick Corbett (July 29, 1812)

Home District

Lieutenant John Johnston
Captain Stephen Jarvis (March 14, 1813), in absence of
Johnston.

Niagara District

Adjutant John Clark, 1st Lincoln (January 25, 1813)
George Shipman, Clerk

QUARTER MASTER GENERAL

Lieutenant Colonel Robert Nichol (June 27, 1812)
Daniel Spilman, Clerk

ASSISTANT QUARTER MASTER GENERALS

Eastern and Johnstown Districts

William Gilkinson (March 4, 1813), with rank of captain.
Oliver Everts, Clerk

Midland District

Donald McDonell, Kingston

Home District

Captain Jarvie, 3rd York (March 19, 1813)
Captain McLean

Niagara District

Lieutenant James Cummings, 3rd Lincoln (June 28, 1812),
with rank of captain.
Colonel Ralph Clench, Fort George (March 13, 1813)
Joseph Edwards, Right Division (May 12, 1814)

Western District

Colonel Jacques Baby, Sandwich
Francis Baby (March 5, 1813), acted from July 8, 1812.
Shown in the Niagara District, August 25, 1814.
John Watson, Clerk

DEPUTY PAYMASTER GENERAL

Alexander McDonell (February 7, 1813, commission dated
January 25, 1813), taken prisoner at Fort George May 27,
1813 and removed to the United States. Returned in the
spring of 1814.

Robert Grant (acting July 12, 1813)

Samuel Street (acting January 20, 1814), vice Grant from
December 25, 1813.

Alexander McDonell, resumed office May 25, 1814.

DISTRICT PAYMASTERS

Eastern and Johnstown Districts

Stewart

Adiel Sherwood (December 6, 1813), vice Stewart, resigned
June 25, 1813.

Midland District

James Mitchell, resigned September 25, 1813.

Robert Richardson (September 25, 1813)

Home District

William Stanton (acting August 5, 1812)

Andrew Mercer (October 25, 1812), vice Stanton
returned to commissariat.

Niagara District

John Symington (July 12, 1812)

Thomas McCormick, Fort George (October 29, 1812),
resigned January 18, 1813.

Samuel Street, Fort Erie (October 29, 1812)

Henry Caruthers, Clerk

London District

Daniel Ross (September 18, 1812), acted from June 28, 1812.

John Rolph (September 25, 1813), acted to the end of the war.

Romaine Rolph, Clerk

Western District

James Gordon

II

THE MILITIA LIST

N O comprehensive record of the men who held commissions in the militia of Upper Canada during the war has been located. It is very unlikely that any list was ever compiled. Many men were appointed and approved by the regular commanding officer but never received commissions, many others were recommended by the officers commanding the different regiments, but were never officially approved (or commissioned), and yet still acted. Others acted for a part of the war and then disappear from the records.

In the early years of this century, L. Homfray Irving assembled a list of officers of the British forces, including the militia, that drew primarily on the records of men who applied for land grants following the war. In many instances it is notoriously incomplete, but in a few regiments, especially in the Niagara District, there are a great number of men noted for whom no record of service has been located.

A regular sedentary battalion or regiment of ten companies should have had two or three field officers (colonel, lieutenant colonel and major) and 30 regimental officers (captains and subalterns). In most of the county regiments there was relatively little change in the roll of the officers, but in the regimental districts that were most closely engaged in active service, the province west of York, there were a great many changes made — and sometimes noted and sanctioned.

Because promotions were, as a rule, made strictly by seniority, and as there was no age limit, a significant number of the captains were well over 60 and in some instances close to 80. Many were half-pay Loyalist veterans of the "American War" and respected members of the community, but of little use if the regiment were called out on active service. As a result, the regiments that saw the most active service saw a great changeover in officers as the old and infirm were culled out. In addition, a small but significant number either declined to act at all, or in some instances "turned coat."

Where possible names are spelled as signed by the individual. Dates of commissions or appointment are shown in parentheses. There are often conflicting dates recorded; dates given here are taken from what I considered the best of the primary sources. Note is made of officers who served in flank companies.

EASTERN DISTRICT

1st Glengarry

CAMERON, John. *Lieutenant* (April 15, 1812). See Flank Companies.

CAMPBELL, John Hooke. *Captain* (April 16, 1812). See Flank Companies.

CHISHOLM, Lewis. *Lieutenant* (February 22, 1813).

CORBETT, William. *Captain* (April 15, 1812).

CORBETT, John. *Captain* (April 15, 1812).

CURRY, John. *Ensign* (April 18, 1812).

DICKENSON, Noah. *Surgeon.*

FERGUSON, Peter. *Ensign* (April 17, 1812).

FRASER, Donald No. 1 *Adjutant* and *Lieutenant* (April 15, 1812).

FRASER, Donald No. 2 *Ensign* (February 22, 1813). *Lieutenant* (December 25, 1813).

GRANT, Alexander. *Lieutenant* (1804). *Captain* (April 15, 1812).

GRANT, Alan. *Lieutenant* (April 15, 1812).

GUNN, Ranald. *Ensign* (April 16, 1812).

KENNEDY, John. *Ensign* (April 20, 1812). See Flank Companies.

McDEARMID, Donald. *Lieutenant* (April 15, 1812).

McDONALD, Donald. *Lieutenant* (1812). See Flank Companies.

McDONELL, Alexander. *Captain* (April 17, 1812).

McDONELL (McDonald), Alexander. *Lieutenant* (February 22, 1813). See Flank Companies.

McDONELL, Allan. *Captain* (January 2, 1809).

McDONELL, Duncan. *Captain* (January 2, 1809). See Flank Companies.

McDONELL, James. *Ensign* (April 22, 1812). See Flank Companies.

McDONELL, Peter. *Lieutenant* (January 2, 1809).

McDONELL, Ranald. *Ensign* (1804).

McDOUGAL, Donald. *Ensign.* Not shown June 16, 1814.

McGILLIES, Donald. *Lieutenant* (1804). *Captain* (February 22, 1813).

McGILLIES, Alexander. *Lieutenant* (February 22, 1813).

McINTYRE, John. *Captain* (1804). Resigned (June 3, 1812).

McKENZIE, Duncan. *Lieutenant* (January 2, 1809).

McKENZIE, John. *Quarter Master* (February 22, 1813).

McLEAN, Murdoch. *Lieutenant* and *Adjutant* (June 9, 1794). *Captain* (April 15, 1812).

McMILLAN, Alexander. *Ensign* (April 15, 1812).

McMILLAN, Alexander. *Lieutenant Colonel.* (June 3, 1804, and January 2, 1809).

McMILLAN, John. *Captain* (January 2, 1809).

McPHERSON, Donald. *Lieutenant* (February 22, 1813).

McPHERSON, Murdoch. *Lieutenant* (February 22, 1813).

MURCHISON, Duncan. *Ensign* (April 21, 1812). See Flank Companies.

ROSE, Alexander. *Captain* (June 3, 1809).

SNIDER, Jeremiah. *Ensign* (January 2, 1809).

SUMMERS, Jacob. *Lieutenant* (April 15, 1812). Not shown in 1814.

SUTHERLAND, Joseph. *Captain* (August 31, 1796). *Major* (April 15, 1812).

URQUHART, William. *Ensign* (February 22, 1813).

2ND GLENGARRY

CAMERON, Peter. *Lieutenant* (April 23, 1812).

CAMPBELL, William. *Major* (July 15, 1813).

GRANT, Alexander. *Lieutenant* (April 22, 1812). *Captain* (March 25, 1813).

GRANT, Lewis. *Captain* (April 22, 1812). Resigned March 25, 1813.

KENNEDY, Angus. *Lieutenant* (April 24, 1812). See Flank Companies. *Captain* (March 25, 1813).

MacLEOD, Alexander. *Captain* (April 18, 1812). Resigned March 25, 1813.

McCALLUM, Donald. *Captain.*

McDONELL, Alexander (Greenfield). *Lieutenant Colonel* (April 15, 1812).

McDONELL, Alexander. *Captain* (April 17, 1812).

McDONELL, Alexander. *Ensign* (April 23, 1812) *Lieutenant* (July, 1813).

McDONELL, Alexander. *Lieutenant* (April 18, 1812).

McDONELL, Allan. *Lieutenant* (April 15, 1812). *Captain* (July, 1813).

McDONELL, Allan. *Ensign* (April 25, 1812).

McDONELL (Macdonald), Angus. *Ensign* (April 16, 1812). See Flank Companies.

McDONELL, Angus Roy. *Lieutenant* (April 16, 1812). *Captain.*

McDONELL, Donald. *Captain* (April 15, 1812). See Flank Companies.

McDONELL, Ranald. *Ensign* (April 22, 1812). *Lieutenant* (March 25, 1813).

McDONELL, John. *Captain.*

McDOUGALL, Donald. *Ensign* (April 18, 1812).

McDOUGALD, Duncan. *Lieutenant* (April 21, 1812). Resigned March 25, 1813.

McINTYRE, John. *Major* (April 16, 1812).

McINTYRE, Peter. *Adjutant* (April 15, 1812). *Captain* (May 21, 1814).

McKAY, Donald. *Captain* (April 20, 1812).

McKENZIE, Alexander. *Captain* (April 21, 1812). See Flank Companies.

McLEOD, Alexander. *Captain* (April 18, 1812).

McLEOD, Donald. *Ensign* (July, 1813).

McLEOD, Norman. *Ensign.*

McLEOD, Norman. *Lieutenant* (April 17, 1812). Resigned March 25, 1813.

McLEOD, Roderick. *Ensign* (April 21, 1812).

McLEOD, William. *Captain* (April 24, 1812).

McMARTIN, Alexander. *Ensign* (April 24, 1812). *Lieutenant* (March 25, 1813).

McMARTIN, Donald. *Lieutenant* (April 25, 1812). See Flank Companies.

McMILLAN, Alexander. *Captain* (April 16, 1812). See Flank Companies.

McMILLAN, Allan. *Ensign* (April 15, 1812).

McMILLAN, Donald. *Captain* (April 25, 1812).

McMILLAN, Duncan. *Ensign* (April 20, 1812). See Flank Companies.

SUTHERLAND, John J. *Captain* (April 23, 1812).

SUTHERLAND, Walter R. *Lieutenant* (April 20, 1812).

1ST PRESCOTT

CAMERON, Alexander. *Lieutenant* (February 27, 1812).

COHOON, Thomas. *Ensign* (February 29, 1812).

EDDY, Omri. *Lieutenant* (February 26, 1812).

FORTUNE, Joseph. *Lieutenant Colonel* (February 25, 1812).

GRANT, Alexander. *Captain* (February 27, 1812).

HALL, Philo. *Lieutenant* (February 28, 1812).

HAMILTON, William. *Captain* (February 25, 1812).

HARRIGAN, Jeremiah. *Captain* (Februry 26, 1812).

JOHNSON, William. *Ensign* (February 28, 1812).

JOHNSON, Chancy. *Ensign* (February 25, 1812).

LeROY, Peter F. *Captain* (February 28, 1812).

LOW, William. *Lieutenant* (February 29, 1812).

MEARS, Thomas. *Major* (February 25, 1812).

PATTIE, David. *Captain* (February 29, 1812).

SHERMAN, William. *Ensign* (February 27, 1812).

STORY, Avery. *Ensign* (February 26, 1812).

STORY, Stephen. *Lieutenant* (February 25, 1812).

1ST STORMONT

ANDERSON, George. *Lieutenant.*

ANDERSON, Joseph. *Major* (June 3, 1809).

ANDERSON, Robert. *Ensign.*

AULT, John. *Ensign.*

BURTON, Arthur. *Adjutant* (1812). See Flank Companies.

CAMERON, Alexander. *Ensign.*

CAMPBELL, Stephen. *Ensign* (June 5, 1809). *Lieutenant.*

COZENS, Joshua Young. *Captain* (April 6, 1810).

EAMER, Peter. *Lieutenant* (January 3, 1809). ·

EMPEY (Empie), Phillip. *Ensign* (1812). See Flank Companies.

EMPEY, Phillip F. *Lieutenant* (1812). See Flank Companies.

EMPEY, Philip. *Captain* (1811). See Flank Companies.

EMPEY, Michael. *Ensign.*

FARRAN, Charles. *Captain* (1811).

FARRAND, John L. *Ensign.*

FRASER, Angus. *Captain* (January 2, 1809).

FRENCH, Albert. *Captain* (April 6, 1809).

FRENCH, Benjamin. *Lieutenant* (January 6, 1809).

JAYCOX, David. *Captain* (January 3, 1809).

MACDONELL, Archibald. *Ensign* (January 2, 1809). *Assistant Adjutant General* (April 15, 1814).

McAULY, Donald. *Lieutenant* (April 2, 1810).

McDERMID, Hugh. *Ensign.*

McDONELL, John. *Captain.* (March 1813).

McDONELL, Archibald. *Ensign.*

McDONELL, Donald. *Lieutenant* (January 7, 1809).

McDONELL, Donald. *Ensign.* See Casualties.

McINTOSH, John. *Lieutenant.*

McLEAN, Alexander. *Lieutenant* (1812). See Flank Companies.

McLEAN, John. *Lieutenant* (1812). See Flank Companies. *Captain* (March 1813).

McLEAN, Neil. *Lieutenant Colonel* (April 27, 1812).

MORGAN, Kenzie. *Ensign. Lieutenant.*

MORGAN, William. *Captain* (1804). See Flank Companies.

MORGAN, George. *Ensign* (November 26, 1813).

SHEEK, David. *Captain* (April 4, 1810).

SNETSINGER, Nathaniel. *Ensign* (April 2, 1810).

STEWART, George. *Captain* (January 2, 1809).

STUART, Henry. (Harry Stewart) *Ensign* (June 6, 1809). See Flank Companies.

STUART (Stewart), John. *Captain* (January 5, 1809).

VANKOUGHNET, John. *Lieutenant* (1812). See Flank Companies.

WOOD, Guy C. *Ensign* (April 4, 1810).

1ST DUNDAS

AULT, Michael. *Captain* (January 27, 1810). See Flank Companies.

CARMAN, Michael. *Captain* (January 31, 1810).

CASSELMAN, Servius (Sevrinus). *Ensign* (February 5, 1810). *Lieutenant* (February 22, 1812).

CLARK, Duncan. *Ensign* (February 2, 1810). See Flank Companies.

COONS, Jacob. *Ensign* (February 24, 1812). *Lieutenant* (December 9, 1813).

CRYSLER, John. *Lieutenant* (February 5, 1810). *Captain* (January 28, 1813).

DORAN, Jacob. *Lieutenant* (February 3, 1810). See Flank Companies.

DOREN, John. *Ensign*. (January 28, 1813).

FRASER, James. *Lieutenant* (February 7, 1810). See Flank Companies.

FRASER, Thomas. *Lieutenant Colonel* (February 15, 1812).

FRASER, Richard Duncan. *Captain* (February 25, 1813). See Flank Companies (from the 1st Grenville).

GLASSFORD, Paul. *Lieutenant* (February 21, 1812). *Captain* (December 12, 1813).

HAINS, Christopher. *Ensign* (February 26, 1812).

LOUCKS, William. *Lieutenant* (February 25, 1812).

MERKLEY, Christopher. *Lieutenant* (February 24, 1812). See Flank Companies.

MERKLEY, George. *Captain* (February 20, 1812). See Flank Companies.

MERKLEY, Henry. *Captain* (February 22, 1812).

MERKLEY, Henry. *Major* (February 20, 1812).

MERKLEY, Jacob. *Ensign* (February 25, 1812). See Flank Companies. *Lieutenant* (December 10, 1813).

MERKLEY, Michael. *Ensign* (February 21, 1812).

McDONELL, A. *Ensign* (January 28, 1813).

McDONELL, C. James. *Lieutenant*.

McDONELL, James. *Lieutenant* (February 2, 1810). *Captain* (December 8, 1813).

McDONELL, John. *Captain* (December 25, 1812). See Flank Companies.

McDONELL, John. *Ensign* (January 27, 1810).

MUNROE, John. *Captain* (February 21, 1812).

MYERS, Daniel. *Lieutenant* (July 12, 1813).

ROBINSON, David. 1st Dundas. *Lieutenant* (December 16, 1813).

ROSE, Alexander. *Lieutenant* (January 31, 1810). See Flank Companies.

ROSS, Alexander. *Ensign* (February 20, 1812).

SHAVER, Adam. *Lieutenant* (January 29, 1810).

SHAVER, Jacob. *Ensign* (December 10, 1812). *Lieutenant* (December 8, 1813).

SHAVER, John. *Captain* (January 30, 1810).

SHAVER, Nicholas. *Ensign* (December 10, 1813).

SHAVER, Peter. *Lieutenant* (February 20, 1812).

VANALLEN, Jacob. *Captain* (February 1, 1810).

VANALLEN, Jacob Jr. *Ensign* (February 22, 1812).

WEAGAR, Jacob. *Captain* (January 29, 1810).

WEAGAR, John. *Ensign* (January 29, 1813).

WEART (Wart), George. *Lieutenant* (January 29, 1810).

WELSH, William. *Ensign* (December 9, 1812). Returned as dead in 1814.

WRIGHT, Jesse. *Captain*. Returned March 1813 as deceased.

JOHNSTOWN DISTRICT

1ST GRENVILLE

ADAMS, Andrew. *Lieutenant* (February 19, 1812). See Flank Companies.

ADAMS, Gideon. *Major* (June 4, 1812).

ADAMS, Gideon Jr. *Lieutenant* (February 25, 1812).

ADAMS, Joel. *Captain* (February 17, 1812).

ADAMS, John. *Ensign* (December 24, 1813).

ADAMS, Peter. *Ensign* (February 25, 1812).

ADAMS, Samuel. *Lieutenant* (February 24, 1812).

BOLTEN (Boulton), Abraham. *Captain* (February 20, 1812).

CURRY, Abraham. *Ensign* (February 19, 1812).

DENAULT, Joachim. *Lieutenant* (February 20, 1812). *Captain* (October 24, 1813).

DULMAGE, Philip. *Captain* (March 18, 1811). See Flank Companies.

DULMAGE, Samuel. *Ensign* (February 26, 1812). See Flank Companies.

FORESTER, William. *Cornet.*

FRASER, Daniel. *Ensign* (June 4, 1813).

FRASER, Donell. *Lieutenant* (1812). See Flank Companies.

FRASER, John. *Ensign* (February 24, 1812). See Flank Companies. *Lieutenant* (April 13, 1813).

FRASER, Thomas. *Captain* (February 15, 1812).

FRASER, William Grant. *Captain* (February 18, 1812).

FRASER, William. *Colonel* (June 10, 1812).

FROOM, James. *Ensign* (February 21, 1812). *Lieutenant* (June 4, 1813).

GLASFORD, Lytle. *Lieutenant* (February 18, 1812).
GRANT, Peter. *Captain* (February 19, 1812).
HALL, James. *Lieutenant* (July 12, 1812).
JONES, Dunham (Daniel). *Ensign.*
LAMSON (Lampson), James. *Ensign* (February 20, 1812).
LAURENCE (Lawrence), John. *Lieutenant* (February 17, 1812).
    See Flank Companies.
MAIN, James. *Ensign* (February 17, 1812).
McCARGER, Thomas Jr. *Ensign* (February 18, 1812). *Lieutenant*
    (June 5, 1813).
MERWIN, Justus. *Ensign* (February 22, 1812).
MILLS, James. *Lieutenant* (February 21, 1812).
MUNRO, Hugh. *Captain* (1812). See Flank Companies.
SCOTT, John. *Lieutenant* (February 22, 1812).
SNIDER, Solomon. *Ensign* (February 15, 1812). See Flank
    Companies.
WEATHERHEAD, John. *Ensign* (February 27, 1812). *Lieutenant*
    (October 24, 1813).
WOODCOCK, Jonathan. *Lieutenant* (February 15, 1812).

2ND GRENVILLE

BOTTOM, William Henry. *Lieutenant* (February 24, 1812).
BURRITT, Adoniram. *Captain* (February 26, 1812).
BURRITT, Daniel. *Captain* (February 19, 1812). See Flank
    Companies.
BURRITT, Edmund. *Ensign* (February 18, 1812).
BURRITT, Harry (Henry). *Lieutenant* (February 18, 1812). See
    Flank Companies.
BURRITT, Major. *Lieutenant* (February 20, 1812).
BURRITT, Stephen. *Captain* (February 15, 1812).
CAMPBELL, Thomas D. *Lieutenant* (February 22, 1812).
CAMPBELL, Duncan. *Ensign* (February 15, 1812). Noted in a return
    of December 24, 1814, as having absconded from the province.
CAMPBELL, Archibald. *Ensign* (February 26, 1812).
CHESTER, John. *Ensign* (February 17, 1812).
CLAWSON, Caleb. *Captain* (February 17, 1812).
COLLINS, Stephen. *Lieutenant* (February 25, 1812).
DAVIS, William. *Lieutenant* (February 19, 1812).
DOYLE, Thomas. *Captain* (February 21, 1812).
FRASER, Thomas. *Lieutenant Colonel.* (August 10, 1794, in the
    1st Grenville, and February 15, 1812).
FRASER, Richard Duncan. *Lieutenant* (February 17, 1812).
    See Flank Companies. See Captain Fraser's Troop of Provincial
    Light Dragoons.

GATES, Walter F. *Lieutenant* (February 26, 1812).

HICK, Samuel. *Lieutenant, Captain.*

HURD, Truman. *Ensign* (February 24, 1812).

HURD, Asahel. *Captain* (February 23, 1812).

HURD, Jehial. *Captain* (February 22, 1812).

JONES, Dunham. *Ensign.*

KERR, John. *Ensign* (1812). See Flank Companies.

LAKE, Abraham. *Lieutenant* (February 15, 1812).

LANDON, Reuben. *Ensign* (February 25, 1812).

LANDON, Herman. *Captain* (February 20, 1812).

McCRAE, Thomas. *Ensign* (February 19, 1812). See Flank Companies.

MERRICK, William. *Ensign* (February 22, 1812).

ROSE, Samuel. *Ensign* (February 20, 1812).

SCOTT, Francis. *Captain.*

SCOTT, John. *Lieutenant.*

WALKER, Hamilton. *Captain* (February 24, 1812). See Flank Companies.

WEATHERHEAD, John. *Ensign* (February 21, 1812).

WELLS, William. *Lieutenant* (February 21, 1812).

WRIGHT, Asahel. *Captain* (February 18, 1812).

1ST LEEDS

BOOTH, Samuel. *Captain* (1811).

CARLEY, Bartholomew. *Major* (June 23, 1812).

CARLEY, Duncan. *Ensign.*

COLE, Peter. *Lieutenant* (June 23, 1812).

DAYTON, Abraham. *Ensign* (1812). See Flank Companies. *Lieutenant* (December 26, 1814).

DAYTON, Nathan. *Captain* (June 23, 1812).

DOAK, William. *Lieutenant* (June 23, 1812).

FREEL, Thomas. *Ensign* (June 24, 1812).

FULFORD, Jonathan. *Lieutenant* (1812). See Flank Companies. *Captain* (December 25, 1814).

GRANT, John. *Lieutenant* (June 24, 1812).

GRANT, Allan. *Ensign* (July 1, 1812). *Lieutenant.*

HAGERMAN, John. *Ensign* (1812). See Flank Companies. *Lieutenant* (December 27, 1814).

HOWARD, John. *Captain* (December 15, 1807).

HOWLAND, Thomas F. *Ensign.* (March 15, 1808).

HUBBLE, E. *Surgeon.*

JONES, Charles. *Captain* (June 24, 1812).

JONES, Henry. *Cornet.*

JONES, Jonas. *Lieutenant* (June 25, 1812). See Flank Companies.
LANDON, Asa. *Captain* (June 23, 1812). Resigned February 3, 1813.
McDONALD, Randal. *Lieutenant* (June 23, 1812).
McDONALD, Charles. *Ensign* (June 29, 1812).
McLEAN, Alexander. *Lieutenant* (June 23, 1812).
McLEAN, Archibald. *Captain* (June 23, 1812).
McLEAN, John. *Lieutenant* (June 23, 1812). See Flank Companies.
McLEAN, Robert. *Captain* (June 23, 1812).
McNEIL, John. *Lieutenant* (June 23, 1812).
McNISH, John. *Ensign* (June 23, 1812).
McNISH, Samuel. *Lieutenant* (June 23, 1812).
MORRIS, Alexander. *Lieutenant* (June 24, 1812).
MORRIS, William. *Ensign* (June 30, 1812). See Flank Companies.
PURVIS, Peter. *Lieutenant* (June 23, 1812).
SHERWOOD, Levius P. *Captain* (1811). *Lieutenant Colonel*
    (June 23, 1812).
SHERWOOD, Adiel. *Captain* (June 23, 1812).
SHERWOOD, James. *Ensign* (June 25, 1812).
SHERWOOD, Reuben. *Captain*.
SHIPMAN, Samuel. *Ensign* (June 27, 1812).
SMYTH (Smith), Terence. *Ensign* (June 26, 1812). See Flank
    Companies.
STUART, John. *Captain* (June 4, 1807).
SUNDERLIN, Wallis. *Captain* (June 24, 1812). Noted in a return of
    February 25, 1813, as dead.
WRIGHT, Sylvester. *Captain* (March 3, 1808). See Flank Companies.

2ND LEEDS

ADAMS, Joshua. *Captain* (August 6, 1812).
BATES, George. *Ensign*.
BENEDICT, Joseph. *Captain* (June 15, 1810).
BRADISH, Andrew. *Lieutenant* (1812). See Flank Companies.
BRESEE, Nicholas. *Ensign* (1811). *Lieutenant*.
BRISEE, Peter. *Captain* (June 16, 1810).
BROWN, Daniel. *Lieutenant*.
DAVIS, Walter. *Ensign* (June 16, 1810).
DAY, Jeremiah. *Lieutenant* (June 16, 1810).
HALLIDAY, Samuel. *Ensign* (1811).
HERSKINS, Carey. *Lieutenant*.
HICOCK, Nathan. *Ensign* (1812). See Flank Companies.
JONES, William. *Captain* (1811). See Flank Companies.
KELSEY, Samuel. *Ensign*. See Flank Companies. *Lieutenant*.
    Court-martialled and dismissed from the service March 4, 1814.

KILBORN, James. *Ensign* (June 15, 1810). See Flank Companies.
LIVINGSTONE, Duncan. *Captain* (June 14, 1810).
MUNSELL, Benjamin R. *Captain* (June 13, 1810).
READ, Samuel. *Ensign* (1812). See Flank Companies.
READ, William. *Captain* (1811). *Major.*
READ, William. *Lieutenant.*
SCHOFIELD, Ira. *Captain* (1812). See Flank Companies.
SCHOFIELD, James. *Major* (1811).
SCHOFIELD, James. *Lieutenant* (1811).
SMITH, Henry. *Lieutenant* (1811).
SOPER, Levi. *Lieutenant* (June 14, 1810).
STONE, Joel. *Colonel.*
STRUTHERS, John. *Lieutenant* (June 18, 1810). See Flank
    Companies.
WILTSEE, Benoni. *Captain* (1812). See Flank Companies.
WILTSEE, Benoni. *Lieutenant Colonel* (March 19, 1810).
    Court-martialled and dismissed from the service April 4, 1814.
WILTSEE, John. *Ensign* (1811). *Lieutenant.*
WILTSEE, Joseph. *Lieutenant* (1811). *Captain.*
WILTSEE, James. *Ensign* (June 14, 1810).

MIDLAND DISTRICT

1ST FRONTENAC

BRASS, David. *Captain* (1811).
BRASS, John. *Ensign* (May 18, 1812). See Flank Companies.
CARTWRIGHT, The Hon. Richard. *Colonel.*
COOK, Thomas. *Lieutenant* (May 18, 1812). See Flank Companies.
CUMMING, John. *Captain* (October 25, 1809).
ELLERBACK, Richard. *Ensign* (October 27, 1809).
EVERITT, Charles. *Lieutenant* (October 24, 1809).
EVERITT, John. *Major.*
FORSYTH, Joseph. *Captain* (1811).
GRANT, Peter. *Lieutenant.*
GRASS, Peter. *Lieutenant.*
HERKIMER, Laurence. *Captain* (1811).
KIRBY, John. *Captain* (October 26, 1809).
MACAULAY. John. *Ensign* (June 8, 1813).
MARKLAND, Thomas. *Captain* (1811). See Flank Companies.
MARKLAND, George. *Ensign* (October 25, 1809).
McGUIN, Anthony. *Captain* (1811).
McLEAN, Allan. *Lieutenant Colonel.* Sent in his resignation
    March 26, 1814.
McPHERSON, A. *Ensign* (June 8, 1813).

MITCHELL, William. *Ensign.*

RICHARDSON, Robert. *Ensign* (August 6, 1810). See Flank Companies.

ROBINS, William. *Captain* (October 18, 1809). See Flank Companies.

ROBINSON, Richard. *Lieutenant* (October 25, 1809).

SHELLEY, (?). *Ensign.*

SHIBLEY, Jacob. *Ensign* (May 19, 1812).

SLOOT, Michael. *Lieutenant* (August 7, 1810).

SMITH, Peter. *Captain* (1811).

SMYTH, Patrick. *Lieutenant* (August 6, 1810). See Flank Companies. Resigned May 9, 1813.

SPARHAM, Thomas (Thorney). *Lieutenant* (1812). See Flank Companies.

WARTMAH, Peter. *Lieutenant.*

WASHBURN, Simon. *Ensign* (1812). See Flank Companies.

1ST LENNOX

BARNHART, Charles. *Lieutenant* (February 2, 1809).

BEDELL (Bedall), Reuben. *Lieutenant* (January 4, 1801). See Flank Companies.

BELL, William. *Captain* (July 3, 1794). Resigned January 30, 1816, on account of old age and infirmity.

BELL, Duncan. *Lieutenant* (July 3, 1794).

BENSON, Garret. *Ensign* (January 5, 1809).

BENSON, Jacob. *Ensign* (February 20, 1813).

BRADSHAW, Asahael. *Lieutenant* (February 21, 1812).

CARSCALLEN, George. *Lieutenant* (August 1, 1801).

CARSCALLEN, James. *Lieutenant* (June 1, 1798).

CARSCALLEN, John. *Captain* (July 3, 1794). Died October 10, 1815.

CARSCALLEN, Luke. *Captain* (June 1, 1798).

CHAMBERLAIN, Jacob B. *Lieutenant* (November 11, 1794).

CHURCH, Oliver. *Ensign* (1800). See Flank Companies.

CLAP, Gilbert. *Ensign* (1812). *Lieutenant* (May 29, 1813)

CLARK, Alexander. *Captain* (July 3, 1794).

CRAWFORD, William. *Major* (July 3, 1794). *Lieutenant Colonel* (May 29, 1813).

CRAWFORD, Brian. *Captain* (July 3, 1794).

DEFOE, Abraham. *Lieutenant* (June 1, 1798).

DEFOE, John. *Lieutenant* (February 22, 1812).

DETLOR, Samuel. *Ensign* (August 1, 1803).

DORLAND, Samuel. *Ensign* (February 25, 1812).

DORLAND, Thomas. *Captain* (January 3, 1801). See Flank Companies.

EMBURY, John. *Captain* (June 4, 1802).

EMBURY, Andrew. *Captain* (February 22, 1812).

HAGERMAN, Nicholas. *Captain* (1812). See Flank Companies. *Major* (May 29, 1813).

HAGERMAN, Christopher Alexander. *Ensign* (February 24, 1812). See Flank Companies.

HAWLEY, Martin. *Ensign* (1813). Resigned June 14, 1813, and noted as left the country.

HESFORD, Frederick. *Ensign* (August 2, 1803).

KEMP, John. *Cornet.* (May 29, 1813).

KIMMERLEY, Andrew. *Ensign* (February 22, 1812).

PARKES, Cyreneus. *Captain* (February 21, 1812).

PHILIPS, Elisha. *Captain* (August 20, 1801). See Flank Companies.

PRINDLE, Joseph. *Ensign* (February 21, 1812).

RAMBOUGH, William. *Lieutenant* (February 24, 1812).

RYCKLEY, Andrew. *Ensign* (January 2, 1809).

SMITH, William. *Lieutenant* (August 20, 1801). Resigned June 14, 1813, on account of age and health.

SPENCER, Benjamin Conger. *Ensign* (August 4, 1803). See Flank Companies.

SPENCER, Hazelton. *Colonel.* Died February 6, 1813.

THOMPSON, Timothy. *Lieutenant Colonel. Colonel* (May 29, 1813).

TROMPOUR, John. *Lieutenant* (1812). *Captain* (May 29, 1813).

TROMPOUR, Paul. *Captain* (1812).

1ST ADDINGTON

AMEY, Abraham. *Ensign* (February 22, 1813).

AMEY, Joseph. *Ensign* (February 22, 1813).

BOICE, Stephen. *Lieutenant* (1810). Noted in a return of 1815 as "Resigned long since for conduct unbecoming an Officer."

BOOTH, Joshuah. *Captain* (1811). Died October 27, 1813.

BOWERS, Adam. *Lieutenant* (October 14, 1809).

BRISCO, Norris. *Captain* (October 14, 1809).

CLARK, John C. *Ensign* (1812). See Flank Companies.

CLARK, Robert. *Captain* (January 2, 1809).

CLARK, Matthew Clark. *Captain* (January 2, 1809). See Flank Companies.

DAILEY, Peter. *Captain* (October 17, 1809).

DAVEY, Henry. *Lieutenant* (October 20, 1809). See Flank Companies.

DUSENBURY, John. *Major* (January 2, 1809).

FRALICK, John C. *Cornet* (February 22, 1813).

FRALICK, Christopher. *Captain* (January 2, 1809).

FRASER, Daniel. *Lieutenant* (October 16, 1809). See Flank Companies.

FRASER, Isaac. *Lieutenant* (February 22, 1813).
FRASER, Thomas. *Captain* (January 3, 1809).
HAM, George. *Adjutant* (February 22, 1813).
HAWLEY, Jeheal. *Ensign* (October 18, 1809). See Flank Companies.
HAWLEY, Sheldon. *Captain* (October 16, 1809). See Flank Companies.
HAWLEY, Davis. *Captain* (February 22, 1813).
HAWLEY, Ichabod. *Captain*. Noted as deceased in a return of
    June 16, 1814.
JOHNS, Solomon. *Lieutenant* (February 22, 1813).
JOHNSTON, William. *Colonel* (January 2, 1809).
LOCKWOOD, David. *Ensign* (October 19, 1809).
MACKENZIE, Colin. *Lieutenant* (February 22, 1813).
McKAY, William J. *Ensign* (February 22, 1813).
MILLER, George. *Ensign* (February 22, 1813).
PARROT, James. *Lieutenant Colonel* (January 2, 1809).
PERRY, David. *Ensign* (February 22, 1813).
RICHARDS, John. *Lieutenant* (October 17, 1809).
SHARP, John. *Lieutenant* (February 22, 1813).
SIMMONS, Daniel. *Ensign*.
STARK, John. *Ensign* (probably same as John Sharp noted above).
WILLIAMS, Robert. *Lieutenant* (October 19, 1809).

1ST HASTINGS

BELL, William. *Lieutenant Colonel* (November 1, 1804).
CHARD, Boice. *Ensign* (April 25, 1813).
CHISHOLM, Alexander. *Captain* (September 5, 1807).
CHISHOLM, Archibald. *Ensign* (January 4, 1809). *Lieutenant*
    (March 25, 1813).
CUNNINGHAM, Hugh. *Ensign* (March 25, 1813).
FAIRMAN, Hugh. *Ensign*. See Flank Companies. Noted in a return
    of 1819 as having served 31 days and resigned.
FERGUSON, John. *Colonel* (November 1, 1804).
GILBERT, Abel. *Lieutenant* (July 28, 1812).
GILBERT, Samuel Birdseye. *Captain* (September 7, 1807).
HAGERMAN, Henry. *Ensign* (August 2, 1812).
HARRIS, Gilbert. *Captain* (August 4, 1800). See Flank Companies.
HOLMS, Peter. *Ensign* (April 25, 1813).
KETCHESON, Benjamin. *Ensign* (April 25, 1813).
KETCHESON, William. *Ensign* (September 9, 1807). See Flank
    Companies. *Lieutenant* (July 28, 1812).
KETCHESON, Thomas. *Ensign* (March 25, 1813).
LEMOINE, Joseph. *Ensign* (December 25, 1812). See Flank
    Companies. *Lieutenant* (April 25, 1813).

McINTOSH, John. *Captain* (November 1, 1800). See Flank
Companies. *Quarter Master.*
McMICHAEL, John. *Lieutenant* (September 8, 1807). See Flank
Companies. *Captain* (March 25, 1813).
McNABB, Simon. *Captain* (September 6, 1807).
MEYERS, George Walden. *Major* (September 5, 1807).
MYERS, Peter W. *Ensign.*
MYERS, Jacob Walden. *Captain* (September 5, 1807). See Flank
Companies.
REID, John. *Ensign* (September 7, 1807). *Lieutenant* (July 28, 1812).
TAYLOR, Allan. *Ensign* (July 28, 1812). *Lieutenant* (April 25, 1813).
THOMPSON, John. *Lieutenant* (September 6, 1807). See Flank
Companies. *Captain* (March 25, 1813) and *Adjutant.*
VANDERVOORT, Francis. *Ensign* (January 3, 1809). *Lieutenant*
(March 25, 1813).
WEST (Weist), John. *Lieutenant* (1812).
ZWICK, Philip. *Lieutenant* (September 9, 1807).
ZWICK, William. *Ensign* (August 1, 1812).

1ST PRINCE EDWARD

ALLEN, John. *Captain* (June 4, 1811). See Flank Companies.
BLAKELY, Samuel. *Lieutenant* (March 24, 1814).
BLAKELY, William. *Ensign* (June 4, 1811).
BLAKELY, William. *Ensign* (June 4, 1811).
CONGER, Peter. *Captain* (December 24, 1813).
CONGER, Stephen. *Lieutenant* (June 4, 1811).
COTTER, James. *Captain* (June 4, 1811).
CUMMING, James. *Lieutenant* (June 4, 1812).
DAVERN, Daniel. *Ensign* (February 24, 1813).
DEMERIAT, Gilliam. *Lieutenant* (June 4, 1811).
DINGMAN, Henry *Ensign* (February 24, 1813).
DORLAND, Daniel B. *Ensign* (February 24, 1813).
FERGUSON, Hazel. *Quarter Master* (June 4, 1811).
FERGUSON, Farrington. *Lieutenant* (March 24, 1814).
GARDNER, Richard. *Ensign* (December 24, 1813).
GOLDSMITH, Thomas. *Captain* (1813).
HICKS, Joshua. *Ensign* (March 24, 1814).
HOWARD, Thomas. *Lieutenant* (March 24, 1813).
HOWELL, Jacob. *Ensign* (March 24, 1814).
HOWELL, John. *Captain.* Court-martialled and services dispensed
with April 3, 1813.
HOWELL, Richard. *Ensign* (1812). See Flank Companies.
McDONELL, Archibald. *Colonel* (January 2, 1800).

McINTOSH, Donald. *Lieutenant* (July 14, 1807). See Flank
Companies.

NALOE, Hilerbrant. *Lieutenant* (January 2, 1809).

PLATT, Caleb. *Cornet* (December 24, 1813).

RICHARDS, Owen. *Captain* (June 1, 1801). See Flank Companies.
Noted as served the whole war.

SEGAR, David. *Captain* (March 24, 1813).

STINSON, John. *Captain* (July 14, 1807).

VANALSTINE, Cornelius. *Captain* (July 14, 1807).

WALDBRIDGE, William. *Ensign* (March 24, 1813).

WASHBURN, Simeon. *Lieutenant* (1812). *Captain*
(December 24, 1813).

WASHBURN, Simon. *Ensign* (February 24, 1813). See Flank
Companies.

WAY, Benjamin. *Ensign* (1812). *Lieutenant* (December 24, 1813).

WRIGHT, James. *Captain* (June 1, 1801).

WRIGHT, William. *Lieutenant* (June 4, 1811).

WRIGHT, Daniel. *Lieutenant Colonel.* (June 2, 1801).

YOUNG, Daniel. *Major* (December 24, 1813).

YOUNG, Guy B. *Ensign* (March 24, 1814).

YOUNG, Henry. *Lieutenant* (1812). See Flank Companies.
See Casualties.

YOUNG, James. *Lieutenant* (1812). See Flank Companies. *Captain*
(June 4, 1812?).

YOUNG, Robert. *Ensign* (1812). See Flank Companies. *Lieutenant*
(March 24, 1814).

NEWCASTLE DISTRICT

1ST NORTHUMBERLAND

BLANCHARD, Archibald. *Adjutant* (May 25, 1812).

BROCK, Samuel. *Ensign.*

BURNHAM, Asa. *Captain* (June 21, 1810). See Flank Companies.
Noted as deceased in return of March 24, 1813.

BURNHAM, John. *Ensign* (June 27, 1810).

BURNHAM, Zacheus. *Captain* (June 23, 1810).

BAYS, Manchester Eddys. *Lieutenant* (June 27, 1810). *Captain* (1816).

EWING, Benjamin. *Quarter Master* (June 28, 1810).

GROVER, John. *Lieutenant* and *Adjutant* (June 28, 1810).
Captain (1816).

HARE, Richard. *Captain* (June 20, 1810).

JONES, Elias. *Major.*

JONES, Elisha. *Lieutenant* (June 26, 1810). *Captain* (1816).

KEELER (Kerlie), Joseph A. *Ensign* (June 26, 1810). See Flank
  Companies. *Lieutenant.*
KELLY, John. *Ensign* (May 25, 1812).
LOSIE (?), Joseph. *Ensign.*
McKIES, Barnabas. *Lieutenant* (May 25, 1812). *Captain* (1816).
MEYERS, Adam Henry. *Ensign* (June 26, 1810). See Flank
  Companies.
NORRIS, James. *Lieutenant* (May 25, 1812). See Flank Companies.
  Noted in a return of 1816 as resigned and moved to the
  United States.
PETERS, John. *Lieutenant Colonel* (June 20, 1810).
PETERS, John. *Ensign* (May 26, 1812).
PORTER, Timothy. *Captain* (June 20, 1810). Noted as deceased in a
  return of 1816.
RICHARDSON, John. *Ensign* (June 25, 1810) *Lieutenant.* Noted in a
  return of 1816 as an ensign and reported to have moved to the
  United States.
RUTTAN, Henry. *Ensign.*
SIMMONS, Abraham. *Lieutenant* (June 23, 1810). *Captain* (1816).
SPALDING, Thomas M. *Ensign.*
SPENCER, John. *Captain* (June 20, 1810). See Flank Companies.
  Noted in a return of 1816 as resigned.
VAUGHAN, John. *Lieutenant* (June 21, 1810). *Captain* (March 1813).
  Noted in a return of 1816 as resigned as unable to serve.
WARD, Thomas. *Captain* (May 25, 1812). Noted in a return of 1816
  as resigned and moved to County Durham.
WILKINS, Robert Charles. *Captain* (June 20, 1810). See Flank
  Companies. Noted in a return of 1816 as moved to Lower Canada.
WOOLCUT, Roger. *Lieutenant* (June 22, 1810). See Flank Companies.
  Captain (December 1813).

1ST DURHAM

BALDWIN, Robert. *Colonel* (1801).
BALDWIN, William W. *Lieutenant Colonel* (June 26, 1812).
BATES, James. *Lieutenant* (April 16, 1812).
BURNS, John. *Lieutenant* (April 13, 1812). *Captain* (July 11, 1812).
  See Flank Companies.
CARR, John. *Lieutenant* (October 25, 1812). See Flank Companies.
CLARK, Robert. *Ensign* (July 11, 1812). *Lieutenant* (July 30, 1812).
FLETCHER, Alexander. *Captain* (April 13, 1812). *Major* (1816).
HARTWELL, John. *Lieutenant* (April 11, 1812). *Captain*
  (July 31, 1812).
HARRIS, Thomas. *Ensign* (October 25, 1813).
HASKELL (Haskil), Josiah. *Ensign* (August 10, 1812).

MARSH, Benjamin. *Lieutenant* (April 10, 1812).

SMITH, John D. *Ensign. Lieutenant* (July 11, 1812). *Captain* (July 30, 1812).

SOPER, Leonard. *Captain* (April 10, 1812).

TAYLOR, John. *Ensign* (1812). See Flank Companies. *Lieutenant* (October 25, 1813).

WALTON, Nathan. *Captain* (April 11, 1812). Resigned July 1812.

HOME DISTRICT

1ST YORK

ARNOLD, John. *Captain* (October 1812).

BOSTWICK, John. *Ensign* (December 25, 1812).

BUTTON, John. *Captain* (1812).

FENWICK, James. *Lieutenant* (June 9, 1809). *Captain* (December 25, 1812).

GAMBLE, Nathaniel. *Lieutenant* (July 1814).

GRAHAM, William. *Lieutenant Colonel* (November 23, 1807).

HAMPTON, Thomas. *Ensign* (December 25, 1812).

HOLLEY, Elijah. *Ensign* (December 25, 1812).

LEMON, George. *Ensign* (March 1814).

MERCER, Andrew. *Ensign.*

MILES, James. *Lieutenant.*

MUSTARD, James. *Captain* (June 10, 1809).

MUSTARD, George. *Ensign* (June 13, 1809). *Lieutenant* (December 25, 1812).

PINGLE, Henry. *Ensign* (December 25, 1812).

RICHARDSON, Reuben. *Lieutenant* (October 1812). See Flank Companies. *Captain* (December 25, 1812).

ROBINSON, Peter. *Captain* (October 1812).

ROSS, William. *Lieutenant* (1812). Resigned November 4, 1812.

SCHUTZ, John George. *Lieutenant* (October 1812).

SELBY, Thomas. *Captain* (June 9, 1809). See Flank Companies.

SHEETS, John G. *Lieutenant* (October 1812).

SMALLEY, Arad. *Ensign* (December 25, 1812).

THOMPSON, Andrew. *Ensign* (December 25, 1812).

TRAVIS, Jeremiah. *Lieutenant* (June 6, 1809). *Captain* (December 25, 1812).

TYLER, William. *Ensign* (December 25, 1812).

VANDERBURG, Barnet. *Lieutenant* (October 1812). See Flank Companies.

WIDIMAN, Ludiwick. *Ensign* (November 1812).

WILLSON, John. *Captain.*

WILMOT, Samuel S. *Major* (April 16, 1812).

APPLEGARTH, William. *Captain* (May 8, 1811). See Flank Companies.

APPLEGARTH, John. *Lieutenant* (June 6, 1809). See Flank Companies.

ATKINSON, Thomas. *Lieutenant* (May 10, 1811). See Flank Companies.

BATES, William. *Captain* (May 29, 1806).

BEASLEY, Richard. *Colonel* (January 2, 1809).

BEASLEY, David. *Ensign* (September 1813).

CHISHOLM, John. *Captain* (May 10, 1811). See Flank Companies.

CHISHOLM, George. *Ensign* (1812). See Flank Companies.

CHISHOLM, William. *Ensign* (1812). See Flank Companies.

COODY, Philip. *Ensign* (September 1813).

DETLOR, George H. *Ensign* (October 26, 1812).

HEPBURN, William G. *Captain* (May 11, 1811).

HEPBURN, William. *Ensign* (May 14, 1811). See Flank Companies.

JARVIS, Frederick Star. *Lieutenant* (April 15, 1812).

KING, George. *Lieutenant* (May 9, 1811). See Flank Companies. See Casualties.

LUCAS, Thomas. *Ensign* (May 11, 1811).

MACKAY, Hector Sutherland. *Captain* (April 14, 1812).

McCARTY, William. *Ensign* (July 1814). Noted as a prisoner of war.

MERRIGOLD, Thomas. *Captain* (June 5, 1809).

MILLS, James. *Ensign* (May 9, 1811).

MORDEN, James. *Captain* (May 9, 1811).

O'REILLY, Daniel. *Lieutenant* (May 8, 1811). Noted as a prisoner of war.

OVERFELD, Manuel. *Lieutenant* (May 11, 1811).

ROSE, Hugh. *Ensign* (May 10, 1811).

ROUSSEAUX, J. B. *Lieutenant Colonel* (May 16, 1811).

RYCKMAN, Samuel. *Captain* (May 29, 1806).

SIMONS, John K. *Adjutant* (September 1813).

SIMONS, Titus Geer. *Major* (June 4, 1811).

SMITH, Thomas. *Lieutenant* (May 13, 1811).

THOMPSON, William. *Captain* (April 15, 1812). Noted as a prisoner of war.

VAN EVERY, David. *Lieutenant* (March 1, 1804).

ALLAN, William. *Major* (April 15, 1812).

BAYNES, Charles. *Quarter Master* (May 18, 1812).

BOULTON, D'Arcy Jr. *Ensign* (June 30, 1812).

BROOKS, Daniel. *Ensign* (July 2, 1812).

CAMERON, Duncan. *Captain* (June 7, 1809). See Flank Companies.

CARFRAE, Hugh. *Sergeant Major* (April 15, 1812).

CHEWITT, James. *Ensign* (July 1, 1812).

CHEWITT, William. *Lieutenant Colonel* (April 15, 1812).

DENISON, Charles. *Ensign* (December 25, 1812).

DENISON, John. *Captain* (June 29, 1799).

DENISON, George. *Ensign* (December 25, 1812).

DENISON, Thomas. *Ensign* (December 25, 1812).

DUGGAN, George. *Adjutant* (April 17, 1812).

ENDICOTT, John. *Lieutenant* (May 18, 1812).

HAMILTON, Thomas. *Captain* (April 27, 1812).

HEWARD, Stephen. *Captain* (April 16, 1812). See Flank Companies.

HUMBERSTONE, Thomas. *Ensign* (December 25, 1812).

JARVIE, William. *Lieutenant* (April 16, 1812). See Flank Companies.
Captain (December 25, 1812).

JARVIS, Samuel. *Ensign* (April 27, 1812).

JARVIS, Samuel P. *Ensign* (June 30, 1812). See Flank Companies.

JARVIS, William. *Ensign* (May 20, 1812). *Lieutenant*
(December 25, 1812).

KUCK, George. *Ensign* (December 25, 1812).

MATTHEWS, Thomas. *Lieutenant* (May 18, 1812).

McARTHUR, Donald. *Ensign* (May 18, 1812).

McLEAN, Archibald. *Ensign* (April 16, 1812). *Lieutenant*
(May 18, 1812). See Flank Companies.

McMAHON, Edward. *Ensign* (April 29, 1812). See Flank Companies.

MERCER, Andrew. *Ensign* (October 21, 1812).

PLAYTER, Eli. *Lieutenant* (June 30, 1812).

PLAYTER, John. *Captain* (June 8, 1809).

RIDOUT, George. *Ensign* (April 28, 1812, or June 30, 1812). See
Flank Companies.

RIDOUT, Samuel. *Captain* (May 15, 1812).

ROBINSON, John Beverly. *Ensign* (April 17, 1812). See Flank
Companies. *Captain* (December 25, 1812).

SCARLET, John. *Ensign* (May 21, 1812). *Lieutenant*
(December 25, 1812).

SECOR, Isaac. *Lieutenant* (May 18, 1812).

SMITH, William. *Ensign* (May 19, 1812). *Lieutenant*
(December 25, 1812).

STANTON, Robert. *Ensign* (April 17, 1812). *Lieutenant*
(May 18, 1812). See Flank Companies.
THOMPSON, David. *Captain* (January 19, 1810).
THOMPSON, Edward. *Ensign* (December 25, 1812).
WILSON, John. *Ensign* (May 22, 1812). *Lieutenant*
(December 25, 1812).

NIAGARA DISTRICT

1ST LINCOLN

ADAMS, George. *Lieutenant* (May 6, 1812). See Flank Companies.
See Casualties.
BALL, Jacob A. *Captain* (July 2, 1812).
BALL, John C. *Lieutenant* (May 12, 1811).
BALL, George Augustus. *Lieutenant* (May 6, 1806). *Captain*
(July 2, 1812).
BALL, Peter. Jr. *Ensign*. See Flank Companies. *Lieutenant*.
BROWN, Adam. *Ensign* (January 5, 1809). *Lieutenant* (July 2, 1812).
CAMERON, Alexander. *Lieutenant* (May 6, 1812).
CLARK, John. *Adjutant*. *Lieutenant* (June 28, 1812).
CLAUS, William. *Colonel* (June 1812).
CLEMENT, Joseph. *Ensign* (July 2, 1812).
CLENCH, Ralfe. *Colonel* (1812). No record of his resignation, but
William Claus apparently succeeded him in the late spring of 1812.
CROOKS, James. *Captain* (May 13, 1807). See Flank Companies.
See Casualties.
FOSTER, Anlsem. *Lieutenant* (January 5, 1809). See Flank
Companies. *Adjutant* (July 2, 1812).
GEORGE, James. *Ensign* (February 8, 1813). See Casualties.
HAINER, George. *Ensign* (May 6, 1812). *Lieutenant*
(October 25, 1812).
HAMILTON, George. *Captain*.
JONES, John. *Captain* (1812).
LAW, George. *Captain* (1812).
LAWRENCE, George. *Captain*. Resigned July 1812.
MAY, John. *Ensign* (1812). *Lieutenant* (July 2, 1812). See Casualties.
McCLELLAN, Martin. *Lieutenant* (1812). See Flank Companies.
Captain (July 2, 1812). See Casualties.
McEWEN, John. *Captain* (May 13, 1811). See Flank Companies.
See Casualties.
McKEE, Alexander. *2nd Lieutenant*.
PAULING (Pawling), Henry. *Ensign* (May 14, 1806). *Lieutenant*
(July 2, 1812).
POWELL, John. *Captain* (1812).

POWER (Powers), William. *Lieutenant* (January 4, 1806). See Flank
    Companies.
ROBERTSON, John. *Ensign* (October 25, 1812).
ROBERTSON, William. *Major* (June 28, 1812).
RUNCHY, Robert. *Lieutenant*. See Flank Companies. Later taken to
    command the Coloured Corps.
SECORD, James. *Ensign* (July 2, 1812).
SECORD, Van Cortland. *Ensign* (July 2, 1812). See Flank Companies.
SECORD, Elijah. *Ensign* (May 23, 1806) *Lieutenant* (July 2, 1812).
SERVOS, John D. *Captain* (July 2, 1812).
SERVOS, D. K. *Ensign* (July 2, 1812).
SERVOS, William. *Lieutenant* (1812). See Flank Companies.
SMITH, Lewis. *Lieutenant* (1814).
SMITH, William L. *Ensign* (May 6, 1812). *Lieutenant*
    (October 25, 1812).
STEPHENSON, Simcoe. *Ensign* (May 15, 1806). *Lieutenant*
    (July 2, 1812).
WARNER, Peter. *Ensign* (October 25, 1812).

2ND LINCOLN

ASKINS, Charles. *Captain* (1812).
BALL, Jacob J. (A. ?). *Lieutenant* (1813).
BALL, Henry C. *Ensign* (March 17, 1814).
BASTEDO, David. *Captain* (June 26, 1812).
BOUGHNER, Christopher. *Ensign* (1812). See Flank Companies.
    Lieutenant (March 11, 1814), vice Roraback, promoted.
BOWMAN, Abraham. *Lieutenant* (June 26, 1812). See Flank
    Companies. See Casualties.
BROOKS, Robert. *Ensign* (1812).
BRYSON, Alexander. *2nd Lieutenant*.
BURCH, John. *Lieutenant* (1812). See Flank Companies. *Captain*.
    (March 10, 1814), vice Macklem removed to London District.
    See Casualties.
CAMPBELL, Robert. *Captain*. (June 4, 1811).
CANBY, Benjamin. *Ensign* (1812).
CAVERS, Ebenezer. *Ensign* (March 16, 1814).
CLARK, Thomas. *Lieutenant Colonel* (1811).
CLEMENT, Lewis. *Lieutenant* (June 26, 1812), vice Brown resigned.
COOPER, James. *Lieutenant* (1812). See Flank Companies. *Captain*
    (July 4, 1812).
COUCK, John. *Ensign* (1812). *Lieutenant* (March 10, 1814), vice
    Burch, promoted. *Captain*.
CHRYSLER, John. *Captain* (1811).
CUMMINGS, James. *Captain* (1814).

DAVIS, Thadeus. *Lieutenant* (1812). See Flank Companies.

DAVIS, Hall. *Ensign* (March 19, 1814).

DECOU, John. *Captain* (April 16, 1812), prisoner of war.

DICKSON, Thomas. *Lieutenant Colonel* (January 5, 1814).

FRALIGH, John. *Ensign* (1814).

GRANT, Robert. *Captain* (April 17, 1812). See Casualties.

HAINER, John Jr. *Lieutenant* (March 15, 1814).

HAMILTON, Robert. *Captain* (1812). See Flank Companies.

KEEFER (Keever), George. *Lieutenant* (June 4, 1811). *Captain*
(March 9, 1814), vice Campbell resigned.

KERBY, James. *Adjutant* (June 4, 1811). *Captain*.

KIRKPATRICK, Robert. *Ensign* (March 14, 1814). Wounded in the
action at Chippewa, July 5, 1814.

LYONS, James. *Ensign* (June 30, 1812).

MACKLEM, James. *Captain* (1812). Noted as removed to District of
London by March 1814.

McCLELLAN, John. *Lieutenant* (1813).

McDONELL, Christian. *Lieutenant* (1813). Killed in action at
Chippewa, July 5, 1814.

McMICKING, John. *Lieutenant* (June 26, 1812). See Flank Companies.

MEISNER, John. *Ensign* (1812). *Lieutenant* (March 9, 1814), vice
Keefer, promoted.

NELLES, Warner. *Lieutenant* (1812).

PHELPS, Elijah. *Captain* (June 4, 1811).

REILLY, John. *Captain* (June 4, 1811).

RORABACK, Andrew. *Adjutant* (1812). *Captain* (March 11, 1814),
vice Hamilton, absent.

ROW, John. *Captain* (1812). See Flank Companies. See Casualties.

ROW, George. *Ensign* (March 20, 1814).

SECORD, David. *Major* (1813).

SECORD, James Jr. *Ensign* (March 21, 1814).

SMITH, Nicholas. *Lieutenant* (1812). Resigned May 12, 1813.

STREET, John. *Ensign* (March 18, 1814).

STULL, Latham. *Captain* (June 4, 1811).

TURNEY, George. *Captain* (June 4, 1811). See Casualties.

THOMPSON, David. *Adjutant* (March 12, 1814), vice Roraback.

THOMPSON, James. *Ensign* (June 29, 1812). See Flank Companies.

UPPER, Jacob. *Ensign* (June 26, 1812).

UPPER, Anthony. *Lieutenant* (1812). See Flank Companies.

VANDERBURGH, Garret. *Ensign* (1814).

WARREN, John Jr. *Ensign* (March 15, 1814). See Casualties.

WEISHAHN, Henry. *Ensign* (1813).

WILSON, John. *Ensign* (June 27, 1812). *Lieutenant* (March 12, 1814),
vice Smith, resigned.

3RD LINCOLN

ALEXANDER, Hugh. *Lieutenant* (January 25, 1813).

ANGOR, Augustus. *Ensign* (1810). *Lieutenant* (January 25, 1813).

BAXTER, John. *Lieutenant* (1812). *Captain* (January 25, 1813).

BENNER, John Jr. *Ensign* (January 25, 1813).

BUCHNER, Henry. *Captain* (January 2, 1809).

BUCHNER, Ozias. *Lieutenant.* (January 25, 1813).

BUCHNER, Chris. *Ensign* (1812).

CUMMINGS, James. *Captain* (January 25, 1813).

CUMMINGS, Thomas. *Major* (June 25, 1802).

DAVIS, David. *Ensign* (January 25, 1813).

GANDER, Jacob. *Lieutenant* (January 25, 1813).

HARDISON, Benjamin. *Ensign* (1812). See Flank Companies. *Lieutenant* (January 25, 1813).

HARDY, John. *Captain* (January 2, 1809).

LEFERTY, John Johnston. *Lieutenant* (1812). See Flank Companies.

MILLER, William Duff. *Ensign* (1812). See Flank Companies. *Lieutenant* (January 25, 1813).

MILLER, John. *Ensign* (January 25, 1813).

MORGAN, David. *Lieutenant* (1812). Court-martialled and superceded January 20, 1813.

MUIRHEAD, John. *Captain* (January 2, 1809).

PARKS, Shubel. *Lieutenant* (1812). See Flank Companies. *Captain* (January 25, 1813).

POWELL, William. *Lieutenant* (1812). *Captain* (January 25, 1813). See Flank Companies.

PUTMAN, John. *Ensign* (1812). See Flank Companies. *Lieutenant* (January 25, 1813).

REILLY, Patrick. *Lieutenant* (1812).

ROBERTSON, James. *Lieutenant* (1813).

STREET, Samuel. *Captain* (January 2, 1809).

THOMPSON, James. *Ensign* (January 25, 1813).

TROUT, Henry. *Lieutenant* and *Adjutant* (January 25, 1813).

WARREN, John. *Colonel* (June 29, 1802).

WARREN, John. *Captain* (1812). See Flank Companies. *Lieutenant Colonel* (April 16, 1813).

WARREN, Henry. *Major* (1812).

WEAVER, Peter. *Lieutenant* (1812). Court-martialled and superceded January 20, 1813.

WHITEHEAD, George. *Ensign* (January 25, 1813).

WINTERMUTE, Philip. *Ensign* (1812). See Casualties.

WISEHUHN, Henry. *Ensign* (January 25, 1813).

BELL, Nathaniel. *Quarter Master* (July 3, 1812). See Casualties.

BUTLER, Johnson. *Major* (1804). *Lieutenant Colonel* (May 16, 1806). See Casualties.

BUTLER, Thomas. *Lieutenant* (1812). See Flank Companies. *Captain* (November 2, 1812). Resigned October 8, 1814.

CAMPBELL, James. *Ensign* (1814).

CARPENTER, William. *Lieutenant* (1804). *Captain* (June 28, 1812).

CHISHOLM, William. *Ensign* (June 28, 1812).

COMFORT, Robert. *Lieutenant* (1804). *Captain* (June 29, 1812).

CROOKS, Francis. *Ensign* (June 28, 1812).

CROOKS, Matthew. *Ensign* (May 22, 1811). *Lieutenant* (July 8, 1812). See Flank Companies.

CROOKS, William. *Captain* (1806). See Flank Companies.

DITTRICK (Dederich), James. *Lieutenant* (June 28, 1812). See Flank Companies. *Captain*.

DEDERICH, Walter. *Ensign* (June 28, 1812). *Lieutenant*.

DOCKSTATER, Henry. *Lieutenant*. (July 1, 1813).

GRIFFIN, Edward. *Ensign* (1804). *Lieutenant* (June 28, 1812).

HARE, Peter. *Ensign* (June 28, 1812). *Lieutenant* (January 1814).

HENRY, James. *Captain*. Resigned April 1813.

HENRY, John. *Lieutenant* (July 1, 1812). See Flank Companies.

HIXON, Henry. *Lieutenant* (July 3, 1812). See Flank Companies. *Captain* (September 20, 1814).

HOUSE, Philip. *Captain* (1812).

KENNEDY (Canada), Charles. *Ensign* (July 5, 1813).

LEWIS, Daniel. *Ensign* (June 28, 1812).

LYONS, William. *Captain* (October 25, 1812).

McCOLLUM, John. *Ensign* (July 4, 1814).

McCALLUM, Peter. *Lieutenant* (1812). See Flank Companies.

McKAY, John. *Major* (May 16, 1806).

MERRITT, William Hamilton. *Ensign* (May 23, 1811).

MOORE, John. *Ensign* (July 8, 1813).

MOORE, Jonathan. *Captain* (1812). See Flank Companies.

MUIRHEAD, John B. *Ensign* (June 28, 1812). *Lieutenant* (May 22, 1814).

NELLES, Abraham. *Captain* (1797). See Flank Companies. *Major* (October 16, 1814).

NELLES, Henry. *Lieutenant* (1812). See Flank Companies. *Captain* (July 1, 1813).

NELLES, Robert. *Lieutenant Colonel* (October 16, 1814).

NELLES, William. *Captain* (June 25, 1802).

NIXON, Allan. *Captain* (May 22, 1811).

OWEN, Abner. *Lieutenant* (July 4, 1814).

PAWLING, Henry. *Ensign* (1812). *Lieutenant* (September 18, 1813).

PETTIT, Jonathan A. *Lieutenant* (January 3, 1809). *Captain* (July 4, 1813).

PETTIT, Jonathan. *Ensign* (July 4, 1814).

PETTIT, Robert. *Ensign* (1812). *Lieutenant* (September 20, 1813).

SERVOS, William. *Lieutenant* (1812). See Flank Companies.

SIMMERMAN, Adam. *Ensign* (1812). *Lieutenant* (July 4, 1814).

SMITH, Israel. *Ensign* (July 3, 1813).

TAYLOR, John J. *Adjutant* (1812).

TEN BROECK, Jacob. *Captain* (1804). *Major* (June 28, 1812). Resigned October 16, 1814.

TURNEY, John. *Ensign* (July 6, 1813).

WRONG, Gilbert. *Ensign* (July 7, 1813).

5TH LINCOLN

AIKMAN, John. *Captain* (1813).

AIKMAN, John. *Lieutenant* (June 25, 1802).

BARNUM, Ezra. *Quarter Master* (1812).

BIGGAR (S), William. *Ensign* (May 7, 1812). *Lieutenant* (1812). Court-martialled and superceded January 20, 1813.

BIRNEY, Joseph. *Ensign* (May 1, 1812). See Flank Companies.

BOWMAN, Peter. *Captain* (January 2, 1809).

BRADT, Andrew. *Lieutenant Colonel* (January 2, 1809).

BRADT, John. *Ensign* (May 7, 1812). Noted as taken a prisoner of war on June 7, 1813.

CAIRN (Karn), David. *Ensign* (1812).

CARPENTER, Gersham. *Captain* (1813).

CHISHOLM, William. *Ensign*. See Flank Companies.

DAVIS (Davie), William. *Lieutenant* (January 2, 1809). See Flank Companies.

DEPEW, Charles. *Captain* (January 4, 1809).

DOWDY, Israel. *Captain* (May 2, 1812).

DURAND, James. *Captain* (May 1, 1812). See Flank Companies.

GARDINER, Lebius. *Lieutenant* (1812).

HATT, Samuel. *Captain* (January 2, 1809). See Flank Companies.

HATT, Richard. *Major* (January 2, 1809). See Casualties.

HESS, Peter. *Lieutenant* (1812).

HORNING, Lewis. *Lieutenant* (1812).

HOUSE, Joseph. *Lieutenant* (May 2, 1812).

HOWARD, Frederick. *Captain*.

KERR, David. *Ensign* (January 11, 1809).

KRIBBS, David. *Ensign* (September 1813).

LAND, Abel Sr. *Lieutenant* (May 1, 1812).

LAND, Abel Jr. *Ensign* (May 4, 1812).

LAND, Ephraim. *Lieutenant* (July 29, 1813).

LAND, Robert. *Lieutenant* (January 2, 1809). See Flank Companies. *Captain*.

LOTTRIDGE, John. *Captain* (May 3, 1812). See Casualties.

LOTTRIDGE, William. *Captain* (January 2, 1809).

McDOUGALL, Allan. *Ensign* (September 29, 1813).

McINTYRE, John W. *Adjutant*. See Casualties.

NEWTON, David. *Adjutant* (1812). Court-martialled and superceded January 20, 1813.

PERRIN, Thomas. *Captain*.

RACEY, Thomas. *Ensign, Lieutenant* (1812).

RACEY, Thomas. *Lieutenant* (1812).

ROUSSEAUX, George. *Ensign* (May 6, 1812).

RYMALL, Jacob. *Lieutenant* (May 2, 1812).

RYMALL, Philip. *Ensign.* (May 2, 1812).

SHOWERS, Michael. *Lieutenant* (1812).

SHOWERS, Daniel. *Ensign* (May 3, 1812). See Flank Companies.

SMITH, George F. *Ensign* (October 17, 1813).

SMITH, John. *Captain* (January 2, 1809).

SPRINGSTED, Jacob. *Ensign* (May 5, 1812).

YOUNG, Daniel. *Captain* (January 2, 1809).

WESTBROOK, John. *Captain.* (June 19, 1814).

LONDON DISTRICT

1ST NORFOLK

BACKHOUSE, John. *Captain* (February 18, 1812).

BACKHOUSE, Thomas. *Ensign* (February 17, 1812).

BOSTWICK, John. *Captain* (February 11, 1812). See Flank Companies.

BOWEN, William D. *Major* (February 11, 1812).

DEDRICK, John. *Lieutenant* (February 17, 1812).

DILL, William. *Lieutenant* (February 18, 1812).

GLOVER, Francis. *Ensign* (February 15, 1812).

GORDON, William. *Adjutant*.

MABEE, Oliver. *Captain* (February 13, 1812).

McCALL, Daniel. *Captain* (February 12, 1812). See Flank Companies.

McCALL, Duncan. *Captain* (February 14, 1812).

McCALL, James. *Ensign* (February 14, 1812). See Flank Companies.

MITCHELL, James. *Lieutenant* (February 12, 1812). *Captain* (June 30, 1812).

POTTS, Jacob. *Ensign* (February 13, 1812). *Lieutenant* (September 25, 1813).

ROLPH, George. *Lieutenant* (February 14, 1812). See Flank Companies.

ROLPH, Romain. *Ensign* (February 12, 1812).

ROSS, Daniel. *Lieutenant* (February 15, 1812).

RYERSON, George. *Lieutenant* (February 11, 1812). See Flank Companies.

RYERSON, Samuel. *Ensign* (February 11, 1812). See Flank Companies. *Lieutenant* (September 25, 1813).

RYERSON, Joseph. *Lieutenant Colonel* (February 11, 1812).

SHAW, Michael. *Captain* (February 17, 1812).

SMITH, William. *Lieutenant* (February 13, 1812).

TISDALE, Mathew. *Ensign* (February 18, 1812).

TISDALE, Samuel. *Adjutant* (October 25, 1814).

WALSH, Aquilla. *Ensign* (September 25, 1813).

WALSH, Francis Leigh. *Quarter Master* (February 11, 1812).

WHITE, Nathaniel. *Captain* (February 15, 1812).

2ND NORFOLK

AUSTIN, Jonathan. *Lieutenant* (February 14, 1812). See Flank Companies.

BEEMER, Abraham. *Lieutenant* (February 19, 1812). Never served, possibly superceded.

BEEMER, Philip. *Ensign* (February 12, 1812). Never served, possibly superceded.

BERDAN, Albert. *Quarter Master.* (July 4, 1812).

BOSTWICK, Henry. *Captain* (February 13, 1812).

COLLVER, Nesbit. *Lieutenant* (February 15, 1812).

COLLVER, Timothy. *Ensign* (February 15, 1812). Returned as having deserted to the enemy.

CONROD, John. *Ensign* (April 25, 1814).

DAVIS, James. *Ensign* (February 11, 1812).

DAVIS, Thomas. *Lieutenant* (February 17, 1812).

DRAKE, William. *Captain* (May 19, 1812).

FRANCIS, Thomas. *Ensign* (April 25, 1814).

GILBERT, Isaac. *Ensign* (May 19, 1812). See Flank Companies.

GORDON, William. *Lieutenant* (May 19, 1812). *Adjutant* (May 19, 1812). See Flank Companies.

LEMON, Jacob. *Ensign* (September 25, 1813).

McCRACKEN, William. *Captain* (May 19, 1812). See Flank Companies.

McQUEEN, James. *Ensign* (April 25, 1814).

MEAD, Benjamin. *Lieutenant* (June 30, 1812).

MEDCALF, Henry. *Lieutenant. Captain* (January 21, 1814).

MESSACCAR, Abraham. *Ensign* (February 13, 1812).

NICHOL, Robert. *Lieutenant Colonel* (February 11, 1812). Appointed *Quarter Master General* (July 3, 1812).

PARK, William. *Captain* (February 14, 1812).

RAPELJE, Abraham. *Captain* (February 11, 1812). See Flank Companies.

READ, Benjamin. *Lieutenant* (May 20, 1812).

ROBINSON, (Robertson) William. *Lieutenant* (February 18, 1812). *Captain* (September 25, 1813).

ROSS, Daniel. *Lieutenant* (February 13, 1812).

RYERSE, Samuel. *Captain* (February 12, 1812).

RYERSE, George. *Ensign* (October 25, 1814).

SALMON, George C. *Major* (February 11, 1812).

SHOAFF, Denis. *Ensign* (February 14, 1812).

WHITE, Nathaniel. *Captain* (February 15, 1812). See Flank Companies.

WILLIAMS, Titus. *Ensign* (February 17, 1812). *Lieutenant* (July 13, 1812). See Flank Companies. See Casualties.

WILSON, McFarlane. *Ensign* (May 20, 1812).

1ST OXFORD

AMES, Brockway. *Lieutenant* (June 25, 1814).

BAKER, Joseph. *Ensign. Lieutenant* (July 11, 1812). See Flank Companies. Deserted to the enemy.

BOSTWICK, Henry Bostwick. *Lieutenant Colonel* (May 19, 1812).

BOTSFORD, William. *Lieutenant* (July 11, 1812). See Flank Companies. Noted in a return of 1819 as having gone to the enemy.

BOWEN, William Daniel. *Major* (February 11, 1812).

BRIGHAM, Belah Brewster. *Lieutenant* (July 13, 1812). See Flank Companies. *Captain* (November 5, 1812).

BROWN, Daniel. *Ensign* (July 15, 1812). *Lieutenant* (April 25, 1814).

BURDICK, Isaac. *Ensign* (July 11, 1812).

CARROL, John. *Captain* (July 11, 1812). See Flank Companies. See Casualties.

CARROL, Henry. *Ensign* (July 13, 1812). *Lieutenant* (October 22, 1812).

CARROL, James. *Ensign* (July 14, 1812). *Lieutenant* (February 24, 1814).

CURTIS, David. *Captain* (July 11, 1812).

DECOU, Abner. *Ensign* (July 16, 1812).

EAKINS, John. *Adjutant* (July 11, 1812).

HALL, Ichabod. *Captain* (July 11, 1812).

HARRIS, James. *Lieutenant* (July 14, 1812).

KINDRICK, Isaac. *Lieutenant* (October 25, 1813).

MALCOLM, Finley. *Ensign* (July 17, 1812). *Lieutenant* (April 25, 1814).

MALCOLM, John. *Lieutenant* (July 15, 1812). *Captain* (April 25, 1814).

McCARTNEY, *Ensign* William. *Lieutenant* (acting).

MARTIN, Peter. *Ensign* (June 25, 1814).

OWEN, Abner. *Lieutenant*.

PIPER, Joel. *Ensign*.

SECORD, John. *Captain* (July 11, 1812).

TEEPLE, William. *Lieutenant* (January 25, 1814).

TOWSELY, Sykes. *Major* (May 19, 1812). See Casualties.

WATSON, Edward. *Captain* (October 22, 1812).

WHITE, Marvil. *Captain* (1812). See Flank Companies.

WILLIAMS, John. *Lieutenant* (September 25, 1812). See Flank Companies.

YEIGH, Jacob. *Lieutenant* (July 11, 1812).

1ST MIDDLESEX

AXFORD, Samuel. *Lieutenant* (February 17, 1812).

BIRD, William. *Lieutenant* (February 12, 1812). See Flank Companies.

BURWELL, Mahlon. *Lieutenant Colonel* (February 13, 1812).

DAVIS, David. *Ensign* (February 13, 1812).

DEFIELD, Joseph. *Ensign* (February 14, 1812). See Flank Companies.

EDISON, Samuel. *Captain* (February 17, 1812).

HARRIS, Samuel. *Ensign* (February 17, 1812).

McINTYRE, Daniel. *Ensign* (February 12, 1812).

NEVILL, James. *Adjutant* (April 25, 1814).

PATTERSON, Leslie. *Captain* (February 15, 1812). See Casualties.

POTTS, John. *Adjutant* (1812).

RAPELJE, Daniel. *Captain* (May 1814).

REYNOLDS, Sylvanus. *Quarter Master* (1812).

RICE, Moses. *Lieutenant* (February 15, 1812).

SAXTON, William. *Lieutenant* (February 13, 1812). See Flank Companies.

SECORD, David. *Captain* (February 12, 1812). See Flank Companies.

SPRINGER, Daniel. *Captain* (February 13, 1812). See Flank Companies.

TALBOT, Thomas. *Colonel* (February 12, 1812).

TIFFANY, Gideon. *Lieutenant* (February 14, 1812).
WILSON, Benjamin. *Ensign* (February 15, 1812). See Flank
    Companies.
WILSON, Gilman. *Captain* (February 14, 1812). See Casualties.

WESTERN DISTRICT

1ST ESSEX

ALLAN, James. *Lieutenant Colonel* (August 7, 1807). Died
    November 2, 1817.
BARTHE, Jean Baptiste. *Captain.*
BELL, John. *Captain* (1811).
BONDY Laurent. *Captain.* See Casualties.
BONFORD,(Bouffard) Antoine. *Ensign* (1812) *Lieutenant.*
BOUCHERVILLE, Thomas. *Lieutenant* (1812).
BRUSH, John. *Lieutenant* (June 5, 1809).
BUCHANAN, William. *Captain.* See Casualties.
CALDWELL, Francis. *Ensign* (July 12, 1812).
CALDWELL, William Jr. *Captain* (May 8, 1807). See Flank Companies.
CALDWELL, Thomas. *Ensign* (1812). See Flank Companies.
    Lieutenant (1812).
DUFF, William. *Adjutant.*
ELLIOTT, Matthew. *Lieutenant Colonel* (1804).
ELLIOTT, William. *Captain* (August 18, 1807) See Flank Companies.
FORTIER, Charles. *Ensign* (1812).
GIRTY, Thomas. *Ensign* (1812) See Flank Companies. Died
    September 18, 1812.
GIRTY, Prideaux. *Ensign* (1816).
GORDON, James. *Lieutenant* (June 6, 1809). See Flank Companies.
    See Casualties. Promoted *Captain.*
GRANT, Robert. *Captain* (January 1, 1809).
HALL, George Benson. Late of the Provincial Marine
    (September 21, 1813).
INNIS, Robert. *Quarter Master.*
LAFERTE, Alexis. *Lieutenant.* (1812).
LAPORTE, Alexis. *Lieutenant.*
LITTLE (Lytle), James W. *Ensign.* See Flank Companies.
LITTLE (Lytle), John. *Lieutenant* (1812). See Flank Companies.
LYTTLE, Nicholas. *Ensign* (July 12, 1812). See Flank Companies.
MAISONVILLE. *Captain.*
McCORMICK, William. *Lieutenant* (1812). See Flank Companies.
    See Casualties.
McCORMICK, John. *Ensign* (July 12, 1812).

MILLS, William. *Captain*. See Casualties.
REAUME, Charles. *Lieutenant*.
REYNOLDS, Ebenezer. *Major, Lieutenant Colonel*
  (September 21, 1813). Shown as Major in 1816.
REYNOLDS, Robert. *Captain* (1811).
SCRATCH, Peter. *Ensign*.
STOCKWELL, James. *Ensign*.
WAGLEY (Weighly), Windle (Wendal). *Ensign, Lieutenant*.

2ND ESSEX

ASKIN, James. *Captain* (1812). See Flank Companies.
ASKIN, Alexander D. *Lieutenant* (July 9, 1812). See Flank Companies.
ASKIN, John. *Major* (September 22, 1813).
BABY, Jean Baptiste. *Lieutenant Colonel* (August 1, 1806).
BARTHE, Jean Baptiste. *Captain* (1812).
BATISHON, Dedine. *Lieutenant*.
EBERTS, Joseph. *Ensign* (July 9, 1812). See Flank Companies.
ELLIOTT, William.
GARVIN, Claude. *Ensign*. See Casualties.
GENTLE, John. *Ensign*.
GENTLE, John, *Adjutant* (July 25, 1812).
GOUIN, Claude. *Ensign* (July 17, 1812).
HANDS, William Jr. , *Ensign* (July 9, 1812). See Flank Companies.
JANISSE, Hypolite. *Ensign* (acting).
LABADIE, Jean Baptiste. *Lieutenant*.
LABUTE, Pierre. *Captain*.
LABUTE, Alexis. *Captain* (1812).
LABUTE, Julien. *Captain* (July 9, 1812).
MAISONVILLE, Toussaint. *Captain* (July 9, 1812).
MAISONVILLE, Alexis. *Captain* (1812). See Flank Companies.
McGREGOR, James. *Lieutenant*.
McINTOSH, James. *Quarter Master* (1812).
McINTOSH, Duncan. *Lieutenant* (July 9, 1812).
McKEE, Thomas. *Major* (1811).
OUILLETTE, Jean Baptiste. *Ensign* (July 9, 1812).
PARENT, Alexis. *Lieutenant* (1812).
PARENT, Joseph. *Lieutenant* (July 9, 1812). See Flank Companies.
PARENT, Jacques. *Ensign* (acting).
PATTINSON, Richard. *Captain* (1812).
PETRE, Jean Baptiste. *Lieutenant*.
PRINGLE, Alexander, *Paymaster* (1812). *Quarter Master*
  (July 3, 1812).

PRINGLE, Alexander. *Ensign* (July 9, 1812).
REAUME, Thomas P. *Lieutenant.*
REAUME, Pierre. *Lieutenant.*
SHAW, William. *Ensign* (acting).
SMITH, William, *Adjutant* (acting) (July 2, 1812). *Captain.*
SMITH, Charles. *Ensign* (July 9, 1812).
WOODS, James. *Captain* (July 9, 1812).
WOODS, Bryce. *Ensign* (July 9, 1812).

1ST KENT

BABY, The Hon. James. *Colonel.*
DOLSEN, Isaac. *Lieutenant.*
DOLSEN, John. *Lieutenant* (1811). *Captain.*
JACOB, George. *Captain* (1811). See Flank Companies.
McKERIGAN, David. *Lieutenant* (1811).
McRAE, Thomas. *Captain* (1811).
PECK, Robert. *Ensign* (1811).
PECK, Robert. *Lieutenant* (1811).
PECK, John. *Lieutenant.* See Flank Companies.
PECK, John. *Ensign* (1810).
SHAW, William. *Captain* (1811).
SHAW, William. *Ensign.*
STERLING, William. *Lieutenant* (1811). See Flank Companies.
TRAXLER, Peter. *Ensign* (1811).
WILLIAMS, John. *Lieutenant* (1811).

III

THE FLANK COMPANIES

I N regular regiments of the line there were two companies
that were considered the elite of each regiment. They were
designated the "grenadier" and "light" companies and were
positioned on the right and left of the line respectively. Flank
companies had been authorized in the militia in the 1790s; the
1st York and 1st Norfolk, for example, had both light and
grenadier companies in the early 1800s.

A principal objective of General Brock's supplementary
Militia Act of February 1812 had been the establishment of a
better trained, loyal and dependable core in each militia regiment, one that could be called on to give effective support to his
all-too-few regulars in the defence of the colony. Apparently he
envisaged something quite different than what the legislature
eventually accepted. He was disappointed by the limited periods
of service allowed.

The supplementary Militia Act called for flank companies to
be established in every regimental division; they were to consist
of no more than 100 men from 18 to 50 years of age, and in no
case to exceed one-third of the total strength of any battalion.
The companies were to be called out for training and exercise six
days in each month until they were considered "duly instructed,"
after which the commanding officer would call them out for training one day a month. When the different regimental commanding

officers were ordered to form the new flank companies in the spring of 1812, they were instructed to fill them to only 25 to 35 rank and file, and not the maximum allowed by law.

As a result, only a small proportion of the flankers who were called out on active service in July had actually received any training. When the different companies were filled up to the limit allowed by law at the beginning of July, a ballot had to be used in Leeds, Northumberland, Durham, and Norfolk to fill their quotas. A second subaltern officer was appointed at the same time.

The Militia Act called for a maximum of eight months' continuous service, and in December volunteers and drafted men were called on to relieve the men who were still on duty. The men who had served as flankers were then put at the bottom of their company rolls and were not to be drafted until all others in their divisions had served.

In a number of instances the officers were relieved every two or three months and so more officers than authorized were returned as having served in the first campaign.

Until actually called out on active service these men were not paid or clothed by the government, but they were armed and accoutred wherever possible.

Companies of flankers were often referred to by the name of their commanding officer. The following guide to the flankers consists of two parts: the first lists flank companies by county (arranged from east to west) and the names of men holding commissions in them; the second is a roll of all men who served at some point in each company.

FLANK COMPANIES AND OFFICERS

EASTERN DISTRICT

Lieutenant Colonel Neil McLean
Adjutant Arthur Burton

1ST GLENGARRY

1st Flank Company
Captain John Hooke Campbell
Lieutenant John Cameron
Ensign James McDonell

2nd Flank Company
Captain Duncan McDonell
Lieutenant Donald McDonald
Ensign John Kennedy

3rd Flank Company
Captain Duncan McDonell (same as 2nd Flank Company)
Lieutenant Alexander McDonald
Ensign Duncan Murchison

2ND GLENGARRY

1st Flank Company
Captain Donald McDonell. Served in 1812.
Captain Alexander McMillan. Served in 1813.
Lieutenant Angus Kennedy. Served two months as a captain.
Ensign Alexander Macdonald

2nd Flank Company
Captain Alexander MacKenzie
Lieutenant Donald McMartin
Ensign Duncan McMillan

1ST STORMONT

1st Flank Company
Captain William Morgan
Lieutenant Philip Empey
Lieutenant Alexander McLean
Ensign Henry Stewart

2nd Flank Company
Captain Philip Empey
Lieutenant John McLean
Lieutenant John VanKoughnet
Ensign Philip Empey

1ST DUNDAS

1st Flank Company
    Captain Michael Ault
    Lieutenant James Fraser
    Lieutenant Jacob Dorin
    Ensign Duncan Clark

2nd Flank Company
    Captain George Merkley
    Lieutenant Alexander Rose
    Lieutenant Christopher Merkley
    Ensign Jacob Merkley

JOHNSTOWN DISTRICT

Adjutant William Fraser, Prescott

1ST GRENVILLE

1st Flank Company
    Captain Hugh Munro
    Lieutenant Andrew Adams
    Lieutenant John Fraser
    Ensign Solomon Snyder

2nd Flank Company
    Captain Philip Dulmage
    Lieutenant Donell Fraser
    Lieutenant John Lawrence
    Ensign Samuel Dulmage

2ND GRENVILLE

1st Flank Company
    Captain Daniel Burritt
    Lieutenant Henry Burritt
    Ensign Thomas McRae

2nd Flank Company
    Captain Hamilton Walker
    Lieutenant Richard D. Fraser
    Ensign John Kerr

1ST LEEDS

Flank Companies
    Captain John Stuart
        Jonas Jones served a short time as captain.
    Captain Sylvester Wright
        Reuben Sherwood served a short time as captain.
        Allan Grant served a short time as captain.
    Lieutenant Jonathan Fulford
    Lieutenant John McLean
    Ensign Abraham Dayton
    Ensign John Hagerman
    Ensign William Morris
    Ensign Terence Smith

2ND LEEDS

Flank Companies
    Captain Ira Schofield to February 16, 1813, relieved by
    Captain William Jones from February 16, 1813.
    Captain Benoni Wiltsee to February 16, 1813, relieved by
    Lieutenant Andrew Bradish from February 16, 1813.
    Lieutenant John Struthers
    Lieutenant Andrew Bradish to February 16, 1813, then relieved by
    Lieutenant Samuel Kelsey from February 16, 1813.
    Ensign Nathan Hicock
    Ensign Samuel Read to March 1, 1813, then relieved by
    Ensign James Kilborn from March 1, 1813.

MIDLAND DISTRICT

Colonel Richard Cartwright

1ST FRONTENAC

Flank Companies
    Captain Thomas Markland
    Captain William Robins
    Lieutenant Patrick Smith. Resigned May 9, 1813.
    Lieutenant Thorney Sparham
    Lieutenant Thomas Cook
    Ensign Robert Richardson
    Ensign John Brass
    Ensign Simon Washburn

1ST LENNOX

Flank Companies
Captain Nicholas Hagerman
Captain Thomas Dorland
Captain Elisha Phillips
Lieutenant Reuben Bedell
Ensign Oliver Church
Ensign Benjamin Conger Spencer
Ensign Christopher Alexander Hagerman

1ST ADDINGTON

Flank Companies
Captain Mathew Clark
Captain Sheldon Hawley
Lieutenant Daniel Fraser
Lieutenant Henry Davey
Ensign Jehial Hawley
Ensign John C. Clark

1ST HASTINGS

Flank Companies
Captain Gilbert Harris
Captain John MacIntosh
Captain Jacob Walden Meyers
Lieutenant John Thompson
Ensign Hugh Fairman
Ensign William Ketcheson
Ensign Joseph LeMoine

1ST PRINCE EDWARD

Flank Companies
Captain John Allen. To December 31, 1812.
Captain Owen Richards. Served the whole war.
Lieutenant Donald McIntosh. Served to December 4, 1814.
Lieutenant James Young
Lieutenant Henry Young. Died on service in 1812.
Ensign Robert Young
Ensign Richard Howell
Ensign Simon Washburn

NEWCASTLE DISTRICT

1ST NORTHUMBERLAND

Flank Companies
Captain John Spencer, relieved in 1812 by
Captain Robert G. Wilkins.
Captain Asa Burnham. Died in March 1813.
Lieutenant Roger Woolcut
Lieutenant James Norris
Ensign Joseph A. Keeler
Ensign Adam H. Meyers

1ST DURHAM

1st Flank Company
Captain John Burn
Lieutenant John Karr
Ensign John Taylor

HOME DISTRICT

Major William Allan
Adjutant John Johnston

1ST YORK

1st Flank Company
Captain John Selby
Lieutenant Reuben Richardson
Lieutenant Barnet Vanderburgh

2ND YORK

1st Flank Company
Captain John Chisholm
Lieutenant George King. Died on service in 1812.
Ensign George Chisholm. Joined after death of Lieutenant King.
Ensign William Hepburn

2nd Flank Company
Captain William Applegarth
Lieutenant Thomas Atkinson
Lieutenant John Applegarth. Joined as a supernumerary officer
    November 1, 1812.
Ensign William Chisholm

3RD YORK

1st Flank Company
Captain Duncan Cameron
Lieutenant William Jarvie
Lieutenant Archibald McLean
Lieutenant George Ridout
Lieutenant Edward McMahon. On duty attached to General Brock.

2nd Flank Company
Captain Stephen Heward
Lieutenant John B. Robinson
Lieutenant Robert Stanton
Lieutenant Samuel P. Jarvis

NIAGARA DISTRICT

Colonel William Claus, Fort George

1ST LINCOLN

1st Flank Company
Captain James Crooks
Lieutenant Martin McClellan. Promoted to a battalion company.
Lieutenant William Powers
Lieutenant Anslem Foster. Vice McClellan, promoted.
Ensign Van Courtland Secord

2nd Flank Company
Captain John McEwen
Lieutenant Robert Runchy. Taken to command the
    Coloured Corps.
Lieutenant William Servos. Vice Runchy, promoted.
Lieutenant George Adams

2ND LINCOLN

Flank Companies
Captain John Row
Captain Robert Hamilton
Lieutenant James Cooper. Promoted to a battalion company,
    July 4, 1812.
Lieutenant Anthony Upper
Lieutenant John Burch. From July 4 to October 29, 1812.
Lieutenant John McMicking. From October 29 to end of the year.
Lieutenant Thadeus Davis. To July 4, 1812.
Lieutenant Abram Bowman. From July 4 to the end of the year.
Ensign Christopher Boughner
Ensign James Thompson

3RD LINCOLN

Flank Companies
- Captain John Warren
- Captain William Powell
- Lieutenant Shubal Park
- Lieutenant John Johnson Lefferty. From June 26 to August 1, 1812.
- Ensign Benjamin Hardison Jr.
- Ensign William Duff Miller
- Ensign John Putman

4TH LINCOLN

1st Flank Company
- Captain Abraham Nelles
- Lieutenant Thomas Butler
- Lieutenant James Dedrick
- Lieutenant Mathew Crooks. From October 16, 1812.

2nd Flank Company
- Captain Jonathan Moore. From June 27 to August 24, 1812.
- Captain William Crooks. From August 24, 1812.
- Lieutenant Henry Hixon. To August 24, 1812.
- Lieutenant John Henry. To August 24, 1812.
- Lieutenant Henry Nelles. From August 24, 1812.
- Lieutenant William Servos. From August 24, 1812.
- Lieutenant Peter McCollum. Promoted and joined in October 1812.

5TH LINCOLN

1st Flank Company
- Captain Samuel Hatt
- Lieutenant Robert Land
- Ensign Daniel Showers

2nd Flank Company
- Captain James Durand
- Lieutenant William Davie
- Ensign Joseph Birnie

LONDON DISTRICT

Major George C. Salmon, Adjutant (June 30, 1812)

1ST NORFOLK

1st Flank Company
Captain John Bostwick
Lieutenant George Ryerson
Lieutenant George Rolph
2nd Flank Company
(sometimes referred to as a rifle company)
Captain Daniel McCall
Lieutenant Samuel Ryerson
Ensign James McCall

2ND NORFOLK

Flank Companies
Captain Nathaniel White
Captain Abraham A. Rapelje
Captain William McCracken
Lieutenant William Gordon
Lieutenant Jonathan Austin
Lieutenant Titus Williams
Ensign Isaac Gilbert

1ST OXFORD

1st Flank Company
Captain Marvil White
Lieutenant Joseph Baker
Lieutenant John Williams
2nd Flank Company
Captain John Carrol
Lieutenant Bela B. Brigham
Lieutenant William Botsford

1ST MIDDLESEX

Flank Companies
Captain David Secord
Captain Daniel Springer
Lieutenant William Saxton
Lieutenant William Bird
Ensign Benjamin Willson
Ensign Joseph De Fields

WESTERN DISTRICT

Major Ebenezer Reynolds
Adjutant William Duff

1ST ESSEX

1st Flank Company
Captain William Caldwell
Lieutenant James Gordon. Appointed to command a gunboat
    July 10, 1812.
Lieutenant William McCormick
Ensign Thomas Caldwell. On staff of Quarter Master General's
    department from July 12, 1812.
Ensign Nicholas Lytle. Promoted from private July 12, 1812.
2nd Flank Company
Captain William Elliott
Lieutenant John Little
Ensign Thomas Girty. Died September 18, 1812.
Ensign James Little

2ND ESSEX

1st Flank Company
Captain James Askin
Lieutenant Alexander D. Askin
Ensign William Hands Jr.
2nd Flank Company
Captain Alexis Maisonville
Lieutenant Joseph Parent
Ensign Joseph Eberts

1ST KENT

Flank Company
Captain George Jacob
Lieutenant John Peck
Lieutenant William Sterling

NOMINAL ROLL OF THE FLANKERS

EASTERN DISTRICT

1ST GLENGARRY

1st Flank Company

ALGERRIE, John. Private.
ARGUIT, Michael. Private.
ARGUIT, Peter. Private.
ARGUIT, Joseph. Private.
ASHBURN, John. Private.
BANTER, William. Private.
BRINKMAN, John. Private.
BROWN, Josephus. Private.
CAMERON, John. Private.
CAMERON, John. *Lieutenant.*
CAMERON, Hugh. Private.
CAMPBELL, Donald. Private.
CAMPBELL, John Hooke.
  Captain.
CAMPBELL, John. Sergeant.
CAMPBELL, William. Sergeant.
CLARK, John. Private.
CLARKE, Alexander. Private.
CROSS, James. Private.
DOGHERTY, John. Private.
GLASSFORD, Benjamin. Private.
GLASSFORD, Mathaniel. Private.
GRANT, Ranald Sr. Private.
GRANT, Richard. Private.
GRANT, Donald (Front). Private.
GRANT, Duncan (Dutoryan).
  Private.
GRANT, Alexander Sr. (Front).
  Private.
GRANT, Donald (Dutoryan).
  Private.
GRANT, John. Sergeant.
HAY, William. Private.
HAY, Alexander. Private.
HEWITT, John. Private.
HUDSON, William. Private.
KENNEDY, Donald. Private.
KENNEDY, Angus. Private.

LAVOY, Joseph. Private.
MALLOT, Stephen. Private.
MARTIN, Francis. Private.
McCARTHUR, Donald. Private.
McDONELL, Ranald (T. L.).
  Private.
McDONELL, Allan (L. B.).
  Private.
McDONELL, Alexander
  (Samuel). Private.
McDONELL, Donald (Brown).
  Private.
McDONELL, James (L. B.).
  Private.
McDONELL, John Private.
McDONELL, James. *Ensign.*
McDONELL, Donald (T. L.).
  Private.
McDONELL, John Jr. Private.
McDONELL, Alexander
  (Bridge). Private.
McDONELL, Angus (Black).
  Private.
McDONELL, Ranald (Front).
  Private.
McGEE, Oliver. Private.
McGEE, James. Private.
McINTYRE, John. Private.
McLAUCHLIN, William. Private.
McLELLAN, Donald. Private.
McLENNAN, Hugh. Private.
McLENNAN, Donald. Private.
MYRES, Joseph. Private.
  Deserted to the enemy.
ROBINS, Robert. Private.
SANTIMORE, John. Private.
SMITH, William Sr. Private.
SMITH, John. Private.
SNYDER, Francis. Private.

SULLIVAN, George. Private.
SUMMERS, Andrew. Private.
TYO, Pero. Private.
TYO, Francis. Private.
TYO, Marset. Private.
WOOD, Hiram. Private.
WOOD, Roger. Private.
YOUNG, George. Private.
YOUNG, Allan. Private.

2nd Flank Company
BETHUNE, John. Private.
BETHUNE, Angus. Private.
CALDER, William. Private.
CAMERON, Donald Sr. Private.
CAMERON, Donald. Private.
CAMERON, James. Sergeant.
CAMERON, Donald Jr. Private.
CAMPBELL, Alexander. Private.
CHISHOLM, Alexander. Private.
FALKNER, James. Private.
FALKNER, Henry. Private.
FALKNER, William. Private.
FERGUSON, Alexander. Private.
FERGUSON, Alexander. Private.
FERGUSON, William. Private.
FERGUSON, Duncan. Private.
FERGUSON, George. Private.
FINY, George. Private.
GERDRIN, Antony. Private.
GRANT, John. Private.
KENNEDY, John. *Ensign.*
LEU, John. Private.
McARTHUR, John. Private.
McBEAN, Farquhar. Private.
McBEAN, Laughlin. Private.
McDONALD, Donald. *Lieutenant.*
McDONELL, Duncan. *Captain.*
McDONELL, Duncan. Sergeant.
McDONELL, Donald. Sergeant.
McDOUGALL, Donald. Private.
McGILLIS, Duncan. Private.
McGILLVORY, Malcolm. Private.
McGLIS, Alexander. Private.

McGREGOR, John. Private.
McGREGOR, James. Private.
McINTOSH, Alexander. Private.
McINTOSH, Duncan. Private.
McLENNAN, Angus. Private.
McLENNON, Peter. Private.
McLENNON, Farquhar. Private.
McLENNON, Donald. Private.
McLENNON, Rook. Private.
McNAUGHTON, John. Private.
McNAUGHTON, Alexander.
  Private.
McNAUGHTON, Duncan.
  Private.
McPHERRON, Neil. Private.
MORRISON, Donald. Private.
MUCHMORE, John. Private.
MULLOY, Barney. Private.
MUNRO, John. Private.
PERROULT, Joseph. Private.
ROSS, Donald. Private.
SNYDER, David. Private.
SNYDER, William. Private.
VOUDRE, Francis. Private.
WESTLEY, Charles. Private.
WILLIAMS, Walter. Private.
WILLIAMS, John. Private.

3rd Flank Company
BOSTON, Richard. Private.
BULLARD, George. Private.
CALDER, John. Private.
CHISHOLM, Archibald. Private.
DUNN, John. Private.
DUSA, James. Private.
FALKNER, William. Private.
FERGUSON, Donald. Private.
FERGUSON, Alexander. Private.
FERGUSON, James. Private.
FERGUSON, James. Private.
GERDIN, Baptist. Private.
GRANT, John. Private.
GRANT, Alexander. Private.
McBEAN, Laughlin. Private.

McDONALD, Alexander.
  Lieutenant.
McDONELL, Duncan. *Captain.*
McDONELL, Alexander. Private.
McDOUGALL, John. Private.
McGILLIS, John. Private.
McGILLIS, Donald. Private.
McGREGOR, Gregor. Sergeant.
McGREGOR, Alpin. Private.
McINTOSH, John. Private.
McINTOSH, John. Private.
McKAY, Hugh. Private.
McKILLOP, Malcolm. Private.
McKOY, William. Private.
McLENNON, Donald. Private.
McLENNON, Nathaniel.
  Private.
McLENNON, John. Sergeant.

McNAUGHTON, John. Private.
McPHERSON, Alexander.
  Private.
MILLAR, George. Private.
MULLOY, Thomas. Private.
MUNROE, Thomas. Private.
MUNROE, Thomas. Private.
MURCHISON, Duncan. *Ensign.*
PATINGAL, Enias. Private.
ROSS, Donald. Private.
ROSS, David. Private.
ROSS, Alexander. Private.
ROSS, Donald Jr. Private.
ROSS, George. Private.
ROSS, Donald Sr. Private.
SNYDER, John. Private.
SUNVA (?), Peter. Private.
WOOD, Alexander. Sergeant.

2ND GLENGARRY

1st Flank Company
BARBRAU, Gabriel. Private.
BARDIE, Austin. Private.
CAMERON, Angus. Private.
CAMERON, John. Private.
CAMERON, William. Private.
CAMERON, John. Private.
DE ROCHE, Antoine. Private.
DEWAR, Ronald. Private.
ERMITINGER, George. Private.
FRASER, Alexander. Private.
GURGOE, Pierre. Private.
KENNEDY, John. Private.
KENNEDY, Donald. Private.
KENNEDY, Ewn. Private.
KENNEDY, Angus. Private.
KENNEDY, Alexander. Private.
KENNEDY, Angus. *Lieutenant.*
KENNEDY, Allan. Private.
MACDONALD, Archibald. No. 1
  Sergeant.
MACDONALD, Archibald. No. 2
  Sergeant.

MACDONALD, Alexander.
  Ensign.
MACDONALL, Angus. No. 4
  Private.
MACDONELL, John. No. 6
  Private.
MACDONELL, Duncan. Private.
MACDONELL, Finlay. Private.
MACDONELL, Finlay. Private.
MACDONELL, Angus. Private.
MACDONELL, Donald. No. 6
  Private.
MACDONELL, Donald. No. 7
  Private.
MACDONELL, Ronald. Private.
MACDONELL, Allan. No. 1
  Private.
MACDONELL, Allan. No. 2
  Private.
MACDONELL, Ewn. Private.
MACDONELL, Peter. Private.
MACDONELL, Angus. Private.
MACDONELL, Donald. Private.

MACDONELL, Donald. *Captain.*
MACDONELL, Angus. Sergeant.
MACDONELL, Kenneth. Private.
MACDONELL, John. Private.
MACDONELL, Archibald.
Private.
MACDONELL, Ewn. Private.
MACDONELL, Donald. Private.
MACDONELL, John. Private.
MACDONELL, John. No. 5
Private.
MACDONELL, Donald. No. 2
Private.
MACDONELL, Ronald. Private.
MACDONELL, Donald. No. 1
Private.
MACDONELL, Angus. No. 2
Private.
MACDONELL, Lachlin. Private.
MACDONELL, Donald. No. 3
Private.
MACDONELL, Angus. No. 1
Private.
MACDONELL, Donald. No. 5
Private.
MACDONELL, Donald. No. 4
Private.
MACDONELL, Archibald.
Private.
MACDONELL, Alexander.
Private.
MACDONELL, John. Private.
MACDONELL, Angus. No. 3
Private.
MACDOUGALL, Ronald. Private.
MACDOUGALL, John. Private.
MACDOUGALL, John. Private.
MACDOUGALL, Angus. Private.
MACDOUGALL, Angus. Private.
MacINNIS, John. Private.
MacINTOSH, John. Private.
MACINTOSH, Angus. Private.
MACINTOSH, Neil. Private.
MACINTOSH, Donald. Private.

MacMILLAN, John. No. 1 Private.
MacMILLAN, Ewn. Private.
McCORMICK, John. Private.
McDONELL, Donald. No. 8
Private.
McDONELL, Donald. Private.
McDONELL, John. Private.
McDOUGALL, John. Private.
McDOUGALL, Roderick. Private.
McDOUGALL, Donald. Private.
McDOUGALL, Angus. Private.
McGEE, William. Private.
McGILLIS, Angus. Private.
McGILLIS, William. Private.
McGILLIVRAY, Duncan. Private.
McGILLIVRAY, Murdoch. Private.
McGILLIVRAY, Angus. Private.
McGILLIVRAY, Hugh. Private.
McGILLIVRAY, William. Private.
McKINNON, Angus. Private.
McKINNON, Duncan. Private.
McKINNON, Donald. Private.
McKINNON, John. Private.
McKINNON, Allan. Private.
McLEAN, Duncan. Private.
McLENNAN, Farquhar. Private.
McLENNAN, Farquhar. Private.
McLENNON, Duncan. Private.
McLEOD, Alexander. No. 2
Private.
McLEOD, Alexander. No. 1
Private.
McLEOD, Kenneth. Private.
McLEOD, Norman. Private.
McLEOD, Roderick. Private.
McLEOD, William. Private.
McLEOD, Neil. Private.
McLEOD, Alexander. Private.
McLEOD, Roderick. Private.
McMILLAN, John. No. 4 Private.
McMILLAN, Alexander. *Captain.*
McMILLAN, John. No. 2 Private.
McMILLAN, Duncan. Private.
McMILLAN, Duncan. Private.

McMILLAN, Donald. Private.
McMILLAN, Ewn. Private.
McMILLAN, Ewn. Private.
McMILLAN, Duncan. Private.
McMILLAN, Ewn. Private.
McMILLAN, Ewn. Private.
McMILLAN, Angus. Private.
McMILLAN, John. No. 3 Private.
McMILLAN, Duncan. Private.
McMILLAN, John. Private.
McMILLAN, Duncan. No. 2
  Private.
McPHEE, Ronald. Private.
McPHEE, Dougal. Private.
McPHEE, Donald. Private.
McPHEE, Duncan. Private.
McPHEE, James. No. 1 Private.
McPHEE, James. No. 2 Private.
McQUAIG, John. Private.
McRAE, John. Private.
McRAE, Duncan. Private.
MUNRO, Finlay. Private.
PICARD, Alexis. Private.
ST. PIERRE, Francis. Private.

2nd Flank Company
BUREAU, Francis. Private.
BUREAU, Louis. Private.
CAMERON, William. Private.
CAMERON, Angus. Private.
CAMERON, John. Private.
CAMPBELL, Alexander. Private.
CULBERT, James. Private.
FOSTER, Nathan. Private.
GRANT, Peter. Private.
GRANT, Angus. Private.
GRAY, Angus. Private.
KENNEDY, Alexander. Private.
KENNEDY, Donald. Private.
LEMMON, John. Private.
MACDONALD, Alexander.
  Private.
MACDONALD, Neil. Private.
MACDONALD, Angus. Private.

MACDONALD, John. Private.
MACDONALD, Donald. Private.
MACDONALD, John. Private.
MACDONALD, Donald. Private.
MACDONALD, Duncan. Private.
MACDONALD, Malcolm. Private.
MACDONALD, Angus. Private.
MACDONELL, Archibald. Private.
MACDONELL, Donald. Private.
MACDONELL, Rodrick. Private.
MACDONELL, Angus. Private.
MACDONELL, Archibald. Private.
MACDONELL, John. Private.
MACDONELL, Hugh. Private.
MACDONELL, Ronald. Private.
MACDONELL, Angus. Private.
MACDONELL, John. Private.
MACDONELL, John. Private.
MACDONELL, Donald. Private.
MACDONELL, Roderick.
  Sergeant.
MACDONELL, Allan. Private.
MACDONELL, Ronald. Private.
MACDONELL, Alexander.
  Private.
MACDONELL, Donald. Private.
MACDONELL, Angus. Private.
MACDONELL, Duncan. Private.
MACDONELL, Alexander.
  Private.
MACDONELL, Neil. Private.
MACDONELL, Donald. Private.
MACDONELL, Donald. Private.
MACDONELL, Donald. Private.
MACDONELL, Alexander.
  Private.
MACDONELL, Archibald. Private.
MACDONELL, Hugh. Private.
MACDONELL, Roderick.
  Sergeant.
MACDONELL, Angus. Private.
MACDONELL, Alexander.
  Private.
MACDONELL, Angus. Private.

MACDONELL, Kenneth. Private.
MACDONELL, Angus. Private.
MACDONELL, Neil. Private.
MACDONELL, John. Sergeant.
MACDONELL, Alexander.
  Private.
MACDONELL, John. Sergeant.
MACDONELL, Dougal. Private.
MACDOUGAL, Angus. Private.
MACDOUGALL, Alexander.
  Private.
MACDOUGALL, Angus. Private.
MACDOUGALL, Archibald.
  Sergeant.
MACDOUGALL, Duncan. Private.
MACINTOSH, Donald. Private.
MacKENZIE, Alexander. *Captain*.
MacKINNON, Donald. Private.
MacKINNON, Donald. Private.
MacMARTIN, Donald. *Lieutenant*.
MacNIEL, John. Private.
MacRAE, John Jr. Private.
MacRAE, John. Private.
MacRAE, John Sr. Private.
McCALLUM, Duncan. Private.
McCALLUM, Donald. Private.
McDIARMID, Duncan. Private.
McDIARMID, Malcolm. Private.
McDIARMUD, John. Sergeant.
McDOUGALL, Donald. Sergeant.

McGILLIS, John. Private.
McGILLIS, Finlay. Private.
McGILLIS, John. Private.
McGILLIS, Donald. Private.
McGILLIS, Angus. Private.
McGILLIS, Angus. Private.
McKINNON, Charles. Private.
McKINNON, John. Private.
McLARREN, Duncan. Private.
McLAUGHLIN, Alexander.
  Private.
McLAUGHLIN, John. Private.
McMARTIN, John Sr. Private.
McMARTIN, John Jr. Private.
McMILLAN, John. Private.
McMILLAN, Duncan. *Ensign*.
McMILLAN, Alexander. Private.
McMILLAN, Donald. Private.
McMILLAN, Alpin. Private.
McNAUGHTON, Donald. Private.
McNEIL, Donald. Private.
McPHALL, Alexander. Private.
McRAE, Alexander. Private.
McRAE, Donald. Private.
MORRISON, Lodevic. Private.
MORRISON, Malcolm. Private.
MUNRO, Donald. Private.
MUNRO, David. Private.
URQUHART, John. Private.
WISEMAN, William. Sergeant.

1ST STORMONT

1st Flank Company
ALGIRE, Martin. Private.
AULT, Peter. Private.
AULT, Nicholas. Private.
BAXTER, John. Private.
BELLONE (Bellore), Joseph.
  Private.
BINGHAM, Martin. Private.
BOCKUS, David. Private.
BRADSHAW, William. Sergeant.
BROWELL, Steven. Private.

BROWNELL, John. Private.
CAMPBELL, James. Private.
CAPEL, Henry. Private.
CRAMER, Henry. Private.
CUTLER, Sewell. Private.
DEFOE, William. Private.
DUSDAR (Dusclar), William.
  Sergeant.
ELIGH, Peter. Private.
ELIGH, David. Private.
ELIGH, George. Private.

EMON, John. Private.
EMON, George. Sergeant.
EMPEY, Jacob P. Private.
EMPEY, Philip. *Lieutenant.*
EMPEY, John. M. Private.
EMPEY, David J. Private.
EMPEY, Adam W. Private.
EMPEY, Jacob W. Private.
EMPEY, Richard J. Private.
FERGUSON, John. Sergeant.
FETTERLY, John. Private.
FETTERLY, Rudolph. Private.
GERALDS, Asail. Private.
GRANT, Robert. Private.
GRANT, John. Sergeant.
GRANT, Daniel. Sergeant.
HAINES, William. Private.
HAWN, Peter. Private.
HELMER, Aron. Private.
HOLLISTER, Charles. Private.
HOOPLE, John. No. 3 Private.
HOWARD, Levi. Private.
HOWARD, Steven. Private.
HUTCHINS, John. Private.
LEROU (Seron), David. Private.
LINK, Mathias. Private.
LOUCKS, Jacob. Private.
MABEE, John. Private.
MARKLE, Richard. Private.
MATTICE, Nicholas. Private.
McDONELL, Jacob. Private.
  See Casualties.
McLEAN, Alexander. *Lieutenant.*
McLEAN, Hector. Private.
McMILLAN, John. Private.
McPHEE, John. Private.
  See Casualties.
MEIKER, Benjamin. Private.
MOKE, Simon. Private.
MORGAN, William. *Captain.*
MOSS, Thomas. Private.
MOSS, Peter. Private.
OTTO, Peter. Private.

PITTS, Chesley. Private.
PITTS, Joseph. Sergeant.
PROSSER, Jesse. Private.
RAMBOUGH, Jacob. Private.
RAMBOUGH, David. Private.
RANEY, John. Private.
REDICK, Adam. Private.
RONIONS, George. Private.
ROSS, Michael. Private.
RUNIONS, Philip. Private.
RUNNIONS, Henry. Private.
SAINT PIERRE, Joseph. Private.
SHAEN, William. Private.
SHAVER, Henry. Sergeant.
SHAVER, John F. Private.
SHAVER, Jacob. Private.
SHAVER, John N. Private.
SMITH, James. Private.
SNIDER, Conrath. Private.
STADLY, Andrew. Private.
STEENBERG, John. Private.
STEENBOURGH, Martin.
  Private.
STEWART, Henry. *Ensign.*
STEWART, John. Sergeant.
STUART, James. Private.
TUPPER, Mayhew. Private.
WALDRIFFE, Martin. Sergeant.
WALDRIFFE, Adam. Private.
WARNER, Adam. Private.
WARNER, Godfrey. Private.
WART, George. Private.
WART, John J. Private.
WART, Conrat. Private.
WART, John E. Private.
WART, John A. Private.
WIAT, William. Private.
WINTER, Frederick. Private.
WINTERS, George. Private.
  See Casualties.
WINTERS, Henry. Private.
WOOD, Roger. Private.

2nd Flank Company
ALGUIRE, Henry. Private.
BAKER, Steven. Private.
BARNHART, Lewis. Private.
BARNHART, Benjamin. Private.
BERNIE, Lewis. Private.
BLARE, Theodore. Private.
BOUSHIE, Baptiste. Private.
BRUCE, Alexander. Corporal.
BRUCE, William, Jr. Private.
BRYAN, Thomas. Private.
CAIN, Steven. Private.
CAMERON, Charles. Private.
CAMERON, Alexander. Private.
CAMERON, Angus. Private.
CAMPBELL, Daniel. Private.
CARPENTER, Peter. Private.
CHESLEY, John. Private.
CHISHOLM, David. Corporal.
CHISHOLM, John. Private.
CHISHOLM, Alexander. Corporal.
CHRISTY, Andrew. Private.
CRIDERMAN, Harmonius.
  Private.
CRIDERMAN, John. Private.
CUMMINGS, John. Private.
DIXON, Robert. Private.
EASTMAN, Samuel. Sergeant.
EMPEY, Philip. *Ensign.*
EMPEY, Philip. *Captain.*
EMPEY, Philip J. Private.
EMPEY, William. Drummer.
FITZPATRICK, Richard. Private.
FITZPATRICK, Hugh. Private.
FLAWNY, Alexander. Private.
FLINN, William. Private.
FORSYTH, William. Private.
GALLINGER, George. No. 10
  Private.
GALLINGER, Joseph. Private.
GALLINGER, Henry. Private.
GALLINGER, Philip. Private.
GALLINGER. George. Private.
GROVES, James. Private.

HART, Jacob. Private.
HARTLE, John, Jr. Private.
HARTLE, John. Private.
KAY, John. Private.
LILEBARE, Gabriel. Private.
LINK, John. Private.
LINK, Mathias. Sergeant.
LINK, Michael. Private.
McBEAN, Donald. Private.
McBEAN, Benjamim. Private.
McDERMID, Hugh. Sergeant.
McDONELL, Allan. Private.
McDONELL, Alexander. Private.
McDONELL, Archibald. Private.
McDONELL, Allan. Private.
McDONELL, Hugh. Private.
McDONELL, John. Private.
McDONELL, Duncan. Private.
McDONELL, Alexander. Private.
McDONELL, Alexander. Private.
McDONELL, John. Private.
McDONELL, Alexander. Private.
McDONELL, John. Private.
McDONELL, Alexander. Private.
McDONELL, James. Private.
McDONELL, John. Private.
McDONELL, Duncan. Private.
McDONELL, Lauchlan. Private.
McDONELL, Allan. Private.
McDONELL, Archibald. Corporal.
McDONELL, Ronald. Sergeant.
McGILLIS, Donald. Private.
McGILLIS, Angus. Private.
McGUIRE, Angus. Private.
McINTIRE, Robert. Private.
McINTOSH, William. Private.
McLEAN, John. *Lieutenant.*
McLELLAN, Neil. Private.
McNERRIN, William. Private.
McPHALE, Donald. Private.
McQUARIE, Neil W. Sergeant.
MITCHELL, William. Private.
MYERS, Philip. Private.
PETERSON, Samuel. Private.

PUTMAN, Robert. Private.
RAMOND, Oliver. Private.
SCOTT, Duncan. Private.
SILMOEN (Silmser), Henry.
  Private.
SINCARTIER (Lincartier),
  Joseph. Private.

STONEBURNER, John. Private.
STONEBURNER, Lenard.
  Private.
SWITSINGER, George. Private.
VAN KOUGHNETT, John.
  Lieutenant.
WOOD, William. Private.

1ST DUNDAS

1st Flank Company
AULT, John. Sergeant.
AULT, Michael. Captain.
AVICKHAWSER, Godfrey.
  Private.
BARKLEY, Michael. Private.
BROUCE, Jacob. Private.
  GSM, Chrysler's Farm.
BROUCE, Michael. Private.
CARNS, Jacob. Private.
CASLEMAN, John. Private.
CLARK, Duncan. *Ensign.*
COLLISON, John. Private.
COONS, Jacob. Private.
COONS, Henry. Private.
COONS, John. Private.
COONS, George. Private.
DORIN, Jacob. *Lieutenant.*
DORIN, David. Private.
DORIN, John. Private.
DULMAGE, Jacob. Corporal.
FADDLE, Samuel. Private.
FORRESTER, Gabriel. Private.
FORRESTER, Isaac. Sergeant.
FOSTER, Edward. Private.
FRALICK, John. Private.
FRASER, James. *Lieutenant.*
FREECE, Michael. Private.
FREECE, David. Private.
FREECE, Peter. Private.
FROLICK, David. Private.
GLASFORD, Robert. Private.
GODARE, Lewis. Private.
JOHNSON, George. Private.

KEAVARE, Alexander. Private.
KINTNER, Conrad. Private.
LAJOY, Baptiste. Private.
LENNOX, James. Private.
LEONEX, Elijah. Private.
LOCK, Joseph. Private.
RATHBORN, Faxton. Private.
REDMAN, Robert. Private.
RULER, John. Sergeant.
SAVER, John. Private.
SEALY, David. Private.
SERVOS, William. Private.
SHAVER, Edward. Private.
SHAVER, Nicholas J. Sergeant.
SHAVER, John H. Private.
SHAVER, John. A. Private.
SHAVER, Nicholas N. Corporal.
SHAVER, George H. Private.
SIPES, Jacob. Private.
SNYDER, Farquer. Corporal.
STAMP, James. Private.
STAMP, Jacob. Private.
STEWART, William. Private.
STEWART, John. Private.
STRADER, Jacob. Private.
SURCHEA, Joseph. Private.
SURCHEA, Peter. Private.
TADER, Jacob. Private.
VAN CAMP, John. Private.
VAN CAMP, Peter. Private.
WALCH, John. Private.
WALLACE, Antony. Private.
WEAGER, Henry. Private.
WICKWARE, Jonathan. Private.

2nd Flank Company
ALGIRE, Jacob. Private.
AULT, Nicolas. Private.
  GSM, Chrysler's Farm.
BAKER, Frederick. Private.
BAKER, Nicholas. Private.
BARGER, Andrew. Private.
BEDSTEAD, Alexander. Private.
BERKLEY, Joseph. Private.
BERLKEY, Martin. Private.
BURGER, John. Private.
CASSELMAN, John. Private.
CASSLEMAN, William. Private.
CASSLEMAN, Conrad. Private.
COOK, John. Private.
CROWBARGER, Andrew. Private.
CROWBARGESS, John. Private.
CROWDEN, Anthony. Private.
DE PENZIER, Luke. Sergeant.
DILLABACK, Nicholas. Private.
FETTERBY, Peter. Private.
FROAH, John. Private.
FRYMIRE, Conrad. Private.
FRYMIRE, Philip. Private.
GARLOUGH, Stephen. Private.
HANES, Frederick. Private.
HANES, John. Private.
HANES, Joseph. Private.
HANES, David. Private.
HELMER, Joseph. Private.
HICKEY, John. Private.
HOLMES, Peter. Private.
HUNT, Stephen. Private.

KNIGHT, William. Private.
LASART, Charles. Private.
LOUX, Philip. Private.
LOUX, William. Sergeant.
LOUX, Peter. Private.
MARSAILES, Garret. Private.
McCRAGEN, Hugh. Private.
MERKLEY, Christopher.
  Lieutenant.
MERKLEY, Jacob, Jr. Private.
MERKLEY, Jacob. Sergeant.
MERKLEY, George. *Captain.*
MERKLEY, Adam. Sergeant.
MERKLEY, Jacob. *Ensign.*
MURSALIS, Peter. Private.
MYERS, Tobias. Private.
NEEDLE, Adam. Private.
O'BRIEN, James. Private.
OUDERKIRK, Frederick. Private.
PILLER, John. Private.
POLLY, John. Private.
PRUNEN, Peter. Private.
ROSE, Alex. *Lieutenant.*
ROSENBARGER, Jacob. Private.
SCOTT, William. Private.
SHAVER, John. Private.
SHELL, Daniel. Private.
STERNER, Mathew. Private.
SWERTSFAGER, Lewis. Private.
VAN ALLEN, John. Private.
VAN ALLAN, Henry. Private.
WOOD, Moses. Private.

DISTRICT OF JOHNSTOWN

1ST GRENVILLE

1st Flank Company
ADAMS, John. Private.
ADAMS, Andrew. *Lieutenant.*
ADAMS, William, Jr. Private.
ANDERSON, William. Private.
ANDERSON, John. Private.
BEACH, Malum. Private.

BEAUPORT, Constant. Private.
BLAIR, John. Corporal.
BOICE, David. Private.
BOLTON, Abraham. Private.
BOLTON, Henry. Private.
BONISTEEL, Jacob. Private.

BOSTWICK, Albia. Private.
See Casualties.
BOYD, James. Private.
BOYD, Augustus. Private.
BOYD, Andrew. Private.
BYRANT, John. Sergeant.
CAMERON, Duncan. Private.
CHURCH, Samuel. Private.
COCKBURN, Syman (Lyman).
Private.
CULBREATH, James. Private.
CUMMINGS, Abraham. Private.
CUMMINGS, Daniel. Private.
CURRY, James. Private.
See Casualties.
CURRY, John. Private.
DODGE, Abner. Private.
FLAG, Elzea. Private.
FRASER, John. *Lieutenant.*
FRASER, Simon Sr. Private.
GAGER, Noah. Private.
GRANT, James. Private.
GREEN, William. Private.
HALL, Samuel. Private.
HELMER, John. Private.
HOLTON, Samuel. Private.
HUMPHREY, James. Sergeant.
HUNTER, Samuel. Private.
JACKSON, Henry. Private.
JACKSON, Peter. Private.
KING, Stephen. Private.
KING, Jacob. Corporal.
LALONE, Joseph. Private.
LEE, George. Private.
LEMAN, William. Private.
LEWIS, William. Private.
McCARGAR, Hugh. Private.
McCARGAR, Robert. Private.
McCLATCHIE, James. Private.
McDONELL, Daniel. Private.
McLAUGHLIN, William. Private.
McNEAL, William, Jr. Private.
McNEAL, William, Sr. Private.
MILLS, Jacob. Private.
MOOR, Peter. Private.

MORISE, Jaques. Private.
MUNRO, Hugh. *Captain.*
NETTLETON, Stephen. Private.
NEWLAN, Henry. Private.
RAVEN, Adam. Private.
RENEAU, Joseph. Private.
RUNIONS, Michael. Private.
SEYMOUR, Peter. Private.
SMITH, David. Private.
SMITH, Peter. Sergeant.
SNIDER, John. Private.
SNYDER, Solomon. *Ensign.*
SPENCER, David. Private.
SPENCER, William. Private.
STONE, Lyman. Private.
TAUGH, Thomas. Private.
TENDREAU, Charles. Corporal.
THRASHER, Charles. Private.
VAN BUREN, Henry. Private.
VAN CAMP, Jacob. Private.
See Casualties.

2nd Flank Company
BARGER, Francis. Private.
BEWKER, Melvin. Private.
BEWKER, Taylor. Private.
BISHOP, James. Private.
BISHOP, Buel. Private.
BROWN, David. Private.
BUNKER, Alexander. Private.
CALL, Rufus. Private.
DRUMMOND, George. Private.
DULMAGE, Philip. *Captain.*
DULMAGE, Samuel. *Ensign.*
EASTMAN, Joseph. Private.
FELL, David. Private.
FELL, John. Private.
FELL, Frederick. Private.
FRASER, Donell. *Lieutenant.*
GLASSFORD, John. Private.
GLASSFORD, Thomas. Private.
GRIFFITH, Daniel. Private.
HAZLETON, Charles. Private.
HENDERSON, Isaac. Private.

ISABELL, Andrew. Private.
LAMABLE, Joseph. Private.
LANE, Cornelius. Private.
LANE, Henry. Private.
LAVIGURRE, Joseph. Private.
LAWRENCE, John. *Lieutenant.*
MACK, Peter. Sergeant.
MARTIN, Richard. Private.
McNEAL, Henry. Private.
McNEAL, John. Sergeant.

MOLAT, Abraham. Private.
MORRISON, William. Private.
MOSHER, Rice. Private.
PROSSER, William. Private.
ROWLAND, Thomas. Private.
RUDE, John. Private.
STREET, Timothy. Private.
STREET, Alford. Private.
WALTER, Jacob. Private.
WILEY, Richard. Private.

2ND GRENVILLE

1st and 2nd Flank Companies
ALDRICK, David. Sergeant.
ANDREWS, Alhana. Private.
BARBER, Benjamin, Sr. Private.
BARTON, William. Private.
See Casualties.
BEEMAN, Sibra. Private.
BISSELL, William. Private.
BISSELL, Gilbert. Private. Joined
the Incorporated Militia.
BLACK, William. Private.
BLODGETT, Orin. Private.
BROWN, Thomas. Private. Joined
the Glengarry Regiment.
BROWN, Jesse. Private.
BROWN, Jesse. Private. Joined
the Glengarry Regiment.
BROWN, Samuel. Private.
BULLIS, John. Drummer.
BULLISS, Richard. Private.
BULLISS, Jeremiah. Private.
BULLISS, Daniel. Private.
BULLISS, Jubez. Private.
BURRITT, Calvin. Private.
BURRITT, Henry. *Lieutenant.*
Joined the Incorporated Militia.
BURRITT, Daniel. *Captain.*
BUTTERFIELD, John. Private.
CHESTER, Thomas. Private.
CLIFLIN, Suther. Corporal.
COLEMAN, John. Private.

COLLER, Elisha. Sergeant.
COVILL, Henry. Private.
CROSS, Daniel. Private. See
Casualties.
DOPP, Henry. Private.
DUDLEY, Charles. Private.
ELWOOD, Abraham. Private.
EVERTS, David. Private.
FRASER, Richard D. *Lieutenant.*
GIFFORD, Edman. Private.
GILLMAN, David. Private.
See Casualties.
GOODWIN, Simeon. Private.
GRIPPIN, Ethan. Private.
HAMBLIN, John. Private.
HAMBLIN, Silas. Private.
HANES, John. Private.
HARRIS, Daniel. Private.
HICKS, Thomas. Private.
HICKS, Joseph. Drummer.
HISS, Jacob. Private.
HOLMBECK, Jacob. Private.
JACKSON, Thomas. Sergeant.
JONES, David D. Private.
KEELER, Daniel. Private.
KERR, John. *Ensign.* Joined the
Incorporated Militia.
LAKE, Garret. Private.
LAKE, John. Private.
LAKE, Thomas. Private.
LINSS, Bartholomew. Private.
LINSS, John. Private.

MALLORY, Joseph. Private.
MARTIN, Timothy. Private.
MASHER, Nicholas. Private.
McCATHRAN, John. Private.
McCREA, Alexander. Private.
McCREA, James. Private.
McCREA, Thomas. *Ensign.*
McDONELL, Baviack. Private.
McINTIRE, Simeon. Private.
McINTIRE, William. Private.
See Casualties.
MERRICK, Isaac. Corporal.
MITCHEL, George C. Private.
MITCHELL, Zalman. Private.
MOORE, James. Private.
MOREY, Samuel. Private.
NETTLETON, Barnabas. Private.
NETTLETON, Samuel. Private.
Joined the Incorporated Militia.
NICHOLSON, Robert. Private.
OLMSTED, Ephrain. Private.
OLMSTED, Richard. Private.
OSBORN (?), Jeremiah. Private.
OWEN, Hus. Private.
PHILLIPS, Ziba M. Sergeant.
PHILLIPS, Thomas. Private.
Joined the Incorporated Militia.
PHILLIPS, Samuel. Private.
Joined the Incorporated Militia.
RANDOLPH, Samuel. Private.
See Casualties.

ROBINSON, John. Private.
ROBINSON, Joseph B. Private.
See Casualties.
ROBINSON, Garret. Private.
SMITH, Darling. Private.
SMITH, John. No. 2 Private.
SMITH, William B. Private.
SMITH, John. No. 1 Private.
SPEN, Lawrence. Private.
Joined the Incorporated Militia.
STRATTON, Silvanus. Sergeant.
STREET, Peter. Private.
TALLMAN, Charles. Private.
THOMAS, Daniel. Sergeant.
THOMPKINS, Obadiah. Private.
THOMPKINS, George. Private.
See Casualties.
THOMPKINS, Nathan. Private.
THROOP, Calvin. Private.
TURNER, David L. Corporal.
Joined the Incorporated Militia.
UMPHREY, William. Private.
UMPHREY, Alexander. Private.
Joined the Glengarry Regiment.
VAN ARNAM, William. Private.
WALKER, Hamilton. *Captain.*
Joined the Incorporated Militia.
WOOD, Amasa. Private.
WOOD, Anthony. Corporal.
WRIGHT, Abel. Private.
WRIGHT, Asahal. Private.

1ST LEEDS

1st and 2nd Flank Companies
ADAMS, Samuel. Private.
ADAMS, Walter. Private.
ADAMS, Elija. Private.
ALLAN, Alva. Private.
ANDREWS, Michael. Private.
ARMSTRONG, Adolphus. Private.
ARNOLD, John. Private.
AUSTIN, Mauris. Private.
AYLEBOYNE, John. Private.

AYRES, Clossen. Private.
BABCOCK, Amos. Private.
BAKER, John. Private.
BAKER, Elisha. Private.
BAND, Andrew. Private.
BARKER, Stephen. Private.
BAXTER, Nathan. Private.
BEACH, Jobez. Private.
BEACK, Stephen. Private.
BENEDICK, John. Private.

BILLINGS, Elkanah. Private.
BISSENETTE, Stephen. Private.
BLANCHARD, Aron. Private.
BLUKE, Joseph. Private.
BLUNCHARD, Selah. Private.
BOEN, John S. Private.
BOGENT, William. Private.
BOICE, James. Private.
BOICE, Abiatha. Private.
BOOK, Isaac. Private. Served
    as sergeant.
BOOTH, John. Sergeant.
BOTSFORD, Alunson. Private.
BOULTON, Hugh. Private.
BOULTON, Thomas. Private.
BOULTON, Daniel. Private.
BOULTOU, Benjamin. Private.
BRASS, Abraham. Private.
BRAYTON, Freeborn. Private.
BRISTOL, Joseph. Private.
BROOKER, William. Private.
BROOKER, Elisha. Private.
BROWN, Benjamin. Private.
BROWN, Henry. Private.
BROWN, Mordecai. Private.
BROWN, James. Private.
BUCK, Joseph. Private.
BUELL, Timothy. Private.
BUELL, William. No. 3 Private.
    Served as sergeant. GSM,
    Chrysler's Farm.
BUELL, Rynalda. Private.
BUELL, William Jr. Private.
BYINGTON, Daniel. Private.
BYRANT, William. Private.
BYRANT, John. Private.
CAIN, John, Jr. Private.
CAMERON, Richard. Private.
CAMERON, John. Private.
CAMERON, James. Private.
CARLY, James. Sergeant.
CARLY, Duncan. Private.
    Served a short time as ensign.
CASWELL, Zachiess. Private.
CASWELL, Stephen. Private.

CHURCH, Daniel. Private.
CHURCH, Jonathan M. Jr. Private.
CLARK, Nathan Jr. Private.
CLOW, John. Private.
CLOW, Peter. Private.
CLOW, William. Private.
COLE, Isaac. Private.
COLE, George. Private.
COLE, Peter. Private.
CONNELL, James. Private.
CORUVILL, Samuel. Private.
COVILLE, John. Private.
CROMWELL, Samuel. Private.
CROSS, John. Private.
CUMSTOCK, William. Private.
CUMSTOCK, Aron. Private.
CURTIS, Daniel. Private.
CURTIS, John. Private.
CURTIS, John. Private.
CURTIS, Allan. Private.
DAVIS, William. Private.
DAVISON, John. Private.
DAY, John. Private.
DAY, Albert H. Private.
DAY, Alonza. Private.
DAY, William. Private.
DAYTON, Abraham. *Ensign*.
DEMMING, John. Private.
DEMMINGS, Elisha. Private.
DENSMORE, William. Private.
DENSMORE, Moses. Private.
DOCKUM, Herman. Private.
DOZENBURY, John. Private.
DUKELOSE, Claudius. Private.
DUKELOU, Adam. Private.
DYER, John. Private.
DYER, Richard. Private.
EARL, Robert. Private.
ELLIOTT, Stephen. Private.
ELLIOTT, Moses. Private.
FAUSHETTE, Joseph. Private.
FAVE, Benjamin. Private.
FERGUSON, Joseph. Private.
FIELDS, Russel. Private.

FIELDS, John. Private.
FITZGERALD, Thomas. Private.
FLETCHER, Archbald. Private.
FRASER, William. Private.
FRASER, Collins. Private.
FREDINBURGH, John. Private.
FREDINBURGH, Nathan. Private.
FREEL, David. Private. See
Casualties.
FULFORD, Jonathan. *Lieutenant.*
GARDNER, George. Sergeant.
GARRY, Cornelius. Private.
GAVAY, John. Private.
GILLET, Silas. Private.
GORDON, Thomas. Private.
GORDON, Abraham. Private.
GRAHAM, John. Private.
Joined the Glengarry Regiment.
GRANT, Duncan. Private.
GRANT, Allan. *Lieutenant.* Noted
as having served a short time.
GRAY, Samuel. Sergeant.
GRIFFIN, Calvin. Private.
GRIFFIN, John. Private.
GRISWOLD, Freeman. Private.
GROSSMAKER, John. Private.
HACKET, Josiah. Private.
HAGERMAN, John. *Ensign.*
HANS, Peter. Private.
HAUS (Hans), Edward. Private.
HENDERSON, William. Private.
HENDERSON, John. Private.
HOOVER, David. Private.
HORTON, Nicholas. Private.
HORTON, Adam. Private.
HORTON, John. Private.
HORTON, John Jr. Private.
HOWARD, James B. Private.
HOWE, Daniel. Private.
HUBBARD, David. Private.
HUBBELL, Justus. Private.
HUMBLEN, William. Private.
HUNTER, Marvin. Private.
HUNTLEY, Thomas. Private.

HUTCHINSON, Elias. Private.
HUTCHINSON, Joah. Private.
JOHNES, Rueben M. Private.
JOHNES, Edward. Private.
JONES, Jonas. *Captain.* Noted
as having served a short time.
JUNE, David. Private.
JUNE, Levi. Private.
KETCHAM, John Jr. Private.
KEYS, Asahel. Private.
KIELER, Isaiah. Private.
KIELER, Nathan. Private.
KILBORN, Hiram. Private.
KILBORN, John. Private.
Acted as sergeant.
KINCAID, Archibald. Private.
KINCAID, John. Private.
KINION, Thomas O. Private.
LADD, Archibald. Private.
LANDON, Jessee. Private.
LANDON, Luthur. Private.
LARNE (Lame), Cuness. Private.
LEE, Noah. Private.
LIDDLE, Andrew. Private.
LIVINGSTON, Silas. Private.
MALLOEY, Isaac. Private.
MALLOEY, Samuel. Private.
MALLOEY, John. Private.
MALLOEY, David. Private.
MALLOEY, Daniel. Private.
MANHART, David Jr. Private.
MARCHART, Henry. Private.
MARSHAL, Ira. Private.
MARSHAL, John. Private.
McBEAN, Gillis. Private.
McCAIN, Stephen. Private.
McCUE, John. Private.
McCUE, Abraham. Private.
McGOWEN, Thomas. Private.
McLEAN, John. *Lieutenant.*
McREADY, Anthony. Private.
MILLER, Robert M. Private.
MOORE, Frederick. Private.
MOORE, James. Private.

MOORE, Ebenezar. Private.
MORRIS, William. *Ensign.*
MOTT, Edmond. Private.
MOTT, Rueben. No. 2 Private.
MOTT, Jeremiah. Private.
  See Casualties.
MUNROE, Israel. Private.
MYRES, John. Private.
OLDS, Moses. Private.
PAGE, Reubin. Private.
PALLARD, John M. Private.
PALMER, Neil. Private.
PATTERSON, James. Private.
PATTERSON, Ira. Private.
PATTERSON, William. Private.
PATTERSON, Thovin. Private.
PATTERSON, William. Private.
PATTERSON, Robert. Private.
PEARSON, Silas. Private.
PECK, Elias. Private.
PENNOCK, Abelee. Private.
PHILIPS, Davis. Private.
PLUMB, Harvey. Private.
PREVOST, Andrew. Private.
PURVIS, George. Private.
PURVIS, Thomas. Private.
PURVIS, John. Private. Acted as
  sergeant.
PUTVA (Putra), Baptist. Private.
RANDOLPH, Abel. Private.
RAY (Kay), John. Private.
RENRICK, David. Private.
RICE, Joel. Private.
ROBERTSON, William. Private.
ROBINS, John. Private.
ROBINSON, James. Private.
ROBINSON, John. Private.
ROBINSON, William. Private.
ROOT, Daniel Jr. Private.
RORICK, Gaspser. Private.
SELEE, Ira. Private.
SELEE, John. Private.
SHANK, John. Private.
SHEPHERD, George. Private.

SHERWOOD, Reuben. *Captain.*
  Noted as having served a short
  time.
SHIPMAN, Samuel Jr. Private.
SHIPMAN, Daniel. Private.
SHIPMAN, David. Private.
SHIPMAN, Joel. Private.
SMITH, Terence. *Ensign.*
SMITH, John. Private.
SMYTH, Peter. Private.
SOVEREN, Iasiah. Private.
STANTS, Henry. Private.
STEPHENS, Nathan. Private.
STEPHENS, William. Private.
STEPHENSON, Symore. Private.
STEVENSON, David. Private.
STUART, John. *Captain.*
STUFFORD, David D. Private.
STUNTS (?), Peter. Private.
STURDEPHANK, Soloman.
  Private.
STURDIPHANT, William. Private.
TAPLIN, Walter. Private.
THOMPSON, Thomas. Private.
THOMPSON, Benjamin. Private.
TREEDAY, James. Private.
TRICKEY, Peter. Private.
TRICKEY, Christopher. Private.
TRICKEY, William O. Private.
TUFFS, Winthropp. Private.
  Deserted to the enemy.
TUTTLE, Levi. Private.
TUTTLE, Newman. Private.
VAUGHAN, John. Private.
VAUGHAN, Charles. Private.
WAIT, Henry. Private.
WALKER, Summers. Private.
WALKER, John. Private.
WARNER, Oliver. Private.
WARNER, Asa. Private.
WARNER, Ralph. Private.
WATSON, James. Private.
WEBSTER, Ephraim. Private.
WELLER, Elijah. Private.
WHITAMORE, Harvey. Private.

WHITAMORE, Samuel. Private.
WHITE, John Jr. Private.
WHITNEY, Peter. Private.
WHITNEY, William. Private.
WICKWIN, Philip. Private.
WILCOX, Stephen. Private.

WOOLEY, Joseph. Private.
WRIGHT, Timothy. Private.
WRIGHT, Sylvester. *Captain.*
WRIGHT, David. Private.
WRIGHT, Abraham. Private.
WRIGHT, William H. Private.

2ND LEEDS

The Flank Companies
ABELS, Lyman. Private.
ABINATHY, James. Private.
ADAMS, David. Private.
  See Casualties.
ALLEN, William. Private.
ALLEN, Aaron. Private.
ALLEN, David. Private.
BACHELOR, Simeon. Private.
BARNES, John Jr. Private.
BARRY, Patrick. Private.
BEACH, Elisha. Private.
BENEDICT, John. Private.
BENSAY (?), William B. Private.
BIRDSALL, Annanias. Private.
BLASEDILL, John. Private.
BOGATT, Gersham. Private.
BRADISH, Andrew. *Lieutenant.*
BRESEE, Peter. Sergeant.
BROWN, David H. Private.
BROWN, Henry. Private.
BROWN, William W. Private.
BULLARD, Josiah. Private.
BURGES, Jesiah D. Private.
BURGES, John. Private.
BURGES, John. Private.
BYNIGTON, James. Private.
CHACE, Benjamin. Private.
CHACE, John. Corporal.
CHAPIN, Almer. Private.
CHIPMAN, Henry. Private.
CHIPMAN, Elon. Private.
CHIPMAN, Truman. Private.
CHURCH, Oliver. Private.
CHURCHALL, Joseph. Private.

CHURCHIL, Mark. Private.
CONLY, Nicholas. Private.
CONLY, Solomon Jr. Private.
CONLY, Solomon. Private.
COOPER, William. Sergeant.
CORBEN, Abijah. Private.
CORNWALL, George. Private.
DAVISON, Robert. Sergeant.
DAY, John. Private.
DAY, Robert. Corporal.
DAY, Jacob. Private.
DAY, John. Private.
DAY, Moses. Private.
DELONG, George. Corporal.
DURFEY, Trueman. Corporal.
EATON, Oliver. Corporal.
EATON, Fabey. Private.
EATON, Aaron. Private.
ELSWORTH, Israel. Private.
ELSWORTH, Benjamin. Private.
FAGERSON, John. Private.
FAGERSON, Samuel. Private.
FAINAM, John. Private.
FARNAM, Archalus. Private.
  See Casualties.
FERRY, Daniel. Private.
  Armourer.
FOX, Jeremiah. Private.
FRASER, Jeremiah. Private.
FRUECK (French), Charles.
  Private.
FUMAN, Henry. Corporal.
GEVILE, Amos. Private.
GILBERT, John. Private.
GILBERT, Enos E. Private.

GILMORE, John. Private.
GILMORE, John. Private.
HALLADA, Henry. Corporal.
HALLIDA, Alvin. Corporal.
HALLIDA, James. Private.
HARRISS, William. Corporal.
HERRICK, Henry. Private.
HETCHUSON (?), Nathaniel.
Private.
HICOCK, Nathan. *Ensign.*
HOTCHKISS, Levi. Corporal.
HUIT, James. Private.
HUIT, Jacob. Private.
IRELAND, Isaac. Private.
IRELAND, (Locy). Private.
JACKSON, Samuel. Corporal.
JAQUE, Richard. Private.
JONES, William. *Captain*
JONES, Asa. Corporal.
KELSY, Samuel. *Lieutenant.*
KILBORN, James. *Ensign.*
LAMB, Isaac. Private.
LAMPSON, Alvin. Private.
LANE, Daniel. Private.
LANE, Samuel. Private.
LAWRENCE, Elihu. Private.
LAWRENCE, Robert. Private.
LEAMON, Stephen. Private.
LEAMON, David. Private.
LEE, David Jr. Private.
LEE, Palmer. Private.
LEE, Zenos. Private.
LINSAY, Thomas. Private.
LYMAN, Barnabas. Private.
MAN, James. Private.
MARTIAL, James. Private.
MARVIN, Calvin. Private.
MATHERSON, Nathan. Private.
MATTERSON, Jesse. Private.
MITCHEL, John. Private.
MITCHEL, Hyman. Private.
MITLER, John. Corporal.
MOCK, Henry. Corporal. Joined
the Glengarry Regiment.
MOTT, Squire, Private.

NICHOLS, Clark. Private.
NICHOLS, Elisha. Private.
NICHOLS, Benjamin. Private.
NICKSON, John. Private.
ORAGAN, Edmond Jr. Private.
OREGAN, Edmond. Private.
PALMER, Jacomiah. Private.
PALMER, Darias. Private.
PALMER, David. Private.
PARISH, William Jr. Private.
PARKER, John. Corporal.
PARKER, Charles. Private.
PARRISH, Harris. Private.
Joined the Incorporated Militia.
PATTERSON, Daniel Jr. Private.
PENAK, Aaron. Private.
PHILIPS, William. Sergeant.
POPE, Jonathan. Private.
PRATT, George. Private.
PRATT, Grovi. Private.
PROCTOR, Isaac. Private.
RAYMOND, Trueman. Private.
Assistant Surgeon.
READ, Samuel. *Ensign.*
READ, John. Private.
READES, Jabez. Private.
RIPLEY, Thomas. Private.
ROBERTSON, William. Sergeant.
ROCKWOOD, Elijah. Corporal.
SANFORD, Soloman. Private.
SANFORD, Peter. Private.
SAXTON, Jonathan. Private.
SCHOFIELD, Ira. *Captain.*
SEAMAN, Samuel. Quarter
Master Sergeant.
SHAMWAY, Francois. Private.
SHEAMAN, Prince. Sergeant.
SHOOK, Philip. Sergeant.
SIMPSON, Isaac. Private.
SIWAY, Ephraim. Private.
SLACK, Joseph. Private.
SLY, John. Private. See Casualties.
SMITH, Silas. Private.
SMITH, Timothy. Private.
SMITH, Samuel. Private.

SNIDER, Mathew. Private.
STAYTON, Charles. Corporal.
STEVENS, Isaac. Corporal.
STEVENS, Abraham. Private.
  Joined the Glengarry Regiment.
STEVENS, Jonathan Jr. Private.
STEVENS, Alford. Corporal.
STODARD, Arvin. Private.
STODDARD, Jackson. Private.
STRATTON, Daniel P. Corporal.
STRUTHERS, John. *Lieutenant.*
SUTHERLAND, German.
  Corporal.
SWEET, Allen. Corporal.
SWEET, Land. Sergeant.
SWEET, Eli T. Private.
SWIND, Trueman. Private.
TALMAN, Abial. Private.
TEAD, Jeremiah. Private.
THELP (Shelp), Patrick. Private.

THORNTON, John. Private.
TITUS, William. Private.
TITUS, Gilbert. Private.
  See Casualties.
TUPPER, Horrace. Private.
TWOCKY, Abraham. Private.
WAGER, Joseph. Private.
WARD, Abel. Private.
WARREN, Artemies. Corporal.
WARREN, Gideon. Private.
WHALEN, John. Private.
WHITE, James. Private.
WHITE, William. Private.
WHITE, Isaac. Private.
WILTSE, Cornelius. Private.
WILTSEE, Leonard. Corporal.
WILTSEE, Benoni. *Captain.*
WILTSEE, Henry. Corporal.
YATES, William. Private.
YATES, Philip. Private.

MIDLAND DISTRICT

1ST FRONTENAC

The Flank Companies
ALDRIDGE, Thomas. Private.
ALEXANDER, James. Private.
ALLEN, William. Private.
ANSLEY, Henry. Sergeant.
ANSLEY, Daniel. Sergeant.
ANSLEY, Samuel Jr. Private.
ARCHAMBAULT, Louis. Private.
ARKLAND, Charles. Private.
  GSM, Chrysler's Farm.
ARKLAND, Richard. Private.
ARMSTRONG, Thomas. Private.
ARMSTRONG, John. Private.
ASHLEY, William Jr. Private.
BABCOCK, Samuel. Private.
BABCOCK, David. Private.
BABCOCK, Peter. Private.
BAKER, William. Private.
BAKER, Henry. Private.
BAKER, Palmer. Private.
BARRET, Isaac. Private.

BARRET, Jesse. Private.
BARRET, Joseph. Private.
BATES, John. Private.
BEAUSOLIEL, Francois. Private.
BENNET, Alva. Private.
BEUNEL, Angel. Corporal.
BISSEL, Erastus. Private.
BOND, Isaac. Private.
BORISON, James. Sergeant.
BOUCHE, (Lary). Private.
BOUDAIR, Toussaint. Private.
BOURDETTE, David. Private.
BRADLY, Thomas. Private.
BRASS, Henry. Sergeant.
BRASS, William. Corporal.
BRASS, John. *Ensign.*
BRASS, David. Corporal.
BUCK, George. Private.
BUNDAY, Willard. Private.
BURIEL, Emanuel. Corporal.
BURLEY, Samuel. Private.

BURLEY, William. Private.
BURLEY, Emerson. Private.
BUTT, Bries. Sergeant.
BUTTERWORTH, John. Private.
CAMPBELL, John. Private.
CAMPBELL, Isaac. Private.
CANNON, Abraham. Private.
CASSIDY, Henry. Private.
CAVERLY, Joseph. Private.
CAVERLY, Nathaniel. Private.
CESARE, Baptiste. Private.
CHARBONEA, Paul. Private.
CHARBONEAU, Amable. Private.
CHARBONEAU, Peter. Private.
CHATTERTON, David. Private.
CLEMENT, John. Private.
CLEMENT, Baptiste. Private.
CLEMENT, Joseph. Private.
COIN, Gardiner. Private.
COLLINS, John. Private.
CONKLIN, Thomas. Private.
CONNER, David. Private.
CONNOLLY, John. Private.
COOK, Thomas. *Lieutenant.*
COON, John. Private.
CRONSE, Oliver. Private.
CUMMING, Alexander. Private.
DAGNE, Louis. Private.
DAVIS, John. Private.
DAVIS, Peter. Private.
DAVIS, Thomas. Private.
DAWSON, John. Private.
DAWSON, William. Private.
DEACON, Thomas. Private.
DOUGLASS, George. Private.
DRAPER, Clark. Private.
DUBEAU, Bernard. Private.
DUCHARME, Louis. Private.
DUFOE, Louis. Private.
DUFOE, Francois. Private.
DUFOE, Michael. Private.
DUFOE, Joseph. Private.
EARLES, Jeremiah. Private.
ELLERBECK, John. Private.
ELLERBECK, James. Private.

EVERITT, John. Private.
EVERITT, Daniel. Private.
FAVEREAU, Toussaint. Private.
FENIS, Corey. Private.
FENON, Peter. Private.
FERRIES, Willeh. Private.
FERRIES, Daniel. Private.
FORTIER, Charles. Private.
FORTIER, Joseph. Private.
FOURNIER, Augustus. Private.
FRANKLIN, Henry. Private.
FRANKLIN, John. Private.
FRANKLIN, William. Private.
FREEMAN, Simeon. Private.
FURRAND, Joseph. Private.
GIBBO, Edward. Private.
GORDENEAU, Jacob. Private.
GOSS, Asa G. Private.
GOWAN, Thomas. Private.
GRAHAM, William. Private.
GRAHAM, John. Private.
GRANT, James. Private.
GRENIER, Joseph. Private.
GROOMS, James. Private.
HARDY, Thomas. Private.
HARPUM, George. Corporal.
HARRIS, Abner. Private.
HARVEY, John. Private.
HOGAN, Michael. Private.
HOWE, Peter. Private.
HOWE, William. Private.
HUETSON (?), Cornelius. Private.
HUFF, Samuel. Private.
HUNTLY, William. Private.
JACKSON, Jethro. Private.
JACKSON, John. Sergeant.
JACQUES, Francois. Private.
JIBEAU, Jean. Private.
KELLAR, Isaac. Private.
KNAPP, Samuel. Private.
L'ESTAGE, Toussaint. Private.
LA PRISE, John. Private.
LA MARCHE, Baptiste. Private.
LA PORTE, Louis. Private.
LA BELLE, Joseph. Private.

LA BLANC, Francois. Private.
LA MONTAIGNE, Amable. Private.
LIGHTHATT, William. Private.
LUCIEN, Christopher. Private.
MACHAN, William. Corporal.
MADONE (Madore), Alexander. Private.
MARKLAND, Thomas. *Captain.*
MASON, James. Corporal.
MATTON, Joseph. Private.
McCAULAY, John. Sergeant.
McINTOSH, Laughlin. Private.
McLAUGHLIN, William. Private.
McMICHAEL, Albert. Private.
McNAB, John. Private.
McPHERSON, Allen. Private.
MERNET, George. Private.
METCALF, Apollas. Private.
MILES, Stephen. Private.
MITCHELL, George. Private.
MORIN, Nicholas. Private.
MORLU, Jean B. Sergeant.
MOSHER, Nicholas. Private.
MOSHER, Louis. Private.
MOSHER, John. Private.
MOSHER, Thomas. Private.
NORTON, Loomis. Private.
O'BRYAN, George. Private.
OBLE, Charles. Private.
OLCOT, Benjamin. Private.
OLIVER, George. Private.
ONIEL, John. Private.
ORSER, Gabriel. Private.
ORSER, Joseph. Private.
ORSER, Isaac. Private.
OTTHOUSE, Peter. Private.
PAXTON, Thomas. Sergeant.
PEMLEER, Thomas. Private.
PERNBER, Francis. Sergeant.
PERRON, Paul. Private.
PERRY, Emery. Private.
PETRIE, Alexander. Sergeant.
PIXLEY, Asa. Private.
POWERS, Alexander. Private.

POWLEY, Francis. Private.
PRINCE, Frederick. Private.
RANDAL, William. Private.
RECORD, Jacob. Private.
RICHARDSON, Robert. *Ensign.*
ROBINS, William. *Captain.*
ROBINSON, Hugh. Private.
ROCHELEAU, Francois. Corporal.
ROGERS, Moses. Private.
ROOD, Harvey. Private.
ROSEGNOT, Antoine. Private.
RUTTER, John. Private.
SANCIER, Theodore. Private.
SANSONCER, Francois. Private.
SEAMAN, Smith. Private.
SHAW, Samuel. Sergeant.
SHEFFIELD, Soloman. Private.
SHELDON, Peter. Private.
SIMONCAU, Joseph. Private.
SMITH, Thomas. Private.
SMITH, Patrick. *Lieutenant.*
SMITH, Darius. Private.
SNOOK, George. Private.
SPAFFORD, Moses. Private.
SPARHAM, Thorney. *Lieutenant.*
SPONCER, John. Private.
SPOONER, Jonathan. Private.
SPOONER, Barnabas. Private.
STARK, Andrew. Private.
STEPHENSON, William. Private.
STOUGHTON, James. Private.
STOUGHTON, John. Private.
TACHEBURY, W. H. Private.
TALBOT, Robert. Private.
THOMPSON, Joseph. Private.
TINDALE, Robert Jr. Private.
TINNEY, Elisha. Private.
TURNER, James. Private.
VALIERE, James. Private.
VALIERE, Charles. Private.
VALIERE, Joseph. Private.
VAMILIER, William. Private.
VAN COTT, Cornelius. Private.
VAN BLACK, Henry. Private.
VAN ORDER, Isaiah. Private.

VANEST, James. Private.
VIENNE, Antoine. Private.
WAGGONER, Emanuel. Private.
WAGGONER, John. Private.
WALKER, Edward. Private.
WALLACE, John. Private.
WASHBURN, Simon. *Ensign.*
WILCOCK, Huzard. Private.
WILLIAMS, Cornelius. Private.

WILLIAMS, Daniel. Corporal.
WILLIAMS, Daniel. Private.
WIRNELL, Stephen. Private.
WOOD, Daniel. Sergeant.
WOODCOCK, John. Private.
WOODCOCK, Abraham. Private.
WORDEN, Jarvis. Private.
WYCOT, Richard. Private.
YOUNG, Elijah. Private.

1ST LENNOX

The Flank Companies
ABBOT, Samuel. Private.
ABBOT, John. Private.
AIREHART, William. Private.
AIRHART, Asa. Private.
ALLISON, Joseph. Private.
ANDERSON, Alexander. Corporal.
BARNHART, Samuel. Private.
BARNHART, John. Private.
BARTLEY, Josiah. Private.
BEDELL, Rueben. *Lieutenant.*
BELL, John. Sergeant.
BENSON, David. Private.
BINN, Peter. Private.
BOGERT, John. Private.
BOWEN, Daniel. Private.
BRADSHAW, John. Private.
BRADSHAW, William. Private.
BRADSHAW, James. Corporal.
BRADSHAW, Jeptha. Private.
BRANDY, William. Private.
BROWN, Robert. Private.
BRUSH, Robert. Private.
CADMAN, Joshua. Private.
CANIFF, Jonas. Sergeant.
CANIFF, John. Private.
CARNAHAN, Moses. Sergeant.
CASEY, Robertson. Private.
CAYLE, Michael. Private.
CHAPMAN, Timothy. Private.
CHAPMAN, Jeremiah. Private.

CHARD, Joseph. Private.
CHURCH, Oliver. *Ensign.*
CLUTE, John J. Sergeant.
COLE, Henry. Private.
CORNELIUS, John. Private.
CORNELIUS, Nicholas. Private.
CRONKWRIGHT, Jacob. Private.
DAFOE, Zenas. Private.
DAFOE, Michael. Private.
DAFOE, William. Private.
DAVIS, John. Private.
DAVIS, Henry. Private.
DEFOE, John. Private.
DELLINGBECK, Henry. Private.
DEMOREST, William. Private.
DIAMOND, Marcus. Private.
DORLAND, Thomas. *Captain.*
DRAPER, Clark. Private.
DULYEA, Isaac. Private.
DULYEA, Peter. Private.
DUNHAM, Israel. Private.
DURYES (?), Peter. Private.
EDGAR, William. Private.
EMBURY, Valentine. Sergeant.
ERMAND, Enoch. Private.
ETONY, Mercee. Private.
FOX, Charles. Sergeant.
FRASER, Jacob. Private.
FREDERICK, John. Private.
FRY, Abner. Private.
GARDENEAR, Daniel. Private.
GERMAN, Mathew. Private.

GRANT, Horrace. Private.
GRIFFITH, Philip. Private.
GRIFFITH, Stephen. Private.
GROOMS, Zepheniah. Private.
HAGERMAN, Christopher
Alexander. *Ensign.*
HAGERMAN, Nicholas. *Captain.*
HAINES, George. Private.
HARLOW, Samuel. Private.
HARRIS, Noxen. Sergeant.
HART, John. Corporal.
HAWLEY, John. Private.
HELLER, John. Private.
HELLER, Daniel. Private.
HENDRICK, David. Private.
HESS, John. Private.
HICKS, Joseph. Private.
HOLBERT, James. Private.
HOLCOMB, John. Private.
HOUGH, Jacob. Private.
HOUGHNET, Peter. Private.
HOUGHNET, John. Private.
HUDGINS, William. Private.
HUDGINS, Daniel. Private.
HUDGINS, John. Private.
HUFF, Peter. Private.
HUFF, Solomon Jr. Private.
HUFF, William Jr. Private.
HUFF, Peter. Private.
HUFF, Asa. Private.
HUFF, Samuel. Private.
HUMMERLY, David. Private.
HUSNAIL, Andrew. Private.
JAYNES, Joseph. Private.
JOHNSON, John. Private.
KELLER, Samuel. Private.
KELLER, John. Private.
KELLER, Frederick. Private.
KERNELL, Daniel. Private.
KERNELL, John. Private.
KIMMERLY, John. Corporal.
KIMMERLY, Henry. Private.
KIMMERLY, Statts. Private.
KIMMERLY, Jacob. Private.
KIMMERLY, Garret. Private.

KING, Harmonies. Private.
KIRBY, Absalom. Private.
LABET, Anthony. Private.
LANSING, John. Private.
LASHER, Andrew. Private.
LOYD, John. Corporal.
LOYD, Edward. Private.
MARRICLE, Gilbert. Private.
MASLE, Benjamin. Private.
MATT, Aaron. Private.
McBRIDE, Thomas. Private.
McCABE, Peter. Private.
McCUMBER, Jarvis. Private.
McGRATH, Christopher. Private.
McGRATH, John. Private.
McMASTERS, James. Private.
MILLER, Michael. Private.
OCHERMAN, Jacob. Private.
OUTWATERS, Joseph. Private.
PARKS, Cyreue. Private.
PARKS, David. Private.
PARKS, William. Private.
PATERSON, John. Private.
PAXTON, Thomas. Private.
PENNY, Ebenezar. Private.
PETERMORE, Baptiste. Private.
PETERSON, Christopher. Private.
PETERSON, Paul. Private.
PETERSON, Nicholas. Private.
PHILIP, Peter. Private.
PHILIP, James. Private.
PHILLIPS, Elisha. *Captain.*
POTTER, Peter. Private.
PRICE, John. Private.
PRINDEL, Joseph. Private.
RICHARDSON, Thomas. Private.
RICHARDSON, Asa. Private.
RIKELY, Andrew. Private.
ROBLIN, William Moore. Private.
ROBLIN, Jacob. Private.
RUTTAN, Peter. Sergeant.
RUTTAN, John. Private.
RUTTAN, Joseph. Private.
RUTTES, Alexander. Private.
SAGER, William. Private.

SAGER, Garret. Private.
SAGER, Adam. Private.
SAVROWAY (?), John. Private.
SCHAMAHORN, Benjamin.
  Private.
SCHAMEHORN, William.
  Private.
SCHAMEHORN, Amas. Private.
SCHUTLHOFS (?), James.
  Private.
SCRIVER, John. Private.
SEDORE, Isaac. Private.
SEDORE, Abraham. Private.
SERIVEN, George. Private.
SHAW, Alexander. Private.
SILLS, Peter. Private.
SIMMONS, Coonrod. Private.
SORRACE, Peter. Private.
SPARROW, Joseph. Corporal.
SPENCER, Benjamin Conger.
  Ensign.
SPENCER, John. Private.
SPENCER, William. Private.
SPENCER, Richard. Private.
STERRING, Jacob. Private.
STUDSON, John. Private.
TAYLOR, William. Private.
TOBY, John. Private.
TYLER, Soloman. Private.
UNGER, Philip. Private.
UNGER, John. Private.
VALIER, James. Private.
VAN COTE, Cornelius. Private.

VAN VOLKENBURG, Peter.
  Private.
VANACTAM, Jacob. Private.
VANALSTINE, James. Private.
VANALSTINE. James. Private.
VANBLARICUM, Isaac. Private.
VANBLARICUM, Benjamin.
  Private.
VANDEBOGERT, William.
  Private.
VANDEWATERS, Peter. Private.
VANDUKYDEN, Peter. Sergeant.
VANDYCK, John. Sergeant.
WAGER, Thomas. Private.
WILLIAMS, John. Private.
WINDOVER, John. Private.
WOODCOCK, Abraham Jr.
  Private.
WOODCOCK, John. Private.
WOODCOCK, Abraham. Private.
WORDOFF, John. Private.
WRIGHT, Wait. Private.
WRIGHT, George. Private.
YORK, David. Private.
YOUNG, Jacob. Private.
YOUNG, Henry Jr. Private.
YOUNG, Daniel. Private.
YOUNG, Christopher. Private.
YOUNG, George. Private.
YOUNG, John. Corporal.
YOUNG, Richard. Private.
YOUNG, Henry Jr. Private.
YOUNG, Elijah. Private.

1ST ADDINGTON

The Flank Companies
ABRAMS, John. Sergeant.
ALCOT, Henry. Private.
AMEY, Joseph. Private.
ANDERSON, John. Sergeant.
AREHART, Simon. Private.
AREHART, John. Private.
ARHART, William. Private.

ASSELSTINE, Michael. Private.
ASSLOTINE, Peter. Private.
BABCOCK, William. Private.
BABCOCK, Henry. Private.
BABCOCK, Peter. Private.
BAKER, Peter. Corporal.
BALL, Solomon. Private.
BARNARD, Alexander. Private.

BELL, Thomas. Private.
BOICE, Joseph. Private.
BOICE, Abraham. Private.
BOWER, Peter. Private.
BRASS, John. Private.
BREZEE, John. Private.
BRISTOL, Coleman. Private.
BURDAN, John. Private.
BURLEY, Cornelius. Private.
CALDWELL, William. Private.
CAN (Car), Daniel. Private.
CASTLE, John. Private.
CASTLEOU, James. Private.
CASTON, Henry. Private.
CATON, Thomas. Private.
CHATTERSON, James. Private.
CHATTERSON, Jacob. Private.
CHATTERSON, David. Private.
CLARK, Chancy. Private.
CLARK, John C. *Ensign.*
CLARK, Robert. Sergeant.
CLARK, Samuel. Corporal.
CLARK, Rufus. Private.
CLARK, Mathew. *Captain.*
CLEMENT, Lewis. Private.
CLOW, Peter. Private.
COMEE, John. Private.
CORL, Richard. Private.
CRONK, Stephen. Private.
CRONK, John. Private.
CUMMING, Eyler. Private.
DAFOE, John. Private.
DALY, Philip. Corporal.
DARBY, Dudley. Private.
DAVEY, Peter. Private.
DAVEY, Henry. *Lieutenant.*
DAVEY, Michael. Private.
DIMOND, Jacob. Private.
DUSENBERRY, John. Corporal.
FAIRFIELD, John. Private.
FERGUSON, John. Private.
FINKLE, George. Private.
FISH, Milton. Private.
FORBS, Adam. Private.
FRALICK, Martin. Private.

FRALICK, John. Private.
FRASER, Daniel. *Lieutenant.*
FREANDS, Joseph. Private.
FROIMAN, David. Private.
GALLOWAY, Henry. Corporal.
GARDINEER, Lewis. Private.
GEORGE, Thomas. Private.
GEORGE, William. Private.
GIBBARD, John. Private.
GIBBARD, William. Private.
GILCHRIST, Archibald. Private.
GOROON, John. Sergeant.
GROOMS, Elijah. Private.
GUIN, Isaac. Private.
GUN, Theron. Private.
HALL, Isaac. Private.
HAM, Peter. Private.
HAM, George. Sergeant.
HANES, Jacob. Private.
HASTMAN, Adam. Private.
HAWLEY, Sheldon. *Captain.*
HAWLEY, Jehial. *Ensign.*
HAWLEY, Johnston. Sergeant.
HAWLEY, Tyrus. Private.
HICKS, John. Private.
HICKS, Isaac. Private.
HICKS, Benjamin. Private.
HILLER, Jacob. Private.
HOUGH, John. Private.
HOUGH, Samuel. Private.
HUNTLY, Jason. Private.
HUTCHINS, Henry. Private.
IRISH, Abraham. Private.
JOHNSTON, Conrad. Private.
JOHNSTON, James. Private.
JOHNSTON, Andrew. Corporal.
JOHNSTON, Nathan. Private.
KELLER, Frederick. Private.
KELLY, Samuel. Private.
KNOULTON, Erastus. Private.
LANE, Benjamin. Private.
LAPP, Anthony. Private.
LARD, William. Private.
LATIMORE, Francis. Private.
LAUGHLIN, Jacob. Corporal.

LEE, Levi. Private.
LEE, Edward. Private.
LEE, William. Private.
LEEMAN, James. A. Private.
LESTER, Daniel H. Private.
LOCKWOOD, Joseph. Sergeant.
LOCKWOOD, Theophilus.
  Private.
LOUKS, John. Private.
LOVELASS, Marshal. Private.
MANTEN, Jeremiah. Private.
MARTEN, Amos. Private.
MARTEN, William. Private.
McCREMMON, Duncan. Private.
McGINNIS, William. Private.
McGINNIS, George. Private.
McKERN, Thomas. Private.
McKIM, James. Private.
McLAUGHLIN, John. Sergeant.
McPHERSON, Peter. Private.
McPHERSON, Duncan. Private.
McPHERSON, Malcolm. Private.
MILIGAN, Samuel. Private.
MONEY, George. Private.
MORAK, Peter. Private.
NEILY, John. Private.
NICHOLSON, Chester. Private.
NOBLE, Mark. Private.
NORTON, Leeman J. Private.
OUTERCERK, Nicholas. Private.
OUTWATERS, Barnard. Private.
PARROTT, Jonathan. Private.
PECKINS, George. Private.
PEEKINS, Martin. Private.
PERRY, William. Private.
PURDY, Micajah. Private.
RAYMOND, John. Private.
REDDING, Simon. Private.
ROBERTSON, George W. Private.
ROGERS, Joseph. Private.
ROSE, William. Private.
ROSINAL, Francis. Private.
ROSS, Hatter. Private.
SAMKINS, Oliver. Private.

SCOTT, Samuel. Private.
SHOREY, Elisha. Private.
SHOVEY (Shorey), Rufus.
  Sergeant.
SHUTTS, William. Private.
SIMMONS, Nicholas. Private.
SMITH, Jacob. Private.
SMITH, Parker. Private.
SNIDER, Jonas. Private.
SNIDER, John. Private.
SNIDER, Philip. Private.
SNIDER, John B. Private.
SNIDER, Jeremiah. Private.
SNIDER, Jacob. Private.
SNIDER, Abraham. Private.
SOLES, Benjamin. Private.
SPAFFORD, John. Private.
STALKER, James. Private.
STOVEN, Martin. Private.
STOVER, Martin. Private.
STOVER, Jacob. Corporal.
SWEET, James. Private.
THOMAS, Peter. Private.
THOMPSON, John. Private.
TRYON, William. Private.
TYFARE, Francis. Private.
VAN VALKINBUNG, Adam.
  Private.
VANALSTINE, Duncan. Private.
VANLUVAN, Benjamin. Private.
VANLUVAN, Henry. Private.
WALKER, John. Private.
WALKER, Daniel. Private.
WARD, Moses. Private.
WEIS, David. Private.
WELCH, David. Private.
WETSEL, Peter. Sergeant.
WICKLIN, John V. Private.
WILLIAMS, Joseph. Private.
WILLIAMS, James. Private.
WILLIAMS, Robert S. Private.
WOODS, Bradford. Private.
WRIGHT, William. Private.
YOUNG, John. Private.

The Flank Companies

ACKERMAN, John. Private.
BADGELY, Lawrence. Private.
BADGELY, Samuel. Private.
BARKER, William. Private.
BARNUM, Israel. Private.
BARNUM, John. Private.
BOICE, John. Private.
BROWN, James. Private.
CANIFF, Abram. Sergeant.
CARSCALLEN, Edward. Private.
CARTER, John. Private.
CAV?, Stephen. Private.
CHRYSDELL, Joshua. Corporal.
COOK, William. Private.
COTTER, David. Private.
COX, Spencer. Drummer.
CR?, David. Private.
CRAM, Edward. Private.
DIXON, Francis. Private.
EMBURY, Phillip. Private.
FAIRMAN, HUGH. *Ensign.*
FINKLE, George. Private.
FORSTER, Shubal. Private.
FULTON, John. Private.
GEMALES, Cornelius. Private.
GEMER, Jean Baptiste. Private.
GLOVER, Isaac B. Private.
GREEN, Ebenezer. Private.
GRIFFEN, John. Private.
HARRIS, Gilbert. *Captain.*
HENDRIX, Jacob. Private.
HENNEREY, John. Private.
HIGLEY, Philo. Private.
HOLTON, Timothy. Private.
HUBBLE, Reuben. Private.
HUBBLE, Peter. Drummer.
INGERSOLL, John. Private.
KETCHERON, Thomas. Sergeant.
KETCHERON, William. *Ensign.*
KETCHERON. Benjamin.
  Sergeant.
KETCHESON, Elijah. Private.

L?, William. Private.
LAKE, James. Private.
LAWRENCE, Stephen. Private.
LEAVINS, Rosewell. Private.
LEMMON, Nicholas. Private.
LeMOINE, Joseph. *Ensign.*
LIDDEL, Robert Dennison.
  Corporal.
LINE, William. Private.
LINE, Thomas. Private.
LOT, Bolten. Private.
MACINTOSH, John. *Captain.*
MARSHAL, Solomon. Drummer.
MARTIN, James. Private.
McCONNELL, Edward. Private.
McMICHAEL, John. *Lieutenant.*
McMULLEN, George. Private.
McMULLEN, Stephen. Private.
MEYERS, Peter Walden. Private.
MEYERS, Jacob Walden.
  Captain.
MILLER, Jacob. Private.
MOTT, Solomon. Private.
NOARD, William. Private.
OSTRUM, Simon. Private.
OSTRUM, Benjamin. Private.
PALMER, Daniel. Private.
PARKER, Thomas. Sergeant.
PATRICK, Spencer. Sergeant.
PERRY, Jacob. Private.
PITMAN, Martin. Private.
POTTER, Rowland. Private.
PURDY, Ruloff. Private.
REID, Solomon. Private.
REID, Daniel. Private.
ROBLIN, David. Corporal.
ROREBUSH, Samuel. Private.
ROREBUSH, Joseph. Private.
ROSE, Jacob. Private.
ROSS, Zenas. Private.
ROSS, Obijah. Private.
SEELEY, David. Private.
SELDON, Jonathan. Private.

SHELDON, David. Private.
SHELDON, George. Private.
SHERARD, Nathaniel. Private.
SIMPKINS, Benjamin. Private.
SMITH, John R. Private.
SMITH, Jacob. Private.
SMITH, Ammi. Private.
SMITH, John. Private.
STIMERS, Isaac. Corporal.
STREETER, Rufus. Private.
THOMPSON, Robert. Private.
THOMPSON, John. *Lieutenant.*

THRASHER, Cornelius. Private.
THRASHER, John. Private.
TIVNER, Gideon. Private.
VANDERVOORT, Peter. Private.
VANDERWATER, John. Private.
VANSKUN, Peter. Private.
VEELEY, Henry. Private.
WEST, Ira. Private.
WESTFALL, George. Private.
WHITTICK, John. Private.
YEOMAN, James. Sergeant.
YOUNG, George. Private.

1ST PRINCE EDWARD

The Flank Companies
ALGER, Charles. Corporal.
ALLEN, John. *Captain.*
ALLESON, John. Sergeant.
ANDERSON, William. Private.
AVERY, John S. Private.
BADGELY, Stephen. Private.
BENSEN, Jacob. Private.
BICK, John. Sergeant.
BLACK, William Jr. Private.
BRYANT, John. Private.
BURLINGHAM, Vernon. Private.
CHAUSER, Abraham. Private.
CLAPP, Joseph. Private.
CLARK, David. Private.
CLARK, Jacob. Private.
COLE, John. Private.
CORBMAN, Jacob. Private.
COVERT, Samuel. Private.
COVERT, David. Private.
CRENK, Enoch. Private.
CRYDERMAN, Jacob. Private.
DAVIES, James. Private.
DELONG, David. Private.
DEMELL, John. Private.
DINGMAN, Henry. Sergeant.
DOORES, Thomas. Private.
DORLAND, Daniel B. Sergeant.
DREADES, Jacob. Private.
DULMADGE, John. Sergeant.

DULMADGE, Phillip. Private.
ECKERT, Tunis. Private.
EXUEN, Jeremiah. Private.
FAIRMAN, George. Private.
FARNYEN, Andrew. Private.
FERRY, Isaac. Private.
FLAGER, Thomas. Sergeant.
GARRET, Caleb. Private.
GARRETSEE, Henry. Private.
GREEN, Jacob. Private.
GRIMMON, Robert. Private.
GROOMS, Joseph. Private.
HANESS, John. Private.
HARISON, John. Private.
HARLOW, Joshua. Private.
HEAD, Jonathan. Private.
HICKS, John. Private.
HICKS, William. Private.
HOWELL, Richard. *Ensign.*
HUFF, Joshua. Private.
HULL, Daniel. Private.
HUYCK, John. Private.
HUYCK, Cornelius. Private.
HUYCK, John H. Private.
JOHNSON, John. Private.
JONES, David. Private.
JONES, Thomas. Private.
KEMP, John. Private.
KETCHUM, Thadeus. Private.
LANE, John. Private.

LATHAM, James. Private.
LATURE, Lewes. Private.
LAWSON, John. Private.
LAZIER, James. Private.
LAZIER, Abram. Private.
LEAVENS, Daniel. Private.
LEAVENS, William B. Private.
LEW, John. Private.
LOSIE, Isaac. Private.
LOVELESS, Esrim. Private.
MABIE, Abraham. Private.
MARTEN, John. Private.
McCARTNEY, Thomas. Sergeant.
McCARTNEY, Samuel. Private.
McCARTNEY, Robert. Private.
McCONNEL, James. Private.
McDONELL, Alex. Private.
McDONELL, John. Private.
McDONELL, Francis W. Private.
McDONELL, Daniel. Private.
McFALL, Peter. Private.
McGUIRE, Peter. Private.
McINTOSH, Donald. *Lieutenant.*
MERDEN, George. Private.
MERDEN, Joseph. Sergeant.
MERDEN, Joseph R. Private.
MERDEN, John R. Private.
MERDEN, Joseph. Private.
MEWERSON, Abraham. Private.
MEWERSON, Isaac. Private.
MEWERSON, Jacob. Private.
MILLEN, Elisha. Private.
MORGAN, Thomas Jr. Private.
MYNEKER, Charles. Private.
NORTH, John. Sergeant.
NORTH, James. Sergeant.
ORSER, Jesse. Private.
OSBORNE, Nemiah. Private.
OSBURN, Nathaniel. Private.
OSBURN, William. Private.
PALMER, James. Private.
PERSONS, James. Private.
PETTIT, Isaac. Private.
POTTER, Jesse. Private.
POWIS, Edward. Private.

QUACKENBUSH, Isaac. Private.
RICHARD, Owen. *Captain.*
RICHARDSON, William. Private.
RIDNER, Peter. Private.
RIDRICK, George. Private.
RIDRICK, David. Private.
ROBINSON, Hugh. Private.
ROWE, John. Private.
RUSH, John. Private.
RUSSELL, Richard. Private.
RYCKMAN, John. Private.
RYCKMAN, Samuel. Private.
RYCKMAN, John. Private.
SCRIVER, Henry. Private.
SHAFFORD, Henry. Private.
SHIARMAN, Rowland. Private.
SHIFFIELD, Solomon. Private.
SHULER, William. Private.
SKINKLE, John. Private.
SMITH, Lyman. Private.
SMITH, William. Corporal.
SMITH, Kenneth. Private.
SOLMES, Samuel. Private.
SPIER, John. Private.
STAPLETON, Benjamin.
   Sergeant.
STERNS (Sterm), Elisha. Private.
STICKLES, Peter. Private.
STREMP, James. Private.
STRIKER, Garret. Private.
STRING, John. Private.
SWITZER, Christopher. Private.
TAYLOR, Robert. Private.
TRIPP, Richard. Private.
TUBS, Isiah. Private.
VAIL, Thomas. Private.
VANDEBEGART, Francis. Private.
VANDERSON, John. Private.
VANDUSEM, Henry. Private.
VANTASSEL, Henry. Private.
VINCENT, Leonard. Private.
WANNAMAKER, William. Private.
WASHBURN, Simon. *Ensign.*
WATERS, Joshua. Private.
WATTERS, Daniel. Private.

WAY, Ruben. Private.
WAY, John R. Private.
WAY, Lawrence D. Private.
WAY, Jacob. Private.
WAY, John B. Private.
WERDEN, Asa. Private.
WESSELS, Owen. Private.
WESSELS, Nicholas. Private.
WEST, John. Private.
WHITE, Gilbert. Private.
WHITE, Moses. Private.

WHITE, Cornelius. Private.
WILLIAMS, Nicholas. Private.
WRIGHT, David. Private.
YOUNG, William. Private.
YOUNG, James. *Lieutenant.*
YOUNG, John Jr. Private.
YOUNG, Robert. *Ensign.*
YOUNG, Henry. *Lieutenant.*
YOUNG, John. Sergeant.
YOUNG, Guy Henry. Private.
ZERT, William. Private.

DISTRICT OF NEWCASTLE
1ST NORTHUMBERLAND

1st and 2nd Flank Companies
ABBOTT, George. Private.
ALGER, Peter. Private.
ASH, Joseph. Sergeant.
ASH, Hiram. Corporal.
BABCOCK, Benjamin. Private.
BADSLEY, Rosel. Private.
  Volunteer.
BATES, Levi. Private.
BATTY, David F. Private.
BLAKELY, Samuel. Private.
BRADLEY, William. Private.
BRADLY, George. Private.
BRADLY, Samuel H. Private.
BRADLY, Eli. Private.
BRINTNAL, Asa. Private.
BURNHAM, Asa. *Captain.*
CAMP, Daniel. Private.
CAMPBELL, William. Private.
COFFIELD, Nathaniel. Private.
COLKINS, Silba. Private.
CRANDAL, Benjamin. Private.
CRONKITE, Samuel. Private.
CULVER, Isaac. Private.
CUMMINGS, Abel. Private.
DEAN, Joel Jr. Private.
DEAN, Benjamin. Private.
DICKSON, Nathaniel C. Private.
DINGMAN, Jacob. Private.

DINGMAN, John Jr. Private.
DOOLITTLE, Isaac. Private.
DRAPER, Carr. Private.
EDDY, Allen. Private.
ELSWORTH, Noel. Corporal.
ELSWORTH, George. Private.
FAIRMAN (Furman), John.
  Private.
FAND, Ephraim. Private.
FISHER, Henry. Private.
FISHER, James F. Private.
GARRETT, Mott. Corporal.
GIDEONS, Chester W. Corporal.
GOHEAN, Samuel. Private.
GOHEAN, Thomas. Private.
GOHEAN, Charles. Private.
GOULD, Seth B. Private.
HARNDEN, Jeshua. Private.
HARRISON, Thomas. Private.
HASES, Enoch. Corporal.
HINDS, Daniel L. Corporal.
HOLLINBUK, Jacob. Private.
HUBBERT, John. Private.
IRISH, John. Private.
IVES, Atwater. Private.
JEROME, Asael. Private.
JOHNSON, William. Private.
KEELER, Joseph A. *Ensign.*
KELLY, Charles. Sergeant.

LINCOTT, (Hamden). Private.
LITTLE, David. Private.
LOSIE, Abraham. Private.
MALLORY, Caleb. Private.
MASTERS, William. Private.
McCARTY, John. Private.
McCARTY, David. Private.
McDONALD, Walter. Private.
McDOUGAL, Walter. Private.
McEVERS, Benjamin. Private.
McKENNY, Samuel L. Sergeant.
McKENZIE, Daniel. Private.
McNUTT, Garret. Private.
MERRIAM, Johnson. Drummer.
MERRILL, Russell. Private.
MEYERS, Adam H. *Ensign*.
NAPP, Jesse. Private.
NICHOLS, John G. Private.
NICKERSON, Nathaniel. Sergeant.
NICKERSON, Levi. Private.
NIX, John Jr. Private.
NORRIS, James. *Lieutenant*.
OWENS, Michael. Private.
PALMER, Elijah. Private.
PARLIAMENT, Jacob. Corporal.
PIKE, Daniel. Private.
PURDY, Nathaniel. Private.
PURDY, Gilbert. Private.
RAMOND, William. Private.
RAMONT, William. Private.
RANDALL, John P. Private.
RICHARDS, Whiting. Private.
RIDER, Elvyer. Drummer.
ROGERS, John. Private. Volunteer.
ROGERS, William. Private.

RUSS, James. Private.
RUSS, Joshua. Private.
SCRIBNER, Nathan. Private.
SHERWOOD, Samuel H. Private.
SIMSON, John. Private.
SIMSON, John Jr. Private.
SMITH, John. Private.
SMITH, William. Private.
SOLES, Daniel. Private.
SPENCER, John. *Captain*.
SQUIRES, Eliakim. Sergeant.
STAFFORD, Annanias. Private.
THOMPSON, Henry Jr. Private.
TOMPKINS, Caleb. Private.
TRIPP, Solomon. Private.
TRIPP, Russel. Private.
TURK, Isaac. Private.
VAN WICKLER, Cornelius.
   Private.
VAN WICKLER, John. Private.
VAN WICKLER, Abraham.
   Private.
WAIT, Isaac. Private.
WAIT, Criel. Private.
WAIT, Jinks. Private.
WAIT, George. Private.
WARFIELD, Ephraim. Private.
WEAVER, John. Private.
WHITE, James. Private.
WILKINS, Robert C. *Captain*.
WILSON, Walter. Private.
WILSON, William. Private.
WOOLENT, Roger. *Lieutenant*.
YOUNG, Benjamin. Sergeant.
YOUNG, John B. Private.

1ST DURHAM

The Flank Companies
ABBE, Nathaniel. Private.
BEBEE, Aron. Private.
BEDFORD, Benjamin. Private.
BEDFORD, Stephen. Private.
BEDFORD, David. Private.

BEDFORD, John. Private.
BEEBEC, Steadman. Private.
BEEBER, Ebenezer. Private.
BOICE, John. Private.
BORLAND, William Sr. Private.
BORLAND, William. Private.

BOWEN, Israel. Private.
BROWN, George. Private.
BURN, John. *Captain.*
CULVER, Raswell. Private.
FENTON, Erastus. Private.
FRANKLIN, Elisha. Private.
FREEZE, Abraham. Private.
GAGE, David. Private.
GIFFORD, Ora. Private.
GIFFORD, Samuel. Private.
GIFFORD, Ezra. Private.
GIFFORD, Gardner. Private.
GRAND, Rueben. Private.
GRANT, James. Private.
HARRIS, Myndert. Private.
HARRIS, Thomas. Private.
HASKEL, Jadathan. Private.
HASKILL, William D. Private.
HERON, Joseph. Private.
HILL, Moses. Private.
HOGABOON, James. Private.
HUEYS, John. Private.
JOHNSON, Justice. Private.
JOOFERY, Pascal. Private.
KARR, John. *Lieutenant.*

LEE, James. Private.
MATHEWS, Christopher. Private.
MATTISON, Caleb. Private.
MILLER, Jacob. Private.
MORSE, Abner. Private.
MUNSON, Eathen. Sergeant.
MUNSON, William. Private.
O'REILY, Patrick. Private.
ODELL, Zachariah. Private.
OLMSTEAD, Charles. Private.
PEACOCK, Samuel. Private.
POIRYIEA (?), Amable. Private.
POTTER, Elias. Private.
PRESTON, Benjamin O. Private.
PRESTON, Benjamin Sr. Sergeant.
ROOT, Benjamin. Private.
SAXTON, George. Sergeant.
SAXTON. Zephaniah. Private.
SERON, David. Private.
SMADES, Luke. Private.
SMITH, Ebenezer. Private.
SMITH, William. Sergeant.
TAYLOR, John. Private.
TAYLOR, John. *Ensign.*
WOOD, John. Private.

HOME DISTRICT

1ST YORK

The Flank Companies
BOSTICK, John. Sergeant.
BRIDGEFORD, David. Sergeant.
CASTOR, Jacob. Private.
CHAPMAN, Jeremiah. Private.
CLARK, Nathaniel. Private.
COOK, Stephen. Private.
CORBINE (Corbier), Lewis.
   Private. GSM, Fort Detroit.
CORNELL, Stephen. Private.
CRITTENDON, William. Private.
CURTZ, Abraham. Private.
DAVIS, William. Private.
DENNY, Francis. Private.
DITSMAN, John. Private.

EVANS, John. Private.
FISHER, Jacob. Private.
FONTAIN, Lewis. Private.
GERNON, Richard. Private.
GRAHAM, William. Private.
GRONNEAU (Grovrau), Richard.
   Private.
HADLOCK, Joseph. Private.
HAMILTON, Edward. Private.
HOWMAN, John. Private.
HULTZ, George G. Private.
JOHNSTONE, Nicholas. Private.
KENNEDY, John R. Private.
KENNY, Joel. Private.
KEOPKEY, Frederick. Private.

LONGHOUSE, Peter. Private.
MARSH, James. Private.
McGUIRE, Thomas. Private.
MILLEGEN, Benjamin. Private.
OSBORNE, Joseph. Private.
PARKS, John. Private.
PHILIPS, Henry. Private.
RAWN, Jacob. Private.
READ, George. Private.
REYNOLDS, William. Private.
RICHARDSON, Ruben.
  Lieutenant.
ROBINS, Henry. Private.
SELBY, Thomas. *Captain.*
SHAVER, John. Private.
SHAW, William. Private.

SHELL, Henry. Private.
SMALLY, Ralfe. Private.
SMALLY, Asa. Private.
STOOKS, John C. Sergeant.
TEAL, Francis. Private.
TEEL, Simeon. Private.
TERRY, Moses. Private.
TRAVIS, William. Private.
TYLER, William. Sergeant.
VANBERBURGH, Isaac. Private.
VANDERBURGH, Barret.
  Lieutenant.
VERNON, Nathaniel. Private.
WAGGONER, William. Private.
WHITE, Moses. Private.
WILLSON, John H. Private.

2ND YORK

1st Flank Company
ALBERSON, William. Private.
ANGEN, Frederick. Private.
BADGER, Thomas B. Private.
  Deserted to the enemy.
BARNES, Elisha. Sergeant.
BATES, Walter. Private.
  See Casualties.
BEEKER, Benjamin G. Private.
BISTIDO, Abraham. Private.
CHISHOLM, George. *Ensign.*
CHISHOLM, John. *Captain.*
CONNER, Thomas. Private.
COUPLIN, Robert. Private.
CRAMER, William. Private.
DAVIS, Asahel. Private.
DEPEW, James. Private.
ELOTT, Aaron. Private.
EMMONS, Johm. Private.
  Deserted to the enemy.
FONGER, John. Private.
GABLE, John. Private.
GREEN, Alexander. Private.
GRENNAS, Daniel. Private.
GRIGS, John. Private.

HAINES (Karnes), Jacob. Private.
HAINES (Harnes), John. Private.
HEPBURN, William. *Ensign.*
HOWELL, Samson. Private.
HUGGINS, Robert. Private.
  Deserted to the enemy.
HULL, Richard. Private.
INGERSON, Thomas. Private.
IRELAND, John. Private.
KENNY, Peter. Private.
KENNY, Joseph. Private.
KING, Daniel B. Private.
  Deserted to the enemy.
KING, George. Private.
KING, James V. Private.
  Deserted to the enemy.
KING, James. Private.
KING, George. *Lieutenant.*
  See Casualties.
KINTON, Thomas. Private.
LEOPARD, Jacob. Private.
LONDON, Aaron. Private.
LONG, William. Private.
LOREE, Timothy. Private.
MACKLIN, Samuel. Private.

McCORMICK, Robert. Private.
McGEE, James. Private.
Deserted to the enemy.
McGEE, William. Private.
Deserted to the enemy.
McKAY, William. Private.
GSM, Fort Detroit.
MITCHEL, Elisha. Private.
MOLAT, George. Sergeant.
See Casualties.
NELSON, David. Private.
OLIFANT, Aaron. Private.
PALMETEER, John. Private.
Deserted to the enemy.
PATTERSON, Jacob. Private.
POLLARD, Joshua. Private.
RAMBO, Elisha. Private.
REYNOLDS, Ryer. Private.
ROBENET, Thomas. Private.
SAVERCOOL, John. Private.
Deserted to the enemy.
SEALY, Hopkins. Private.
Deserted to the enemy.
SHELER, John. Private.
SHOOK, Peter. Sergeant.
SILVERTHORN, Thomas. Private.
SILVERTHORN, Aaron.
Sergeant. GSM, Fort Detroit.
SMITH, John. Private.
STEWART, Charles. Private.
STREET, Timothy. Private.
See Casualties.
THOMSON, James. Private.
TIPS, Cornelius. Private.
TROBRIDGE, David. Private.
UPDIGROVE (Updegrove),
Peter. Private.
UTTER, John. Private.
VANNORMAN, Joseph. Private.
Deserted to the enemy.
VANNORMAN, Abraham. Private.
WHALIN, Walter. Private.
Deserted to the enemy.
WIBSEL, Nicholas. Private.

WILCOX, Amos. Private.
GSM, Fort Detroit.
WOLF, Peter. Private.

2nd Flank Company
APPLEGARTH, John. *Lieutenant.*
Volunteer. GSM, Fort Detroit.
APPLEGARTH, William. *Captain.*
ARMSTRONG, Charles. Private.
ATKINSON, Thomas. *Lieutenant.*
BALDWIN, Gilbert. Private.
BEATTY, John. Sergeant.
BUCK, Jacob. Private.
BUCKLURY, George. Private.
CHISHOLM, William. *Ensign.*
COOK, Robert. Private.
See Casualties.
COPE, Henry. Private.
See Casualties.
COPE, Joshua. Private.
CORNWALL (Cornell), Aaron.
Private. GSM, Fort Detroit.
CORNWALL, Moses. Private.
CORNWALL, Thomas. Private.
COUCHNER, Jacob. Sergeant.
CRAMER, Adam. Private.
CUMMINS, William. Private.
CUMMINS, Jacob. Private.
ELLIS, William. Sergeant.
FERGUSON, Richard. Private.
FREEMAN, Clarkson. Private.
GABLE, John. Private.
GREENE, William. Private.
HAGY, John. Private.
HANUBERGER (Hanaberger),
John. Private.
HOPKEN (Slopher), Abraham.
Private.
HUTCHINSON, John. Private.
LAMB, Henry. Private.
LARRISON, John. Private.
LEWIS, William. Private.
Deserted to the enemy.
LONTIES, Jacob. Private.

McCARTHY, James. Private.
McCARTHY, Adam. Private.
See Casualties.
McMAHON, James. Private.
McMANNESS, David. Private.
MEDDOW, James. Private.
MEEDON, Moses. Private.
MERICLE, Jacob. Private.
MERICLE, William. Private.
MERRICLE, Benjamin. Private.
MORDON, James. Private.
MORDON, Thomas. Private.
MUMA, Christian. Private.
PEER, Jacob. Private.
ROSEBROOK, William. Private.
ROSEBROOK, Thomas. Private.
SEVERGOOD, Jacob. Private.

SEVERGOOD, Peter. Private.
SEVERGOOD, George. Private.
SHANNON, William. Private.
SHAVER, Isaac. Private.
SHIRKE, George. Private.
SMITH, Ward. Private.
SMITH, Joseph. Private.
SUPES (Sipes), Jacob. Private.
SURRANAS, Jacob. Private.
TEEPLE, John. Private.
Deserted to the enemy.
THORPE, Adam. Private.
THORPE, John. Private.
VAN EVERY, Michael. Private.
VAN EVERY, Peter. Private.
WARNER, Henry. Private.
WEDGE, James. Private.

3RD YORK

1st Flank Company
ALTON (Allen), George. Private.
ANDERSON, Elias. Private.
BAYNES, Charles. Quarter
Master
BRIGHT, Thomas. Sergeant.
BRIGHT, Robert. Private.
GSM, Fort Detroit.
BURKHOLDER, Abraham.
Private.
CAMERON, Duncan. *Captain.*
CAUL, Stephen. Private.
CAUL, Richard. Private.
CAWTHRA, John. Private.
GSM, Fort Detroit.
CAWTHRA, Johnathan. Private.
COCHRAN, Samuel. Private.
COOK, Seth. Private.
CORNELL, William. Private.
COVELLION, John. Private.
COX, Osborn. Private.
CRAWFORD, Joseph. Private.
CROSS, Hazon K. Private.
CULVER, Abraham. Private.
GSM, Fort Detroit.

DENNISON, Charles. Private.
DEVINS, Simeon. Private.
DOYLE, Michael. Private.
ELSWORTH, Harden. Private.
FLUMMERFELT (Plomerfelt),
Cornelius. Private. GSM, Fort
Detroit.
GRAHAM, Richard. Private.
GSM, Fort Detroit.
HALE, Henry. Private.
HARLEY, William. Private.
HOWE, George. Sergeant.
HUMBERSTON, Thomas.
Sergeant. GSM, Fort Detroit.
JARVIE, William. *Lieutenant.*
JOHNSTON, Henry. Private.
JOHNSTON, John. Adjutant.
JONES, William. Private.
GSM, Fort Detroit.
KENNEDY, Andrew. Private.
GSM, Fort Detroit.
KENNEDY, John. Private.
LAWRENCE, Edward. Private.
GSM, Fort Detroit.
LAWRENCE, William. Private.

LEE, Francis. Private.
GSM, Fort Detroit.
LEE, Asa. Private.
GSM, Fort Detroit.
LEWIS, Samuel. Private.
LUDDEN (Sudden), Eli. Private.
Deserted to the enemy.
MAJOR, Thomas. Private.
See Casualties.
MATHEWS, John. Private.
GSM, Fort Detroit.
McBRIDE, Edward. Quarter
Master Sergeant.
McDONELL, Roderick. Private.
McLEAN, Archibald. *Lieutenant.*
McMAHON, Edward. *Lieutenant.*
MILLER, Jacob. Private.
GSM, Fort Detroit.
MITCHEL, David. Private.
MOORE, Robert. Sergeant Major.
MYERS, William. Private.
GSM, Fort Detroit.
PHILIPS, Philip. Private.
PILKINGTON, Isaac. Private.
POWELL, Henry. Private.
RANSOM, Ebenezer. Private.
RIDOUT, George. *Lieutenant.*
ROSS, John. Private.
GSM, Fort Detroit.
ROWLINS, Luther. Private.
RUNNIONS, Benjamin. Private.
GSM, Fort Detroit.
SECORD, Joseph. Private.
SHAW, William. Private.
SIMPSON, Thomas. Private.
GSM, Fort Detroit.
SMALLMAN, George. Private.
SMITH, Thomas. Private.
STIVER, Henry. Private.
STONER, Peter. Private.
GSM, Fort Detroit.
THOMPSON, Andrew. Private.
GSM, Fort Detroit.
THOMPSON, John. Sergeant.

THOMPSON, Richard. Private.
GSM, Fort Detroit.
THOMPSON, Edward. Private.
TIVEY, John. Private.
TWILLIGER, Mathias. Private.
WARD, Adam. Private.
WHIPPLE, Jeremiah. Private.
WHITE, Isaac. Private.
GSM, Fort Detroit.
WRIGHT, Simcoe. Private.
GSM, Fort Detroit.
YEOMANS, Johnston. Private.

2nd Flank Company
ADAMS, Thomas. Private.
GSM, Fort Detroit.
ANDERSON, Cornelius. Private.
GSM, Fort Detroit.
ANDERSON, Jacob. Private.
GSM, Fort Detroit.
BOND, George. Sergeant.
GSM, Fort Detroit.
BOSSELL, John. Sergeant.
BROCK, William. Private.
BURK, John. Private.
CALL, John. Private.
CARY, George. Private.
GSM, Fort Detroit.
CHASE, George. Private.
CLOCK, John. Private.
COLE, Charles. Private.
GSM, Fort Detroit.
COLLINS, Richard. Private.
COZENS, Benjamin. Private.
DAVES, Aaron. Private.
DAVIS, Calvin. Private.
GSM, Fort Detroit.
DEHART, Thomas. Private.
DEMAREY, David. Private.
DENNISON, Thomas. Private.
DEXTER, Elisha. Drummer.
DIVER, Andrew. Private.
GILGORY, Anthony. Private.
GLENNON, Barnard. Private.
GSM, Fort Detroit.
HAMILTON, William A. Private.

HAMILTON, Thomas G. Private.
HARRISON, William. Private.
GSM, Fort Detroit.
HENDRICK (Kendrick), James.
Private.
HENRY, David. Private.
HEWARD, Stephen. *Captain.*
HUBBARD, Andrew. Private.
GSM, Fort Detroit.
HUCK (Kuck), George. Sergeant.
HUNTINGDON, William.
Private.
JARVIS, George. Private.
JARVIS, Samuel Peters.
Lieutenant. GSM, Fort Detroit.
JOHNSTON, Thomas. Private.
GSM, Fort Detroit.
KNOTT, William. Sergeant.
GSM, Fort Detroit.
LACKEY, Robert. Private.
LACOMPT, Joseph. Private.
GSM, Fort Detroit.
LEMEREUX, Andrew. Private.
MARSH, Leonard. Private.
McDONELL, James. Private.
McDONELL, Charles. Private.
GSM, Fort Detroit.
McINTOSH, John. Private.
GSM, Fort Detroit.
MERCER, Andrew. Private.
MOORE, William. Private.
GSM, Fort Detroit.
MOORE, Thomas. Private.

MOORE, George. Private.
GSM, Fort Detroit.
PATRICK, Ruben. Private.
PATTERSON, George. Sergeant.
PHILIPS, Jacob. Private.
PHILIPS, John. Private.
ROBINSON, John Beverely.
Lieutenant. GSM, Fort Detroit.
ROSS, James. Private.
SAUNDERS, John. Private.
SINCLAIR, Samuel. Private.
GSM, Fort Detroit.
SMITH, William. Private.
STANTON, Robert. *Lieutenant.*
STIMSON, Aaba. Private.
STONER, Abraham. Private.
GSM, Fort Detroit.
STONER, John. Private.
GSM, Fort Detroit.
STOUTENBURRGH, Martin.
Private.
VARNUM, Abraham. Private.
WALKER, William. Private.
WEBSTER, Timothy. Private.
WELLS, Robert. Private.
GSM, Fort Detroit.
WEYLEY, Joseph. Private.
WHITNEY, Peter. Private.
WILLS (Wells), John. Private.
GSM, Fort Detroit.
WRIGHT, Edward. Private.
GSM, Fort Detroit.
YOUNG, John. Private.

DISTRICT OF NIAGARA
1ST LINCOLN

1st Flank Company
ALLEN, Alexander. Private.
BALL, Peter Jr. Private.
BARNS, Cornelius. Private.
BRADY, John. Private.
Joined the Dragoons.
BROWN, William. Private.
See Casualties.

BROWN, Henry. Private.
BUNTING, Samuel. Private.
BURNS, David. Drummer.
CAMERON, William. Private.
See Casualties.
CAMPBELL, John Jr. Private.
CAMPBELL, John. Private.
CHISHOLM, John Jr. Private.

CLEMENT, John (son of James).
Private.
CLEMENT, Samuel Thompson.
Private.
CLEMENT, Joseph. Private.
CLEMENT, John (son of Joseph).
Private.
COOK, William. Private.
COOK, William. Private.
Joined the Artillery.
COLLARD, Richard Private.
See Casualties.
COTRINGTON, Samuel. Private.
COUGHILL, John, Jr. Private.
COUGHILL, George, Jr. Private.
CROOKS, James. *Captain.*
CROSS, John. Acting Lance
Sergeant. Joined the Marine
Department.
CUDNEY, Caleb. Private.
See Casualties.
CUDNEY, Ezekiel, Jr. Private.
CUDNEY, Joshua. Private.
CUDNEY, Daniel. Private.
DE CLUTE, Jeremiah. Private.
DeBONE, Michael. Private.
DuBAYE, Joseph. Private.
DURHAM, Elias. Private.
EGBERT, Garnet (Garret).
Private.
EGBERT, John. Private.
EMUEL, Frances. Private.
FIELDS, John. Private.
FOSTER, Anselm. *Lieutenant.*
GOODSON, Edward. Private.
GORING, Hamilton. Private.
GRAHAM, David. Private.
GRANT, Isaac. Private.
HOGHTELLEN, Jacob. Private.
Joined the Provincial Dragoons.
HUNT, John. Private.
HURST, Isaac. Private.
KELLY, Nathaniel. Private.
Joined the Artillery.
KELLY, George. Private.

KELLY, Ebenezer. Private.
KRYSLER, Ralph Mordant.
Private.
LAMPMAN, John. Sergeant.
LAMPMAN, Peter. Private.
See Casualties.
LAWE, George William. Private.
See Casualties.
LAWRENCE, David. Private.
See Casualties.
LAWRENCE, Francis. Private.
LAWRENCE, George B. Private.
LOWELL, Francis. Private.
MACKLE, Benjamin. Private.
MANN, Elkannah. Private.
MARKLE, Solomon. Private.
MARTEL, Francis. Private.
McCLELLAN, Martin.
Lieutenant. See Casualties.
McDONELL, David. Private.
McFARLAND, James. Private.
McKINNY, Elijah. Private.
McNABB, James. Acting Lance
Sergeant. Joined the Artillery.
McNABB, John. Private.
Designated "French."
McSWAIN, Daniel. Private.
MEED, Ezekiel. Private.
Deserted to the enemy.
MERRILL, Charles. Private.
MINO, John. Private.
MUIRHEAD, John Butler.
Private.
OSBURN, John. Private.
PARKER, Samuel. Private.
PARSONS, Isaac. Private.
Joined the Car Brigade.
PATTERSON, Lancelot. Private.
PICKHARD, Frederick. Private.
POWERS, William. *Lieutenant.*
PRICE, William. Private.
ROBLIN, Archibald. Private.
ROGERS, Joseph. Private.
ROSE, Lewis. Private.
ROSS, Alexander. Sergeant.

SAUNDERSON, Robert. Private.
SECORD, Edwin. Private.
SECORD, Isaac. Private.
SECORD, Van Cortland. *Ensign.*
SERVOS, Daniel Kerr. Private.
SHAVER, John. Private.
SKINNER, Asa. Private.
SOPER, John. Private.
SPARKMAN, Philip. Private.
SPARKMAN, John, Jr. Private.
SPILMAN, Daniel. Private.
STEVENS, Nicholas. Private.
STEVENS, Adam. Private.
STEVENS, Francis. Private.
  Joined the Artillery.
STEWART, Daniel. Private.
  See Casualties.
TAYLOR, Robert. Private.
  See Casualties.
THOMPSON, Frederick. Private.
THOMPSON, John. Private.
THOMPSON, Robert Jr. Private.
VROOMAN, Adam. Private.
WARNER, Mathew. Private.
WARREN, John Jr. Private.
WHALEN, Patrick. Private.
  Joined the Artillery.
WILSON, James. Acting Lance
  Sergeant.
WINTERBOTTOM, George.
  Sergeant.
WOODRUFF, William. Private.
WOODRUFF, Henry. Private.
YOUNG, Alexander. Private.

2nd Flank Company
ACKEN, George. Private.
ACKER, Peter. Private.
  Joined the Artillery.
ADAMS, Geoge. *Lieutenant.*
ATLAN, Western. Private.
BALL, Jacob H. Private.
BALL, Peter, Jr. *Ensign.*
BARNES, Christian. Private.
BARTRAN, Cornelius. Private.
BEAMER, Henry. Private.

BEBEE, Joshua. Private.
BEBIE, Emisley. Private.
BENNET, John. Private.
BORDEAUX, John. Private.
  Joined the Artillery.
BOSSIEN, David. Private.
BOSSIEY, John, Sr. Private.
BRADT, Isaac. Private.
  Joined the Artillery.
BRADT, Mathias. Private.
BRADT, Hice. Private.
BRADT, Isaac, Sr. Private.
BRADT, Albert. Private.
  Joined the Artillery.
BRADT, David. Private.
BUNCH, Levia. Private.
BURNS, Samuel. Sergeant.
CAMPBELL, Robert. Private.
  Joined the Artillery.
CAMPBELL (Camble), Peter.
  Private.
CASS, David. Private.
CHATTISON, Joseph. Private.
CLENDENING, Walter. Private.
CLENDINNING, John. Sergeant.
COCHO, Nathan. Private.
  See Casualties.
COLE, John Jr. Private.
COTTINGTON, Joseph. Private.
CRUM, Cornelius. Private. Joined
  the Artillery.
CUBE, John, Sr. Private. Joined
  the Artillery.
DEFOREST, John. Private.
DETTRICK, Walter. Private.
DETTRICK, Robert. Private.
DETTRICK, Jacob. Sergeant.
DEXTER, William. Private.
DONES, Benjamin. Private.
DURHAM, Jeremiah. Private.
EMMET, Frances. Private.
EMMIT, John. Private. Joined the
  Artillery.
FERGUSON, Robert. Private.
FLETCHER, John. Private.

FORCE, Henry. Private.
FORCE, John. Private.
GILMORE, Moses. Private.
GOLD, John. Private.
GOLD, Jacob. Private.
GOODWIN, William. Private.
GRASS, George. Private.
See Casualties.
GRASS, Jeremiah. Private.
GRIFFES, Bannero. Private.
See Casualties.
HAINER, (Henry). Private.
HAINER, Isaac. Private.
HAINER, John. Private.
HAINS, Peter. Private.
HAINS, Harmonis. Private.
HAINS, John. Private.
HANSENGER, John. Private.
HANTSWELL, Jacob Private.
HEWLTS, Joseph, Jr. Private.
HURST, Isaac. Private.
KELLY, Nathan. Private.
KELLY, Ebenezer. Private.
LARAWAY, Jonas. Private.
LAWTON, Cornelius. Private.
LEBUNN, John. Sergeant.
MARVIN, Isaac. Private.
Joined the Artillery.
MAY, James. Private.
MAY, William. Private.
McCAMBO, Samuel. Private.
McCAMLER, John. Private.
McCLAUGHLIN, James. Private.
Joined the Artillery.
McEWEN, John. *Captain.*
McGREGOR, Daniel. Private.
McLAUGHLAN, Jeremiah.
Private. Joined the Artillery.
MERATT, Joseph. Private.
OSTERHAUT, Marlin. Private.
OVERHATT, John, Sr. Private.
OVERHATT, John, Jr. Private.
See Casualties.
PAWLING, Peter. Private.
PENNALL, William. Private.
PHENIX, Abraham. Private.

PICKARD, William. Private.
PICKARD, Benjamin. Private.
PIDO, James. Private.
PLUMERFELT, Benedick
(Frederick). Private.
See Casualties.
PLUMERFELT, John. Private.
PRICE, Robert. Private.
PRICE, David. Private.
RAIL, Isaac. Private.
REID, Cornelius. Private.
RUNCHEY, George. Sergeant.
RUNCHY, Robert. *Lieutenant.*
SCRAM, Frederick. Private.
SCRAM, Peter. Private.
Joined the Artillery.
SERVOS, William. *Lieutenant.*
SHAVER, John. Private.
SHAVER, Jacob. Private.
SHIPMAN, Grange. Private.
SINGER, Peter. Private.
SLACK, Peter. Private.
SLAUKWEATHER, John. Private.
Joined the Incorporated Militia.
SMITH, Elijah. Private.
SMITH, John, Jr. Private.
SMITH, William. Private.
SMITH, Benjamin. Private.
SMITH, John. Private.
STANELY, Lewis. Private.
STEPHENSON, John. Private.
STULL, Adam. Private.
STULL, William. Private.
THOMPSON, Agustine. Private.
TURNEY, John. Sergeant.
VANALSTINE, John. Private.
VANATA, Peter. Private.
Joined the Artillery.
VANATA, Abraham. Private.
Joined the Artillery.
WAGGNER, Abraham. Private.
WALROD, Jonas. Private.
Joined the Artillery.
WEAVER, John. Private.
Joined the Artillery.
WHEELER, James. Private.

WILLEY, James. Private.
WILLSON, Benjamin. Private.
WILLSON, Andrew. Private.
WILLSON, John. Private.
YOCUM, Henry. Sergeant.

YOUKUM, George. Private.
  Joined the Dragoons.
YOUNG, Philips. Private.
  Joined the Artillery.
YOUNG, Peter. Private.

2ND LINCOLN

The Flank Companies
ADAMS, Samuel. Private.
  See Casualties.
AIGLER, William. Private.
ANDERSON, Martin. Private.
ANDERSON, Charles. Private.
BABCOCK, Benjamin. Private.
BACON, Asa. Private.
BACON, Gasham. Private.
BALD, Thomas. Private.
BALL, Henry C. Private.
BASTIDO, John. Private.
BASTIDO, Peter. Private.
BENNET, James. Private.
BIRDSELL, Jacob. Private.
BIRDSELL, Benjamin. Private.
BLANCHETTE, Louis. Private.
  See Casualties.
BLOOMFIELD, Thomas. Private.
  See Casualties.
BOUCHNER, John. Private.
BOUCK, Frederick. Private.
BOUCK, David. Private.
BOUGHNER, Christopher.
  Ensign.
BOWMAN, Adam. Private.
BOWMAN, John (Thorold).
  Private.
BOWMAN, Abram (Abraham).
  Lieutenant.
BOYDEN (Bryden), Asa. Private.
BRADSHAW, Amos. Sergeant.
BROOKS, Barns. Private.
BROOKS, Thomas. Private.
BULLARD, Isaac. Private.
BURCH, John. *Lieutenant.*
CAINE, Thomas. Private.
CAIRNS, Peter. Private.

CARL, James. Private.
CARL, John. Private.
CARL, Jacob. Private.
CHAMPLIN, John. Private.
CHASE, George. Private.
CHRYSLER, Adam. Private.
COOK, Calvin. Private.
COOPER, James. *Lieutenant.*
COSBY, George. Private.
DAVIS, Daniel. Private.
DAVIS, Thadeus. *Lieutenant.*
DAVIS, Hall. Private.
DEFIELD, Edward. Private.
DERRICK, Morris. Private.
  See Casualties.
DEUSE, Caleb. Private.
DISHER, William, Jr. Private.
DOAN, Jonathan. Private.
DORCHIMER, John. Private.
DOWDIE, Jeremiah. Private.
DUQUETTE, Antoine. Private.
  See Casualties.
EMERICK, Francis. Private.
EVANS, Edward. Private.
FLUELLAN, James M. Private.
FORTIER (Fortner), Thomas.
  Private.
FORTIER (Fortner), Andrew.
  Private.
FRELIGH, Robert. Private.
GALLIPOT (Galliport), John.
  Private. See Casualties.
GARNER, William. Private.
GILLMORE, Moses. Private.
GILLMORE, William. Private.
GOLD, Abel. Private. Drummer.
GREEN, Reuben. Private.
GRIFFITH, Richard. Private.

HAGGERTY, Hugh. Private.
HAMILTON, Robert. *Captain.*
HARDER, Adam. Private.
HAUSLER, Jacob. Private.
HICKS, Samuel. Private.
HODGKISS, David. Private.
HOOVER, Henry. Sergeant.
HOPKINS, Robert. Private.
  Deserted to the enemy.
HOPKINS, Caleb. Private.
HUMPHREY, Benjamin. Private.
HUTT, Adam. Private.
HUTT, John. Private.
  See Casualties.
JOHNSTON, Cornelius. Private.
JOHNSTON, Elijah. Private.
KEELER, John. Private.
KELLY, John. Private.
KELLY, Isaac. Private.
KILLMAN, Adam. Private.
KIRBY (Kerby), James. *Adjutant.*
LAMPMAN, Frederick. Private.
LAMPMAN, Mathias. Private.
LAYTON, Job M. Private.
LOUTS, John. Private.
LUNDY, Thomas. Private.
LUNDY, Benjamin. Private.
  See Casualties.
LUNDY, Azariah. Private.
MARLAT, George. Private.
MARR, Allen. Private.
MARTIN, John. Private.
MARTIN, Christian. Private.
McINTOSH, Arthur. Sergeant.
McLAUGHLIN, Dougal. Private.
McLAUGHLIN, Laughlin. Private.
McMICKING, John. *Lieutenant.*
METLAR, George. Private.
METLAR, Daniel. Private.
METLAR, Philip. Private.
MILLARD, Joseph. Private.
MILLER, Henry. Private.
NEAR, Frederick. Private.
NEVILLS, Andrew. Private.
NEVILLS, Jacob. Private.
NEVILLS, James. Private.

NEVILLS, Isaac. Private.
OIL, George. Private.
OLDFIELD, Joseph. Private.
OSTRANDER, James. Private.
PARK, James. Private.
PEIV (Pew), Henry. Private.
PEIV (Pew), Samuel. Private.
PETRIE, Philip. Private.
  See Casualties.
PETTIT, John. Private.
PETTY, William. Private.
PETTY, Francis. Private.
PHILLIPS, Daniel. Private.
PIER, Stephen. Private.
  See Casualties.
POLLARD, Francis. Private.
PRINE, Herman. Sergeant.
REILLY, James. Private.
RHEA, John. Sergeant.
  See Casualties.
RIBBLE, Henry. Private.
RICE, Eber. Private.
ROBINS, Joshua. Private.
ROBINS, John. Private.
ROBINS, Daniel. Private.
ROLLS, William. Sergeant.
  Joined the Incorporated Militia.
RORBACK, Andrew. *Adjutant.*
ROW, John. *Captain.*
  See Casualties.
SCRAM, Jacob. Private.
SEABURN, William. Private.
SEGAR, John. Private.
SKINNER, John (Colin). Private.
  Joined the Artillery.
SLACK, James. Private.
SLAWMICK, Henry. Private.
SMITH, John. Private.
SMITH, Gabriel. Private.
SMITH, Isaac. Private.
SMITH, James. Private.
SMITH, James. Private.
SMITH, Andrew. Private.
  Deserted to the enemy.
SMOKE, John. Private.
SUMMERS, James. Private.

SUMMERS, John. Private.
SUTTON, John. Private.
SUTTON, Aaron. Private.
SWARTS, George. Private.
SWARTS, William. Private.
SWAYZE, Obediah. Private.
SWAYZE, Heram. Private.
SWEARS, Peter. Private.
TALLOW, Garret. Private.
TEETER, Andrew. Private.
TEETER, Abram. Private.
THOMAS, Henry. Private.
THOMPSON, Joshua. Private.
THOMPSON, David. Sergeant.
THOMPSON, Richard. Private.
THOMPSON, James. *Ensign.*
THOMPSON, John. Private.
See Casualties.
UPPER, Anthony. *Lieutenant.*
UPPER, George. Private.
VANDERBARRACK, Andrew.
Private.
VANWYKE, Gilbert. Private.
VROOMAN, John. Private.
WATERHOUSE, John. Private.
Deserted to the enemy.

WATERHOUSE, Robert. Private.
Deserted to the enemy.
WATERS, John. Private.
See Casualties.
WEAVER, Paul. Private.
WEAVER, George. Private.
WHEELER, James. Private.
Joined the Glengarry Regiment.
WIGGINS, Samuel. Private.
WILKINSON (Wilkerson),
Robert. Private.
WILLIAMS, Darius. Private.
WILLIAMS, John. Private.
WILLIS, John. Private.
Joined the Incorporated Militia.
WILSON, Robert. Private.
Noted as acted as a sergeant.
WILSON, John (son of Thomas).
Private.
WILSON, Andrew (Thorold).
Private.
WILSON, Andrew (Pelham).
Private.
WILSON, Patrick. Private.
WILSON, John. Private.

3RD LINCOLN

The Flank Companies
ANGER, George. Private.
ANGER, Frederick Jr. Private.
ANGER, George Frederick.
Private.
BARNES, Joseph. Private.
BARNS, David. Private.
BAXTER, William. Private.
BAXTER, Thomas. Sergeant.
BEACH, Nathan. Private.
BEAM, John. Private.
BENNER, Phillip. Private.
BENNET, Elias M. Private.
BOWEN, Cornelius. Private.
BOWEN, Adam. Private.
BROWN, Walter. Private.
BUCHNER, Martin. Private.

BUCHNER, Daniel. Private.
BUCHNER, Ozias. Sergeant.
BUCHNER, Lewis. Private.
BUCK, Peter. Private.
BUCK, John. Private.
BUCK, Adam. Private.
CANFIELD, Aza. Private.
CARTER, Nicholas. Private.
CARTER, William. Private.
CHAMBERS, John. Private.
CLARK, Benjamin. Private.
COLERAKE, William. Private.
COOK, Jacob. Private.
COOK, William. Private.
COOK, Jonathan. Private.
COOK, Moses. Private.
CORASANT, Christopher. Private.

CRAWSON, William. Private.
CROW, Jacob. Private.
CUAGOR, William. Private.
DAVIS, Thomas. Private.
DAVIS, William. Private.
De LAMACE, Pierre. Private.
  See Casualties.
DEFIELDS, James. Private.
DELL, Peter. Private.
DELL, Martin. Private.
DELL, Henry. Private.
DOAN, Titas. Private.
DOAN, William. Private.
DOAN, Levi. Private.
DOAN, John. Private.
DOAN, David. Private.
DODGE, Benjamin Pitt. Private.
DURHAM, Joseph. Private.
EDSALL, John. Private.
EDSALL, James Jr. Private.
EDWARDS, John. Private.
ELSWORTH, George. Private.
EVERINGHAM, Jacob. Private.
FERGUSON, Hugh. Private.
FORSYTH, James. Private.
  See Casualties.
FORSYTH, Ezekiel. Private.
FOX, Edward. Private.
FURRAY, John. Private.
GAUGH, Jeremiah. Private.
GRAHAM, James. Private.
  See Casualties.
HARDISON, Benjamin, Jr. *Ensign.*
HARINGTON, Cyres. Private.
HARINGTON, Zenas. Private.
HARP, Jeremiah. Private.
HARP, John. Private.
HARTNEY, Michael. Private.
HELMES, John. Private.
HODGKINS, William. Private.
HOFFMAN, Jacob Jr. Private.
HOFFMAN, George. Private.
HOWEY, Daniel. Private.
HUMPHREY, Ezekiel. Sergeant.
HUMPHREY, HIRAM. Private.
JOHNSON, James. Private.

JOHNSON, Jehoiacum. Private.
LAUR, George. Private.
LAUR, John Jr. Private.
LAWE (Laur), Peter Jr. Private.
Le LOAN, George. Private.
LEARN, Benjamin. Sergeant.
LEFFERTY, John Johnson.
  Lieutenant.
LEMONS, John. Private.
MARTIN, James. Private.
  See Casualties.
McCALL, Preserved. Private.
McCARTY, James. Private.
McCARTY, Charles. Private.
McCLINTOCK, Robert. Private.
McDONELL, Peter. Private.
McDONELL, William. Private.
McDONELL, Christopher.
  Private.
McGOWAN (McCowan,
  McEwen), John. Private.
McINTOSH, John. Private.
McINTOSH, John. Sergeant.
McINTOSH, Alexander. Private.
McINTYRE, Angus. Sergeant.
McNAIR, Adam. Private.
MEISNER, Leonard. Private.
MEISNER, John. Private.
MEISNER, Peter. Private.
MILLER, John. Sergeant.
MILLER, William Duff. *Ensign.*
MONTAUNIA, Elisha. Private.
MOON, Edward. Private.
MOORE, Abraham. Private.
MUDGE, Elisha. Private.
NEAR, Henry Jr. Private.
NEAR, Nicholas. Private.
NEAR, John. Private.
NIGHT, John. Private.
NIGHTEN, David. Private.
OLIVER, Zimri. Private.
PARK, Shubael. *Lieutenant.*
PARK, Alexander. Private.
PARKER, William. Private.
PETTIT, Stephen. Private.
PLATO, Christian Jr. Private.

PLUMMERFELT, David. Private.
POWELL, William. *Captain.*
PRICE, David. Private.
PUTMAN, John. *Ensign.*
RAMSAY, James. Private.
RHEMY, David. Private.
RHEMY, Lawrence. Private.
ROCK, John. Private.
SCARLET, John. Private.
SEGAR, Henry. Private.
SENN, Joseph. Sergeant.
SHEINHOLTS, Daniel. Sergeant.
SHEINHOLTS, Martin. Private.
SHUFELT, Casper. Private.
  See Casualties.
SILVERTHORN, John. Private.
SNIVELY, George. Private.
SNIVELY, Jacob. Private.
SNIVELY, Abraham. Private.
SNIVELY, Conrad. Private.
STEEL, Solomon. Private.
STEINHOOF, Leo. Private.

STRINGER, Henry. Private.
STROHM, Jacob. Private.
TEAL, Zachariah. Private.
THERON, Hugh. Private.
TROUT, Henry. *Lieutenant* and
  Adjutant.
TURRILL, Uriah. Private.
VANFLEET, Isaac. Private.
VINCENT, Lewis. Private.
WALTON, Thomas B. Private.
WARREN, John. *Captain.*
WEISHUHN, Henry. Sergeant.
WEISHUHN, James. Private.
WHITEHEAD, George. Sergeant.
WIGGINS, Thomas. Private.
WINDECKER, Henry. Private.
WINTERMUTE, Philip. Private.
YOKUM, John. Private.
YOKUM, Lemuel. Private.
YORK, Jeremiah. Private.
YORK, Stephen. Private.
YOUNG, George. Private.

4TH LINCOLN

1st Flank Company
ADAIR, David. Private.
  Joined the Artillery.
ADAIR, John. Private.
ADAIR, William. Private.
BEAM, James. Private.
BEAMER, John Jr. Private.
BELL, Benjamin. Private.
BOOK, Jacob. Private.
BOUSLAUGH, Peter Jr. Private.
BUSKIRK, Lawrence. Private.
  Joined the Artillery.
BUTLER, Thomas. *Lieutenant.*
CARPENTER, Ashman. Private.
CARPENTER, Charles. Private.
CLENDINNEN, Daniel. Private.
CLINE, Henry. Private.
CLOUSE, Nicholas. Private.
CONDON, Briant. Private.
CONKLE, Adam. Private.

COON, Isaac. Private.
CORNWELL, Thomas. Private.
  Joined the Artillery.
CORSON, Robert. Private.
COURSON, Lawrence. Private.
COUSE, Frederick. Private.
COUSE, John. Private.
CROOKS, Mathew. *Lieutenant.*
CURTIS, Alanson W. Sergeant.
DEDRICK, James. *Lieutenant.*
DOWNS, Timothy. Private.
DUNMEAD, John. Private.
DURHAM, James. Private.
ENGLEHARD, John. Private.
  Joined the Artillery.
ENSLY, Christopher. Private.
FORBES, George. Private.
GLOVER, Francis. Private.
HERON, David. Private.
HILL, Abraham. Private.

HOUSE, John. Private.
HOUSE, Patrick. Private.
KARVER, Peter. Private.
 Deserted to the enemy.
KENNEDY, Morris. Private.
KENNEDY, Samuel. Private.
 Joined the Artillery.
KENTNER, Jerry T. Private.
KINNY, John. Private.
LAMBERT, Thomas. Private.
LAMBERT, John. Private.
LAMBERT, Philip. Private.
 Joined the Artillery.
LEWIS, James S. Private.
LEWIS, James. Private.
LOW, Richard. Private.
LYMBURNER, Christopher.
 Private.
LYON, Daniel. Private.
MARKLE, John. Private.
MARSELES, Stephen. Private.
MARSELES, John. Private.
McKAY, William. Private.
McLEAN, John. Private.
MILLS, Joseph. Private.
MILLS, John Jr. Private.
 Joined the Artillery.
MOORE, William. Private.
MOORE, John. Sergeant.
NELLES, Abraham. *Captain.*
NIXON, William. Private.
OSBORNE, William. Private.
OVERHAULT, John. Private.
OVERHAULT, Christopher.
 Private.
PATTERSON, John. Private.
PETTIT, Charles. Private.
PETTIT, Andrew Jr. Private.
PETTIT, Ashman. Private.
PICKARD, James. Private.
POSTLE, Francis. Private.
 Deserted to the enemy.
SHEPPARD, Henry. Private.
SILLS, Jabez. Private.
 Deserted to the enemy.
SILLS, John. Private.
 Deserted to the enemy.

SIMMERMAN, Mathias. Private.
SIMMERMAN, Adam. Sergeant.
SKELLY, Daniel. Private.
 See Casualties.
SMITH, Annanias. Private.
SMITH, Daniel. Private.
SMITH, Silas Jr. Private.
SMITH, Israel. Sergeant.
SWACKHAMMER, Jacob.
 Private.
TALLMAN, Joel. Private.
TEETZELL, Jonathan. Private.
THORN, William. Private.
TUFFARD, George. Private.
TUFFARD, Philip. Private.
 Deserted to the enemy.
VANETTA, Benjamin. Private.
 Joined the Artillery.
VANETTA, William Jr. Private.
VANSICKEL, Lambert. Private.
VANSICKLE, John. Private.
 Joined the Artillery.
WATE (Wade), Bryant. Private.
WILLSON, Caleb. Private.
WINEGARTNER, George.
 Private.
WOOLVERTON, Dennis. Private.
YOUNG, William. Sergeant.

2nd Flank Company
AERE, Adam. Private.
AUREY, John Jr. Private.
AURT, Henry. Private.
BATRAN, James. Private.
BATRAN, David. Private.
BERUP, John. Private.
BOUGHNER, Christopher.
 Private.
BROWN, Benjamin. Private.
CARLE, Abraham. Private.
CLENDENNAN, John. Sergeant.
COCKLE, David. Private.
CROOKS, William. *Captain.*
DEEN, Philip. Private.
DEEN, David. Private.
DEMOREE, Charles A. Private.
 Deserted to the enemy.

ELLICE, John. Private.
EVERITT, John. Private.
FELKER (Saltfleet), Frederick.
  Private.
FLEMMING, James. Private.
GALLINO, Joseph. Private.
GEE, Henry. Private.
GEE, David. Private.
HAGERMAN, Joseph. Private.
HAGERMAN, William. Private.
HANSMAN, Robert. Private.
HARKISON, Robert. Private.
HARRIS, Stephen. Private.
  Deserted to the enemy.
HEASLIP, Samuel. Private.
HENRY, John. *Lieutenant.*
HERON, Patrick. Sergeant.
HILL, Benone. Private.
HILL, Solomon. Private.
HIXON, Henry. *Lieutenant.*
HODGES, Edmond. Private.
HOWEY, John. Private.
JOHNSON, James. Private.
  See Casualties.
JOHNSTON, Frederick. Private.
  Deserted to the enemy.
JOHNSTON, Henry. Private.
KENNEDY, John. Sergeant.
KENNEDY, William. Private.
KENNEDY, Charles. Sergeant.
LANE, Gilbert. Private.
LANE, Ezekiel. Private.
LANE, Nathan. Private.
LANE, Jeremiah. Private.
LINDEBERRY, Christopher.
  Private.
LINDEBERRY, John. Private.
LYMBURNER, Mathew. Private.
LYON, Reuben. Private.
LYON, Nathan. Private.
LYON, Joseph. Private.
McCAMP, John. Private.
McCOLLUM, Peter. *Lieutenant.*
McGAW, John. Private.

McGAW, William. Private.
MERIDETH, John. Private.
MERRILL, Jacob. Private.
MERRITT, Moses. Private.
MERRITT, Martin. Private.
MERRITT, Joseph. Private.
MERRITT, Isaac. Private.
MERRITT, Elizah. Sergeant.
MOORE, Jonathan. *Captain.*
MOOTE, Richard. Private.
MOOTE, Jacob. Private.
  Deserted to the enemy.
MOYERS, James. Private.
NELLES, Henry. *Lieutenant.*
NUNN, Samuel. Private.
NUNN, Benjamin. Private.
OSBOURN, Isaac. Private.
PISHER, Zachariah. Private.
QUICK, Solomon. Private.
  Joined the Artillery.
QUICK, Moses. Private.
  Joined the Artillery.
ROBBINS, Job. Private.
ROBBINS, Thomas. Private.
SERVOS, William. *Lieutenant.*
SHADOWICK (Shadwick), Philip.
  Private. GSM, Fort Detroit.
SIMMERMAN, Philip. Private.
SMITH, Abraham. Private.
SNYDER, Henry. Private.
SNYDER, Philip Jr. Private.
SNYDER, John. Private.
  Joined the Artillery.
STAFFORD, Amos. Private.
SWAZEY, Caleb. Private.
SWAZEY, James. Private.
TAYLOR, Richard. Private.
TAYLOR, William. Private.
TEETER, Isaac. Private.
TEETER, Michael Jr. Private.
  See Casualties.
TUFFORD, John Jr. Private.
VAUGHAN, Jacob. Private.
WARDELL, Joshua. Private.
WRONG, John. Private.

1st Flank Company
BOOK, George. Private.
BOOK, John. Private.
BOOK, Adam. Private.
BUCKBOROUGH, Hugh. Private.
BUCKBOROUGH, John. Private.
BYCRAFT, James. Private.
CAMPBELL, John. Private.
COOK, John. Private.
CORNWALL, John. Private.
CRANDLE, Jesse. Private.
DARBY, Joseph. Private.
DEFOREST, Simon. Private.
FILMAN, William. Private.
FONGER, John. Private.
FORSYTH, Caleb. Private.
GORDON, John. Private.
See Casualties.
GORDON, Nathaniel. Private.
GREEN, John. Private.
HAMMEL, John. Sergeant.
HAMMEL, Patrick. Private.
HATT, Samuel. *Captain.*
HENDERSHOT, John. Private.
See Casualties.
HENRY, Christopher. Private.
HORNING, Peter. Private.
HOUSE, Peter. Private.
HOWEL, James. Private.
HOWEL, Isaac. Private.
HOWEL, Sampson. Private.
HOWELL, Peter. Private.
HOWELL, Jonah. Private.
HUGHSON, George. Sergeant.
KELLY, John. Private.
KEMP, David. Private.
KERR, Robert S. Private.
Deserted to the enemy.
KETRUM, David. Private.
KITCHEN, Henry. Private.
KITCHEN, Moses. Private.
KNOWLS, George. Private.
LAND, Robert. *Lieutenant.*
GSM, Fort Detroit.

LARRISON, Thomas. Private.
(Lawrason) GSM, Fort Detroit.
LONG, Michael. Private.
LOWNSBURY, Solomon. Private.
LYKINGS, Archeis (Archer).
Private. See Casualties.
MARCHEAUX, Joseph. Private.
MARKLE, William. Sergeant.
See Casualties.
MARKLE, Henry. Private.
See Casualties.
MARKLE, Isaac. Private.
McAFFE, Samuel. Private.
McINTYRE, John. *Adjutant.*
McKAY, Henry. Private.
MILLAR, William. Private.
MILLER, Adam. Private.
MISENER, Peter. Private.
OLMSTEAD, Russell. Private.
OLMSTEAD, Benjamin. Private.
PEER, John. Private.
REVEAUX, Loui. Private.
RULISSON, John. Private.
SECORD, Abraham. Private.
SECORD, David. Private.
SHOWERS, Daniel. *Ensign.*
SMITH, John. Private.
SMITH, Mathias. Private.
See Casualties.
SMITH, Samuel. Private.
STILLS, Anthony. Private.
SYDAN, Humphry. Private.
TEMPLAR, Samuel. Private.
VANEVERY, Peter. Private.
GSM, Fort Detroit.
VANNICKLE, David. Private.
See Casualties.
WANDECKER, Solomon. Private.
WEAVER, John D. Private.
WILL, George. Private.
WILSON, Levi. Private.
YOUNG, David. Private.
Joined the Dragoons.
YOUNG, David (of Barton).
Private.

2nd Flank Company
AIKMAN, Alexander. Private.
AIKMAN, John. Sergeant.
ALMAS, Adam. Private.
BATES, John. Private.
BEADLE, Stephen. Private.
BERHAM, Geriat. Private.
BIGGAR, Amos. Private.
BIGGAR, Robert. Private.
BIGGAR, William. Private.
BIRNIE, Joseph. *Ensign.*
BOWSLAUGH, John. Private.
BRADT, Simon. Private.
BROWN, Abel. Private.
BUTT, Vandal. Private.
CHISHOLM, George. Sergeant.
CHOUTE, Thomas. Private.
CLEMENT, Paul. Private.
COMBS, John. Private.
CORMAN, Isaac. Private.
CROSTHWAITE, Daniel. Private.
CROWELL, Nathaniel. Private.
DAVIS, William. *Lieutenant.*
DEGEAR, Michael. Private.
DEPEW, John. Private.
DEPEW, John. Private.
DURAND, James. *Captain.*
EARLS, Oliver. Private.
FERGUSON, John. Private.
FINK, Christian. Private.
FISHER, James. Private.
GAGE, Andrew. Private.
GAGE, James. Private.
GALBREATH, John. Private.
GARVIN, Hugh. Private.
GILLET, James. Private.
GREEN, John. Private.
  See Casualties.
GREEN, Freeman. Private.
HANNAN, Thomas. Private.
HARMAN (Hannan), William.
  Private. See Casualties.
HOTRUM, Frederic. Private.
HUFFMAN, Jacob. Private.
HUGHSON, Nathaniel. Private.

HUGHSON, Robert. Private.
JONES, Peter. Private.
JONES, Stephen. Private.
KRIBS, John. Private.
LABAR, Andrew. Private.
LAND, William. Private.
LEE, John. Private.
LONDON, Joseph. Private.
  GSM, Fort Detroit.
LUCAS, Robert. Private.
MARKLE, Zachariah. Private.
MARKLE, William. Private.
McDAVID, John. Private.
McFEE, Daniel. Private.
McPHEE, Angus. Sergeant.
MULHOLLIN, John. Private.
POTORFF, John. Private.
REYNOLDS, William. Private.
  GSM, Fort Detroit.
REYNOLDS, David. Private.
RICHARDS, John. Private.
  Deserted to the enemy.
ROW, Christopher. Private.
RYCHMAN, James. Private.
SCRAM, William. Private.
SHAFER, Daniel. Private.
SHAFER, Joseph. Private.
SHAW, Gilbert. Private.
SMITH, Jonas. Private.
SMITH, Jacob. Private.
SMITH, Henry. Private.
SMOKE, Peter. Private.
SNIDER, Frederic. Private.
SNIDER, John. Private.
SPRINGSTED, John. Private.
STEAVES, Joshua. Private.
STEWART, John. Private.
STORMS, Henry. Private.
SUMMERS, Absolom. Private.
SYPES, Jacob. Private.
TRAINER, David. Private.
  See Casualties.
TRAYNER, James. Private.
WEDGE, Thomas. Private.
WEDGE, Andrew. Private.

WHITAKER, Thomas. Private.
WHITE, Seth. Private.
YEAGER, John. Private.

YOUNG, Henry. Private.
YOUNG, Adam. Private.
YOUNG, John. Private.

DISTRICT OF LONDON
1ST NORFOLK

1st Flank Company
ALGIE, William. Private.
  See Casualties.
BACKHOUSE, John. Private.
BARNINGER, Daniel. Private.
BOSTWICK, John. *Captain.*
  GSM, Fort Detroit.
BOUGHNER, Alexander.
  Corporal.
CALDWELL, John. Private.
CLINE, Henry. Private.
  Joined the Dragoons.
COPE, Jacob. Private.
CRONK, William. Private.
DAVIS, Robert. Private.
  GSM, Fort Detroit.
DELL, Richard. Private.
DUSTIN, Paul. Sergeant.
FRANKLIN, George. Private.
GLOVER, Charles. Private.
  (perhaps John) GSM, Fort
  Detroit.
HOGGADONE, Peter. Private.
HORTON, Peter. Private.
LEMON, James. Private.
LONG, David. Private.
  GSM, Fort Detroit.
MANUEL, Frederick. Private.
  See Casualties.
MATHEWS, George. Private.
MATHEWS, James. Private.
McMICHAEL, George. Sergeant.
  See Casualties.
MORE, William. Private.
POWELL, William. Corporal.
POWELL, Jacob. Sergeant.
ROLPH, George. *Lieutenant.*
  GSM, Fort Detroit.
RYERSON, George. *Lieutenant.*

SILVERTHORNE, William.
  Private.
SILVERTHORNE, Jonathan.
  Private.
SILVERTHORNE, Thomas.
  Private.
VAIL, William. Private.
WEBB, Parnell. Private.
  GSM, Fort Detroit.
WILLIAMS, Samuel. Private.
WILSON, Usual. Private.
WILSON, Samuel. Private.
  See Casualties.
WILSON, Philip. Sergeant.
WINEGARDEN (Vinegarden),
  Conrad. Private.
WOOD, Joseph. Private.
WOOD, Robert. Private.

2nd Flank Companies
ALWAY, Robert. Private.
ANDERSON, John H. Private.
ANDREWS, Joseph. Private.
BOUGHNER, Mathias. No. 2
  Private.
BOUGHNER, Mathias. No. 1
  Private.
BOUGHNER, Martin. Private.
BOUGHNER, Joseph. Private.
BOUGHNER, John. Sergeant.
BROWN, Victor. Private.
BROWN, George. Private.
BROWN, John. Private.
DERICKSON, Thomas. Private.
  GSM, Fort Detroit.
DEWITT, Peter D. Private.
  Deserted to the enemy.
FINCH, George. Private.
  GSM, Fort Detroit.

FONGER, Philip. Private.
  See Casualties.
HATCH, William. Private.
KENNEDY, James. Private.
  Joined the Incorporated Militia.
KENNEDY, Reuben S. Private.
KITCHEN, Joseph. Sergeant.
LAUNING, Richard. Private.
MABEE, Pelham. Private.
MANUEL, John. Private.
McCALL, James. *Ensign.*
McCALL, Daniel. *Captain.*
McCALL, Hugh. Private.
MILLARD, Squire. Private.
PALMERSTON, Benjamin.
  Private.

RORAH, Martin. Private.
RYERSON, Samuel. *Lieutenant.*
SKINNER, Solomon. Private.
SMITH, John. Private.
SMITH, Abraham. Private.
SMITH, Samuel. Private.
SOVEREEN, Morris. Private.
SPRINGER (Spurgin), Aron.
  Private.
WALSH, Aquela M. Sergeant.
VANATTER, John. Private.
  Deserted to the enemy.
WILSON, Andrew. Private.
WILSON, Peter. Private.
WOOD, Thomas. Private.
  GSM, Fort Detroit.

2ND NORFOLK

The Flank Companies
ADAMS, Uriah. Private.
  Deserted to the enemy.
ADAMS, Evi. Private.
ALWOOD, Reuben. Private.
  See Casualties.
AUSTIN, Jonathan. *Lieutenant.*
BARBER, Elisha. Private.
BEAMER, John. Private.
BEAMER, Joseph. Private.
BERDAN, Jacob. Private.
BOODLY, Mathias. Private.
BOUGHNER, John. Private.
BOWLBY, Axford. Private.
BUTLER, John. Private.
  Joined the Incorporated Militia.
CANFIELD, Ransler N. Private.
CAZED, Jacob. Private.
CHAMBERS, James. Private.
  GSM, Fort Detroit.
CHERIE, Leon. Private.
CLARK, William. Private.
COLE, John. Private.
COLTON, James. Private.
  Deserted to the enemy.

COMBS, Peter. Private.
  Deserted to the enemy.
CONRAD, John. Private.
CONRAD, David. Private.
  See Casualties.
CULVER, Jabez. Private.
CULVER, Michael. Private.
CULVER, Benjamin. Private.
DEWITT, Philip. Private.
  Deserted to the enemy.
DINGMAN, Jabez. Private.
DISBROW, Almond. Private.
  Deserted to the enemy.
DISBROW, Israel. Private.
DOUGAL, William. Private.
  GSM, Fort Detroit.
DOUGLAS, Levi. Private.
DRAKE, Richard. Private.
  See Casualties.
FAIRCHILD, James D. Private.
  Deserted to the enemy.
GILBERT, Isaac. *Ensign.*
GILLESPY, William. Private.
GILMORE, Samuel. Private.
  GSM, Fort Detroit.

GORDON, William. *Lieutenant.*
GREEN, John. Sergeant.
GREEN, Jeremiah. Private.
GREEN, Elisha. Private.
    Deserted to the enemy.
HANNERS, Charles. Private.
HAVERLAND, Benjamin. Private.
HERON, Andrew Jr. Private.
    GSM, Fort Detroit.
JAY, Samuel. Private.
    GSM, Fort Detroit.
JEWELL, James. Private.
    Joined the Incorporated Militia.
KITCHEN, Wheeler. Private.
    GSM, Fort Detroit.
LEFLER, Peter. Private.
LEMON, Alexander. Private.
    GSM, Fort Detroit.
MABEE, Pinkney. Private.
MABEE, Simon. Private. Traitor.
MARKLE, John. Private.
MATHEWS, Philip. Private.
MATHEWS, John. Private.
    See Casualties.
McCRACKEN, William. *Captain.*
McQUEEN, James. Private.
MESSICAR, Henry. Private.
MESSICAR, Jacob (Job). Private.
    GSM, Fort Detroit.
MESSICAR, Abraham. Private.
MESSINGER, Giles. Private.
METCALF, Henry. Sergeant.
    GSM, Fort Detroit.
MILLARD, Peter. Private.
MILLARD, Daniel. Private.
MISNER, Adam. Private.
MUCKLE, James. Private.
NELLIS, Abraham. Private.
PERRY, William. Private.
    GSM, Fort Detroit.
PERSALL, Henry. Private.
    Deserted to the enemy.

PETTIT, Isaac. Private. Traitor.
POTTS, John. Sergeant.
RAPELJE, Abraham A. *Captain.*
    Joined the Incorporated Militia.
ROBERRE, Joseph. Private.
RUSLE, Isaac. Private.
    Deserted to the enemy.
SCHOFUTT, John. Private.
    Deserted to the enemy and
    noted as killed.
SERLS, Moses. Private.
SHAW, Michael. Private.
SLAGHT, John. Private.
    Deserted to the enemy.
SLAGHT, Aaron. Private.
    GSM, Fort Detroit.
SLAGHT, Cornelius. Private.
SOVERIEN, John. Private.
SOVERIEN, Antony. Private.
    GSM, Fort Detroit.
SOVREIN (?), Robert. Private.
TAGERT, Alexander. Private.
TEEPLE, Edward. Private.
    GSM, Fort Detroit.
TROUP, Samuel. Private.
WHITE, Nathaniel. *Captain.*
WHITE, William. Private.
    GSM, Fort Detroit.
WICOFF, John. Private.
    See Casualties. GSM, Fort
    Detroit.
WILLIAMS, Benjamin. Sergeant.
WILLIAMS, Henry. Private.
WILLIAMS, Titus. *Lieutenant.*
    GSM, Fort Detroit.
WILLIAMS, Elija. Private.
WINEGARDNER, William.
    Private.
WOOLEY, Peter. Private.
WOOLLEY, Joseph. Private.
    GSM, Fort Detroit.
WYNONS, John. Private.

1st Flank Company

AVERILL, David. Private.
Deserted to the enemy.
BABCOCK, Henry. Private.
Deserted to the enemy.
BAKER, Joseph. *Lieutenant.*
Deserted to the enemy.
BARNES, Hirman. Private.
BROWN, Josiah. Private.
BROWN, Neal Jr. Private.
BURTCH, Ethan. Private.
CHAPEL, Gideon. Private.
CHAPEL, Samuel. Private.
DAVIS, Joseph. Private.
DECOU, Abner. *Ensign*
but volunteered and served
as a private.
DECOW, Abraham. Private.
DOUGLAS, Stephen. Private.
DOYLE, Samuel. Private.
Deserted to the enemy.
EMMENS, John. Private.
FOWLER, Horatio. Private.
GRAHAM, Jonathan. Private.
GRAHAM, John. Private.
GREASON, Robert. Private.
GREEN, John. Private.
Deserted to the enemy.
KIPP, Jonathan. Private.
Deserted to the enemy.
KIPP, Isaac. Private.
Deserted to the enemy.
LAFLER, Jacob. Private.
LAFLER, David. Private.
LANDON, Nathaniel. Private.
LANE, George. Private.
LESTER, John. Private.
Deserted to the enemy.
MALCOLM, Hugh. Private.
MALCOLM, Duncan. Private.
MALCOLM, Peter. Private.
MARTIN, Peter. Sergeant.
MARTIN, Earl. Private.
PEASE, Andrew B. Private.

PELTON, James. Private.
Deserted to the enemy.
PHILIPS, Peter. Private.
ROUNDS, Abraham. Private.
ROUSE, George. Private.
ROUSE, Joshua. Private.
STEPHENS, Jonathan. Private.
UPTERGROVE, Jesse. Private.
Deserted to the enemy.
WHITE, Marvil. *Captain.*
WICKAM, Samuel. Private.
WILLIAMS, John. *Lieutenant.*
WILSEY, Henry. Private.
WOODLEY, George. Private.
WOODLEY, John. Private.
YEIGH, Adam. Sergeant.
GSM, Fort Detroit.

2nd Flank Company

BOTSFORD, William. *Lieutenant.*
Deserted to the enemy.
BRIANT, John. Private.
Deserted to the enemy.
BRIGHAM, Bela B. *Lieutenant.*
BURDICK, Caleb. Private.
BURTCH, Nathan. Private.
BURTCH, Daniel. Private.
CARROLL, Daniel. Private.
CARROLL, John. *Captain.*
See Casualties.
CLARK, Robert. Private.
CORTWRIGHT, Abraham. Private.
DYGART, Warner. Private.
FLANNIGAN, Barnabas. Private.
FULLER, Ira. Private.
FULLER, Ethan. Private.
GRAHAM, David. Private.
HARRIS, Elijah. Private.
HUFFMAN, Godfrey. Private.
JANES, James. Private.
Deserted to the enemy.
JOHNSON, Truman. Sergeant.
See Casualties.
LEWIS, Samuel. Private.

LIVINGS, John. Private.
LOGAN, Edward. Private.
  Joined the Incorporated Militia.
MARKS, Cornelius. Sergeant.
  See Casualties.
MATHER, Samuel. Private.
McNAMES, Peter. Private.
McNAMES, Isaac. Private.
NORTON, Benjamin. Private.
NORTON, Henry. Private.
SAGE, Comfort. Private.
SALES, Hiram. Private.
SHAW, Daniel. Private.
  Supposed to have deserted
  to the enemy.

STEPHENS, Garret. Private.
  GSM, Fort Detroit.
SUDDINGTON, Alva. Private.
SWINGS, Henry. Private.
THORNTON, Jabez. Private.
  Deserted to the enemy and
  killed by the Indians.
TOWSLEY, Alanson. Private.
UNDERWOOD, William.
  Private.
WILLIAMS, George. Private.
  Deserted to the enemy.
WILLIAMS, Silas. Private.

1ST MIDDLESEX

The Flank Companies
ARMSTRONG, John. Private.
  Deserted to the enemy.
AXFORD, John. Private.
  Deserted to the enemy.
BACKUS, Stephen. Private.
BARTOU (Bartow), Edwin.
  Private. See Casualties.
BELLES, Samuel. Private.
BENEDICT, Elisha. Private.
  See Casualties.
BENEDICT, Charles. Private.
BIRD, William. *Lieutenant.*
BOWMAN, Jacob. Private.
BRADLY, Prusimus Gould.
  Private.
BROOKS, William. Private.
BROTHERHOOD, Samuel.
  Private.
BURWELL, John. Sergeant.
BURWELL, Samuel. Private.
BURWELL, Lewis. Private.
BURWELL, Robert. Private.
  See Casualties.
BURWELL, Adam Hood.
  Sergeant.
CALUTE, Henry. Private.
  Joined the Dragoons.

CASCADDEN, Alexander. Private.
CHASE, Mark. Private.
CHASE, James. Private.
COOK, John. Private.
CRANDLE, Eber. Private.
CRANDLE, William. Private.
  Joined the Rifle Company.
CRANE, George. Sergeant.
CRANMER, Jeremiah. Private.
CURTIS, Thomas. Private.
DAVY, John. Private.
DE FIELDS, Joseph. *Ensign.*
DECOW, Joseph. Private.
  Deserted to the enemy.
DINGMAN, David. Private.
DINGMAN, Lawrence. Private.
DINGMAN, William. Private.
DOTY, David. Private.
DUTTON, Seth. Private.
DUTTON, David. Private.
EDWARDS, John. Private.
EDWARDS, James. Private.
EDWARDS, Thomas. Private.
EVELAND, Frederick. Private.
FOURNAIS, Luther. Private.
GALBRAITH, Walter. Private.
GIBBONS, James. Sergeant.
GOFF, Alexander. Private.

GOFF, Elijah. Private.
GREGORY, John. Private.
  Deserted to the enemy.
GREGORY, William. Private.
GRIFFITH, Nathan. Private.
GRIFFITH, Ezra. Private.
GRINNEL, Richard. Private.
HACKNEY, Ralph. Private.
HACKNEY, Joseph. Private.
HEBBETT, William. Private.
  Deserted to the enemy.
HEBLER, Peter. Private.
HIGLEY, John. Private.
  Deserted to the enemy.
HOUSE, Mathew. Private.
HOUSE, Henry. Private.
HOUSE, Abraham. Private.
JOHNSON, William. Private.
  Joined the Rifle Company.
JOHNSON, Benjamin. Private.
JONES, John. Private.
  Deserted to the enemy.
KERR, Edward. Private.
KILBOURN, Aaron. Private.
KILBOURN, Timothy. Private.
LAWRENCE, George. Private.
LEE, Hiram Davis. Private.
LEE, John. Private.
LEE, William B. Private.
LEE, Riverius Hooker. Private.
LIBBY, William. Private.
LUTON, William. Private.
MANDEVILLE, Henry. Private.
MATHEWS, Thomas. Private.
McLYMAN, John. Private.
McNAIR, John. Private.
McNAIR, Neil. Private.
McNEAL, Archibald. Private.
MOREHOUSE, Isaiah. Private.
MORTON, Harvey. Private.
NEAL, Timothy. Private.
NEVILLE, Thomas. Private.
NEVILLE, John. Private.
NIGHTMAN, Abraham. Private.
NORTON, William. Private.

NORTON, George. Private.
ODEL, Joseph L. Private.
ODEL, John. Private.
ODELL, Joshua. Private.
PATRICK, Abraham. Private.
PEARCE, John. Private.
PEARCE, David. Private.
PEASE, Allanson B. Private.
  See Casualties.
PERVOOST, Joseph. Private.
PERVOOST, William. Private.
PETTIT, Abadiah. Private.
PETTIT, William. Private.
PORTER, Augustus. Private.
  Deserted to the enemy.
PUTNAM, William. Private.
RAPELJE, George James.
  Private.
REYNOLDS, Sylvanus. Private.
REYNOLDS, Henry. Private.
REYNOLDS, George. Private.
  Deserted to the enemy.
RICE, William. Private.
RICHARDS, Charles. Private.
RICHARDS, Alfred. Private.
  Deserted to the enemy.
SAXTON, William. *Lieutenant.*
SCHRAM, William. Private.
SCHRAM, Benjamin. Sergeant.
  See Casualties.
SEARS, James. Private.
SECORD, Silas. Private.
SECORD, William Peter.
  Private.
SECORD, David. *Captain.*
SPEAR, George. Private.
  Deserted to the enemy.
SPRINGER, Daniel. *Captain.*
STORY, Walter. Private.
SUMNER, John D. Private.
SWISKER, Burgess. Private.
THAYER, Jarvis. Private.
THOMPSON, Hugh. Private.
  Joined the Rifle Company.
TOLES, William. Private.

TREADWELL, Anson. Private.
TURREL, Jesse Jr. Private.
  Joined the Dragoons.
UNDERWOOD, William. Private.
  Joined the Kent Volunteers.
VAIL, James. Private.
  See Casualties.
VAN CISE, Joseph. Private.
WALLACE, David. Private.
WELLS, John. Sergeant.
WELLS, Riley. Private.
WESTBROOK, James. Private.
WESTBROOK, Nicholas. Private.

WHITCOMB, Ira. Private.
WIDNER, John. Private.
  Joined the Incorporated Militia.
WILCOCKS, Justus. Private.
WILLCOX, William. Private.
WILLSON, Benjamin G. Private.
WILLSON, Benjamin. *Ensign*.
  GSM, Fort Detroit.
WOOD, George. Private.
YOUNGLOVE, Ezekial. Private.
YOUNGLOVE, John. Private.
YOUNGLOVE, David. Private.
  Joined the Incorporated Militia.

WESTERN DISTRICT

1ST ESSEX

1st Flank Company
ARMSTRONG, John. Private.
AUGUSTINE, Alexander. Private.
BALDWIN, Russel. Private.
  GSM, Fort Detroit.
BALDWIN, Benjamin. Private.
  GSM, Fort Detroit.
BALDWIN, Cyrus. Private.
  GSM, Fort Detroit.
BELLAIRE, Paul. Private.
  GSM, Fort Detroit.
BERGERON, Pierre. Private.
BRUSH, Jarvis. Private.
  GSM, Fort Detroit.
BUCHANNAN, Gordon.
  Sergeant Major.
CALDWELL, Thomas. *Ensign*.
  GSM, Fort Detroit.
CALDWELL, Francis. Private.
  GSM, Fort Detroit.
CALDWELL, William. *Captain*.
  GSM, Fort Detroit.
CASIDY, Peter. Private.
  GSM, Fort Detroit.
CLINGERSMITH, Jacob.
  Sergeant.
COMERFORD, John. Private.
  GSM, Fort Detroit.

DOWLER, Richard. Private.
  GSM, Fort Detroit.
FERRIS, Isaac. Private.
  GSM, Fort Detroit.
FERRIS, John. Corporal.
FRIEND, Charles. Corporal.
GLASSNER, William. Private.
GORDON, James. *Lieutenant*.
  GSM, Fort Detroit.
HARDON (Harding), John.
  Private.
HARPER, Thomas. Private.
HUFFMAN, Henry. Private.
JOHNSON, Moses. Private.
  GSM, Fort Detroit.
KENT, Jacob. Private.
KNAPP, Benjamin. Private.
LIEBEAU, John. Private.
  GSM, Fort Detroit.
LOCKHART, Jeremiah. Private.
  GSM, Fort Detroit.
LOCKHART, James. Private.
  GSM, Fort Detroit.
LYTLE, Nicholas. *Ensign*.
MALLOTTE, Joseph. Private.
McCORMICK, John. Private.
McCORMICK, William.
  Lieutenant.

McKENZIE, Alexander. Corporal.
McLEAN, Thomas. Private.
 GSM, Fort Detroit.
MICKLE, John. Corporal.
NEVIL, Edward. Private.
 GSM, Fort Detroit.
O'NEIL, Joseph. Private.
 GSM, Fort Detroit.
PARDOE, William. Private.
 GSM, Fort Detroit.
PARDOE, Samuel. Private.
PRICE, James. Sergeant.
QUICK, John. Private.
 GSM, Fort Detroit.
QUICK, Joseph. Private.
QUICK, Alexander. Private.
 GSM, Fort Detroit.
REYNOLDS, Ebenezer. *Major.*
 GSM, Fort Detroit.
ROACH, Morris. Private.
 GSM, Fort Detroit.
ROBERTS, Robert. Private.
 GSM, Fort Detroit.
SCHAMEHORN, David. Private.
 Deserted to the enemy.
SCRATCH, Leonard. Private.
SIPPS (Lipps), Henry. Private.
 GSM, Fort Detroit.
ST. AUBIN, Joseph. Private.
STEWART, Charles. Private.
 GSM, Fort Detroit.
STOCKWELL, John. Private.
 GSM, Fort Detroit.
SWERGOOD, George. Private.
TOFFLEMIRE, William. Private.
 GSM, Fort Detroit.
VICKERS, Benjamin. Private.
WHITE, David. Private.
 GSM, Fort Detroit.
WHITE, Thompson. Private.
WHITE, Silas. Private.
WHITTLE, Thomas. Private.
 GSM, Fort Detroit.
WILCOX, Asa. Private.
WILFONG, Jonas. Private.
 GSM, Fort Detroit.

WILFONG, Joseph. Private.
 GSM, Fort Detroit.
WILLIAMS, Isaac. Private.
WRIGHT, William. Sergeant.
WRIGHT, Henry. Private.
 GSM, Fort Detroit.
WRIGHT, Philip. Private.
YOUNG, Peter. Sergeant.

2nd Flank Company
ANTAILLA, Thomas. Corporal.
BARBE, Francis. Private.
BARILLE, Francis. Private.
BARNES, George. Private.
BASTION, Eustache. Private.
BEATRICE, Michel. Private.
BEAUCHAMP, Pierre. Private.
 See Casualties.
BELAND, Robert. Private.
BELAND, Francis. Private.
BERGERON, Joseph. Private.
BERNARD, Jean Baptist. Private.
 GSM, Fort Detroit.
BERTRAND, Jean Baptist.
 Private.
BERTRAND, Simon. Private.
BILLET, Francis. Private.
 Deserted to the enemy.
BONDY, Gabriel. Private.
BONDY, Charles. Private.
BOUFFARD, Laurent. Private.
BOUTHILLIER, Francis. Private.
BRISBOIS, Jean Baptist. Private.
BUTLER, Edward. Private.
BUTLER, Francis. Private.
 See Casualties.
CANADIEN, Jean Baptist.
 Private.
CHAPEU, Benjamin. Private.
CHOISIE, Francis. Private.
CLARK, John. Private.
CLOUTIER, Antoine. Private.
CONSTANTINO, Jean B.
 Sergeant. GSM, Fort Detroit.
DELISLE, Denis. Private.
DENEAU, Baptiste. Private.
 GSM, Fort Detroit.

DEPAUCA, Vincent. Private.
DESCARE, Joseph. Private.
DESCORRY, Francis. Private.
DUCLOS, Antoine. Private.
DUROCHER, Charles. Private.
ELLIOTT, William. *Captain.*
  GSM, Fort Detroit.
ESTE, Amable. Private.
GAGNION, Pierre. Private.
GALERNEAU, Pierre. Private.
GENEREUX, Peter. Corporal.
  See Casualties.
GIRTY, Thomas. *Ensign.*
  See Casualties.
GOULLET, Francis. Private.
  GSM, Fort Detroit.
GROSBEC, James. Private.
HEARTLY, Jonathan. Private.
JAMES, Thomas. Sergeant.
JOLIE, Michel. Private.
KEMP, David. Private.
L'ORME, Pierre. Private.
LA ROSE, Pierre. Private.
  GSM, Fort Detroit.
LA VIOLLETTE, Francis. Private.
LA LIBERTE, Baptist. Private.
  GSM, Fort Detroit.
LAFERTE, Antoine. Private.
LAFRAMBOISE, Paul. Private.
LAJEUNESSE, Louis. Private.
LALONGE, Baptist. Private.
LAMARCHE, Charles. Private.

LANGLOIS, Joseph. Private.
  GSM, Fort Detroit.
LITTLE, James. *Ensign.*
  GSM, Fort Detroit.
LITTLE, John. *Lieutenant.*
LONSON, Francis. Private.
LYONS, Benjamin. Private.
MALLETTE, Gabriel. Private.
MARSAC, George. Private.
McDONELL, John. Sergeant.
MELOCHE, Francis. Private.
  GSM, Fort Detroit.
MELOCHE, Baptist. Private.
MELOCHE, Alexis. Private.
MONFORTON, Francis. Private.
MORIN, Joseph. Private.
PAPPIN, Michel. Private.
PERROT (Perrault), Louis.
  Private. GSM, Fort Detroit.
PLANTE, Antoine. Private.
POIRIER, Baptist. Private.
PRONOVEAU, Francis. Private.
RACICOT, Antoine. Private.
REAUME, Paschal. Corporal.
  See Casualties.
RENEAU, Baptiste. Private.
ROBINSON, John. Corporal.
ROI, Francis. Private.
VALLADE, Jean Baptist. Private.
VASSEUR, Laurent. Private.
VERNIER, Bazel. Private.
VIZINA, Louis. Sergeant.

2ND ESSEX

1st Flank Company
AMELLE, Amable. Private.
ASKIN, Alexander D. *Lieutenant.*
ASKIN, James. *Captain.*
AYOTTE, Francis. Private.
BADISHAW, Pierre. Private.
BADISHAW, Baptiste. Private.
BEKER, Jacob. Private.
BELLAN, Bazil. Sergeant.
BELLEPUCHE, Joseph. Private.

BELLEPUCHE, Jacques. Private.
BENETEAU, Andre. Sergeant.
BERELAW, Pierre. Private.
BLONDIEN (Blondier), Henry.
  Private.
BOLIEU, Julien. Private.
  Deserted to the enemy.
BOUCHE, Francais. Private.
BRUGERE, Charles. Private.
CADET, Joseph. Private.

CAMPEAU, Jean. Private.
CAZAVAN, Pierre. Private.
CLOUTIER, Pierre. Private.
DEMARAY, Francais. Private.
DUCHESNE, Thomas. Private.
DUGAU, Louis. Private.
DUPLICE, Jacque. Private.
FARINEAUX, Joseph. Sergeant.
FORTIEY, Nicholas. Private.
GAUDETTE, Joseph. Private.
GUILLIOTT, Pierre. Private.
HANDS, William Jr. *Ensign.*
LA FARIER, Joseph. Private.
LA BUTTE, Charles. Private.
LADEROUT, Alexis. Private.
LAFORRAIS, Jean Marie. Private.
LANGLOIS, Alexis. Private.
LANGLOIS, Augustine. Private.
LATOURNEAU, Francois.
   Private.
LE DUE Paul. Private.
LeBLANC, Baptiste. Private.
LeBLANC, Joseph. Private.
   Deserted to the enemy.
LeBLANC, Pierre. Private.
   Deserted to the enemy.
LESPERANCE, Charles. Private.
LOGAN, Gabriel. Private.
   See Casualties.
MAISONVILLE, Bernard.
   Private.
McDOUGAL, Peter. Private.
MELOCHE, Baptiste. Private.
MIREAU, Joseph. Private.
MORIN, Pierre. Private.
NADEAU, Baptiste. Private.
PARRE, Felix. Private.
PELTIER, Alexis. Private.
PERA, Baptiste. Private.
PILLETTE, Baptiste. Private.
REAUME, Charles. Private.
SIMBRIETTE, Claude. Private.
   Deserted to the enemy.
SOULIER, Bernard. Private.
SOULIER, Baptiste. Private.

ST. LOUIS, Pierre. Private.
TRAMBLE, Baptiste. Private.

2nd Flank Company
BANGLE, William. Private.
BEAUGRAND, Charles. Private.
BENETEAU, Charles. Private.
BERTRAND, Antoine. Private.
   GSM, Fort Detroit.
BERTRAND, Jean Baptiste.
   Private. GSM, Fort Detroit.
CARTIER, Pierre. Private.
CHAMBERLAN, Jacques.
   Private.
CHAUVIN, Jean Baptiste. Private.
CLEMENT, Jean Baptiste.
   Private.
COTTE, Pierre. Private.
DROUILLARD, Francois. Private.
DROUILLARD, Thomas. Private.
DUFOUR, Jean Baptiste. Private.
   See Casualties.
DUFOUR, Antoine. Private.
DULAC, Joseph. Private.
DUMOUCHEL, Pierre. Sergeant.
EBERTS, Joseph. *Ensign.*
EBERTS, Henry. Private.
   See Casualties.
FIELDS, James. Sergeant.
GABRIAN, Albert. Private.
HODIENNE, Joseph. Private.
JANISSE, Joseph. Private.
JANISSE, Nicholas. Private.
JOLIBOIS, Louis. Private.
LABELLE, Eustache. Private.
LABOURIN, Francois. Private.
LAJEUNESSE, Pierre. Private.
   See Casualties.
LURANJO, Jacques. Private.
MAILLAUX, Joseph. Private.
MAISONVILLE, Alexis. *Captain.*
MARANTEL, Joseph. Private.
MARANTEL, Antoine. Private.
MARANTEL, Francois. Private.
MARANTEL, Benjamin. Private.

MARANTEL, Pierre. Private.
MERCURE, Jean Baptiste.
  Private.
MONTREUIL, Luc. Private.
NORMANDIN, Louis. Private.
PARENT, Joseph. *Lieutenant.*
PARENT, Jacques. Private.
PARENT, Laurent. Private.
PARENT, Hypolite. Private.
PARENT, Nicholas. Private.
PARENT, Antoine. Private.
PINEAU, Joseph. Private.

PRATT, Theodore. Private.
PRATTE, Francois. Private.
PRATTE, Dominique. Private.
RAE (Roe), John. Sergeant.
REAUME, Louis. Private.
RENEAU, Joseph. Private.
ST. DENNYS, Nicholas. Private.
TALLARD, Jean Baptiste. Private.
TOURNEAUX, Victor. Private.
TOURNEAUX, Dominique.
  Private.
TOURNEAUX, Charles. Private.

1ST KENT

Flank Company
ALWARD, Daniel. Private.
ARMOR, Jacob. Private.
ARQUOITTE, Pierre. Private.
BALLAR, Nicholas. Private.
BARKER, Ephraim. Private.
  See Loyal Kent Volunteers.
BLACKBURN, Isaac. Private.
BLACKBURN, Leonard. Private.
CADDY, Joseph. Private.
CALDWELL, William. Private.
CHARON, Jacques. Private.
COSTA, Peter. Private.
COURTNEY, Jean B. Private.
COUTIER, Simon. Private.
CRAWFORD, James. Private.
  See Loyal Kent Volunteers.
CROW, Robert. Private.
CULBERTSON, Samuel. Private.
CULL, Samuel. Private.
CULL, Daniel. Private.
CULL, John. Private.
DAVIS, John. Private.
DELISLE, Antoine. Private.
DOBIN, Jean B. Private.
DOLSEN, Jacob. Private.
DONNAR, Antoine. Private.
DRAGON, Louis. Private.
  GSM, Fort Detroit.

DRAKE, Francis. Private.
  GSM, Fort Detroit.
DRUILLARD, Dennis. Private.
EVERETT, David. Private.
  See Loyal Kent Volunteers.
FENNELL, Daniel. Private.
  See Loyal Kent Volunteers.
FIELD, Daniel. Private.
  See Loyal Kent Volunteers.
  GSM, Fort Detroit.
FIELD, George. Private.
  See Loyal Kent Volunteers.
  GSM, Fort Detroit.
FRAXTER, Michael. Private.
FRAXTER, Peter. Private.
FRUDELLE, Jean B. Private.
FURUES, Maurice. Private.
GREAR, Thomas. Private.
HAMLIN, Isaac. Private.
HITCHCOCK, Daniel. Private.
HOLMES, Hugh. Sergeant.
HOLMES, John. Private.
JACOB, George. *Captain.*
JAMES, Henry. Private.
JOHNSON, James. Private.
JOHNSON, Joseph. Private.
KILBURN, Anthony. Private.
LADOUCEUR, Jean Marie.
  Private.

LAFORAIS, Jean B. Private.
LAFORAIS, Antoine. Private.
LAIRD, George. Private.
LAUGHLON, Augustus. Private.
LAUGHTON, John. Sergeant.
LEWDES, Nicholas. Private.
MAIJON, Pierre. Private.
McCALLUM, Hugh. Sergeant.
   GSM, Fort Detroit.
McDOUGALL, Hector. Private.
   See Loyal Kent Volunteers.
McDOUGALL, Angus. Private.
   See Loyal Kent Volunteers.
MESSIMON, Jacob. Private.
MINOR, Allan. Private.
OLBAN, Robert. Private.
PARSON, Edward. Private.
PARSTONE, John. Private.
PATTERSON, William. Private.
   See Loyal Kent Volunteers.
PECK, John. *Lieutenant.*

PETITE, Bazil. Private.
PHARON, Andre. Private.
RALSTON, Peter. Private.
REAUME, Pierre. Private.
REAUME, Thomas. Private.
RICHARDSON, Joseph.
   Private.
ROE, William. Private.
ROY, Joseph. Private.
SHAW, William. Private.
   See Loyal Kent Volunteers.
STACY, Lewis. Private.
STERLING, William. *Lieutenant.*
STUBBLE, Jacob. Private.
VALAIDE, Joseph. Private.
WARD, John. Private.
WARD, Anthony. Private.
WEBSTER, Milo. Private.
WILCOX, Elisha. Private.
WISE, Charles. Private.
   See Loyal Kent Volunteers.

IV

THE VOLUNTEER CORPS
1812 ~ 1813

I N 1812 there were a number of volunteer corps raised in
addition to the flank companies. Artillery companies were
raised in the Niagara and Midland Districts; troops of horse
in the Western, Niagara, Home, Newcastle, Midland and
Johnstown Districts; and rifle companies in the London, Home
and Johnstown Districts. In several instances, militiamen were
simply attached to the regular forces to assist in serving the
guns or to act as dispatch riders.

An artillery company had been organized in the 1790s, and
at least one troop of cavalry had been officially reported by
1802. Some correspondence exists that refers to pre-war flank
companies, but for the overwhelming majority of Upper
Canadians, their militia obligations were met in enrolling in the
local infantry companies of the sedentary organization.

In the spring of 1812 the situation changed. General Brock
actively encouraged the formation of separate troops of cavalry,
a car brigade (artillery drivers), artillery companies and rifle
companies, all in addition to the newly authorized flank companies. These new corps filled a very pressing need to augment
the regular establishment, to maintain lines of communication
across the province, and to aid in the manning of the "great
guns" at the posts and intermediate strong points along the vulnerable sections of the frontier.

When returns of the volunteers and flankers were made in 1819 and 1820, note was specifically made that only those who had been called out on active service were to be noted. Because a number of the corps east of York were never called on, no roll enumerating them was made. Other muster rolls from the Western District have disappeared, and so information is incomplete.

We know, for instance, that about 30 militia dragoons were employed by Major General Henry Procter in the winter of 1812–13 in the Western District, that one company was designated a marine company in Essex, and that a number of others were manning gunboats on the St. Lawrence, but as yet no other information has been found about who they were or how long they were active.

References also indicate that the militia were employed manning gunboats on the St. Lawrence in 1813 and 1814, and that dozens of mounted men were employed carrying dispatches throughout the war, but no returns have been located.

Rifle companies were authorized in a Militia General Order of May 25, 1812. These were to consist of no more than 30 rank and file (all volunteers), a captain and one subaltern. As no note has been found of them after the spring of 1813, it would appear that they were dissolved with the expiration of the Militia Act of 1812 in March 1813.

The volunteers corps are listed opposite, together with officers known to have acted or held commissions in them. Immediately following this brief guide are the rolls of volunteers that have been located.

The Coloured Corps and the Car Drivers are described in Section VII, but it should be noted that they were also active in this earlier period.

VOLUNTEER CORPS AND OFFICERS

MARINE COMPANIES

1ST ESSEX

No return found.
Captain William Buchanan
Ensign John McCormick (July 9, 1812)

TROOPS OF HORSE

1ST LEEDS

Captain Charles Jones (June 24, 1812)
Lieutenant John Grant (June 24, 1812)
Lieutenant Jonas Jones (June 25, 1812)
Cornet Henry Jones (June 24, 1812)

2ND GRENVILLE

Captain Herman Landon
Lieutenant Thomas D. Campbell
Lieutenant Dunkan Campbell

1ST LENNOX

Captain Paul Trompour. Died March 1813.
Lieutenant John Trompour. Promoted captain (June 7, 1813).
Cornet Gilbert A. Clapp. Promoted lieutenant (June 7, 1813).
Cornet John Kemp (June 7, 1813).

1ST ADDINGTON

Captain Christopher Fralick
Lieutenant Isaac Fraser
Cornet John Fralick

1ST PRINCE EDWARD

Captain John Stinson
Lieutenant Simeon Washburn
Cornet Benjamin Way

1ST YORK

Captain John Button

District of Niagara
Major Thomas Merritt (April 24, 1812). Commanding officer.

1ST TROOP OF LINCOLN CAVALRY

Captain Alexander Hamilton (May 1, 1812)
Lieutenant William Hamilton Merritt (May 1, 1812)
Cornet William Merritt (May 1, 1812)

2ND TROOP OF LINCOLN CAVALRY

Captain George Hamilton (June 1, 1812). From the 1st Lincoln.
James Cummings, Lieutenant (June 1, 1812)
John Pell Major, Cornet (June 1, 1812)

2ND ESSEX

No return found.
Captain William Smith (July 9, 1812)

1ST KENT

No return found.
Captain George Jacobs
Cornet Charles Fisher (July 10, 1812)

ARTILLERY

1ST FRONTENAC ARTILLERY

Ensign Robert Richardson. Commanding officer.
Ensign Simon Washburn

1ST LINCOLN ARTILLERY

Captain John Powell
2nd Captain Alexander Cameron (June 28, 1812)
1st Lieutenant William Servos (June 28, 1812)
1st Lieutenant John Ball (June 28, 1812)
2nd Lieutenant Alexander McKee (June 28, 1812).
    Resigned (December 1, 1812).

2ND LINCOLN ARTILLERY

Captain James Kerby
1st Lieutenant Lewis Clement
1st Lieutenant John McClellan
2nd Lieutenant Jacob A. Ball
2nd Lieutenant Alexander Bryson

RIFLE COMPANIES

1ST GRENVILLE RIFLE COMPANY

No return found.
Captain William Fraser (July 12, 1812)
Lieutenant James Hall (July 12, 1812)
Ensign Daniel Jones (July 12, 1812)

1ST LEEDS RIFLE COMPANY

No return found.
Captain Reuben Sherwood
Lieutenant Alexander Morris
Lieutenant Jonas Jones. Transferred to Troop, June 22, 1812.
Ensign Allan Grant

2ND LEEDS RIFLE COMPANY

No return found.
Captain Benjamin Munsell
Lieutenant Levi Soper
Ensign Samuel Kelsey

1ST YORK RIFLE COMPANY

Captain Peter Robinson
Lieutenant William Ross
Ensign Ludowic Wideman

1ST NORFOLK RIFLE COMPANY

Captain Daniel McCall. See Flank Companies.

1ST OXFORD AND RIFLE COMPANY

(sometimes 1st Oxford and 1st Middlesex Rifle Company)
Captain Bela Brewster Brigham (November 5, 1812)
Lieutenant Abner Owen

NOMINAL ROLL OF VOLUNTEERS

TROOPS OF HORSE

1ST LEEDS

Served in the Johnstown District July 2, 1812 to April 24, 1813. According to the official return of this troop, of the 46 men, all ranks, who served in the troop, 11 deserted to the enemy sometime following its reduction in the spring of 1813.

BAXTER, Daniel L. Private.
BAXTER. Hiram. Private.
BLACKMORE, Rowland. Private.
BRAYTON, Freeborn. Private.
BURKHAM, Guy C. Sergeant. Deserted to the enemy after reduction.
BURRETT, Ruben. Private. Deserted to the enemy after reduction.
CASWELL, Stephen. Private. Sergeant.
CLAPSON, Asa. Private.
CLEMENT, Philip. Private.
CORLMAN, John. Private. Deserted to the enemy after reduction.
CROMWELL, James. Private.
CROMWELL, Samuel. Private.
DEARBORN, Benjamin. Private.
DOCKHAM, Enock. Private.
DUCOLON, Stephen. Private.
DUCOLON, Peter. Private.
EASTWOOD, John. Private. Deserted to the enemy after reduction.
EASTWOOD, Abraham. Private. Deserted to the enemy after reduction.
FIELD, Roswell. Private. Deserted to the enemy after reduction.
FRANKLIN, Mathew. Private. Deserted to the enemy after reduction.
GRANT, John. *Lieutenant.*
GRIFFIN, Isaiah. Private.
HENDERSON, Caleb Jr. Private.
HUTCHISON, Aaron. Private.
JONES, Alpheus. Sergeant.
JONES, Charles. *Captain.*
JONES, Henry. *Cornet.*
JONES, Jonas. *Lieutenant.*
KILBORN, Whiting. Corporal.
LAMBKIN, Jobe N. Private. Deserted to the enemy after reduction.
LEWIS, Ira. Private.
LIDDLE, Andrew. Private.
MANHART, George. Private.

MARSHAL, Isaac. Corporal.
MARSHALL, Isaac. Private.
MATTISON, Jesse. Private. Deserted to the enemy after reduction.
McDANIEL, Randy Jr. Private.
McDANIEL, John. Private.
McDANIEL, James. Private.
MOSIER, Thomas. Private.
MOTT, Clement. Private. Deserted to the enemy after reduction.
MOTT, Reuben. No. 2 Private.
PEARSON, Silas. Private.
RAYMOND, Samuel. Private.
SELYE, Joseph. Private. Deserted to the enemy after reduction.
STONE, Uri. Private.

2ND GRENVILLE

ACLAND (?), James. Private.
ADAMS, Abel. Private.
BOUNDIGE, Joseph. Private.
BROWNE, Himan. Private.
BURK, Peter. Private.
CAMPBELL, Thomas D. *Lieutenant.*
CAMPBELL, Dunkan. *Lieutenant.*
DENING, Amos. Private.
EVERTS, William. Sergeant
EVERTS, George. Private.
FROOM, Elijah. Private.
HUNSDELL, John. Private.
LANDON, John. Sergeant
LANDON, Himan. *Captain.*
LANDON, William. Private.
McELENEY, George. Private.
MOSIER, Silas. Private.
PERIN, William. Private.
PERIN, Marchus. Private.
PERIN, Solomon. Private. See Incorporated Militia.
SPENCER, Charles. Sergeant
STONE, Lyman. Private.
STONE, Ransom. Private.
TAUSLEY, Herman. Private.
THOMAS, Samuel. Private.
THROOP, Ely. Private.
VININGE, John. Private.

The 1st Lennox alternated month on and month off with the troop of the 1st Addington while serving in the garrison at Kingston.

BEADLE, William. Private.
BEADLE, Enock. Private.
BEADLE, Daniel. Private.
BEADLE, James. Private.
BELL, Frederick. Private.
BROWEN, William L. Private.
BRUNSON, Samuel. Private.
CASEY, Samuel. Private.
CLAPP, Dorland. Sergeant.
CLAPP, Thomas. Private.
CLAPP, John. Sergeant.
CLAPP, Paul. Private.
CLAPP, Gilbert A. *Cornet*.
CLEMENT, Martin. Private.
COLE, Barnard. Private.
DAFOE, Michael. Private.
DETTON, Jacob. Private.
DORLAND, Philip. Private.
DORLAND, Peter. Private.
FRITTS, John Jr. Private.
GARRISON, Elias. Private.
GARRISON, Marvels. Private.
GARRISON, Jonas. Private.
HART, James. Private.
HERNS, Thomas. Private.
HERNS, George. Private.
HUFF, William M. Private.
HUYKE, Burger. Private.
JACKSON, Joseph. Private.
KEMPP, Abraham. Private.
KEMPP, John. Sergeant. *Cornet* (June 7, 1813).
KOUGHNET, Christian. Private.
LONG, Joshua. Private.
LOSEY, Dorland. Private.
LOSEY, Joseph. Private.
LOSEY, Abraham. Private.
MORE, John. Private.
NILES, Stephen. Private.
PETERSON, John. Private.
PETERSON, Nicholas. Private.
SCOTT, Amos. Private.

SHARP, Lawrence. Private.
SMITH, Jacob A. Private.
SMITH, George Sr. Private.
SMITH, Elias. Private.
SMITH, Amos. Private.
SMITH, George Jr. Private.
SMYTH, Mathias. Sergeant.
SOSEY, James. Private.
THORP, Henry. Private.
TRUMP, Joseph. Private.
TRUMPOUR, John. *Lieutenant. Captain* (June 7, 1813).
TRUMPOUR, Paul. *Captain*. Died March 1813.
VANALSTINE, Lambert Jr. Private.
VANCLEFT, John. Private.
VANHORN, John. Private.
VANHORN, Peter. Private.
WARNER, Stephen. Private.
WOOD, Peter H. Private.

1ST ADDINGTON

ALCOMBRACK, Cornelius. Private.
ALKENBRACK, William. Private.
AYLESWORTH, Job. Private.
AYLESWORTH, Neil. Private.
BOOTH, Benjamin. Sergeant.
BROWN, George. Private.
BURLEY, Cornelius. Private.
COOK, John. Private.
CUSHMAN, Artimas W. Private.
FINKLE, William. Private.
FRALICK, Jacob. Private.
FRALICK, Levius. Private.
FRALICK, Thomas L. Private.
FRALICK, John. *Cornet*.
FRALICK, Christopher. *Captain*.
FRASER, Daniel. Private.
FRASER, Abraham. Private.
FRASER, Isaac. *Lieutenant*.
GARDINEAR, John. Private.
GORSLIN, Samuel. Private.
HATCH, Nathaniel. Sergeant.
HAWLEY, William. Private.
HESS, John. Private.
HOGLE, John. Private.

KELLER, Zachariah. Private.
KIMERLEY, Henry. Private.
LAKE, James. Private.
MADDEN, Robert. Private.
MARTIN, John. Private. See Casualties.
McARTHUR, Neil. Private.
McGUIN, John. Sergeant.
McMULLEN, William. Private.
McSHOUTEN, Daniel. Private.
MILLER, Jacob. Private.
OVEROCKER, Daniel. Sergeant.
PHILIPS, John. Private.
RICE, Rosewell. Private. Deserted to the enemy.
ROGERS, Armstrong. Private.
ROGERS, John. Private.
ROSE, Mathias. Private.
SHIBLEY, Henry. Private.
SIMMONS, George. Private.
SIMMONS, Philip. Private.
SIMMONS, Bostian. Private.
SIMPSON, John. Private.
STARING, Timothy. Private.
VAN SICKEL, John. Private.
VAN VALKENBURG, David. Private.
WEIS, Peter. Private.
WELLS, James. Sergeant.
WELLS, Jesse. Private.
WHITICK, John. Private.
WILLIAMS, Joshua. Private.
YORK, Frederick. Private.
YORK, Benjamin. Private.

1ST PRINCE EDWARD

BEADLE, William. Private.
BRICKMAN, William. Private.
BRICKMAN, Rynard. Private.
CLARK, Henry. Private.
COLE, Lacharial. Private.
COLE, Isaac. Sergeant.
CROWTER, Anthony. Private.
DEVONPORT, John. Private.
DOXIE, Sylvanus. Private.
DYER, Silas. Private.
DYER, Henry. Private.
ELLIS, Joseph. Private.
ELSWERTH, Caleb. Private.

FAIRMAN, John. Private.
FAIRMAN, Thomas. Private.
FOX, John. Private.
GARDNER, Hezekiah. Private.
GARRETT, Isaac Jr. Private.
GARRETT, Thomas. Private.
GOSLIN, John. Private.
HARE, Daniel. Private.
JOHNSON, Henry H. Private.
JOHNSON, William. Private.
JOHNSON, Andrew. Private.
JONES, Gilbert. Sergeant.
KETCHUM, Lewis. Private.
LAMBERH, Daniel. Private.
LAW, John Jr. Private.
LAZIER, John. Private.
LUFETT, Adam. Private.
LYONS, Thomas. Sergeant.
OYDEN, William. Private.
PLALL, James. Private.
PRENCIE, Baptiste. Private.
RIDNER, Henry. Private.
RIDNER, John. Private.
RIGHT, John. Private.
ROBLIN, Levi. Private.
ROW, John. Private.
SAZIEN, Nicholas. Private.
SAZIER, Peter. Private.
SHORT, Jacob. Private.
SOMES, Richard. Private.
SPENCER, John B. Private.
STAPLETON, John. Private.
STAPLETON, William. Private.
STINSEN, David. Sergeant.
STINSON, John. *Captain.*
TRIPP, Israel. Private.
VANBLARICAM, Peter. Private.
VANBLARICUM, Abraham. Private.
VANSKIVEN, Peter. Private.
WASHBURN, Simeon. *Lieutenant.*
WASHBURN, William. Private.
WAY, Benjamin. *Cornet.*
WHITE, Stephen. Private.
WILLIAMS, John P. Private.
WILLIAMS, Wynot. Private.
WOED, John. Private.

ASHLEY, Leonard. Private.
BEARD, Henry. Private.
BROOKS, Jacob. Private. GSM, Fort Detroit.
BUCK, Philip. Private.
BUCKENDOL, George. Private. GSM, Fort Detroit.
BUTTON, John. *Captain.*
CLARKSON, Joshua. Sergeant.
CONAVER, Peter. Private.
FLETCHER, Silas. Private.
HAGERMAN, Nicholas. Private.
HELMKEY, Frederick. Private.
HENNKEY, Francis. Private.
HOLLINGSHEAD, Anthony. Private.
LAWRENCE, Jacob. Private.
LYMBURNER, William. Private.
MEEKHOM, John. Private.
MOORE, Robert. Sergeant.
MUNSHAW, George. Private.
MURE, William. Sergeant.
PATTEBONE, James. Private.
PHERRIL, Stephen. Private.
PHILIPS, Godfrey. Private.
PLAYTER, George Jr. Private
PRINGLE, Henry. Sergeant. GSM, Fort Detroit.
QUANTZ, George. Private.
REYNOLDS, Asa. Private.
RITTER, Peter. Private.
ROBBINS, Abijah. Private.
SMITH, Alsalem. Private.
SNOOK, Abraham. Private.
SOLES, William. Private.
SPONHOUSE, John. Trumpeter.
SPRING, Peter. Private.
SPRING, Daniel. Private.
STANEM, John. Private.
TAPPIN, Louis. Private.
TOWELLYER, Mathew. Private.
VANHORN, John. Private.
WARREN, James. Private.
WOODRUF, Noadiah. Private.

1ST TROOP NIAGARA LIGHT DRAGOONS

The 1st Troop was embodied from May 1, 1812, to December 24, 1812.

ADAMS, William. Private.
ALLAN, Seneca. Private.
BENDER, John. Private. From the 2nd Troop.
BERGER, David. Private. From the 2nd Troop.
CAMPBELL, Peter. Private.
CASWELL, Nathaniel. Private. From the 2nd Troop.
CASWELL, Daniel. Private. From the 2nd Troop.
CASWELL, Jerotham. Private.
CLINE, Henry. Private. From the 2nd Troop.
CLOW, Duncan. Sergeant. *Quarter Master*, vice Ingersol, promoted.
CORBICE (Corbin), Joshua. Trumpeter. GSM, Fort Detroit.
CRACE, Andrew. Trumpeter.
CUTTLER, Jacob. Private.
CUTTLER, Abram. Private.
DAGGET, Eliazer. Private.
DAVIS, James. Private.
FIELD, Daniel. Private.
FIELD, George. Private.
FULLER, Asa. Private.
GRAHAM, David. Private.
GREEN, William Henry. Private. From the 2nd Troop.
HAMILTON, Alexander. *Captain.*
HAVERLAND (Hoverland), John. Private. From the 2nd Troop.
    See Casualties.
HAWN, Willson. Private. From the 2nd Troop.
HENRY, James. Private.
HINDMAN, Robert. Private.
HODGEKINSON, Samuel. Private.
HORSTIDER, Abraham. Private.
INGERSOL, Charles. *Quarter Master. Cornet*, vice *Major,*
    deceased (October 10, 1812).
KILLINGS, Richard. Private. From the 2nd Troop. GSM, Fort Detroit.
LANE, Thomas. From the 2nd Troop (Sergeant). Private.
LAWRENCE, John. Private.
MAJOR, Pell. *Cornet.* From the 2nd Troop. See Casualties.
MANACLE (Markle), William. Private.
MANN, John. Private.
McKENNY, Amos. Corporal. *Sergeant* (October 10, 1812).
NICHOLS, Charles. Private.
NICHOLS, Abraham. Private.
PAWLING, Henry. Private.

PEW, James. Private. From the 2nd Troop.
PUTMAN, David. Private.
RODGERS, Alexander. Private.
RODGERS, John. Private.
ROSE, Alexander. Private.
RUNCHEY, Robert. Private.
RYKERT, John. Private.
SECORD, David. Corporal.
SHAW, George. Sergeant.
SLATER, Major. Private.
SMITH, John R. Private.
STEINHOOFT, Jacob. Private. From the 2nd Troop.
STREET, Timothy. Saddler.
SUMMERS, William. Private. From the 2nd Troop.
SWAYZIE, Benjamin. Corporal. From the 2nd Troop (Private).
SWAYZIE, Samuel. Private.
TOWLSEY, Alanson. Private.
WIERS, Charles. Private. From the 2nd Troop.
WILLSON, Uriah. Private. From the 2nd Troop.
WILLSON, Benjamin. Private.
WILLSON, William. Private. From the 2nd Troop.
WILLSON, Joseph. Private. From the 2nd Troop.
WINTERMOOT, William. Private. From the 2nd Troop.
WOODRUFF, Richard. Sergeant. GSM, Fort Detroit.
WYNN, William. Private. Promoted corporal October 12, 1812.
YOUNG, David. From the 2nd Troop. Farrier.

2ND TROOP NIAGARA LIGHT DRAGOONS

The 2nd Troop served between Chippewa and Fort Erie from June 21 to July 12, 1812. On reduction, most men joined the 1st Troop.

BENDER, John. Private.
BERGER, David. Private.
CASWELL, Daniel. Private.
CASWELL, Jonathan. Private
CASWELL, Nathaniel. Private.
CLINE, Henry. Private.
COOK, Caleb. Private.
CONN, Andrew. Private.
CUTLER, Abram. Private.
CUTLER, Jacob. Private.
GREEN, William Henry. Private.
HAMILTON, George. *Captain.*
HAVERLAND, John. Private.
HAWN, Willson. Private.

KILLINGS, Richard. Private.
LANE, Thomas. Sergeant.
MAJOR, Pell. *Cornet.*
PEW, James. Private.
SECORD, John. *Lieutenant.*
STEINHOFF, Jacob. Private.
STEVENS, William. Sergeant.
SUMMERS, William. Private.
SWAYZIE, Benjamin. Private.
THOMAS, George. *Quarter Master.*
WEIRS, Charles. Private.
WILLSON, Uriah. Private.
WILLSON, William. Private.
WILLSON, Joseph. Private.
WINTERMOOT, William. Private.
YOUNG, David. Private. 5th Lincoln, 1st Flank Company.

ARTILLERY COMPANIES

1ST FRONTENAC

Ensign Richardson commanded an artillery company that served the guns at Kingston through 1812 and into 1813. It is not clear when it became inactive.

ALDRIDGE, Thomas. Private.
ARCHAMBAULT, Louis. Private.
ARMSTRONG, Thomas. Private.
ASHLEY, William. Private.
BABCOCK, Peter. Private.
BAREIL, Emanuel. Corporal.
CHATTERSON, B. Private.
CONNOLLY, John. Private.
COON, John. Private.
CUMMING, Alexander. Private.
DAWSON, William. Private.
DRAPER, Clark. Private.
DUFOE, Joseph. Private.
DUFOE, Louis. Private.
ELLERBECK, John. Private.
FISH, Joseph. Private.
FORTEN, Charles. Private.
FOUNTAGNE, Louis. Private.
FRANKLIN, William. Private.
FRANKLIN, Henry. Private.
GABRIE, Michael. Private.
GILBO, Edward. Private.

GORDINIER, Jacob. Private.
GRAHAM, Robert. Private.
GROOMS, James. Private.
HOLMES, Peter. Private.
HOPKINS, James. Private.
HUESTON, David. Private.
HUFF, Samuel. Private.
JACQUES, Francis. Private.
KELLAR, Isaac. Private.
LEMARCHE, Baptiste. Private.
LEORTE, Louis. Private.
MASON, James. Corporal.
McLEAN, William. Corporal.
McPHERSON, Allan. Private.
MOSHER, Lewis. Private.
NORTON, Loomis. Private.
O'NIEL, John. Private.
OUTWATERS, Joseph. Private.
PAXTON, Thomas. Sergeant.
PERCE, Frederick. Private.
RANDALL, William. Private.
RICHARDSON, Robert. *Ensign*. Commanding officer.
ROBISON, Henry. Private.
ROSIGNOL, Antoine. Private.
SANSONCI, Germain. Private.
SHAW, Samuel. Sergeant.
SHEFFIELD, Solomon. Private.
SMITH, Thomas. Private.
SPENCER, John. Private.
VANCOTT, Cornelius. Private.
WANNAMAKER, W. Private.
WASHBURN, Simon. *Ensign*.
YOUNGS, Elijah. Private.

1ST LINCOLN

Captain Powell's corps served from the beginning of the war until the fall of Fort George on May 27, 1813. The corps served the guns from Queenstown to the mouth of the Niagara.

ACRE, Peter. Gunner. 1st Lincoln, 2nd Flank Company.
ADAIR, Daniel. Gunner. Perhaps same as David Adair, 4th Lincoln, 1st Flank Company.
ANDERSON, Gilbert. Corporal.
BALL, John. *Lieutenant*.
BELLINGER, David. Gunner.

BOYCE, Jacob. Gunner.
BRADSHAWE, George. Gunner.
BRADT, Mathias. Gunner.
BRADT, Isaac. Gunner. 1st Lincoln, 2nd Flank Company.
BUSHKIRK (Buskirk), Lawrence. Gunner. 4th Lincoln, 1st Flank Company.
CAMERON, William. Gunner. See Casualties.
CAMPBELL, Robert. Gunner. 1st Lincoln, 2nd Flank Company.
CANADA, Samuel. Gunner.
CATHLINE, Mathew. Gunner.
CLINE, Henry Jr. Gunner.
COOK, William. Gunner.
CORNELL, Thomas. Gunner.
COUSE, Frederick. Gunner.
COX, John. Gunner.
CRUML (Crum), Cornelius. Gunner. 1st Lincoln, 2nd Flank Company.
CUSHMAN, William. Sergeant.
DEBONE, Michael. Gunner.
DECLUTE, Jeremiah. Gunner.
DILLS, James. Gunner.
DOWLING, John. Gunner.
DRAKE, Roderick. Gunner.
EGBERT, John. Gunner.
EGBERT, Garret. Gunner.
EMMETT (Emitt), John. Gunner. 1st Lincoln, 2nd Flank Company.
ESTERLY, William. Gunner.
FREEL, Hugh. Gunner.
FREEL, James. Sergeant.
FULLER, Isaac. Gunner.
GODFREY, Peter. Gunner.
GOODSON, Edward. Gunner.
HARRIS, Stephen. Gunner.
JONES, James B. Gunner.
KABLIN, Archibald. Gunner.
KELLY, Nathaniel. Gunner. 1st Lincoln, 1st Flank Company.
KERR, Henry. Gunner.
LAMBERT, Philip. Gunner. 4th Lincoln, 1st Flank Company.
LANE, Edward. Gunner.
LAWRENCE, David. Gunner.
LAWRENCE, Peter. Gunner.
MARVIN, Isaac. Gunner.
MATHEWS, Isaac. Gunner.
McFARLAND, John. Gunner.
McKEE, Alexander. *Lieutenant.*
McLEAN, John. Gunner.

McNABB, James. Gunner. 1st Lincoln, 1st Flank Company.
MERRILL, Jacob. Gunner.
MERRITHEW, Benjamin. Gunner.
MONETTE, Ernest. Corporal.
NUNN, Samuel. Gunner.
POWELL, John. *Captain.*
QUICK, Moses. Gunner. 4th Lincoln, 1st Flank Company.
QUICK, Solomon. Gunner. 4th Lincoln, 1st Flank Company.
RYAN, Isaac. Gunner.
SANGULE, James. Gunner.
SCHRAM, Garret. Gunner.
SCHRAM, Peter. Gunner. 1st Lincoln, 2nd Flank Company.
SCHRAM, Angus. Gunner.
SHAVER, John. Gunner.
SHOLTUS, Bernard. Gunner.
SMITH, John. No. 1 Gunner.
SMITH, John. No. 2 Gunner.
SNYDER, John. Gunner. 4th Lincoln, 1st Flank Company.
STEPHENSON, Jonathan. Gunner.
STEVENS, William. Gunner.
STURGES, Daniel. Gunner.
TEEDER, Isaac. Gunner.
VANATTA, Benjamin. Gunner.
VANSICKLE, John. Gunner. 4th Lincoln, 1st Flank Company
WARDLE, John. Gunner.
WADDLE, Robert. Gunner.
WARDLE, Joshua. Gunner.
WHITTEN, James. Gunner.
WRIGHT, Charles. Gunner. See Casualties.
WULFFE, Conrode. Gunner. See Casualties.
YOUNG, Alexander. Gunner.
YOUNG, George. Gunner.

2ND LINCOLN

Captain Kerby's corps was active from July 1812 until March 1813, serving from Fort Erie to the emplacements at Chippewa and Queenstown.

BALL, Jacob A. *2nd Lieutenant.*
BALL, Henry C. Gunner.
BARNES, Jonas. Gunner.
BENDER, John. Gunner.
BENEDICT, Horace. Gunner.
BENNET, Jesse. Gunner.
BROWN, Christian. Gunner.

BROWN, Daniel. Gunner.

BRYSON, Alexander. *2nd Lieutenant*. See Casualties. Noted as left province in 1812.

CAMPBELL, John. Gunner.

CASSADAY, Levi. Gunner.

CHASE, George. Gunner.

CLEMENT, Lewis. *1st Lieutenant*.

COIL, John. Gunner.

COOK, Charles. Gunner.

COOK, William. Gunner.

CHRYSLER, John. Gunner.

DAVIS, Loyal. Gunner

DOAN, Aaron. Gunner.

DOUGLAS, Nathaniel. Gunner.

FARR, Richard. Gunner.

FORSYTH, William. Sergeant.

FRALICK, Benjamin. Gunner.

GAINER, Thomas. Gunner.

GROFF, William. Gunner.

HAINEY, Matthew. Gunner.

HALL, Cyrenious. Gunner.

HALM, Jonathan. Gunner

HARRIS, John J. Gunner.

HARTWELL, Elijah. Gunner.

HAVENS, George. Gunner.

HERVIE (Hewie), Richard. Gunner.

HICKS, Samuel. Gunner.

HILTZ (Keltz), George. Gunner.

HODGEKINS, Oliver. Gunner.

HOPKINS, Samuel. Gunner.

HORTON, William. Gunner.

HOSHAL, Henry. Gunner.

HOUSE, Nicholas. Gunner.

KERBY, James. *Captain*. See Incorporated Militia.

LACEY, George. Gunner.

MACKLEM, Andrew. Gunner.

MARLAT, Nathan. Gunner.

MARTIN, Daniel. Gunner.

McCALPIN, Aaron. Gunner.

McCLELLAN, John. *1st Lieutenant*.

McCLLELAN, William. Gunner.

McCRACKEN, William. Gunner.

McMILLAN, John. Gunner.

MEDAUGH, Benjamin. Sergeant.

METLAR, Philip Jr. Gunner.

METLAR, Philip Sr. Gunner.
MORIS, Peter. Gunner.
NEVILLS, Abram. Gunner.
OSTRANDER, Thaddeus. Gunner.
OSTRANDER, Isaac. Gunner.
PEW, Robert. Gunner.
POTS, Jacob. Gunner.
RAMSDEN, John. Gunner.
RANNIE, John. Gunner.
SCOTT, John. Gunner.
SEABURN, Matthew. Gunner.
SKINER, Job. Gunner.
SKINNER, Colin. Gunner.
SKINNER, Haggai. Gunner.
SKINNER, Joel. Gunner.
SLAWSON, Henry. Gunner.
SMITH, Henry. Gunner.
SMITH, Joseph. Gunner.
SMITH, Simonson. Gunner.
SMITH, Lewis. Gunner.
SWARTS, Peter. Gunner.
SWAYZIE, Abrah. Gunner.
TOCK, John. Gunner.
TOLAS, Silas. Gunner.
VANDABURG, John. Gunner.
WARD, William. Gunner.
WEAVER, Jeremiah. Gunner.
WEAVER, William. Gunner.
WILKERSON, John. Sergeant.
WILLS, Daniel. Gunner.
WILLSON, Hugh. Gunner.
WINTERMUTE, Abraham. Gunner. See Casualties.
WOOLVERTON, Charles. Gunner.
WRIGHT, Peter. Gunner.

RIFLE COMPANIES

1ST YORK

This company was actively engaged throughout the 1812 campaign. Recruited by Captain Peter Robinson from the northerly part of York County, it included a large number of fur traders. Detachments served as far afield as Michilimakinac, Detroit and along the Niagara. They were reported to have fought at Detroit alongside their Native allies, dressed and painted accordingly.

ARNAUD, Antoine. Private.
BOILEAU, Francis. Private.

BOILS, John. Private.
BORLAND, Andrew. Sergeant. GSM, Fort Detroit.
BURKHOLDER, William. Private.
BURKHOLDER, John. Private
BURN, James. Private.
CHAPPEL, Joseph. Private.
CLANDENNING, Moses. Private.
COOPER, Thomas. Sergeant.
DAVIDSON, James. Private.
DELMAN, Nicholas. Private.
FLANNAGAN, John. Private.
FLURRY, Joseph. Private.
FREDOM, John. Private.
GRAHAM, Edward. Private.
HAYNES, Philip. Private.
HAYNES, John. Private.
HYLYARD, Leno. Private.
JOHNSTON, John. Private.
JOHNSTON, James. Private.
JOHNSTON, Cornelius. Private.
LABELLE, Joseph. Private.
LAMBERT, James. Private.
LAWRENCE, Peter. Private.
MACKLAN, Thomas. Private.
MARKLEM, James. Private.
McLELLAN, Thomas. Private.
McPHERSON, John. Private.
MILLER, Peter. Private.
ROBINSON, Peter. *Captain*.
ROSS, William. *Lieutenant*.
RUSH, William. Private.
RUSH, Peter. Private.
RYENOL, Jacob. Private.
SHEPHARD, Joseph. Private.
SISLAND, George. Private.
SOLES, David. Private.
TURENNE, Antoine. Private.
VANZANTE, John. Private.
WAGGONER, James. Private.
WELDEN, Nathaniel. Private.
WIDEMAN, Philip. Private.
WIDEMAN, Jacob. Private.
WIDEMAN, Lodowick. *Ensign*.
YEAGER, Jacob. Private. GSM, Fort Detroit.

Captain Bela Brewster Brigham, a lieutenant in an Oxford flank company, was permitted to raise a company in early November. It was on active service until the end of that season's campaign in the Fort Erie area.

ALLEN, James. Private.
ALLEN, Seneca. Sergeant.
AVERY, Abner. Private.
BOSTWICK, Gideon. Private.
BRIGHAM, B. Brewster. *Captain*. GSM, Fort Detroit.
CHAPIN, Elam. Private.
CLARK, John W. Private.
CRANDELL, William. Private.
DODGE, Adam. Private.
FASHLOW, James. Private.
POWLIN, Joseph. Private.
TEAPLE, William. Sergeant.
TEAPLE, Edward. Private.
FOWLER, Thomas. Private.
GATES, Henry. Private.
GILLIS, William. Private.
H?, Peter. Private.
HOUSE, Joseph. Sergeant.
JOHNSON, William. Private.
LANCE, Asa. Private. See Casualties.
LANE, George. Private. See 1st Oxford, 1st Flank Company.
MARTIN, Eliab. Private.
MATHER, Samuel. Private.
MILLER, David L. Private.
OMSTEAD, Isaac. Private.
OWENS, Abner. *Lieutenant*.
PANTLAND, William. Private. Deserted to the enemy.
SECORD, James. Private.
SMITH, Chancy. Private.
THOMPSON, Jonathan. Private.
THOMPSON, John. Private.
VANRARTURE, Peter. Private.
WARD, James. Private. See Casualties.

V

THE PROVINCIAL CORPS

THE distinction between the incorporated corps authorized by the Militia Act of 1813 and the provincial corps raised at about the same time is not clear now, and it does not appear to have been very clear at the time. On March 3, ten days prior to the passing of the Militia Act, authorization for the raising of a Troop of Provincial Royal Artillery Drivers, a Company of Provincial Artificers, and a Troop of Light Dragoons was published in the Militia General Orders. In some correspondence, note is made that these units were enlisted under the Articles of War, and so, presumably, not under the Militia Act. The corps that were authorized and raised included: The Niagara Provincial Light Dragoons, commanded by Captain William Hamilton Merritt; Provincial Royal Artillery Drivers, commanded by Captain Swayze; and the Corps of Artificers (the Coloured Corps), commanded by Lieutenant James Robertson. The Michigan Fencibles, and the Western Rangers may also have been considered provincial corps.

Designations were fluid and appear to have reflected the particular clerk's own usages as much as anything else. Of all the corps authorized, only Captain Merritt's was successful in raising the full complement of men called for.

From the Militia General Orders, it is clear that Sir Roger hoped to enlist, for the Provincial Royal Artillery Drivers, 3 commissioned officers and 119 non-commissioned officers and rank and file; for the Provincial Artificers, one commissioned officer and 54 non-commissioned officers and rank and file. As can be seen from the nominal returns, neither corps came close to filling its complement.

It is interesting to note that the Artificers, who would appear to have been all Black men, were paid between four and five times as much as their compatriots called out on regular militia duty.

The provincial corps are listed opposite, together with officers known to have acted or held commissions in them. Immediately following this brief guide is the nominal roll of the provincial corps.

PROVINCIAL CORPS AND OFFICERS

THE NIAGARA PROVINCIAL LIGHT DRAGOONS

Authorized March 3, 1813.
Captain William Hamilton Merritt. Discharged October 24, 1814.
Lieutenant Charles Ingersoll. Discharged October 24, 1814.
Cornet Amos McKenny. Promoted lieutenant and commanding officer (October 24, 1814).

THE ROYAL PROVINCIAL ARTILLERY DRIVERS (THE CAR BRIGADE)

Authorized March 3, 1813.
Captain Isaac Swayze
Lieutenant Robert Richardson. Joined 1814.
Lieutenant Alexander Askin. Transferred to Wagon Department, summer of 1813.
Lieutenant Peter Mann Ball
Lieutenant Charles Anderson

THE CORPS OF ARTIFICERS (THE COLOURED CORPS)

Authorized March 3, 1813.
Lieutenant James Robertson (sometimes Robinson)

NOMINAL ROLL OF THE PROVINCIAL CORPS

THE NIAGARA PROVINCIAL LIGHT DRAGOONS

The troop was put on strength April 24, 1813, and served until October 24, 1814, at which time it was reorganized and redesignated the Niagara Frontier Guides. It was actively engaged in the Niagara area.

ALLEN, Western. Private.
BENDER, John. Trumpeter. See Casualties.
BRADY, John. Private
BRETON, John. Private.
CAIN, John. Private.
CARR, James. Private.
CASSLEMAN, William. Private.
CASWELL, Nathan. Private. Discharged October 24, 1814.
CLEMENT, Paul. Private.
CLUTE, Henry. Private. Discharged October 24, 1814.
DAKINS, Amos. Private. Discharged October 24, 1814.
DEUCE, Frederick. Private.
DONALDSON, Andrew. Private.
DONE, Benjamin. Private.
DOWNS, Timothy. Private.
ELSWORTH, George. Private. Discharged October 24, 1814.
FIELDS, George. Sergeant Major. Discharged October 24, 1814.
FULLER, John. Private.
FURGASON, Hugh. Private.
GILLIS, Elias. Private.
HILTS, Joseph. Private.
HINDMAN, Robert. Private. *Sergeant.* (July 24, 1813).
    Discharged October 24, 1814.
HORTON, David. Private.
HUFFMAN, Godfrey. Private.
INGERSOLE, Charles. *Lieutenant.* Discharged October 24, 1814.
LAMBERT, William. Private.
LANE, Edward. Corporal.
LENCEBOUGH, Jacob. Private.
LOVE, Peter. Private.
McDONALD, David. Private.
McINTOSH, John. Private.
McINTOSH, Alexander. Private.
McKENNY, Amos. *Lieutenant* (October 24, 1814).

McKENNY, Dial. Sergeant.

McKENNY, Elijah Sergeant. Discharged October 24, 1814.

MEDEAUGH, Stephen. Private.

MERRITT, William Hamilton. *Captain*. See Casualties.
   Discharged October 24, 1814.

MILLARD, Jesse. Private. Discharged October 24, 1814.

MILLER, Peter. Private.

MOON, Richard. Private. Sergeant (February 31, 1814).

MOON, Edward. Corporal.

MORESY, Jacob. Private.

MYERS, Peter. Private.

NIGHTON, David. Corporal.

OSBORNE, William. Private.

POSTET, Francis. Private.

RICHARDSON, Joseph. Private.

ROGERS, John. Private.

SENN, Frederick. Private.

STANLEY, Lewis. Private. Discharged October 24, 1814.

STIVER, John. Private.

STIVER, Francis. Private. Discharged October 24, 1814.

SWAZY, Benjamin. Sergeant.

THADAWICK, Philip. Private.

TURREL, Uriah. Private.

TURREL, Jesse. Private. See 1st Middlesex Flank Company.

VANEVERY, David. Private.

WESTOVER, William. Private.

YEOCUM, George. Private.

YORK, Jeremiah. Private.

YOUNG, Henry. Private.

THE ROYAL PROVINCIAL ARTILLERY DRIVERS
(THE CAR BRIGADE)

The Car Brigade was organized immediately before the war. Those men who served in 1812, but apparently did not reenlist in the recon-situted corps of March 1813, designated as the Royal Provincial Artillery Drivers, and authorized as "provincial regulars," are denot-ed with an asterisk. A detachment under the command of Lieutenant A. D. Askin served at York through 1814.

ANDERSON, Charles. *Lieutenant*. Transfered to the Wagon
   Department, summer of 1813.

AURELL, Isaac. Private.

ASKIN, Alexander. *Lieutenant.*
BALL, Peter Mann. *Lieutenant.*
BARTOW, James. Private.
BENNET, James. Private.
BOND, Richard. Corporal.*
BROWN, Stephen. Sergeant.*
BUNBERGER, James. Driver.
CASSADY, Daniel. Staff Sergeant.
CAMPBELLE, James. Private.
CAMPLIN, John. Private.
CARMICHAEL, Dougal. Driver.
CARROL, Joseph. Collar Maker.
CARROL, William. Collar Maker.
CARROL, Thomas. Driver.
CLARK, John B. Driver.
CREECAR (Crucar), John. Private.
DEWGEAW, Lewis. Private.
FIELDS, Alexander. Corporal.*
GABRIEL, Joseph. Driver.*
HARE, George. Driver.
HARRINGTON, Seyrenns. Private.
HARRINGTON, Joshua. Private.
HARRINGTON, Jonathan. Private
HOSS, Philip. Private.
HOLLOCK, James. Private.
JERMAIN, Joseph. Driver.
LANGLEY, James. Driver*
LYON, James. Private.
McDONALD, Charles. Private.
OWLS, Gilbert. Driver.
PELKIE, Francis. Driver.
PETRIE, Philip. Smith.
RABBEE, John B. Private. See Casualties.
REVARD, Lewis. Driver.
RICHARDSON, Robert. *Lieutenant.* Joined 1814.
REES, James. Driver.
REES, John. Driver.
RIFENBURG, George. Private. See Casualties.
ROSS, James. Driver.
RYAN, Charles. Driver.
RYAN, John. Driver.
SECORD, James. Sergeant.*
SMITH, Simeon. Driver.

STEPHENSON, Samuel. Driver.
SUTS, John. Driver.
SWAYZE, Isaac. *Captain*.
TOCK, John. Private.
VAN KOVEN, Joseph. Driver.
VANITTAN, Peter. Driver.*
VOLLICK, Jacob. Driver.
WHELAN, Patrick. Driver.
WIERS, Charles. Driver.
WINTERBOTTOM, Samuel. Private. See Casualties.

THE CORPS OF ARTICIFERS
(THE COLOURED CORPS)

The Coloured Corps was a segregated company primarily recruited in the Niagara District. It was reported as actively engaged at Queenstown in 1812, but would appear to have become a labour company at some subsequent period.

The return made of the corps in 1820 indicates that the company was embodied under the command of Captain Robert Runchey (1st Lincoln) from October 24 to December 24, 1812. Lieutenant Robertson (sometimes Robinson) commanded the Provincial Corps of Artificers raised in March 1813, and it served at Burlington and Fort George until reduced in the spring of 1815. He had served at Black Rock under Bisshopp as the adjutant of militia.

The men who served in both companies are marked with an asterisk; those who served in the company embodied in the 1812 campaign but did not enlist in the provincial corps are marked with a cross; and the men who joined after March 1813 are not marked.

Curiously, of all the volunteer units, this company suffered from one of the highest rates of men deserting to the enemy. The officers were white.

BAKER, James. Private.*
BROWN, Caleb. Private.+
CAUL, John. Private.*
CAUL, Richard. Private.*
CAUL, Stephen. Private.*
CAUGHLY, Daniel. Private.+
CHRISLER, Thomas. Private.+
COLLINS, Richard. Private.*
CRISLAND (Chrysler), Robert. Private.*
DALLEY, John. Private.*
DARBY, Nathanial. Private.

EDMUNDS, Samuel. Private.
EDWARDS, Samuel. Private.+
FLEMMING, George. Private.
FREEMAN, George. Private.+
GARRISON, James. Private.
GOUGH, Edward. Sergeant.*
GREENE, John. Private.*
HAGAR, Henry. Private. Deserted to the enemy.
HARRIS, John. Private.*
HENRY, Prince. Private.
HUNT, Francis. Private.
HUTTS, Anthony. Private.* See Casualties.
JACKSON, Thomas. Private.*
JACKSON, John. No. 1 Private.* Deserted to the enemy.
JACKSON, John. No. 2 Private.*
JOHNSTONE, Michael. Private.*
JONES, William. Private.* Deserted to the enemy.
JUPITER, Robert. Private in 1812. Corporal.*
LEE, Isaac. Private.*
LEE, Peter. Private.*
MANDIGO, William. Private.*
MARTIN, George. Private.*
MONTGOMERY, John. Private.
PEARPOINT, Richard. Private.*
ROBERTSON (Robinson), James. *Lieutenant.*
RUNCHEY, Robert. *Captain.*+ Died in 1812.
RUNCHEY, George. *Lieutenant.*+
SAUNDERS, John. Private.*
SAUNDERSON, Robert. Private.*
SCOTT, Robert. Private.*
SHEPHERD, Richard. Private.*
SHEVALL, Baptiste. Private.
SLOAN, Abraham. Private.
SPENCER, William. Private. Deserted to the enemy.
STANSBERRY, James. Private.
THOMAS, Samuel. Private.*
THOMPSON, William. Private in 1812. Sergeant.*
VANPATTEN, John. Private in 1812. Corporal.*
WATERS, Humphrey. Corporal.+
WATTERS, James. Sergeant.*
WILSON, Francis. Corporal.+
WILLIS, Antrim. Private.+

VI

THE INCORPORATED
CORPS

BEATING orders were sent out in late March from the adjutant general's office at York to militia officers across the province. The most senior men who were invited to recruit for the incorporated corps were Colonels McLean, Sherwood, Clark and Claus. There is no evidence that the authorities expected to raise five or six regiments; these officers were simply invited to participate if they so wished.

At least two companies of Incorporated Militia Artillery were authorized, Captain Alexander Cameron's and 2nd Lieutenant William Munson Jarvis's, but the latter corps was disrupted while in the process of organization when York was taken, and though kept on the books into 1814, never amounted to an effective corps.

Two troops of Incorporated Militia Cavalry, or Provincial Dragoons, were raised in the Eastern and Johnstown Districts, Captain Richard Duncan Fraser's and Captain Andrew Adams's. In early September 1813, Lieutenant Colonel Thomas Pearson, the inspecting field officer stationed at Prescott, was ordered to amalgamate the two troops stationed there (Fraser's and Adams's) to make one effective corps.

Captain Andrew Adams's Troop had been embodied in the District of Johnstown from April 10 to September 24, 1813. It consisted of 3 commissioned officers, 4 non-commissioned officers and 48 privates, of whom only 19 privates elected to join

Captain Fraser's troop. The rest were simply returned to the rolls of the sedentary organization.

The incorporated companies and troops were assembled at the posts at Prescott, Kingston, York and Niagara and attached to the regular establishments at their respective posts: Fort Wellington, York, Fort George, Fort Erie and Chippewa.

Lieutenant Colonel Levius P. Sherwood raised the incorporated militia in the Johnstown District. In a return that he made on May 28, 1813, we can see something of the process in the assembling of the corps. He made a return of the number of recruits that had been engaged, and proposed a slate of officers as follows: Major Charles Jones (late Captain Troop of Dragoons). No. 1 Company: Captain Hamilton Walker (late captain, 2nd Grenville Flank Company); Lieutenant Henry Burritt (late lieutenant, 2nd Grenville Flank Company); Ensign Ziba M. Phillips (late sergeant, 2nd Grenville Flank Company). No. 2 Company: Captain Thomas Fraser (1st Grenville); Lieutenant Daniel Nettleton; Ensign John Kilbourn (late sergeant, 1st Leeds Flank Company). No. 3 Company: Captain Jonas Jones (late lieutenant, Captain Jones's Troop of Dragoons); Lieutenant William Morris (late ensign, 1st Leeds Flank Company); Ensign Alpheus Jones (late sergeant, Captain Jones's Troop of Dragoons). No. 4 Company: Captain Adiel Sherwood (late captain, 1st Leeds); Lieutenant Abraham Dayton (late ensign, 1st Leeds Flank Company); Ensign Duncan Carley (1st Leeds). No. 5 Company: Captain John Kerr (late ensign, 2nd Grenville Flank Company); Lieutenant John Fraser (late lieutenant, 1st Grenville Flank Company); Ensign John Fraser (late 1st Grenville).

Colonel Neil McLean, the officer commanding the Stormont Regiment, was given the responsibility for raising of the corps in the Eastern District. His first reports reveal a fairly good response to the recruiting drive, showing six companies formed and a seventh in the process of being filled up, as some 224 rank and file had been enlisted. In the late spring of 1813, the incorporated militia of the two districts were joined.

Lieutenant Colonel Sherwood was placed in overall command of the incorporated militia of the Eastern and Johnstown Districts when the two units were amalgamated at Fort Wellington (Prescott). On May 19 a total of 329 non-commissioned officers and rank and file, now organized into six companies, were reported to have joined the Eastern and Johnstown Incorporated Militia. The six companies were commanded by Captains John Fraser, Jonas Jones, Archibald McDonell, John McDonell, Archibald McLean, and John Kerr. All the other officers were deemed surplus to requirements and paid off.

The situation at Kingston is less clear. The incorporated corps were under the command of Lieutenant Colonel Allan MacLean as the senior militia officer of the garrison and the officer commanding the embodied militia on duty. However, he is listed as an officer of the incorporated corps in only one return, that of January 25 to February 24, 1814. Three infantry companies were formed at Kingston: Captain Daniel Washburn's, Captain Henry Davey's and Captain Edward Walker's.

The incorporated militia of the Home District was commanded by Major Allan (3rd York). At the time of the capitulation of York, there was a company of infantry in the process of organization under the command of Captain Jarvie, and a company of artillery commanded by 2nd Lieutenant William Munson Jarvis. By April 27, of the 75 men required by regulations, 64 had been enrolled by Major Allan, Captain William Jarvie, Lieutenant Thomas Humberstone, Lieutenant William Jarvis (the artillery company) and Ensign Daniel Brooks from the 3rd York. When York capitulated, 10 were taken prisoner to the United States and about 37 were paroled.

The men raised in the London and Niagara Districts were initially assembled at Fort George and Chippewa under the command of Major Titus G. Simons (2nd York) and Captain James Kerby (2nd Lincoln). Major Simons's pay started March 25, 1813, and he was joined by Captain Abraham A. Rapelje (1st Norfolk) on the 25th of May. Captain James Kerby's pay commenced April 3, 1813, and by April 24 his detachment consisted of 3 sergeants and 34 rank and file. All the divisions were withdrawn to Burlington Heights with the rest of the army after the fall of Fort George on May 27, 1813.

The same factors that frustrated the raising of companies in the Home District plagued the Niagara District. The American invasion in late May disrupted the efforts of the officers attempting to fill their quotas, and the very aggressive — and all-too-successful — American policy of seeking out unarmed men throughout the district to parole effectively neutralized even the loyal classes of the counties of Lincoln and parts of Haldimand and Wentworth.

In July, Major Simons's detachment was reorganized into three companies: Major Simons's, Captain James Kerby's and Captain Abraham A. Rapelje's. Captain Kerby's detachment had been added to the strength of the detachment at the end of June.

From a Militia General Order dated June 9, 1813, it would appear that beating orders had been issued in the Western District, but no record has as yet been found as to who was commissioned for that service, or indeed, if any men were ever actually enrolled. Major General Procter called in the arms of the militia in June of that year, so it is doubtful if any efforts were made to raise any men. The battalion companies were apparently not rearmed and called out on active service again until September 2, 1813. The records presumably were lost when the Right Division was destroyed at Moraviantown in October 1813.

On February 15 the incorporated militia in Kingston and Prescott were ordered to march to York to join the companies of the Niagara and Home Districts at York. The Niagara companies arrived on the 18th, and the rest in mid-March.

General Drummond took a number of steps to improve the efficiency of the corps in early March. On March 5 he ordered Captain William Robinson of the 8th or King's Regiment to take command of the battalion with the rank of lieutenant colonel in the militia. This was dated from the 25th of February. In addition, Adjutant Fitzgerald, Quarter Master George Thrower and Sergeant Major Robinson, all from the 41st, were ordered to serve with the Incorporated Battalion. The following month, on April 25, Lieutenant Kemble of the Glengarry Light Infantry was appointed paymaster, and Grant Powell, surgeon.

The different companies were assembled at York in March 1814 and were organized into 13 companies: The Artillery Company (Lieutenant Jarvis's), No. 1; Major Titus G. Simons's, No. 2; Captain James Kerby's, No. 3; Captain William Jarvie's, No. 4; Captain Abraham A. Rapelje's, No. 5; Captain Daniel Washburn's, No. 6; Captain Henry Davy's, No. 7; Captain Edward Walker's, No. 8; Captain Archibald McLean's, No. 9; Captain Thomas Fraser's, No. 10; Captain John Kerr's, No. 11; Captain

John McDonell's, No. 12; and Captain Hamilton Walker's. Captain Cameron's Company of Incorporated Artillery and Captain Swayze's Company of Provincial Artillery Drivers remained stationed at Burlington and Niagara. Captain Richard Duncan Fraser's Troop of Provincial Dragoons remained stationed in the Johnstown and Eastern Districts, and Captain Merritt's in the Niagara and London Districts.

Lieutenant Jarvis's Artillery Company was reduced and the remaining men transferred to Captain Jarvie's Infantry Company. The infantry companies were reorganized and reduced in number to ten in April. Major Simons's (No. 1) and Captain Davy's (No. 6) were disbanded and the rank and file redistributed. Captain Davy was apparently paid off and returned to Kingston, where he was immediately attached to the embodied militia at that post, and Ensign Robins of Davy's Company was appointed to Captain Washburn's. Major Simons gave up his company, taking field rank in the battalion; Lieutenant William Chisholm went to Captain Kerby's; Ensign John Lampman to Captain Jarvie's; and Ensign Walter Wm. Simons to Captain Walker's. A number of men returned as unfit were discharged on April 5.

Major Simons's Company consisted of 19 rank and file on March 25, 1814. One corporal and two privates deserted March 25; nine more deserted on April 10. Captain Davy's Company proved slightly more accommodating to their change of status; only 6 of the 28 rank and file deserted. Perhaps the fact that they would have had a longer walk (to Frontenac instead of Wentworth) dissuaded them. Most of these men later returned; whether or not of their own volition isn't clear.

In a letter to the adjutant general, Lieutenant Colonel Colley Lucas Foster, dated April 2, Robinson complained that he been able "to make but small progress in the Training of the Militia." Some 46 men had been sent to the artillery and 22 in bateaux to Fort George, and of the remainder, by the time the paroled men working in the commissary and the sick were deducted, there were hardly enough men left for the officers to learn their own duties, let alone train the men in theirs.

The battalion was then composed of ten companies. A change had been made in the field officers of the battalion when Major Simons resigned in June as a result of an altercation in the officers' mess on June 4 and was replaced by Captain James Kerby on July 1. As a result, No. 1 Company was vacant and was commanded by the subaltern, Lieutenant Hamilton.

On June 29, a few days before the Incorporated Battalion was ordered to Niagara, the attached embodied militia were invited to volunteer to go with them to the front lines. A surprising number did. For example, of the 40 privates attached to Captain Kerby's Company, 10 volunteered; of the 40 attached to Captain Jarvie's, 15 volunteered.

The battalion that formed on the field at Lundy's Lane consisted of just under 400 men, all ranks. Of the 294 rank and file present, 16 percent were volunteers from the embodied militia serving in York. Forty other men were noted as sick or on command at York or Prescott.

Note is often made regarding the preponderance of the American-born inhabitants in Upper Canada in the early part of the century. While it is impossible to present an authoritative statement, from the returns of the incorporated companies that have survived we can at the least get a glimpse of the backgrounds of a narrow segment of one particular population — those who served with the incorporated militia — through to the end of the war. The largest single identifiable segment who served were born in the United States in the 1790s. The next largest group were Upper Canadians, and the third were Lower Canadians. The men born in the United Kingdom were an insignificant element in the general mix, comprising at best two or three percent of the whole.

Captain Edward Walker's No. 3 Company, for example, had about 40 percent American-born, 26 percent Upper Canadian, 26 percent Lower Canadian, and the balance from other colonies and the United Kingdom. The farther west, the higher the percentage of American-born. In Captain Jarvie's Company, raised for the most part in the Home District, of the men who served to the end of the war, about three quarters were American-born — that is to say, they can not even by the loosest definition be considered late Loyalists.

Drummond wrote to Sir George Prevost on August 12, "that these two corps [the Glengarry Light Infantry and the Battalion of Incorporated Militia] have constantly been in close contact with the enemy's outposts and riflemen during severe service of the last fortnight and their steadiness and gallantry as well as their superiority as light troops have on every occasion been conspicuous."

While Colonel Robinson remained in titular command of the battalion, he had been severely wounded at Lundy's Lane, and as a result Captain Peter Gibson of the Glengarry Light Infantry was ordered to take immediate command of the battalion on September 1, 1814. On November 5, Colonel John P. Tucker of the 41st was ordered to take the place of Lieutenant Colonel Robinson, who was accompanying his regiment (the 8th, or King's) to Lower Canada. Colonel Tucker was in turn replaced by Captain Glew of the 41st, with the rank of lieutenant colonel, on February 4, 1815.

In late September, 42 of the embodied militia attached to the Incorporated Battalion were discharged and returned to York. The other five either joined or had become casualties over the course of the summer.

On the 10th of October the battalion was withdrawn from its advanced position behind Black Creek and posted with the 6th Foot at Weishuhn's farm, in the fork between Lyon's Creek and the Chippewa. They eventually were withdrawn and went into winter quarters at York, where they were to remain until reduced.

Attention turned once again to recruiting in early 1815 and new orders were issued respecting the bounty to be paid. On the 25th of February, 1815, the Loyal Kent Volunteers was attached to the battalion, but this was to prove a short-lived connection, as the entire battalion was paid off within a month.

General Drummond was highly appreciative of the utility of the battalion and strongly suggested that it be maintained. In addition, given the nature of its contribution to the campaign in 1814, Drummond expressed his desire that it be uniformed in green and designated a rifle corps, to act as light troops, in the same way as the Glengarry Fencibles. In the retrenchment that swiftly followed the cessation of hostilities, Horse Guards deemed otherwise.

The battalion was paid off on March 24, 1815. They were singled out in the Militia General Order of March 15 and were awarded pay for the ensuing month (until April 24), free of deductions for rations. The provincial legislature granted them a gratuity of six months' pay to the whole corps. Swords of honour were sanctioned and presented by the legislature to Colonel Robinson (100 guineas) and Major Kerby (50 guineas). General Drummond, in a last public testimonial, ordered:

> His Honour, the President cannot dismiss that truly deserving Corps, the Battalion of Incorporated Militia, without expressing his warmest approbation of their bravery, steadiness and uniform good conduct on all occasions as the strongest instance of which he had already made application for colours to be granted them by His Majesty's Government upon which and upon their appointments His Honour likewise had humbly solicited the Royal permission that the word *Niagara* might be borne in testimony of His Royal Highness the Prince Regent's gracious consideration of their merits.

On St. George's Day, 1822, seven years after the Battalion of Incorporated Militia had been paid off, colours were presented to an honour guard drawn from the York Militia.

The incorporated corps are listed opposite, together with officers known to have acted in them. This brief guide is followed by a roll of the commissioned officers of the Battalion of Incorporated Militia, and then a review of the chain of succession of the corps, and finally, the nominal roll of the incorporated corps.

INCORPORATED CORPS AND OFFICERS

PROVINCIAL LIGHT DRAGOONS 1813–1814

Captain Richard Duncan Fraser
Lieutenant Allan Grant
Lieutenant Peter Shaver
Cornet George Ault

Captain Andrew Adams
Lieutenant Solomon Snyder
Cornet William Forister

THE PROVINCIAL ARTILLERY COMPANY

Captain Alexander Cameron
Lieutenant John McKinny

BATTALION OF INCORPORATED MILITIA

Commissioned Officers

APPLEGARTH, John. *Ensign* (May 10, 1813).
BURRIT, Henry. *Lieutenant* (November 20, 1813).
CAMPBELL, John. *Ensign*.
CHISHOLM, William. *Lieutenant*.
CLARKE, Duncan. *Lieutenant* (April 15, 1813).
DAVEY (Davy), Henry. *Captain*.
FRASER, Thomas. *Captain* (April 13, 1813).
FRASER, John. *Lieutenant* (April 16, 1813).
FRASER, John. *Ensign* (April 16, 1813).
HAMILTON, James. *Lieutenant* (April 26, 1813). *Captain* (January, 1815).
JARVIS, William. *Lieutenant* (December 25, 1814).
KERBY, George. *Ensign* (April 29, 1813).
KERBY, James. *Captain* (1813). *Major* (July 1, 1814).
KERR, John. *Captain* (May 16, 1813).
KILBOURNE, John. *Ensign* (April 17, 1813).
LAMPMAN, John. *Ensign* (March 26, 1813).
McCOLLUM, Peter. *Lieutenant*.
McDONELL, John. *Captain* (June 15, 1813).
McDONELL, John. *Ensign*.
McDONELL, Duncan. *Lieutenant* (April 6, 1813).
McDOUGALL, Daniel. *Lieutenant* (March 30, 1813).

McLEAN, Archibald. *Captain* (April 14, 1813).

PHILIPS, Ziba M. *Ensign* (March 25, 1813).

RAPELJE, Abraham A. *Captain* (April 24, 1813).

ROBINS, Henry. *Ensign* January 25 to Febuary 24, 1813.

ROSE, Alexander. *Lieutenant* (April 2, 1813).

RUTTAN, Henry. *Lieutenant* (April 24, 1813).

RYERSON, George. *Lieutenant* (April 21, 1813).

SERVOS, Daniel K. *Ensign*.

SHORT, Charles. *Ensign* (April 26, 1813).

SIMONS, Walter W. *Ensign* (October 25, 1813).

WALKER, Edward. *Captain*.

WALKER, Hamilton. *Captain* (June 16, 1813).

WARFFE, Andrew W. *Ensign* (March 27, 1813).

WASHBURN Daniel. *Captain* (April 7, 1813).

SUCCESSION OF INCORPORATED CORPS

Cavalry

Captain Andrew Adams's. Reduced and amalgamated with
    Captain Fraser's.

Captain Richard Duncan Fraser's. Reduced at the end of the war.

Artillery

Captain Alexander Cameron's. Reduced at the end of the war.

2nd Lieutenant W. M. Jarvis's. Reduced February 25, 1814, and men
    transferred to the Incorporated Battalion.

Infantry

Captain Henry Davy's. Reduced and men transferred.

Captain Thomas Fraser's No. 7 Company

Captain William Jarvie's No. 2 Company

Captain Jonas Jones's. Reduced and men transferred.

Captain James Kerby's No. 1 Company

Captain John Kerr's No. 8 Company

Captain John McDonell's No. 9 Company

Captain Archibald McLean's No. 6 Company

Captain John McLean's. Reduced and men transferred.

Captain Abraham Rapelje's No. 3 Company

Major Titus G. Simons. Reduced and men transferred.

Captain Edward Walker's No. 5 Company

Captain Hamilton Walker's No. 10 Company

Captain Daniel Washburn's No. 4 Company

NOMINAL ROLL OF THE INCORPORATED CORPS

DISTRICT OF JOHNSTOWN PROVINCIAL LIGHT DRAGOONS

CAPTAIN R. D. FRASER'S TROOP

Two troops of Light Dragoons were raised in the Johnstown District in the spring of 1813 and were mustered as a part of the Eastern and Johnstown Incorporated Militia. At the suggestion of the inspecting field officer, Lieutenant Colonel Pearson, they were amalgamated in the fall of 1813 under the command of Captain Richard Duncan Fraser. They were on active service until the end of the war, when they were reduced. The troop was broken into small detachments scattered from Kingston to the Lower Province and served as dispatch riders. A small detachment was present at Chrysler's Farm in November 1813.

AVECKCHOUSER, Godfrey. Private. See Captain Adam's Troop.
AULT, Michael. Private.
AULT, George. *Cornet.*
BAKER, John. Private. See Captain Adam's Troop.
BESONEY, Joseph. Private.
BOICE, Joseph. Private.
BOICE, James. Private.
BONE, Peter. Private.
BRINKMAN, John. Private.
BROUCE, Jacob. Private.
BROUSE, Nicholas. Private.
BROWNELL, John. Private.
CALLISON, James. Private.
CAMERON, Duncan. Private. See Captain Adam's Troop.
CARMAN, John. Private. See Captain Adam's Troop.
COLE, Jonathan. Private.
COLE, Titus. Private. See Captain Adam's Troop.
COONS, John. Private.
COONS, Jacob. Private.
DOHERTY, John. Private.
DORIN, Peter. Private.
DULMAGE, Jacob. Sergeant.
FALKNER, Samuel. Private.
FARKNER, William. Private.

FARKNER, Ralph. Private.
FORRESTER, John. Private. See Captain Adam's Troop.
FOSTER, John. Private. See Captain Adam's Troop.
FRASER, Richard Duncan. *Captain.*
FREECE, David. Private.
FREECE, Peter. Private.
FREECE, Nicholas. Private.
FREECE, Michael. Private.
FULFORD, Abel. Sergeant.
GALE, Henry. Farrier. Did no duty as farrier but as sergeant.
GLASFORD, Little. Private.
GODDARE, Lewis. Private. See Captain Adam's Troop.
GRANT, Allan. *Lieutenant.*
GRAUBARIGEN, Andrew. Private.
GRIFFIN, Isaiah. Private.
HAWLEY, Truman. Private.
HAY, Jacob. Private.
HOLENBECK, Jacob. Private.
HOLMES, Joseph. Private.
HUNTER, Jonathan. Private.
JOHNSTON, William. Private.
KEELER, Frederick. Troop Sergeant Major.
KING, Jacob. Private. See Captain Adam's Troop.
KINTNER, Frederick. Private.
KINTNER, Conrad. Private.
LAJAY, Joseph. Private.
LANDOU, John. Private.
LENNOX, James. Private.
LINK, Mathias. Private.
LINK, Jacob. Private.
LORIMEAR (Larimea), Francis. Private. See Captain Adam's Troop.
LOUX, John. Sergeant.
MABY, Frederick. Private.
McDONELL, John. Private.
McDONELL, Adam. Private.
McDONELL (McDonald), Samuel. Private. See Captain Adam's Troop.
McLAUGHLIN, William. Private.
McPHERSON, Donald. Private.
MELOY, John. Private.
MONRO, Samuel. Private. See Captain Adam's Troop.
PARKER, James. Private. See Captain Adam's Troop.

PARKER, John. Private.

PENOE, Nathaniel. Private. See Captain Adam's Troop.

PROCTOR, Joseph. Private. See Captain Adam's Troop.

ROBINSON, William. Private.

SEALY, David. Private.

SHAVER, Peter. *Lieutenant.*

SHAVER, Johon. Private.

SHAVER, Edward. Private.

SMYTH, James. Private.

SMYTH, John. Private.

STAMP, Jacob. Private.

SUMMERS, Andrew. Private.

VANHOWTON, Halmes. Private.

WELCH, John. Private. See Captain Adam's Troop.

YOUNG, David. Private.

CAPTAIN ANDREW ADAM'S TROOP

Served in Johnstown from April 10, 1813, to September 24, 1813. Amalgamated with Captain Richard Duncan Fraser's Troop, September 25, 1813.

ADAMS, Andrew. *Captain.* 1st Grenville.

AULT, John. Sergeant.

AVECKCHOUSER, Godfrey. Private. Joined Captain Fraser's Troop.

BAKER, John. Private. Joined Captain Fraser's Troop.

BEACH, Lavel. Private.

BOICE, Matthew. Private.

BOYCE, James. Private.

BROWNSON, George. Private.

CAMERON, Duncan. Private. Joined Captain Fraser's Troop.

CAMPBELL, James. Private.

CARMON, John. Private. Joined Captain Fraser's Troop.

CLEMENT, Philip. Sergeant.

COLE, Titus. Private. Joined Captain Fraser's Troop.

COOK, Michael. Private.

CULBREATH, James. Private.

EVERTS, William. Sergeant Major.

FORESTER, John. Private. Joined Captain Fraser's Troop.

FORESTER, Gabriel. Private.

FORISTER, William. Cornet.

FOSTER, John. Private. Joined Captain Fraser's Troop.

FULFORD, Abel. Sergeant.

GODARE, Lewis. Private. Joined Captain Fraser's Troop.

GRIFFEN, Isaiah. Private.

HAINES, John. Private.

HUNTER, Jonathan. Private.

JOHNSON, William. Private.

KING, Stephen. Private.

KING, Jacob. Private. Joined Captain Fraser's Troop.

LANDEN, Daniel J. Private.

LANINIGOR, Frederick. Private. Deserted to the enemy.

LARIMEA, Francis. Private. Joined Captain Fraser's Troop.

LARUE, Crinies. Private.

LARUE, James. Private.

LEONARD, Nathaniel. Private.

MATTISON, Jesse. Private.

McDONALD, James. Private.

McDONALD, Samuel. Private. Joined Captain Fraser's Troop.

McDONELL, Andrew. Private.

MONRO, Samuel. Private. Joined Captain Fraser's Troop.

MOSHER, Thomas. Private.

PARKER, John. Private.

PARKER, James. Private. Joined Captain Fraser's Troop.

PENOE, Nathaniel. Private. Joined Captain Fraser's Troop.

PLUMB, Augustus. Private.

PROCTOR, John. Private.

PROCTOR, Joseph. Private. Joined Captain Fraser's Troop.

SEMORE, Peter. Private.

SHEAVER, George H. Private.

SNYDER, Solomon. *Lieutenant*. 1st Grenville.

STONE, Ransom. Private.

THOMAS, Samuel. Private.

VANDOSER, Peter. Private.

WELCH, John. Private. Joined Captain Fraser's Troop.

WOOLEY, Henry. Private.

THE PROVINCIAL ARTILLERY COMPANY

Captain Alexander Cameron was invited to recruit a provincial artillery company in March, 1813. It served throughout the war between Burlington and Niagara and was reduced in the spring of 1815.

ANGER, Philip. Private.

ARMSTRONG, Edward. Sergeant.

BACCHUS, Osias. Gunner. Missing after the battle of Fort George.

BENEDICT, Horace. Bombardier.

BOURDEAUX, John. Gunner. Deserted a short time before peace.

BOWEN, Cornelius. Gunner.

BRETTON, Benjamin. Private. Deserted from Burlington Heights.

CAINE, John. Gunner. Deserted and went to the United States.

CAMERON, Alexander. *Captain.*

CAMPBELL, John. Gunner. See Casualties.

CARPENTER, Ashman. Private. Deserted to the enemy and enlisted in the Canadian Regiment.

CASSADA, Abner. Gunner.

COLE, John. Gunner.

CROLLY, John. Gunner.

DOBIE, James. Gunner.

FIELD, Alexander. Gunner.

FRISEMAN, John. Gunner.

FULLER, John. Gunner.

GRAHAM, Henry. Gunner. Deserted and went to the United States.

HASPLEHEM, George. Gunner. See Casualties.

HOLLIDAY, John. Gunner. See Casualties.

HUGHSON, Robert. Corporal.

LOWE, William. Sergeant.

McDONELL, Roderick. Gunner.

McKINNY, John. *Lieutenant.* Deserted, but apparently not to the enemy.

MILLER (Millen), Conrad. Gunner.

MONTRASS, Benjamin. Gunner. See Casualties. See Battalion of Incorporated Militia.

ROGERS, John. Gunner.

STEVENS, Henry. Gunner.

VROOMAN, Adam. Gunner.

WHEELAN, Patrick. Gunner.

WINTERBOTTOM, Samuel. Gunner. See Casualties.

BATTALION OF INCORPORATED MILITIA

The date of enlistment, the name of officer commanding the incorporated company, initial rank and the company of the Battalion of Incorporated Militia is given where known. If the man served until the end of the war, he was given a regular discharge. If note is not made of being entered on the Incorporated Roll, the man either had deserted or had died.

Information found in this roll is entered chronologically. Where known, the name of the corps in which the militiaman previously served is noted in parentheses. The incorporated militia was raised by company, and in the spring of 1814, reorganized and consolidated into one battalion. Note is made, where known, of the company in which each man enrolled, and a separate note made of the company in the battalion.

ACRE, Peter. Joined March 25, 1813, Major Titus G. Simons's Company. Private. Captain Abraham A. Rapelje's No. 3 Company. Prisoner of war. Discharged and entered on Incorporated Roll.

ADKINS, Daniel Allen. Joined April 12, 1813, Captain Washburn's Company. Sergeant. Discharged March 25, 1815, and entered on Incorporated Roll.

AEQUETTE, Pierre. Private. See Casualties.

AIREHART, William. (1st Addington Flank Company) Captain Henry Davy's Company. Private.

ALBRANT, Henry. Joined before June 25, 1813, Captain John McDonell's Company. Sergeant. Captain John McDonell's No. 9 Company. Discharged March 24, 1815, and entered on Incorporated Roll.

ALCOT, Henry. (1st Addington Flank Company) Joined April 28, 1813. Captain Washburn's Company. Private. Captain Daniel Washburn's No. 4 Company. Discharged and entered on Incorporated Roll.

ALDRIDGE, Thomas. Captain Henry Davy's. Private. Captain Daniel Washburn's No. 4 Company. Discharged and entered on Incorporated Roll.

ALLEN, John. Captain Daniel Washburn's Company. Returned March 10, 1815, as deserted.

ALTHOUSE, Andrew. Captain Edward Walker's Company. Private. Captain Edward Walker's No. 5 Company. Discharged and entered on Incorporated Roll.

AMABLE, Joseph. Private. Captain Hamilton Walker's No. 10 Company.

ANDERSON, Anthony. Joined April 26, 1813, Captain Rapelje's Company. Private. No. 3 Company. Discharged and entered on Incorporated Roll.

ANDERSON, George. Joined April 10, 1813, Captain Jarvie's Company. Private. Captain William Jarvie's No. 2 Company. Prisoner of war. Discharged and entered on Incorporated Roll.

ANDERSON, Martin. Joined April 25, 1813, Captain Kerby's Company. Sergeant. Captain James Kerby's No. 1 Company. Discharged and entered on Incorporated Roll.

APPLE, Christopher. Captain Fraser's Company of Incorporated Miltia. Private. Joined before June 25, 1813, and last noted February 25, 1814.

ARCHAMBO, Louis. Captain Edward Walker's Company. Private. Captain Edward Walker's No. 5 Company. Discharged and entered on Incorporated Roll.

ARMSTRONG, Thomas. Joined May 6, 1813, Captain Henry Davy's Company. Private. Noted as absent without leave May 22, 1813.

AVIKHOUSER (Avichouser), Christian (Christopher). Private. Captain Hamilton Walker's No. 10 Company. Discharged March 24, 1815, and entered on Incorporated Roll.

AVICKHOUSER, John. Captain Fraser's Company. Private. Captain Thomas Fraser's No. 7 Company.

AXLEY, Jacob. Captain Jarvie's Company. Private. Discharged April 5, 1814, as unfit.

BADGEROW, Francis H. Captain Fraser's Company. Private. Corporal (September 25, 1813). Private. Captain Thomas Fraser's No. 7 Company. Discharged March 24, 1815, and entered on Incorporated Roll.

BARBO, Joseph. Captain Fraser's Company. Private. Captain Thomas Fraser's No. 7 Company. Discharged March 24, 1815, and entered on Incorporated Roll.

BARKER, William. Captain Henry Davy's Company. Corporal. Demoted Private. Deserted March 26, 1814.

BARKLEY, Jacob. Joined April 12, 1813, Captain John Kerr's Company. Private. Returned March 9, 1815, as deserted.

BARKLEY, Michael. Captain Fraser's Company. Private. Captain Thomas Fraser's No. 7 Company. Prisoner of war. Discharged March 24, 1815, and entered on Incorporated Roll.

BARRICKER (Barager), Jacob. Captain Fraser's Company. Private. Captain Thomas Fraser's No. 7 Company. Discharged March 24, 1815, and entered on Incorporated Roll.

BARTON, Joseph. Captain Fraser's Company. Private. Captain Thomas Fraser's No. 7 Company. Discharged March 24, 1815, and entered on Incorporated Roll.

BARTRAND, John. Captain Jonas Jones's Company. Drummer. Captain Archibald McLean's No. 6 Company.

BARTROW (Bartrand), Justin (Justice). Captain Fraser's Company. Private. Captain Thomas Fraser's No. 7 Company. Discharged March 24, 1815, and entered on Incorporated Roll.

BASTIAN, Joseph. Joined April 2, 1813, Captain John Kerr's Company. Private. Returned March 9, 1815, as deserted.

BAXTER, Daniel. Joined before June 25, 1813, Captain John McLean's Company. Private.

BAXTER, Donald. Captain John McDonell's Company. Private. Discharged April 5, 1814.

BAXTER, William. Joined before June 25, 1813, Captain John McLean's Company. Corporal. No. 10 Company. Prisoner of war. Discharged March 24, 1815, and entered on Incorporated Roll.

BEACH, Abraham. Captain Fraser's Company. Corporal.

BEAUDVIN (Bodwan, Bodvin), Alexis (Alexander). Joined March 28, 1813, Captain John Kerr's Company. Private. Captain John Kerr's No. 8 Company. Discharged March 24, 1815, and entered on Incorporated Roll.

BEAUPRE, Louis. Captain Archibald McLean's Company. Private. Captain Archibald McLean's No. 6 Company. Prisoner of war. Discharged March 24, 1815, and entered on Incorporated Roll.

BEAUPRE, Peter. Captain Archibald McLean's Company. Private. Captain Archibald McLean's No. 6 Company. Discharged March 24, 1815, and entered on Incorporated Roll.

BEERS, John. Captain Abraham Rapelje's Company. Private. Sergeant.

BEGGS, Alexander. Captain Kerby's Company. Private. Captain James Kerby's No. 1 Company.

BELCHER, John. Joined March 24, 1813. Private. From Lieutenant Jarvis's Artillery Company. Captain William Jarvie's No. 2 Company. Discharged March 24, 1815, and entered on Incorporated Roll.

BELLAMERE, Antoine. Joined before June 25, 1813, Captain John McLean's Company. Private. Captain Fraser's Company. Captain Thomas Fraser's No. 7 Company. Discharged March 24, 1815, and entered on Incorporated Roll.

BELLOIRE (Belore, Belard), Stephen. Joined March 15, 1813, Captain Donald McAulay's Company. Joined before June 25, 1813, Captain John McDonell's Company. Private. Captain John Kerr's No. 8 Company. Discharged March 24, 1815, and entered on Incorporated Roll. See Casualties.

BENJAMIN, Elias. Captain Jarvie's Company. Private. Returned March 9, 1815, as deserted.

BENJAMIN, John. Captain Jonas Jones's Company. Private.

BENSON, Patrick. Joined before June 25, 1813, Captain John McLean's Company. Private. Sergeant. Captain John McDonell's No. 9 Company. Quarter Master Sergeant. Discharged March 24, 1815, and entered on Incorporated Roll.

BERDAN (Burdan), Albert. Joined June 25, 1813, Private Captain Rapelje's Company. Captain Abraham A. Rapelje's No. 3 Company. Prisoner of war. Discharged March 24, 1815, and entered on Incorporated Roll.

BERDAN, John. (1st Addington Flank Company) Joined April 22, 1813. Captain Washburn's Company. Private. Captain Daniel Washburn's No. 4 Company. Discharged March 24, 1815, and entered on Incorporated Roll.

BERNIER (Bornier), Lewis (Louis). Joined March 23, 1813, Captain John Kerr's Company. Private. Captain John Kerr's No. 8 Company. Discharged March 24, 1815, and entered on Incorporated Roll.

BERRY, Emanuel. Captain Edward Walker's Company. Corporal. Captain Edward Walker's No. 5 Company. Discharged March 24, 1815, and entered on Incorporated Roll.

BERTRAND, A. Private. Discharged March 24, 1815, and entered on Incorporated Roll.

BERTRAM (Bertrand), John. Captain Archibald McLean's Company. Drummer. Discharged March 24, 1815, and entered on Incorporated Roll. See Casualties.

BICKHAM, William. Captain Fraser's Company. Private. Drummer. Captain Thomas Fraser's No. 7 Company. Discharged March 24, 1815, and entered on Incorporated Roll.

BIGELOW, Levi (Lewis). Joined April 7, 1813, Captain Daniel Washburn's Company. Sergeant. Captain Daniel Washburn's No. 4 Company. Discharged March 24, 1815, and entered on Incorporated Roll.

BILOW, Michael. Captain Fraser's Company. Private. Discharged April 5, 1814.

BISHOP, Abner. Joined March 20, 1813. Captain Kerr's Company. Private. Captain John Kerr's No. 8 Company. Discharged March 24, 1815, and entered on Incorporated Roll.

BISSELL, Erastus. Joined March 18, 1813. Captain Henry Davy's Company. Corporal. Captain Daniel Washburn's No. 4 Company. Discharged March 24, 1815, and entered on Incorporated Roll.

BISSELL, Gilbert. (2nd Grenville Flank Company) Captain Henry Davy's Company. Private. Captain Edward Walker's No. 5 Company.

BLAIR, John. Joined April 1, 1813, Captain John Kerr's Company. Corporal. Captain John Kerr's No. 8 Company. Discharged March 24, 1815, and entered on Incorporated Roll.

BLONDOO, Joseph. Captain Fraser's Company. Private.

BODREAU, (Budreau) Baptiste. Captain Henry Davy's Company. Private. Discharged April 5, 1814.

BOICE, Joseph. (1st Addington Flank Company) Joined March 30, 1813. Captain Daniel Washburn's Company. Corporal. Captain Daniel Washburn's No. 4 Company. Sergeant. Discharged March 24, 1815, and entered on Incorporated Roll.

BOSCALIE (Bosoliel), John B. Captain Washburn's Company. Private. Captain Daniel Washburn's No. 4 Company. Discharged March 24, 1815, and entered on Incorporated Roll.

BOSOLIEL, Samuel. Captain Edward Walker's Company. Private. Captain Edward Walker's No. 5 Company.

BOUCHER (Bucher), Francis. Joined March 27, 1813, Captain John Kerr's Company. Private. See Bushet.

BOWEN, Peter. Joined April 20, 1813. Captain Washburn's Company. Private. Captain Daniel Washburn's No. 4 Company. Discharged March 24, 1815, and entered on Incorporated Roll.

BOYLE (Bylo, Boileau), Michael Sr. Private. Joined before June 25, 1813, Captain John McLean's Company. Private. Captain Hamilton Walker's No. 10 Company. Discharged March 24, 1815, and entered on Incorporated Roll.

BOYLE, Michael Jr. Joined before June 25, 1813, Captain John McLean's Company. Private.

BRADT, Manuel. Major Titus G. Simons's Company. Private. Drummer. Captain James Kerby's No. 1 Company. Discharged March 24, 1815, and entered on Incorporated Roll.

BRASS, John. (1st Addington Flank Company) Joined May 21, 1813, Captain Henry Davy's Company. Private. Captain Edward Walker's No. 5 Company.

BROCK, Francis. Joined March 20, 1813, Captain Jarvie's Company. Corporal. Captain William Jarvie's No. 2 Company. Private. Discharged March 24, 1815, and entered on Incorporated Roll.

BROCK, William. Captain Jarvie's Company. Private. Captain William Jarvie's No. 2 Company. Discharged March 24, 1815, and entered on Incorporated Roll.

BROOKS, Barns. Joined before April 25, Captain Kerby's Company. Private.

BROOKS, John. Captain Kerby's Company. Private. Captain James Kerby's No. 1 Company. Discharged March 24, 1815, and entered on Incorporated Roll.

BROUGHTON, Asa. Major Titus G. Simons's Company. Private. Noted as deserted April 10, 1814.

BROWN, John. Captain Kerby's Company. Private. Captain James Kerby's No. 1 Company. Prisoner of war. Discharged March 24, 1815, and entered on Incorporated Roll.

BRUCE, John. Captain Jonas Jones's Company. Private. Discharged March 24, 1815, and entered on Incorporated Roll.

BRYANT (Boyant), John. Captain Kerr's Company. Private. Corporal. Captain Thomas Fraser's No. 7 Company. Discharged March 24, 1815, and entered on Incorporated Roll. See Casualties.

BUELL, Renaldo. Captain John McLean's Company. Private.

BULLIS, William. Joined March 28, 1813. Private. Captain John Kerr's No. 8 Company. Discharged March 24, 1815, and entered on Incorporated Roll.

BUNDAY, Willard. Joined May 6, 1813, Captain Henry Davy's Company. Private. Noted as absent without leave May 22, 1813.

BURK, William. Captain Washburn's Company. Private.

BURNS, David. Major Titus G. Simons's Company. Drummer. Captain Abraham A. Rapelje's No. 3 Company. Discharged March 24, 1815, and entered on Incorporated Roll.

BURNS, (Bern) Patrick. Captain Jarvie's Company. Private. Discharged April 5, 1814, as unfit.

BUSHET (Bushey, Bushee), Francis. Captain John Kerr's Company. Private. Captain John Kerr's No. 8 Company. Discharged March 24, 1815, and entered on Incorporated Roll.

BUTLER, John. (2nd Norfolk) Private. Joined June 25, Captain Rapelje's Company. Discharged March 24, 1815, and entered on Incorporated Roll.

CABACIER, Pierre (Peter). Enlisted June 9, 1813, in Captain Henry Davy's Company. Private. Captain Edward Walker's No. 5 Company. Prisoner of war. Discharged March 24, 1815, and entered on Incorporated Roll. See Casualties.

CAIN, Stephen. Captain Hamilton Walker's Company. Private.

CAMERON, Freeman. Captain Kerr's Company. Private. In muster list of August 24, 1813, noted as dead.

CAMERON, John Sr. Captain Jarvie's Company. Private. Discharged April 5, 1814, but paid for the month.

CAMERON, John Jr. Joined April 15, 1813, in Captain Jarvie's Company. Private. Drummer. Captain William Jarvie's No. 2 Company. Discharged March 24, 1815, and entered on Incorporated Roll.

CAMPBELL, John. Joined before June 25, 1813, Captain John McDonell's Company. Private. Captain Archibald McLean's No. 6 Company. Discharged March 24, 1815, and entered on Incorporated Roll.

CANADA, James. Major Simons's Detachment. Sergeant. Shown from May 5 to July 24, 1813.

CANE (Cain), Stephen. Private. Captain Hamilton Walker's No. 10 Company. Discharged March 24, 1815, and entered on Incorporated Roll.

CARDINAL, Francis G. Captain Edward Walker's Company. Private. Captain Edward Walker's No. 5 Company. Discharged March 24, 1815, and entered on Incorporated Roll.

CARLEY, Joseph. Captain Henry Davy's Company. Private. Captain Edward Walker's No. 5 Company.

CASTLE, Carlo D. Captain Kerr's Company. Private.

CAVERLY, James. Captain Washburn's Company. Private. Returned March 10, 1815, as deserted.

CHACE, George. Captain Jarvie's Company. Private. Joined by March 25, 1813. Discharged April 5, 1814.

CHAMBERS, Robert. Major Titus G. Simons's Company. Private. Died April 1, 1814.

CHAPMAN, Jeremiah. Captain Jarvie's Company. Private. Noted as deserted March 25, 1813.

CHAPMAN, Martin. Captain Jarvie's Company. Private. Returned March 9, 1815, as deserted.

CHARLY, Peter. Captain Henry Davy's Company. Private. Discharged April 5, 1814.

CHASE, Elijah. Captain Daniel Washburn's Company. Private. Deserted October 25, 1813, to the enemy.

CHASE, George. Private. See Casualties.

CHASE, Nichol. Private. Discharged March 24, 1815, and entered on Incorporated Roll.

CHISHOLM, William. Major Titus G. Simons's Company. Sergeant. Captain Abraham A. Rapelje's No. 3 Company. Discharged March 24, 1815, and entered on Incorporated Roll. See Casualties.

CHURCH, Samuel. Captain Archibald McLean's Company. Private. Captain Archibald McLean's No. 6 Company. Prisoner of war. Discharged March 24, 1815, and entered on Incorporated Roll.

CLARK, Joseph. Captain Kerby's Company. Private. April 1 to May 24, 1813.

CLEMAUX (Clement), Nicholas. Joined before June 25, 1813, Captain John McDonell's Company. Private. Captain John McDonell's No. 9 Company. Discharged March 24, 1815, and entered on Incorporated Roll.

CLENDENNING, Moses. Captain Jarvie's Company. Private. Joined March 29, 1813. Noted in a return of January 1814 as a prisoner of war in the United States. Returned March 9, 1815, as deserted.

CLOUKIE (Cloukey), Antoine. Joined before June 25, 1813, Captain John McLean's Company. Private. Captain Thomas Fraser's No. 7 Company.

CLOUTIER, Anthony. Private. Captain Thomas Fraser's No. 7 Company. Discharged March 24, 1815, and entered on Incorporated Roll.

CLUNIS, Daniel. Captain Jarvie's Company. Private. Noted as deserted March 25, 1813.

CLUNIS, George. Joined April 1, 1813, Captain Jarvie's Company. Private. Captain William Jarvie's No. 2 Company. Discharged March 24, 1815, and entered on Incorporated Roll.

COLE, John. Private. Captain Rapelje's Company.

COLEMAN, John. Joined March, 1813, Captain John Kerr's Company. Private. Noted as deserted July 23, 1813. Returned March 9, 1815, as deserted.

COLETHAN. Joined February 25, 1815, Captain Jarvie's Company. Private.

COLLARD, Elijah. Major Titus G. Simons's Company. Sergeant. Quarter Master Sergeant. Captain Abraham A. Rapelje's No. 3 Company. Died August 1, 1814.

COLLIER, William. Captain Henry Davy's Company. Sergeant. Captain Edward Walker's No. 5 Company. Discharged March 24, 1815, and entered on Incorporated Roll.

CONEY, Henry. Captain Henry Davy's Company. Corporal. Taken prisoner October 10, 1813.

CONNEL, John. Captain Fraser's Company. Private. Captain Archibald McLean's No. 6 Company. Discharged March 24, 1815, and entered on Incorporated Roll. See Casualties.

CONNOLY, Herman (Harman). Private. Captain James Kerby's No. 1 Company. Discharged March 24, 1815, and entered on Incorporated Roll.

COOK, Jonathan. Captain Kerby's Company. Private.

COOK, Moses. Captain Kerby's Company. Private.

COOK, William. Captain Kerby's Company. Private.

CORBIN, Cyreneus. Captain Hamilton Walker's Company. Private. See Casualties.

CORNWALL, William. Major Titus G. Simons's Company. Private.

COSTELOW, James. (1st Addington Flank Company) Captain Henry Davy's Company. Private. Taken prisoner October 10, 1813. Captain Edward Walker's No. 5 Company. Prisoner of war. Discharged March 24, 1815, and entered on Incorporated Roll.

COWDRAY (Couder), George. Joined April 6, 1813, Captain John Kerr's Company. Private. Captain John Kerr's No. 8 Company. Discharged March 24, 1815, and entered on Incorporated Roll.

COX, Spencer. Joined April 3, 1813. Captain Henry Davy's Company. Private. Captain Daniel Washburn's No. 4 Company. Discharged March 24, 1815, and entered on Incorporated Roll.

CRIM, Peter. Captain Archibald McLean's Company. Private. Captain Archibald McLean's No. 6 Company. Discharged March 24, 1815, and entered on Incorporated Roll.

CRONK (Cram), David. Private. Captain Rapelje's Company. Captain Abraham A. Rapelje's No. 3 Company.

CRONK, William. Private Captain Rapelje's Company. Captain Abraham A. Rapelje's No. 3 Company.

CROSS, Nathan. Captain Archibald McLean's Company. Private. Captain Archibald McLean's No. 6 Company. Discharged March 24, 1815, and entered on Incorporated Roll.

CROSSET, Peter. Captain Archibald McLean's Company. Private. Captain Archibald McLean's No. 6 Company. Discharged March 24, 1815, and entered on Incorporated Roll.

CROSSON, William. Captain Kerby's Company. Private.

CROUCH, Christopher. Captain Hamilton Walker's Company. Private. Noted as deserted June 26, 1813.

CRUM (Crim), Peter. Captain Hamilton Walker's Company. Private.

CURTIS, Daniel. Captain Rapelje's Company. Private.

DARBY, Dexter. Joined No. 3 Company January 22, 1815. Private. Discharged March 24, 1815, and entered on Incorporated Roll.

DAVIDSON (Davison), Andrew. Captain Jarvie's Company. Private. Captain William Jarvie's No. 2 Company. Discharged March 24, 1815, and entered on Incorporated Roll.

DAVIDSON, James. Joined March 24, 1813, Captain Jarvie's Company. Private. Died April 22, 1814.

DAVIS, Elias. Private. Discharged March 24, 1815, and entered on Incorporated Roll.

DAVISON, John. L. Captain Hamilton Walker's Company. Private.

DAY, Moses. Captain Archibald McLean's Company. Private.

DEAN, Isaac. Captain Kerby's Company. Private.

DE CASTLE, Carlos. Corporal. Joined April 6, 1813, Captain John Kerr's Company. Captain John Kerr's No. 8 Company. Sergeant. Discharged March 24, 1815, and entered on Incorporated Roll.

DEGRANA, Joseph. Captain Jonas Jones's Company. Private. Noted as deserted June 26, 1813.

DENNIS (Denne), Baptiste. Private. Captain Hamilton Walker's No. 10 Company.

DENNIS, Obadiah. Captain Kerby's Company. Private.

DENNU, Joseph. Captain Fraser's Company. Private.

DENZ, John. Captain Fraser's Company. Private.

DEROSHE, Stephen. Captain John McDonell's Company. Private. Captain John McDonell's No. 9 Company. Prisoner of war. Discharged March 24, 1815, and entered on Incorporated Roll.

DERRICK, John. Joined before June 25, 1813, Captain John McDonell's Company. Private. Died August 5, 1813.

DERRICK, Moses. Private. Captain Hamilton Walker's No. 10 Company. Discharged March 24, 1815, and entered on Incorporated Roll.

DESROCHES (Durasay), Etienne (Echen). Joined before June 25, 1813, Captain John McDonell's Company. Private.

DEXTER, Derby. Captain Henry Davy's Company. Drummer.

DIETSMAN (Dixman), John. Joined March 30, 1813, Captain Jarvie's Company. Private. See Casualties.

DILLABOUGH, John. Joined before June 25, 1813, Captain John McDonell's Company. Private. Captain John McDonell's No. 9 Company. Prisoner of war. Discharged March 24, 1815, and entered on Incorporated Roll.

DODGE, Abner. Captain Archibald McLean's Company. Private. Deserted October 25, 1813.

DODGE, Peter. Captain Fraser's Company. Private. Captain Thomas Fraser's No. 7 Company. Discharged March 24, 1815, and entered on Incorporated Roll.

DODGE, Sylvester. Major Titus G. Simons's Company. Private.

DRAKE, John. Private. Major Titus G. Simons's Company. Private. Transferred to Captain Rapelje's Company. Noted as a prisoner of war in the United States in a pay list of February 1814. Discharged March 24, 1815, and entered on Incorporated Roll. See Casualties.

DU BUELL, Ronald. Captain Fraser's Company. Private.

DUNN, John. Private. Captain Hamilton Walker's No. 10 Company. Discharged March 24, 1815, and entered on Incorporated Roll.

DUPHY (Duffy), Elijah. Captain John McLean's Company. Private. Captain Archibald McLean's No. 6 Company. Discharged March 24, 1815, and entered on Incorporated Roll.

DUPU, Norbar. Joined before June 25, 1813, Captain John McDonell's Company. Private. Discharged April 5, 1814, as unfit.

DURASAY, Echant. Captain John McDonell's Company. Private.

DURHAM, Elias. Major Titus G. Simons's Company. Private. Sergeant. Captain Abraham A. Rapelje's No. 3 Company. Discharged March 24, 1815, and entered on Incorporated Roll.

DYKE, Vivas. Captain Archibald McLean's Company. Private. Deserted October 25, 1813.

EARHEART (Evehard), John. Joined March 23, 1813. Captain Washburn's Company. Private. Captain Daniel Washburn's No. 4 Company. Discharged March 25, 1815, and entered on the Incorporated Roll.

EARHART, William. Joined April 6, 1813. Captain Washburn's Company. Private. Captain Daniel Washburn's No. 4 Company. Discharged March 25, 1815, and entered on the Incorporated Roll.

EASTMAN, Joseph. (2nd Grenville) Captain Fraser's Company. Corporal. Captain Thomas Fraser's No. 7 Company. Discharged March 25, 1815, and entered on the Incorporated Roll.

ELLIOTT, Luther. Captain Fraser's Company. Private. Captain Thomas Fraser's No. 7 Company. Discharged March 25, 1815, and entered on the Incorporated Roll.

ELLIS, Archibald. Major Simons's Company. Private.

EMMONS, John (Joseph). Private. Captain Rapelje's Company. Captain James Kerby's No. 1 Company. Discharged March 25, 1815, and entered on the Incorporated Roll.

EMPEY, William. Joined March 16, 1813, Captain John Kerr's Company. Private. Captain John Kerr's No. 8 Company. Discharged March 25, 1815, and entered on the Incorporated Roll. See Casualties.

ENNO (Innoe), Peter. Captain Fraser's Company. Private. Captain Archibald McLean's No. 6 Company. Prisoner of war.

EYKE, William. Captain Archibald McLean's Company. Private. Noted as deserted July 26, 1813.

FARE (Fave), Benjamin. Private. Captain Hamilton Walker's No. 10 Company. Discharged March 25, 1815, and entered on the Incorporated Roll.

FENNER, Jacob. Captain Kerby's Company. Private. Discharged March 25, 1815, and entered on the Incorporated Roll.

FERGUSON, Joseph. Captain Henry Jones's Company. Corporal. Captain Hamilton Walker's No. 10 Company. Discharged March 25, 1815, and entered on the Incorporated Roll.

FERRAW, Joseph. Private. Captain Hamilton Walker's No. 10 Company.

FETCHETT (Fitchett), Isaac. Joined April 20, 1813. Captain Washburn's Company. Private. Captain Daniel Washburn's No. 4 Company. Discharged March 25, 1815, and entered on the Incorporated Roll.

FILLEY, Arunel. Captain Kerby's Company. Private.

FISHER, Jacob. Captain Jarvie's Company. Private. Returned December 24, 1813, and February 18, 1814, as dead. Returned March 9, 1815, as deserted.

FOLK, John. Private. Captain Rapelje's Company.

FONTANG (Fontaine), Louis. Captain Edward Walker's Company. Private. Captain Edward Walker's No. 5 Company. Discharged March 25, 1815, and entered on the Incorporated Roll.

FORBES, Abraham. Captain Kerby's Company. Private.

FORBES, Adam. (1st Addington Flank Company) Captain Henry Davy's Company. Taken prisoner October 10, 1813. Captain Daniel Washburn's No. 4 Company. Discharged March 25, 1815, and entered on the Incorporated Roll. See Casualties.

FORTNER, Andrew. Joined April 6, 1813, Captain James Kerby's Company. Private. Corporal (July 25, 1813). Sergeant (January 25, 1814). Captain James Kerby's No. 1 Company. Discharged March 25, 1815, and entered on the Incorporated Roll.

FOX, Jeremiah. Joined January 3, 1814, Captain Henry Davy's Company. Private. Captain Edward Walker's No. 5 Company. Discharged March 25, 1815, and entered on the Incorporated Roll.

FRALICK, David. Captain Archibald McLean's Company. Private. Captain Archibald McLean's No. 6 Company. Discharged March 25, 1815, and entered on the Incorporated Roll.

FRALICK, John. Captain Kerby's Company. Private.

FRALICK, John. Joined April 10, 1813, Captain John Kerr's Company. Private. Captain John Kerr's No. 8 Company. Discharged March 25, 1815, and entered on the Incorporated Roll.

FRASER, Alexander. Captain Archibald McLean's Company. Private. Corporal. Captain Archibald McLean's No. 6 Company. Sergeant. Discharged March 25, 1815, and entered on the Incorporated Roll.

FRASER, Donald. Joined Captain Donald McAulay's Company. Captain Archibald McLean's Company. Private. Deserted August 25, 1813.

FRASER, Hugh. (1st Grenville) Captain Fraser's Company. Sergeant. Captain Thomas Fraser's No. 7 Company. Discharged March 25, 1815, and entered on the Incorporated Roll.

FRASER, Simon. Joined March 25, 1813, Captain Kerr's Company. Private. Captain John Kerr's No. 8 Company. Discharged March 25, 1815, and entered on the Incorporated Roll.

FRASER, Thomas. Private. Discharged March 25, 1815, and entered on the Incorporated Roll.

FRASER, William. Captain Henry Jones's Company. Private. Captain Hamilton Walker's No. 10 Company. Discharged March 25, 1815, and entered on the Incorporated Roll.

FREEMAN, John. Captain Jarvie's Company. Private. Captain William Jarvie's No. 2 Company. Prisoner of war. Discharged March 25, 1815, and entered on the Incorporated Roll.

FREEMAN, Joseph. Captain Jarvie's Company. Private. Returned March 9, 1815, as deserted.

FROOMAN, H. Captain Henry Davy's Company. Private.

FULLER, Daniel. Major Titus G. Simons's Company. Private. Captain Abraham A. Rapelje's No. 3 Company. Discharged March 25, 1815, and entered on the Incorporated Roll.

GAGNE, Charles. Captain Henry Davy's Company. Private.

GALLINGER, Phillip. Captain John McDonell's Company. Private. Captain John McDonell's No. 9 Company. Discharged March 25, 1815, and entered on the Incorporated Roll.

GARDNER, Richard. Major Simons's Company. Private. Died April 1, 1814.

GARRIN (Garvin), Hugh. Major Simons's Company. Private. Captain Abraham A. Rapelje's No. 3 Company. Discharged March 25, 1815, and entered on the Incorporated Roll.

GASTEN (Garston), Joseph. Captain Henry Davy's Company. Private. Captain Edward Walker's No. 5 Company. Discharged March 25, 1815, and entered on the Incorporated Roll.

GATES, Joseph. Captain Edward Walker's Company. Private. Captain Edward Walker's No. 5 Company. Discharged March 25, 1815, and entered on the Incorporated Roll.

GOTIER, Joseph. Joined April 25, 1813, Captain John Kerr's Company. Private.

GENOVELEY, Joseph. Captain Edward Walker's Company. Private. Captain Edward Walker's No. 5 Company. Discharged March 25, 1815, and entered on the Incorporated Roll.

GEROW, David. Captain Fraser's Company. Private. Captain Thomas Fraser's No. 7 Company. Discharged March 25, 1815, and entered on the Incorporated Roll.

GERROW, Allan. Captain Jarvie's Company. Private. Noted as deserted March 25, 1813.

GESMAINE, Ambrose. Captain Jonas Jones's Company. Private.

GOKEA, Benjamin. Captain Fraser's Company. Private. Captain Thomas Fraser's No. 7 Company. Discharged March 25, 1815, and entered on the Incorporated Roll.

GOKEA, Joseph. Captain Fraser's Company. Corporal. Demoted to private. Captain John Kerr's No. 8 Company. Discharged March 25, 1815, and entered on the Incorporated Roll.

GOODRICH, Marvin. Captain Washburn's Company. Private. Captain Daniel Washburn's No. 4 Company. Discharged March 25, 1815, and entered on the Incorporated Roll.

GORDON, Michael. Captain Jonas Jones's Company. Private. Captain John McDonell's No. 9 Company. Discharged March 25, 1815, and entered on the Incorporated Roll.

GOULIE (Goulet), Louis. Joined March 27, 1813. Captain Washburn's Company. Private. Captain Daniel Washburn's No. 4 Company. Discharged March 25, 1815, and entered on the Incorporated Roll.

GRAHAM, William. Joined July 1, 1813, Captain Jarvie's Company. Private. Captain William Jarvie's No. 2 Company. Prisoner of war. Discharged March 25, 1815, and entered on the Incorporated Roll.

GRANT, Duncan. Joined April 1, 1813, Captain Kerr's Company. Private. Captain John Kerr's No. 8 Company. Discharged March 25, 1815, and entered on the Incorporated Roll.

GRANT, James. Joined March 25, 1813, Captain John Kerr's Company. Private. Captain John Kerr's No. 8 Company. Discharged March 25, 1815, and entered on the Incorporated Roll.

GRANT, John. Captain Jonas Jones's Company. Private. Noted as deserted July 29, 1813.

GRANT, John. Captain Hamilton Walker's Company. Private. Discharged April 5, 1814.

GRAY, Angus. Captain Archibald McLean's Company. Private.

GREEN, Alexander. Major Titus G. Simons's Company. Private. Noted as deserted March 25, 1814.

GREEN, Ebenezer. Captain Edward Walker's Company. Private. Captain Edward Walker's No. 5 Company. Discharged March 25, 1815, and entered on the Incorporated Roll.

GRIFFITH, Richard. Captain Kerby's Company. Private.

GRIFFITH, Zebulon. Captain Kerby's Company. Private.

GROOMS, Elijah. Captain Henry Davy's Company. Private. Captain Daniel Washburn's Company. Returned March 10, 1815, as deserted.

GROSSMAKER, John. Captain Henry Jones's Company. Corporal. Sergeant. Captain Hamilton Walker's No. 10 Company. Prisoner of war. Discharged March 25, 1815, and entered on the Incorporated Roll.

GROVES, John. Captain Archibald McLean's Company. Private. Corporal. Sergeant. No. 6 Company.

HAINES, Peter. Major Simons's Company. Private.

HALL, Joseph. Captain Hamilton Walker's Company. Private.

HALL, Samuel. Joined April 18, 1813, Captain John Kerr's Company. Private. Captain John Kerr's No. 8 Company. Discharged March 25, 1815, and entered on the Incorporated Roll.

HALLER, John. Captain Archibald McLean's Company. Private. Absent without leave from November 25th, 1813.

HAMILTON, Edward. Captain Jarvie's Company. Corporal. Died April 1, 1814.

HANES (Hane), Jacob. (1st Addington Flank Company) Joined March 14, 1813. Captain Washburn's Company. Private. Captain Daniel Washburn's No. 4 Company. Discharged March 25, 1815, and entered on the Incorporated Roll.

HARE, George. Captain Kerby's Company. Private.

HARRISON (Harris), Samuel. Major Titus G. Simons's Company. Private. Captain Abraham A. Rapelje's No. 3 Company.

HARTLE, John. Joined before June 25, 1813, Captain John McDonell's Company. Private. Captain John McDonell's No. 9 Company. Discharged March 25, 1815, and entered on the Incorporated Roll.

HARTLE, Lucas. Captain John McLean's Company. Private. Corporal. Captain Hamilton Walker's No. 10 Company. Discharged March 25, 1815, and entered on the Incorporated Roll.

HATTER, John. Private. Captain Archibald McLean's No. 6 Company. Discharged March 25, 1815, and entered on the Incorporated Roll.

HAWES, Edward. Captain Jonas Jones's Company. Corporal. Deserted September 3, 1813.

HAYS (Hase), Henry. Joined No. 3 Company, January 22, 1815. Private. Discharged March 25, 1815, and entered on the Incorporated Roll.

HECKFIELD, John. Captain Jarvie's Company. Private. Returned March 9, 1815, as deserted.

HELMER, Thomas. Joined March 26, 1813. Sergeant. Captain John Kerr's No. 8 Company.

HENRY, David. Captain Jarvie's Company. Private. Noted as a prisoner of war in the United States in a return of January 1814. Returned March 9, 1815, as deserted.

HERRICK, Miles. Captain Jarvie's Company. Private. Noted as deserted March 25, 1813.

HERRIMAN, Luther. Captain Henry Davy's Company. Private. Captain Edward Walker's No. 5 Company. Discharged March 25, 1815, and entered on the Incorporated Roll.

HICKS, Benjamin. Joined March 13, 1813. Captain Washburn's Company. Private. Captain Daniel Washburn's No. 4 Company. Discharged March 25, 1815, and entered on the Incorporated Roll.

HICKS, Edward. Captain Henry Davy's Company. Private. Captain Edward Walker's No. 5 Company. Discharged March 25, 1815, and entered on the Incorporated Roll.

HICKS, John. Captain Henry Davy's Company. Private.

HICKS, Joseph, No. 1. Joined March 4, 1813. Captain Henry Davy's Company. Private. Captain Daniel Washburn's No. 4 Company. Discharged March 25, 1815, and entered on the Incorporated Roll.

HICKS, Joseph, No. 2. Joined March 24, 1813. Captain Daniel Washburn's Company. Private.

HILMER, Thomas. Captain Kerr's Company. Sergeant. Discharged March 25, 1815, and entered on the Incorporated Roll.

HILTZ, Jeremiah. Joined April 22, 1813, Captain Jarvie's Company. Private. Captain William Jarvie's No. 2 Company. Discharged March 25, 1815, and entered on the Incorporated Roll.

HINCHEY, John. Private. Captain Rapelje's Company.

HINTON, Richard. Captain Kerby's Company. Private.

HITCHCOCK, Elam. Captain John McLean's Company. Private. Corporal. Captain John McDonell's No. 9 Company. Discharged March 25, 1815, and entered on the Incorporated Roll.

HOAG, Russel. Captain Jarvie's Company. Private. Returned March 9, 1815, as deserted.

HODGEKIS, Samuel. Private. Discharged March 25, 1815, and entered on the Incorporated Roll.

HOLMES, Charles. Captain John McDonell's Company. Private. Captain John McDonell's No. 9 Company. Discharged March 25, 1815, and entered on the Incorporated Roll.

HOLMES, Elias. Joined May 6, 1813, Captain Henry Davy's Company. Sergeant. Captain John McDonell's No. 9 Company. Discharged March 25, 1815, and entered on the Incorporated Roll.

HOLMES, Peter. Joined before June 25, 1813, Captain John McDonell's Company. Drummer. Demoted to private. Captain John McDonell's No. 9 Company. Discharged March 25, 1815, and entered on the Incorporated Roll.

HOLMES, William. Joined before June 25, 1813, Captain John McDonell's Company. Private. Captain John McDonell's No. 9 Company. Discharged March 25, 1815, and entered on the Incorporated Roll.

HOOVER, Henry. Joined April 20, 1813, Captain James Kerby's Company. Sergeant. Captain James Kerby's No. 1 Company. Discharged March 25, 1815, and entered on the Incorporated Roll.

HOWARD, Abel. Captain Kerby's Company. Private.

HOWE, William. Private. Captain Archibald McLean's No. 6 Company.

HUFFMAN, George. Joined March 4, 1813. Captain Washburn's Company. Corporal. Private. Captain Daniel Washburn's No. 4 Company. Prisoner of war. Discharged March 25, 1815, and entered on the Incorporated Roll.

HUFFMAN, Peter. Joined April 8, 1813. Captain Washburn's Company. Private. Captain Daniel Washburn's No. 4 Company. Discharged March 25, 1815, and entered on the Incorporated Roll.

HULL, Hezeikiah. Major Titus G. Simons's Company. Private. Died November 4, 1813.

HULL, Kiah. Private. See Casualties. Probably same as above.

HULL, Richard. Major Titus G. Simons's Company. Private. Captain Abraham A. Rapelje's No. 3 Company. Discharged March 25, 1815, and entered on the Incorporated Roll. See Casualties.

HUNTINGTON, William. Captain Jarvie's Company. Quarter Master Sergeant. January 25 to February 24, 1814.

HUTCHISON, John. Captain Jarvie's Company. Private. Returned March 9, 1815, as deserted.

INNOE, Peter. Captain Archibald McLean's Company. Private. March 25 to April 24, 1814. Prisoner of war. Discharged March 25, 1815, and entered on the Incorporated Roll.

JACKSON, John. Private. Captain Hamilton Walker's No. 10 Company. Discharged March 24, 1815, and entered on Incorporated Roll.

JACKSON, John. Private Captain Rapelje's Company. Captain Abraham A. Rapelje's No. 3 Company. Discharged March 24, 1815, and entered on Incorporated Roll.

JACKSON, John. Captain Kerby's Company. Private. Probably same as above.

JACKSON, Henry. Captain Kerr's Company. Private.

JARVIE, Joseph. Captain Hamilton Walker's Company. Private.

JEROW, Joseph. Captain Hamilton Walker's Company. Private.

JESMAINE, (Jesmah), Ambrose. Private. Captain Thomas Fraser's No. 7 Company. Discharged March 24, 1815, and entered on Incorporated Roll.

JEWEL, James. (2nd Norfolk) Private. Captain Rapelje's Company. Captain Abraham A. Rapelje's No. 3 Company. Discharged March 24, 1815, and entered on Incorporated Roll.

JOHNSON, Frederick. Major Titus G. Simons's Company. Private.

JOHNSON, George. Captain John McLean's Company. Private. Captain Hamilton Walker's No. 10 Company. Discharged March 24, 1815, and entered on Incorporated Roll.

JOHNSON, William. Private. Discharged March 24, 1815, and entered on Incorporated Roll.

JONES, Asa. Major Titus G. Simons's Company. Private. Discharged March 24, 1815, and entered on Incorporated Roll.

JUDD, Joel. (2nd Leeds) Captain Fraser's Company. Sergeant. Captain Thomas Fraser's No. 7 Company. Discharged March 24, 1815, and entered on Incorporated Roll.

KAY, John. Joined before June 25, 1813, Captain John McDonell's Company. Private. Corporal. Captain John McDonell's No. 9 Company. Sergeant. Discharged March 24, 1815, and entered on Incorporated Roll.

KELLSY, Henry. Captain Kerby's Company. Private.

KELLY, Andrew. Captain Abraham Rapelje's Company. Private. Died September 8, 1813.

KELSEY, Uriah. Captain Kerr's Company. Private. Returned March 9, 1815, as deserted.

KEMP, Daniel. Captain Jarvie's Company. Private. Noted as deserted March 25, 1813.

KENNEDY, James. Returned in the 1st Norfolk Flank Company as having joined the Incorporated Militia and died.

KNAPP, Joseph. Private. Captain Hamilton Walker's No. 10 Company. Discharged March 24, 1815, and entered on Incorporated Roll.

LAPAUL, Dominick. Captain John McDonell's Company. Private.

LADERONT, Toussaint. Joined April 4, 1813, Captain John Kerr's Company. Private. Captain John Kerr's No. 8 Company.

LADEROOT, Toussaint. Captain Hamilton Walker's Company. Private. Noted as deserted August 23, 1813.

LADREA (Ladrae), Baptiste. Captain Jonas Jones's Company. Private. Captain John McDonell's No. 9 Company.

LAGARD, Baptiste. Captain Jonas Jones's Company. Private. Captain John McDonell's No. 9 Company.

LALONDE, Pierre. Captain Jonas Jones's Company. Private. Noted as deserted October 2, 1813.

LALONE, Joseph. Joined April 1, 1813, Captain John Kerr's Company. Private. Captain John Kerr's No. 8 Company.

LAMON, Peter. Captain Kerby's Company. Private.

LAMON (Layman), Richard. Captain Henry Jones's Company. Private. Captain Hamilton Walker's No. 10 Company.

LAMPMAN, Fredrick. Joined April 23, 1813, Captain James Kerby's Company. Private. Captain James Kerby's No. 1 Company. Prisoner of war. Discharged March 24, 1815, and entered on Incorporated Roll.

LANCACIE, Francis. Captain Henry Davy's Company. Private.

LANGARAN, Andrew. Captain John McDonell's Company. Private.

LANGELYEA, Æneas. Captain John McDonell's Company. Private.

LANGLYEA (Lanzelyea), Francis. Joined before June 25, 1813, Captain John McDonell's Company. Private. Captain John McDonell's No. 9 Company.

LANGUELLER (Lanzelea), Æneas (Enis). Captain Jonas Jones's Company. Private. Captain John McDonell's No. 9 Company.

LANNGEVIN, Andrew. Captain John McLean's Company. Private. Captain John McDonell's No. 9 Company.

LANSING, John. Joined May 10, 1813. Private No. 4 Company. Discharged March 24, 1815, and entered on Incorporated Roll.

LAPAUL, Dominick. Private. Captain John McDonell's No. 9 Company.

LAQUE, John B. Captain Jonas Jones's Company. Private.

LAQUEA (Lague), Jean Baptiste (Baptist). Joined April 1, 1813, Captain John Kerr's Company. Private. Captain John Kerr's No. 8 Company. See Casualties.

LAQUEA, John. Captain Fraser's Company. Private. Captain Thomas Fraser's No. 7 Company.

LAQUEYA, Lewis. Captain John McLean's Company. Private. Captain John McDonell's No. 9 Company.

LAROCHE (Larock), Charles. Captain Henry Jones's Company. Private. Captain Hamilton Walker's No. 10 Company.

LAROCHE (Lerock), Francis. Captain Fraser's Company. Private. Captain Thomas Fraser's No. 7 Company. Prisoner of war.

LAROCHE (Lerock), Joseph. Captain Fraser's Company. Private. Captain Thomas Fraser's No. 7 Company. Prisoner of war.

LAROSE, Anthony. Captain Hamilton Walker's Company. Private. Discharged April 5, 1814.

LAROY, Michael. Major Titus G. Simons's Company. Private.

LASHER (Lesher), Andrew. Captain Washburn's Company. Private. Captain Daniel Washburn's No. 4 Company. Discharged March 24, 1815, and entered on Incorporated Roll.

LATULIPE, Joseph. Private. Captain Hamilton Walker's No. 10 Company.

LAUGHLAN, Jacob. (1st Addington Flank Company) Joined April 10, 1813. Captain Henry Davy's Company. Corporal. Captain Edward Walker's No. 5 Company.

LAUGHLIN, Joseph. Private. Discharged March 24, 1815, and entered on Incorporated Roll.

LAYMAN (Leeman), Peter. Private. Captain Rapelje's Company. Captain Abraham A. Rapelje's No. 3 Company. Discharged March 24, 1815, and entered on Incorporated Roll.

LECLARE, Nicholas. Captain Hamilton Walker's Company. Private.

LEE, Francis. Captain Jarvie's Company. Sergeant. Captain John McDonell's No. 9 Company. Discharged March 24, 1815, and entered on Incorporated Roll.

LEEPAUL, Dominick. Captain John McLean's Company. Private.

LEGRO, Antoine (Anthony). Captain Fraser's Company. Private. Captain Thomas Fraser's No. 7 Company.

LEGRO (Legreen), Eustice (Eustach). Captain Fraser's Company. Private. Captain Thomas Fraser's No. 7 Company. See Casualties.

LEGRO, Francis. Captain Fraser's Company. Private.

LEGRO, Peter. Private. Captain Hamilton Walker's No. 10 Company.

LEGRO, Peter. Captain Jonas Jones's Company. Private. Probably same as above.

LEHIGH (Lehay), Abraham. Joined before June 25, 1813, Captain John McLean's Company. Corporal. Private. Captain John McDonell's No. 9 Company.

LEMON, Richard. Captain Hamilton Walker's Company. Private.

LENNOX, Samuel (James). Captain Fraser's Company. Private. Corporal. Captain Thomas Fraser's No. 7 Company. Discharged March 24, 1815, and entered on Incorporated Roll.

LEONARD, Charles. Captain Jarvie's Company. Private.

LESTER (Lesthier), Daniel H. (1st Addington Flank Company) Joined April 24, 1813. Captain Washburn's Company. Sergeant. Demoted April 16, 1814. Private. Captain Daniel Washburn's No. 4 Company. Discharged March 24, 1815, and entered on Incorporated Roll.

LIONNEY, George. Captain Henry Davy's Company. Private. Joined May 1, 1813.

LODEN, Joseph. Private. Captain Rapelje's Company

LODER, Joseph. Captain Kerby's Company. Private.

LOGAN, Edward. Captain Rapelje's Company. Private. Captain Abraham A. Rapelje's No. 3 Company. Discharged March 24, 1815, and entered on Incorporated Roll.

LONG (Loney), George. Captain Henry Davy's Company. Private. Captain Edward Walker's No. 5 Company.

LONG, Joseph. Captain Henry Davy's Company. Private. See Casualties.

LONG, Joseph. Captain Kerby's Company. Private.

LONG, William. Captain Kerby's Company. Private.

LORIE (Loring), Timothy. Major Titus G. Simons's Company. Private. Discharged March 24, 1815, and entered on Incorporated Roll.

LORING, Hezikiah. Captain Kerby's Company. Private.

LOUKS (Lutees), Zebulon. Captain Kerby's Company. Private. Captain Abraham A. Rapelje's No. 3 Company. Discharged March 24, 1815, and entered on Incorporated Roll.

LOUNSBURY, John. Joined April 16, 1813, Captain James Kerby's Company. Private. Captain James Kerby's No. 1 Company. Discharged March 24, 1815, and entered on Incorporated Roll.

LOVELL, Henry. Captain Archibald McLean's Company. Private. Deserted April 6, 1814.

LOVELLE, Henry. Captain Henry Davy's Company. Private. Deserted August 25, 1813.

LUNDY (Lindy), Azariah. Joined March 29, 1813, Captain James Kerby's Company. Private. Captain James Kerby's No. 1 Company. Discharged March 24, 1815, and entered on Incorporated Roll.

MALLARY, William. Captain Jonas Jones's Company. Private. Deserted August 30, 1813.

MALLORY, William. Captain Fraser's Company. Private. Discharged March 24, 1815, and entered on Incorporated Roll. Probably same as above.

MALTIMORE, William. Joined Captain Donald McAulay's Company. Captain John McDonell's Company. Private. Captain John McDonell's No. 9 Company. Discharged March 24, 1815, and entered on Incorporated Roll. See Casualties.

MARKEL (Merikel), Benjamin. Major Titus G. Simons's Company. Corporal. Captain Abraham A. Rapelje's No. 3 Company.

MARKEL, John. Major Titus G. Simons's Company. Private. Discharged March 24, 1815, and entered on Incorporated Roll.

MARKET, John. Captain John McLean's Company. Private.

MARLAT, Joseph. Captain Kerby's Company. Private.

MASHER (Mosher), John. Joined before April 25, 1813, Captain Henry Davy's Company. Private. Died June 12, 1813.

MASON, Jacob. Joined May 14, 1813, Captain Henry Davy's Company. Private. Deserted September 21, 1813. Thought to have gone to the enemy.

MATTICE, John. Joined before June 25, 1813, Captain John McDonell's Company. Private. Captain John McDonell's No. 9 Company. Discharged March 24, 1815, and entered on Incorporated Roll.

McBEAN, Gillis. Joined April 2, 1813, Captain Jonas Jones's Company. Private. Captain John Kerr's No. 8 Company. Discharged March 24, 1815, and entered on Incorporated Roll.

McBRIDE, Edward W. Joined April 15, 1813. Sergeant. From Lieutenant Jarvis's Artillery Company. Captain William Jarvie's No. 2 Company.

McCRANEY, Thomas. Captain Jarvie's Company. Corporal. Noted as deserted in Muster List of July 24, 1813.

McCRIMMON, Daniel. Joined March 4, 1813. Captain Henry Davy's Company. Private. Captain Daniel Washburn's No. 4 Company. Discharged March 24, 1815, and entered on Incorporated Roll.

McCRIMMON, Duncan. (1st Addington Flank Company) Joined March 15, 1813. Captain Washburn's Company. Private. Captain Daniel Washburn's No. 4 Company. Discharged March 24, 1815, and entered on Incorporated Roll.

McCRIMMON, Peter. Captain Washburn's Company. Drummer. Captain Daniel Washburn's No. 4 Company. Discharged March 24, 1815, and entered on Incorporated Roll.

McDONALD, Donald. (2nd Glengarry) Captain Thomas Fraser's Company. Sergeant. Captain Thomas Fraser's No. 7 Company.

McDONELL, Donald. Joined before June 25, 1813, Captain John McDonell's Company. Sergeant. Reduced to the ranks January 2, 1814.

McDONELL, Ewen. Captain Jonas Jones's Company. Quarter Master Sergeant. Reduced October 31 to Private.

McDONELL, Ranald (Randle). Captain Archibald McLean's Company. Private. Captain Archibald McLean's No. 6 Company. Discharged March 24, 1815, and entered on Incorporated Roll.

McDONELL (McDonald), Ronald. Joined before June 25, 1813, Captain John McDonell's Company. Corporal. Sergeant. Captain Hamilton Walker's No. 10 Company. Discharged March 24, 1815, and entered on Incorporated Roll.

McDONELL (McDonald), William. Private. Captain Edward Walker's No. 5 Company. Discharged March 24, 1815, and entered on Incorporated Roll.

McDOUGALL, Angus. Captain Kerr's Company. Sergeant. Captain Daniel Washburn's No. 4 Company. Prisoner of war. Discharged March 24, 1815, and entered on Incorporated Roll. See Casualties.

McDOUGALL, Hugh. Captain Jonas Jones's Company. Private. Noted as discharged October 3, 1813.

McGEE, James. Joined before June 25, 1813, Captain John McDonell's Company. Captain John McDonell's No. 9 Company. Discharged March 24, 1815, and entered on Incorporated Roll.

McGILLIS, Donald. Captain Hamilton Walker's Company. Private.

McGILLVRAY, Angus. Joined April 3, 1813. Captain Kerr's Company. Sergeant. Captain John Kerr's No. 8 Company.

McGINNIS, John. Captain Henry Davy's Company. Private. Deserted July 31, 1813.

McGLOUGHLIN (McLaughlin), John. Joined April 2, 1813, Captain John Kerr's Company. Private. Captain John Kerr's No. 8 Company. Discharged March 24, 1815, and entered on Incorporated Roll.

McGRATH, John. Captain Archibald McLean's Company. Private. Captain Archibald McLean's No. 6 Company. See Casualties.

McGREGOR, Edward. Captain Kerr's Company. Captain Hamilton Walker's No. 10 Company. Discharged March 24, 1815, and entered on Incorporated Roll.

McGUIRE, Daniel. Sergeant. Captain Archibald McLean's No. 6 Company. Discharged March 24, 1815, and entered on Incorporated Roll (may be same as below).

McGUIRE, Donald. Captain Archibald McLean's Company. Sergeant.

McGUIRE, John. Joined March 29, 1813, Captain John Kerr's Company. Private. Noted in a return of July 24, 1813, as absent without leave. Returned March 9, 1815, as deserted.

McINTYRE, Simon. Captain Archibald McLean's Company. Private. Captain Archibald McLean's No. 6 Company. Discharged March 24, 1815, and entered on Incorporated Roll.

McINTYRE, Solomon. Private. Captain Hamilton Walker's No. 10 Company. Discharged March 24, 1815, and entered on Incorporated Roll.

McINTYRE, William. Major Titus G. Simons's Company. Private.

McKAY, Daniel. Major Titus G. Simons's Company. Corporal. Noted as deserted March 25, 1814.

McKAY, Peter. Major Simons's Company. Private.

McLEOD, Alexander. Captain Archibald McLean's Company. Corporal. Demoted December 20, 1813, to private. Captain Archibald McLean's No. 6 Company. Discharged March 24, 1815, and entered on Incorporated Roll.

McLAUGLIN, Robert. Private. See Casualties.

McLEOD, Donald. Captain John McLean's Company. Private. Captain Archibald McLean's No. 6 Company. Prisoner of war. Discharged March 24, 1815, and entered on Incorporated Roll.

McLEOD, Donald. Captain Archibald McLean's Company. Private. Prisoner of war.

McMANNERS, David. Major Titus G. Simons's Company. Private.

McMILLAN, Donald. Captain John McLean's Company. Captain Archibald McLean's No. 6 Company. Discharged March 24, 1815, and entered on Incorporated Roll.

McNEE, Donald. Captain McDonell's Company. Private. Discharged April 5, 1814.

McPHEE, Donald. Joined before June 25, 1813, Captain John McDonell's Company. Private. Deserted September 24, 1813.

McPHEE, Dougald. Joined before June 25, 1813, Captain John McDonell's Company. Private. Deserted September 10, 1813.

McQUARRIE, D. Captain Archibald McLean's Company. Sergeant.

McQUARRIE, Neil. Joined before June 25, 1813, Captain John McLean's Company. Sergeant. Captain John McDonell's Company. Private. Sergeant Major. Captain Archibald McLean's No. 6 Company. Discharged March 24, 1815, and entered on Incorporated Roll.

McQUIRE, Neil. Captain Hamilton Walker's Company. Enlisted March 28, 1813. Sergeant.

MEEKS, Joseph. Joined June 15, 1813, Captain William Jarvie's Company. Private. Noted in a return of January 1814 as a prisoner of war in the United States. Returned March 9, 1815, as deserted.

MELLOT (Millott, Melot), Paul. Joined before June 25, 1813, Captain John McLean's Company. Drummer. Captain Thomas Fraser's No. 7 Company. Discharged March 24, 1815, and entered on Incorporated Roll.

MERRIMAN, John B. Joined before June 25, 1813, Captain John McDonell's Company. Private. Captain John McDonell's No. 9 Company. Discharged March 24, 1815, and entered on Incorporated Roll.

MICKEL, Benjamin. Private. No. 3 Company. Discharged March 24, 1815, and entered on Incorporated Roll.

MILES, Richard. Private. Discharged March 24, 1815, and entered on Incorporated Roll.

MILLARD, Jason (Jacob). Captain Rapelje's Company. Private. Captain Abraham A. Rapelje's No. 3 Company.

MILLARD, Jesse. No. 1 Company. Private. Discharged March 24, 1815, and entered on Incorporated Roll.

MILLARD, John. Captain Rapelje's Company. Private. Captain Abraham A. Rapelje's No. 3 Company. Discharged March 24, 1815, and entered on Incorporated Roll.

MILLARD, Joseph. Captain Kerby's Company. Private.

MILLER, Jacob. Captain James Kerby's No. 1 Company. Private. Returned March 9, 1815, as deserted.

MILLS, Jacob. Captain Fraser's Company. Private. Discharged April 5, 1814.

MILLS, John. Captain Fraser's Company. Drummer. Discharged March 24, 1815, and entered on Incorporated Roll.

MILLS, Richard. Joined April 1, 1813, Captain Jarvie's Company. Private. Deserted April 18, 1814.

MILOTT, Paul. Captain Fraser's Company. Private. Discharged April 5, 1814.

MILOTT, Paul Jr. Captain Hamilton Walker's Company. Drummer.

MITCHELL, David. Joined March 27, 1813, Captain Jarvie's Company. Private. Captain William Jarvie's No. 2 Company. Discharged March 24, 1815, and entered on Incorporated Roll.

MITCHELL, William. Joined April 4, 1813, Captain John Kerr's Company. Private. Captain John Kerr's No. 8 Company. Discharged March 24, 1815, and entered on Incorporated Roll. See Casualties.

MONTROSS, Abraham. Major Titus G. Simons's Company. Private. Captain Abraham A. Rapelje's No. 3 Company.

MOORE, Daniel. Joined March 28, 1813, Captain Jarvie's Company. Private. Captain William Jarvie's No. 2 Company. Discharged March 24, 1815, and entered on Incorporated Roll.

MOORE, George. Joined March 26, 1813, Captain Jarvie's Company. Private. Captain William Jarvie's No. 2 Company. Discharged March 24, 1815, and entered on Incorporated Roll.

MOOR, R. Captain John McLean's Company. Private.

MORIN (Morah), Peter. Captain Henry Davy's Company. Private. Taken prisoner October 10, 1813. Captain Edward Walker's No. 5 Company. Discharged March 24, 1815, and entered on Incorporated Roll.

MORRISON, William. Captain John McLean's Company. Private.

MORRISON, William. Captain Hamilton Walker's Company. Private. Discharged April 5, 1814, as unfit. Probably same as above.

MORRISON, William. Captain Fraser's Company. Private.

MOWERSON, William. Captain Henry Davy's Company. Private.

MULLET, James A. Major Titus G. Simons's Company. Sergeant. See Casualties.

MURPHY, John. Joined April 5, 1813, Captain Jarvie's Company. Private. Noted in a return of January 1814 as a prisoner of war in the United States. Discharged March 24, 1815, and entered on Incorporated Roll. See Casualties.

MURRAY, John. Private. Discharged March 24, 1815, and entered on Incorporated Roll.

MYERS, Joseph. Joined before June 25, 1813, Captain John McDonell's Company. Private. Captain John McDonell's No. 9 Company. Discharged March 24, 1815, and entered on Incorporated Roll.

NAPPIN (Napier), Trueman. Joined April 5, 1813. Captain Washburn's Company. Private. Captain Daniel Washburn's No. 4 Company. Discharged March 24, 1815, and entered on Incorporated Roll.

NETTLETON, Samuel. (2nd Grenville Flank Company) Captain Hamilton Walker's Company. Private.

NETTLETON, Timothy. Captain Hamilton Walker's Company. Private.

NEVILLS, Andrew. Captain Kerby's Company. Private. Corporal. Captain James Kerby's No. 1 Company. Discharged March 24, 1815, and entered on Incorporated Roll.

NEWLAND, Henry. Joined April 7, 1813, Captain John Kerr's Company. Private. Captain John Kerr's No. 8 Company. Discharged March 24, 1815, and entered on Incorporated Roll.

NONEMAKER, Jacob. Private Captain Rapelje's Company. Captain Abraham A. Rapelje's No. 3 Company. Discharged March 24, 1815, and entered on Incorporated Roll.

NORTON, Lumin I. Captain Washburn's Company. Private. Captain Daniel Washburn's No. 4 Company. Discharged March 24, 1815, and entered on Incorporated Roll.

O'CONNER, Edward. Captain Henry Davy's Company. Private. Taken prisoner October 10, 1814. Captain Edward Walker's No. 5 Company. Discharged March 24, 1815, and entered on Incorporated Roll.

O'FLYNN, David. Captain Jarvie's Company. Private. Returned March 9, 1815, as deserted.

O'HARA, James. Captain Jarvie's Company. Private. Discharged April 5, 1814, as unfit.

OLDICK (Obdick), John. Joined April 8, 1813. Captain Washburn's Company. Private. Captain Daniel Washburn's No. 4 Company. Discharged March 24, 1815, and entered on Incorporated Roll.

OUTERKARK (Outerkirk), Henry. Joined before June 25, 1813, Captain John McDonell's Company. Private. Captain John McDonell's No. 9 Company. Discharged March 24, 1815, and entered on Incorporated Roll.

PANGMAN, Sebury (Sebra). Captain Henry Jones's Company. Private. Captain Hamilton Walker's No. 10 Company. Discharged March 24, 1815, and entered on Incorporated Roll.

PANGMAN, Timothy. Captain Archibald McLean's Company. Corporal. Demoted October, 1813, to private. Captain Archibald McLean's No. 6 Company. Discharged March 24, 1815, and entered on Incorporated Roll.

PANKETT, Joseph. Captain Fraser's Company. Private.

PARISH, Horace. Sergeant. Captain Hamilton Walker's No. 10 Company. Died August 1, 1814.

PEALON, Toussaint. Captain Hamilton Walker's Company. Private.

PARISH, Richard. Captain John McLean's Company. Private.

PARKER, Jarus. Captain Jarvie's Company. Private. Noted as deserted March 25, 1813.

PARKER, John. Joined March 25, 1813, Captain John Kerr's Company. Private. Discharged March 24, 1815, and entered on Incorporated Roll.

PARKER, Samuel. Private. Captain Rapelje's Company.

PARKER, Samuel. Captain Kerby's Company. Private.

PARLIAMENT, William. Captain Hamilton Walker's Company. Private. Captain Edward Walker's No. 5 Company. Discharged March 24, 1815, and entered on Incorporated Roll.

PARR, Alexander. Captain Archibald McLean's Company. Private.

PARRISE (Paris), Richard. Captain Fraser's Company. Private. Captain Thomas Fraser's No. 7 Company. Discharged March 24, 1815, and entered on Incorporated Roll.

PEARSON, John. Captain Kerby's Company. Private.

PELON, Yesant. Captain Jonas Jones's Company. Private. Discharged March 24, 1815, and entered on Incorporated Roll.

PERKINS, William. Joined March 28, 1813. Captain Jarvie's Company. Private. Corporal. Captain William Jarvie's No. 2 Company. Sergeant. Discharged March 24, 1815, and entered on Incorporated Roll.

PERRIN, Solomon. Captain Hamilton Walker's Company. Private. Corporal. Discharged March 24, 1815, and entered on Incorporated Roll.

PHILLIPS, Jehiel. Captain Hamilton Walker's Company. Private.

PHILLIPS, Henry. Captain Kerby's Company. Private.

PHILLIPS, Samuel. (2nd Grenville Flank Company) Captain Archibald McLean's Company. Corporal. Captain Archibald McLean's No. 6 Company. Prisoner of war. Discharged March 24, 1815, and entered on Incorporated Roll.

PHILLIPS, Thomas. (2nd Grenville Flank Company) Captain Hamilton Walker's Company. Private. Captain Hamilton Walker's No. 10 Company. Discharged March 24, 1815, and entered on Incorporated Roll.

POLLY, John. Joined before June 25, 1813, Captain John McDonell's Company. Corporal. Private. Discharged March 24, 1815, and entered on Incorporated Roll.

POMAVILLE, Joseph. Captain Fraser's Company. Private. Captain Thomas Fraser's No. 7 Company. Discharged March 24, 1815, and entered on Incorporated Roll.

PONKET (Ponkett), Joseph. Captain Jonas Jones's Company. Private. Captain Thomas Fraser's No. 7 Company. Discharged March 24, 1815, and entered on Incorporated Roll.

PORTER, David. Captain Jarvie's Company. Private. Noted as a prisoner of war in the United States in a return of January 1814. Returned March 9, 1815, as deserted.

POWELL, Royall. Captain Edward Walker's No. 5 Company. Private. Discharged March 24, 1815, and entered on Incorporated Roll.

POWERS, Anthony. Drummer. Discharged March 24, 1815, and entered on Incorporated Roll.

PRAY, Joseph. Captain Henry Davy's Company. Private. Deserted August 5, 1813.

PREMER, Peter. Joined before June 25, 1813, Captain John McDonell's Company. Private. Noted in a return of July 25 as absent without leave.

PRENDERGAST, Richard. Captain Kerby's Company. Private.

PRINGLE, Francis T. Joined April 10, 1813. Captain Henry Davy's Company. Private. Captain Daniel Washburn's No. 4 Company. Prisoner of war. Discharged March 24, 1815, and entered on Incorporated Roll.

PROSSER, Samuel, Captain Archibald McLean's Company. Private. Captain Archibald McLean's No. 6 Company. Discharged March 24, 1815, and entered on Incorporated Roll. See Casualties.

RAMSAY, James. Captain Kerby's Company. Private.

RANDLE, Benjamin. Joined February 2, 1814, Captain Henry Davy's Company. Private. Captain Edward Walker's No. 5 Company. Discharged March 24, 1815, and entered on Incorporated Roll.

RANDLE, Joseph. Captain Hamilton Walker's Company. Private. Noted as deserted April 18, 1814.

RANGER, Baptiste. Captain Jonas Jones's Company. Private. Noted as deserted July 22, 1813.

RANGER, Joseph. Captain Jonas Jones's Company. Private. Noted as deserted July 22, 1813.

RANO (Ranno), Joseph. Private. Captain Edward Walker's No. 5 Company. Discharged March 24, 1815, and entered on Incorporated Roll.

RAVEN, Peter G. Captain Hamilton Walker's Company. Private. Discharged March 24, 1815, and entered on Incorporated Roll.

RAY, Daniel. Major Simons's Company. Corporal.

REED, James. Joined May 19, 1813, Captain Jarvie's Company. Private. Corporal. Captain William Jarvie's No. 2 Company. Discharged March 24, 1815, and entered on Incorporated Roll.

REILLY (O'Reilly), James. Captain Kerby's Company. Private. Corporal. Captain James Kerby's No. 1 Company. Discharged March 24, 1815, and entered on Incorporated Roll.

REILLY, John. Joined April 12, 1813, Captain Kerby's Company. Private. Captain James Kerby's No. 1 Company.

REVEE, Alexander. Captain Fraser's Company. Private. Captain Thomas Fraser's No. 7 Company. Discharged March 24, 1815, and entered on Incorporated Roll.

RICHARDSON, John. Captain John McLean's Company. Private. Captain John McDonell's Company. Discharged April 5, 1814.

ROBBINS, Robert. Joined March 27, 1813, Captain Kerr's Company. Private. Corporal. Captain John Kerr's No. 8 Company. Discharged March 24, 1815, and entered on Incorporated Roll.

ROBERTSON (Robinson), Seth. Captain Rapelje's Company. Private. Captain Abraham A. Rapelje's No. 3 Company. Discharged March 24, 1815, and entered on Incorporated Roll.

ROBINSON, John. No. 3 Company. Private. Discharged March 24, 1815, and entered on Incorporated Roll.

ROBIDEAU, Joseph. Joined before June 25, 1813, Captain John McDonell's Company. Private. Captain John McDonell's No. 9 Company. Discharged March 24, 1815, and entered on Incorporated Roll.

ROBILLARD, Antoine. Captain Hamilton Walker's Company. Private.

ROBILLARD (Reubard), Joseph. Captain Hamilton Walker's Company. Private. Captain Hamilton Walker's No. 10 Company. Discharged March 24, 1815, and entered on Incorporated Roll.

ROCK, Christopher. Captain Henry Jones's Company. Private. Captain Hamilton Walker's No. 10 Company. Discharged March 24, 1815, and entered on Incorporated Roll.

RODGERS (Rogers), Stilman. Joined April 7, 1813. Captain Archibald McLean's Company. Private. Drummer, Drum Major (December 25, 1813). Private. Captain John Kerr's No. 8 Company. Discharged March 24, 1815, and entered on Incorporated Roll.

ROSE, James. Private. Discharged March 24, 1815, and entered on Incorporated Roll.

ROUSSEAU, Antwaine. Captain Archibald McLean's Company. Private.

ROUSSEAU (Russo), Hugh. Joined before June 25, 1813, Captain John McDonell's Company. Private. Captain John McDonell's No. 9 Company. Discharged March 24, 1815, and entered on Incorporated Roll.

ROWLIN (Rowland), Thomas. Captain Fraser's Company. Private. Captain Thomas Fraser's No. 7 Company. Discharged March 24, 1815, and entered on Incorporated Roll.

ROWE, George. Private. Discharged March 24, 1815, and entered on Incorporated Roll.

ROWLS (Rolls), William. (2nd Lincoln Flank Company) Joined March 29, 1813, Captain James Kerby's Company. Sergeant. Captain James Kerby's No. 1 Company. Discharged March 24, 1815, and entered on Incorporated Roll.

RUNNIONS, Michael. Joined April 1, 1813, Captain John Kerr's Company. Private. Captain John Kerr's No. 8 Company.

RUSS, Wilson (William). Joined April 6, 1813. Captain Washburn's Company. Private. Captain Daniel Washburn's No. 4 Company. Discharged March 24, 1815, and entered on Incorporated Roll.

RUSSIGNOL (Rosignol), Antoine (Anthony). Captain Edward Walker's Company. Private. Captain Edward Walker's No. 5 Company. Discharged March 24, 1815, and entered on Incorporated Roll.

RYCKMAN, James. Major Titus G. Simons's Company. Private. Captain Abraham A. Rapelje's No. 3 Company. Discharged March 24, 1815, and entered on Incorporated Roll.

SAGE, William. Captain Jarvie's Company. Private. Joined March 28, 1813. Returned March 9, 1815, as deserted.

SANSOUCI (Sansacie), Francis. Captain Henry Davy's Company. Private. Captain Edward Walker's No. 5 Company.

SARASIN, Jean Baptiste. Captain Hamilton Walker's Company. Private. Noted as absent without leave February 25, 1814.

SAWYER, Jonathan. Captain Archibald McLean's Company. Private. Corporal. Captain Archibald McLean's No. 6 Company. Prisoner of war. Discharged March 24, 1815, and entered on Incorporated Roll.

SCOTT, Abraham. Joined before June 25, 1813, Captain John McDonell's Company. Private. Captain John McDonell's No. 9 Company.

SCOTT, John. Captain Jarvie's Company. Private. Noted as deserted March 25, 1813.

SCOTT, William. Joined before June 25, 1813, Captain John McDonell's Company. Private. Captain John McDonell's No. 9 Company.

SCRAM, Henry. Major Simons's Company. Private. No. 3 Company. Discharged March 24, 1815, and entered on Incorporated Roll.

SEALEY, Abraham. Captain John McLean's Company. Private.

SEATON, Charles. Joined before June 25, 1813, Captain John McDonell's Company. Private. Deserted September 9, 1813.

SEELEY, James. Captain Archibald McLean's Company. Private. Captain Archibald McLean's No. 6 Company. Prisoner of war. Discharged March 24, 1815, and entered on Incorporated Roll.

SEELEY, John. Captain Jonas Jones's Company. Private. Captain Archibald McLean's No. 6 Company. Discharged March 24, 1815, and entered on Incorporated Roll. See Casualties.

SEELEY, Joseph. Captain Archibald McLean's Company. Private.

SENEY, Charles. Joined April 8, 1813, Captain John McLeans's Company. Private. Captain John Kerr's No. 8 Company.

SESMAH, Ambrose. Captain Fraser's Company. Private.

SHANNON, Michael. Joined February 25, 1815, Captain John Kerr's Company.

SHAVER, John. Joined March 29, 1813, Captain Jarvie's Company. Private. Captain William Jarvie's No. 2 Company. Discharged March 24, 1815, and entered on Incorporated Roll.

SHAVER, John. Captain Rapelje's Company. Private.

SHEFFIELD, William. Joined before June 25, 1813, Captain John McDonell's Company. Private. Discharged April 5, 1814, as unfit.

SHELDON, Peter. Joined before April 25, 1813, Captain Henry Davy's Company. Private. Noted as absent without leave May 22, 1813.

SHINHOLT, Martin. Captain Kerby's Company. Private.

SHOFELDT, William. Major Titus G. Simons's Company. Private.

SHOVEAUX (Shevaux), Joseph. Joined April 20, 1813, Captain Jarvie's Company. Private. Captain William Jarvie's No. 2 Company. Discharged March 24, 1815, and entered on Incorporated Roll.

SHULTS (Shulth), Edward. Captain Henry Davy's Company. Private. Captain Edward Walker's No. 5 Company. Discharged March 24, 1815, and entered on Incorporated Roll.

SHUTS (Sheets), John. Joined March 20, 1813, Captain John Kerr's Company. Private. Captain John Kerr's No. 8 Company. Discharged March 24, 1815, and entered on Incorporated Roll.

SIMMONS, David. Major Titus G. Simons's Company. Private. No. 3 Company. Discharged March 24, 1815, and entered on Incorporated Roll.

SIMONS, Walter. Major Simons's Company. Sergeant. Sergeant Major (June 25, 1813).

SLAWSON, Henry. Captain Kerby's Company. Private.

SMALLMAN, George. Joined April 4, 1813, Captain Jarvie's Company. Sergeant. Captain William Jarvie's No. 2 Company. Discharged March 24, 1815, and entered on Incorporated Roll.

SMITH, David. Captain Archibald McLean's Company. Corporal. Private. Captain Archibald McLean's No. 6 Company.

SMITH, John. Captain Jonas Jones's Company. Private. Captain Daniel Washburn's No. 4 Company. Discharged March 24, 1815, and entered on Incorporated Roll.

SMITH, John. Joined April 16, 1813, Captain John Kerr's Company. Private. Captain John Kerr's No. 8 Company. Discharged March 24, 1815, and entered on Incorporated Roll.

SMITH, Samuel. Captain Rapelje's Company. Private. Captain Abraham A. Rapelje's No. 3 Company.

SNYDER, Daniel. Joined April 19, 1813. Private. From Lieutenant Jarvis's Artillery Company. Captain William Jarvie's No. 2 Company. Discharged March 24, 1815, and entered on Incorporated Roll.

SNIDER, John. Captain Henry Davy's Company. Sergeant. Captain Daniel Washburn's No. 4 Company. Died August 1, 1814.

SNYDER, Jacob. Captain Archibald McLean's Company. Private. Captain Archibald McLean's No. 6 Company. Discharged March 24, 1815, and entered on Incorporated Roll. See Casualties.

SOPER, Joseph. Captain Henry Davy's Company. Private. Died June 20, 1813.

SOUTER, William. Joined March 26, 1813, Captain Jarvie's Company. Private.

SOUTHWART, Abner. Captain Kerby's Company. Private.

SPICER, Phillip. Captain Hamilton Walker's Company. Private. Captain Hamilton Walker's No. 10 Company. Prisoner of war.

SPORE, Lawrence. (2nd Grenville Flank Company) Private. Captain Hamilton Walker's No. 10 Company.

SQUIRES, Jonathan. Captain Archibald McLean's Company. Private.

SQUIRES, Robert. Captain Archibald McLean's Company. Private. Deserted October 25, 1813.

St. GERMAIN, Jacob. Private. Captain Thomas Fraser's No. 7 Company. Discharged March 24, 1815, and entered on Incorporated Roll.

St. PIERRE, Francis. Joined April 10, 1813, Captain John Kerr's Company. Private. Captain John Kerr's No. 8 Company. Discharged March 24, 1815, and entered on Incorporated Roll.

St. PIERRE, Joseph Sr. Captain Kerr's Company. Private. Captain John Kerr's No. 8 Company. Discharged March 24, 1815, and entered on Incorporated Roll (or Joseph Jr.).

St. PIERRE, Joseph Jr. Captain Kerr's Company. Private.

St. PIERRE, Martin. Joined September 12, 1813, Captain John Kerr's Company. Private. Captain John Kerr's No. 8 Company. Discharged March 24, 1815, and entered on Incorporated Roll.

St. PIERRE, Peter. Joined April 10, 1813, Captain John Kerr's Company. Private. Captain John Kerr's No. 8 Company.

St. THOMAS, Michael. Captain Hamilton Walker's Company. Private.

STACKHOUSE, John. Captain Henry Davy's Company. Private. Deserted July 31, 1813, from the gunboats.

STALLS, John. Captain Jonas Jones's Company. Private. Noted as deserted July 11, 1813.

STAMP, John. Joined before June 25, 1813, Captain John McDonell's Company. Private. Captain John McDonell's No. 9 Company.

STARKEY, William. Private. See Casualties.

STARKWEATHER, John. Joined March 23, 1813, Captain Jarvie's Company. Private. Captain William Jarvie's No. 2 Company. Discharged March 24, 1815, and entered on Incorporated Roll.

STEPHENSON, Nathan. Captain Kerby's Company. Private.

STEWART, David. Captain Fraser's Company. Private. Captain Thomas Fraser's No. 7 Company. Discharged March 24, 1815, and entered on Incorporated Roll.

STONEBURNER, Leonard. Captain Kerr's Company. Sergeant. Captain John Kerr's No. 8 Company. Discharged March 24, 1815, and entered on Incorporated Roll.

STONEMAN, Leonard. Captain Jonas Jones's Company. Sergeant.

STONER, Henry. Captain Jarvie's Company. Private. Captain William Jarvie's No. 2 Company. Returned March 9, 1815, as deserted.

STORMS, Gilbert. Captain Henry Davy's Company. Private. Taken prisoner October 10, 1813. Captain Edward Walker's No. 5 Company. Discharged March 24, 1815, and entered on Incorporated Roll.

STORMS, William. Captain Henry Davy's Company. Private. Captain Edward Walker's No. 5 Company. Discharged March 24, 1815, and entered on Incorporated Roll.

STORSHAW (Storshew), Lewis. Captain Jarvie's Company. Private. Joined April 13, 1813. Noted in a return of January 1814 as a prisoner of war in the United States. Returned March 9, 1815, as deserted.

SUMMERFIELD, Charles. Major Titus G. Simons's Company. Private.

SUTER, William. Captain William Jarvie's No. 2 Company. Private. Discharged March 24, 1815, and entered on Incorporated Roll.

SWEET, Allan. Captain Archibald McLean's Company. Sergeant. Prisoner of war. No. 6 Company. Discharged March 24, 1815, and entered on Incorporated Roll.

SWEET, James. Joined April 1, 1813. Captain Henry Davy's Company. Private. Captain Daniel Washburn's No. 4 Company. Discharged March 24, 1815, and entered on Incorporated Roll.

TALLMAN, Ephrain. Captain Hamilton Walker's Company. Private. Noted as deserted June 26, 1813.

TAYLOR, Richard. Captain Rapelje's Company. Private.

TAYLOR, William. Captain Henry Davy's Company. Private. Captain Edward Walker's No. 5 Company. Discharged March 24, 1815, and entered on Incorporated Roll.

THOMPSON, John. (1st Addington Flank Company) Captain Henry Davy's Company. Private. Captain Edward Walker's No. 5 Company. Prisoner of war. Discharged March 24, 1815, and entered on Incorporated Roll.

THOMSON, George. Captain Archibald McLean's Company. Private. Captain Archibald McLean's No. 6 Company. Discharged March 24, 1815, and entered on Incorporated Roll.

THOMSON, Robert. Captain Archibald McLean's Company. Private. Captain Archibald McLean's No. 6 Company. Discharged March 24, 1815, and entered on Incorporated Roll.

THOREAUX, Joseph. Captain Jarvie's Company. Private

TIPP, John. Joined April 26, 1813, Captain Jarvie's Company. Private. Captain William Jarvie's No. 2 Company. Discharged March 24, 1815, and entered on Incorporated Roll.

TRADER, Jacob. Joined March 10, 1813. Captain Henry Davy's Company. Private. Captain Daniel Washburn's No. 4 Company. Discharged March 24, 1815, and entered on Incorporated Roll.

TRICKEY, Isaac. Joined before June 25, 1813, Captain John McDonell's Company. Private. Noted in a return of July 25, 1813, as absent without leave.

TRUAX, George. Joined before June 25, 1813, Captain John McLean's Company. Sergeant. Captain Edward Walker's No. 5 Company. Discharged March 24, 1815, and entered on Incorporated Roll.

TRUMBLE, John. Captain Hamilton Walker's No. 10 Company. Drummer. Discharged March 24, 1815, and entered on Incorporated Roll.

TUFTS, Thomas. Captain Archibald McLean's Company. Private. Captain Archibald McLean's No. 6 Company. Prisoner of war. Discharged March 24, 1815, and entered on Incorporated Roll.

TURNER, David L. (2nd Grenville Flank Company) Captain Hamilton Walker's Company. Corporal.

TWINER (Turner), James. Captain Edward Walker's Company. Private. Corporal. Captain Edward Walker's No. 5 Company.

TYRER, John. Captain Jarvie's Company. Private. Noted as deserted March 25, 1813.

VAIL, John. Captain Henry Davy's Company. Private.

VALLADD, Duncan. Captain Fraser's Company. Private. Discharged April 5, 1814.

VAN ALSTINE, David. Captain Henry Davy's Company. Private.

VAN BLARICKER, Martin. Private. Captain Edward Walker's No. 5 Company. Discharged March 24, 1815, and entered on Incorporated Roll.

VAN WICKLER, (Van Wicklen) Adam. Captain Henry Davy's Company. Private. Captain Edward Walker's No. 5 Company. Discharged March 24, 1815, and entered on Incorporated Roll.

VAN BLARICKER, Isaac. Captain Hamilton Walker's Company. Private. No. 5 Company. Discharged March 24, 1815, and entered on Incorporated Roll.

VANALSTINE, Duncan. (1st Addington Flank Company) Joined March 25, 1813. Captain Washburn's Company. Private. Corporal. Captain Daniel Washburn's No. 4 Company. Discharged March 24, 1815, and entered on Incorporated Roll.

VANDAL, Simon. Joined March 31, 1813, Captain John Kerr's Company. Private. Captain John Kerr's No. 8 Company. Discharged March 24, 1815, and entered on Incorporated Roll.

VANLOUEN, Henry. (1st Addington Flank Company) Joined March 12, 1813. Captain Washburn's Company. Private. Captain Daniel Washburn's No. 4 Company.

VANTASSELL, Daniel. Joined April 20, 1813. Captain Washburn's Company. Private. Captain Daniel Washburn's No. 4 Company. Discharged March 24, 1815, and entered on Incorporated Roll.

VASSOUR (Vasar), Joseph. Joined before June 25, 1813, Captain John McDonell's Company. Private.

VEIL, John. Captain Hamilton Walker's Company. Private. Joined March 25, 1814, and deserted April 1, 1814.

VICE, Jacob. Captain Jarvie's Company. Private. Joined March 28, 1813.

VIVELAMOUR, Nicholas. Joined March 20, 1813. Captain Jonas Jones's Company. Drummer. Captain John Kerr's No. 8 Company. Discharged March 24, 1815, and entered on Incorporated Roll.

WALROD, Jonas. Captain Kerby's Company. Private.

WALTERS (Waters), Reuben. Captain Henry Davy's Company. Private. Captain Washburn's Company.

WARNER, Asa. Captain Jonas Jones's Company. Sergeant. Deserted October 5, 1813.

WASHBURN, Gilbert. Captain John Kerr's Company. Private. Noted in a return of July 24, 1813, as deserted. Returned March 9, 1815, as deserted.

WATERS (Walters), Reuben. Joined April 15, 1813, Captain Daniel Washburn's Company. Private. Captain Hamilton Walker's No. 10 Company. Discharged March 24, 1815, and entered on Incorporated Roll.

WEIS (Weese), William. Captain Henry Davy's Company. Private. Taken prisoner October 10, 1813. Captain Edward Walker's No. 5 Company. Discharged March 24, 1815, and entered on Incorporated Roll.

WELLS, Henry. Joined April 27, 1813, Captain Jarvie's Company.

WELLS, Peter. Captain John McLean's Company. Private.

WHITACAR, Peter. Captain Fraser's Company. Private.

WHITAKER, Thomas. Captain Kerby's Company. Private.

WHITE, Isaac. Captain Archibald McLean's Company. Private.

WHITE, Jacob. Joined March 28, 1813, Captain William Jarvie's No. 2 Company. Private.

WHITE, James. Joined April 9, 1813, Captain Washburn's Company. Private. Captain Daniel Washburn's No. 4 Company. Died October 16, 1814.

WICKHAM, John. Captain Jarvie's Company. Private. Returned March 9, 1815, as deserted.

WIDNER, John. (1st Middlesex Flank Company) Returned as having joined the Incorporated Militia.

WILCOX (Willcot), Paul. Captain Jarvie's Company. Private. Noted in a return of January 1814 as a prisoner of war in the United States. Returned March 9, 1815, as deserted.

WILLIAMS, Benjamin. Joined April 4, 1813, Captain Henry Davy's Company. Private. Captain Edward Walker's No. 5 Company. Discharged March 24, 1815, and entered on Incorporated Roll.

WILLIAMS, Robert L. (1st Addington Flank Company) Captain Henry Davy's Company. Private. Captain Edward Walker's No. 5 Company. Discharged and entered on Incorporated Roll.

WILLIAMS, Thomas. Captain Archibald McLean's Company. Private.

WILLIS, John. (2nd Lincoln Flank Company) Joined March 30, 1813, Captain James Kerby's Company. Private. Corporal. Demoted to private. Captain James Kerby's No. 1 Company.

WILLIS, Samuel. Captain Kerby's Company. Private.

WILLSON, Jacob. Captain Kerby's Company. Private.

WINTERMUTE (Wintermoot), Christopher. Major Titus G. Simons's Company. Private. Captain Abraham A. Rapelje's No. 3 Company. Discharged March 24, 1815, and entered on Incorporated Roll.

WINTERS, Asa. Major Titus G. Simons's Company. Private. Corporal. Captain James Kerby's No. 1 Company. Prisoner of war. Discharged March 24, 1815, and entered on Incorporated Roll.

WISE, Allen. Captain Kerr's Company. Drummer. Captain John McDonell's No. 9 Company.

WOLF (or Wolfe), Joseph. Captain Hamilton Walker's No. 10 Company. Private. Prisoner of war. Discharged March 24, 1815, and entered on Incorporated Roll.

WOLFRAM, Philip. Captain Henry Davy's Company. Private. See Casualties.

WOOD, Jonas. Joined before June 25, 1813, Captain John McDonell's Company. Private. Captain John McDonell's No. 9 Company. Discharged March 24, 1815, and entered on Incorporated Roll.

WOOD, Moses. Joined before June 25, 1813, Captain John McDonell's Company. Private. Captain Archibald McLean's No. 6 Company. Corporal (January 1, 1815). Discharged March 24, 1815, and entered on Incorporated Roll.

WOODS, Joseph. Captain Rapelje's Company. Private.

WURTZ, Abraham. Captain Jarvie's Company. Private. Returned March 9, 1815, as deserted.

WYAT, Peter. Joined April 14, 1813, Private.

YORK, Isaac. Captain Henry Davy's Company. Private. Taken prisoner October 10, 1813.

YORK, Stephen. Captain Kerby's Company. Private.

YORKE, Silas. Major Titus G. Simons's Company. Private. Corporal. Captain Abraham A. Rapelje's No. 3 Company. Discharged March 24, 1815, and entered on Incorporated Roll.

YOUNG, Anthony. Captain Hamilton Walker's No. 10 Company. Private. Discharged March 24, 1815, and entered on Incorporated Roll.

YOUNG, Hiram. Captain Archibald McLean's Company. Private. Captain Archibald McLean's No. 6 Company. Captain Hamilton Walker's No. 10 Company. Discharged March 24, 1815, and entered on Incorporated Roll.

YOUNG, William. Captain John McDonell's Company. Private. Captain John McDonell's No. 9 Company. Discharged March 24, 1815, and entered on Incorporated Roll.

YOUNG, William. Captain John McLean's Company. Private. Captain John McDonell's No. 9 Company. Discharged March 24, 1815, and entered on Incorporated Roll.

YOUNGLOVE, David. Captain Kerby's Company. Private. Captain Abraham A. Rapelje's No. 3 Company. Captain Hamilton Walker's No. 10 Company. Discharged March 24, 1815, and entered on Incorporated Roll.

YOUNGLOVE, Ezekiel. Captain Kerby's Company. Private.

YOUREUX, Isaac. Joined April 5, 1813, Captain Henry Davy's Company. Private.

VII

THE MILITIA VOLUNTEERS
1813 ~ 1815

T HE question of raising companies of rangers to fight alongside the Native inhabitants had been raised a number of times in late 1812 and early 1813. The Native allies themselves had asked for units similar to Butler's Rangers, which had proved so effective in the American Revolutionary War. The Western Rangers, with its strong connections with the Indian Department, was formed in an attempt to fill that need. Other companies, the Loyal Kent and the Loyal Essex Rangers, were organized in the fall of 1813 by Loyalists who withdrew from the Western District after it had been occupied by the Americans in October 1813. Following the destruction of the Right Division at Moraviantown on October 5, and the consequent withdrawal of the regular troop toward Burlington, a similar band of Loyalists, the Loyal London Volunteers, banded together and remained active in the field until the sedentary organization was reestablished in February 1814.

The nominal roll of the Militia Volunteers follows the list of corps and officers, on the next page.

MILITIA VOLUNTEER CORPS AND OFFICERS

1813–1814

THE WESTERN RANGERS

Captain William Caldwell. Transferred to Indian Department
  May 24, 1814.
Captain James Askin. Assumed command May 24, 1814.

THE LOYAL KENT VOLUNTEERS, OR KENT RANGERS

Lieutenant John McGregor. Promoted to captain May 28, 1814.
Lieutenant James McGregor
Ensign William Peck

THE LOYAL ESSEX VOLUNTEERS, OR ESSEX RANGERS

Lieutenant Nicholas Lytle
Ensign Prideax Girty

THE LOYAL LONDON VOLUNTEERS

This company was not authorized, but is shown from November 24,
1813, to February 25, 1814. There is no return, and the composition
of corps varied, but its strength was maintained at 50 rank and file for
three months.

Captain William Parks (2nd Norfolk)
Lieutenant Jonathan Austin (2nd Norfolk)
Lieutenant McFarland Wilson (2nd Norfolk)
Ensign Abraham Messacre (1st Norfolk)

NOMINAL ROLL OF THE
MILITIA VOLUNTEERS

THE WESTERN RANGERS

ASKIN, James. *Captain.* See 2nd Essex.
CALDWELL, Thomas. *Lieutenant.* See 1st Essex.
CALDWELL, Francis. *Lieutenant.* See 1st Essex.
CALDWELL, William. *Captain.* See 1st Essex.
COCKLE, John. Private.
DRAKE, Roderick. Private.
EBERTS, Henry. Sergeant. See 1st Essex. See Casualties.
ELLIOTT, William. *Captain.* See 1st Essex.
GOUIN, Claud. *Lieutenant.*
HEWARD, James. *Ensign.*
McCULLUM, Hugh. *Ensign.*
McPHERSON, John. Private.
MOOR, Stephen. Private.
PECK, John. *Lieutenant.* See 1st Kent Flank Company.
PECK, William. Private. See Kent Volunteers.
TOPP, Abraham. Private.
WILLIAM, John. Sergeant.
WILLIAMS, Robert. Private.

THE LOYAL KENT VOLUNTEERS

Mustered from November 25, 1813. Attached to the Incorporated Battalion in early 1815 and reduced at the end of the war.

AMER, Jacob. Private. See Casualties.
ARNOLD, John. Private.
BARKER, Ephriam. Private. See 1st Kent Flank Company.
BROWN, Neil. Private. See Casualties.
BUCHANNAN, Alexander. Private.
COLL, Daniel. Private. See Casualties.
COLL, John. Sergeant. See Casualties.
COLL, Jesse. Private.
COLL, William. Sergeant. See Casualties.
COLL, Samuel. Sergeant. See 1st Kent Flank Company.
COLL, James. Private.
CRANDELL, William. Private.
CRAWFORD, James. Private. See Casualties. See 1st Kent Flank Company.

CRAWFORD, John. Private.

CRAWFORD, Samuel. Private.

CUNTRAMAN, Joseph. Private.

CUTTO, Simon. Private.

DESMOND, William. Private.

DOLSEN, Isaac. Private.

DOLSEN, John. Private.

EVERRITT, David. Private. See 1st Kent Flank Company.

FENNEL, Daniel. Private. See 1st Kent Flank Company.

FIELD, Daniel. Private. See Casualties. See 1st Kent Flank Company.

FIELD, George. Private. See 1st Kent Flank Company.

FIELD, James. Private.

GLASSNER, William. Private.

GORDON, Aron. Private. See Casualties.

GORDON, John. Private.

HACKNEY, Edward. Private.

HOLMES, Daniel. Private. See Casualties.

HUBBLE, Rufus. Private.

JOHNSON, James. Private. See 1st Kent Flank Company.

LASH, John. Private.

LIGHTFOTT, William. Private.

LYONS, John. Private. See Casualties.

McCULLAM, Peter. Private.

McDONALD, Allen. Private.

McDONALD, Archibald. Private.

McDONALD, John. Private. See Casualties. GSM, Fort Detroit.

McDUGLE, Angus. Private. See Casualties. See 1st Kent Flank Company.

McDUGLE, Hectra (?). Private. See 1st Kent Flank Company.

McDUGLE, John. Private.

McDUGLE, Laughlin. Private. See Casualties. GSM, Fort Detroit.

McGREGOR, James. *Lieutenant*. See Casualties. See 2nd Essex.

McGREGOR, John. *Captain*. See Casualties.

McKENZIE, Kenneth. Private.

McPHERSON, Daniel. Private.

MITCHAL, John. Private. See Casualties.

MOODY, James. Private.

PATTERSON, William. Private. See 1st Kent Flank Company.

PECK, William. *Ensign*. See Western Rangers.

PHENCELO (?), John. Private.

QUICK, David. Private. See Casualties.

QUICK, John. Private.

ROACH, Morris. Private. GSM, Fort Detroit. See 1st Essex,
    1st Flank Company.
ROWE, William. Private. See 1st Kent Flank Company.
SHAW, John. Private. GSM, Fort Detroit.
SHAW, William. Private. See Casualties. See 1st Kent Flank Company.
SHUBURG, Francis. Private.
SMALL, Morris. Private.
SPEARS, James. Private. See Casualties.
STEPHENS, Garret. Private.
STERLING, John. Private.
STEWART, James. Sergeant.
SUMMER, George. Private. See Casualties.
UNDERWOOD, William. Private.
WARD, John. Private.
WARD, William. Private. See Casualties.
WEST, George. Private.
WISE, Charles. Private. See 1st Kent Flank Company.

THE LOYAL ESSEX VOLUNTEERS

Lieutenant Nicholas Lytle commanded a company of Essex Volunteers.
The earliest payroll found is from March 25 to April 24, 1814. The last
record of the company is the period ending March 24, 1815. In this last
payroll this corps is referred to as "The Essex Rangers." They were
active in the London and Niagara Districts.

BALDWIN, Russel. Private. Joined April 25, 1814. See 1st Essex,
    1st Flank Company.
BALDWIN, Nathan. Private. Joined April 25, 1814.
BALDWIN, Benjamin. Private. Joined April 25, 1814. See 1st Essex,
    1st Flank Company.
BELL, Thomas. Private. First shown March 25, 1814, not shown
    May 25.
BUTLER, Francis. Private. First shown March 25, 1814. See 1st
    Essex, 2nd Flank Company.
DAVIS, John. Private. Joined April 25, 1814, not shown May 25.
DEGARDEW, Francis. Private. First shown March 25, 1814, not
    shown May 25.
DOULAR, Robert. Private. First shown March 25, 1814.
FALMER, John. Sergeant. Joined May 25, 1814.
GURTY (Girty), Prideaux. *Ensign*. First shown March 25, 1814. Last
    shown October 24, 1814.

LYTLE, Nicholas. *Lieutenant*. First shown March 25, 1814. See 1st Essex, 1st Flank Company.

PARDO, William. Private. First shown March 25, 1814. See 1st Essex, 1st Flank Company.

PHILLIPS, Joseph. Private. Joined May 25, 1814.

PRICE, James. Sergeant. First shown March 25, 1814. See 1st Essex, 1st Flank Company.

QUICK, John. Private. Joined May 25, 1814. See 1st Essex, 1st Flank Company.

WHITE, Thompson. Private. First shown March 25, 1814. See 1st Essex, 1st Flank Company.

WHITE, Silas. Private. First shown March 25, 1814. See 1st Essex, 1st Flank Company.

WILKERSON, Alexander. Private. Joined May 25, 1814.

WILKERSON, James. Private. Joined May 25, 1814.

YOUNG, Peter. Sergeant. First shown March 25, 1814. See 1st Essex, 1st Flank Company.

VIII

CASUALTIES

NO comprehensive return has been found that details the losses of the Upper Canadian militia in the war. It is unlikely that one was ever assembled. A list has survived of those who applied for and were granted pensions, but it is far from complete. The pension list gives a total of 19 killed, 86 died of disease while on duty, and 144 wounded or hurt while on duty. It must be remembered that pensions were only to be paid to those who, if wounded, were incapacitated; and the only claims on the government in the case of a death were those of direct dependents, the militiaman's widow and minor children.

A look at the difference between the pension lists and the killed and wounded of one well-documented action, at Queenston in October 1812, demonstrates the problems in relying on the pension lists as a guide to the militia losses during the war. A return of killed and wounded made after the engagement states that one rank and file of the Lincoln Artillery was wounded; one adjutant, one sergeant and 12 rank and file of the Lincoln Militia were wounded; two rank and file of the York Militia were killed; and one lieutenant, one sergeant and 15 rank and file of the York Militia were wounded. The pension list only includes two rank and file for York wounded and two for Lincoln. That means that neither of the two men who were killed were entered, and of the 32 of all ranks who were wounded, only four are noted.

This is a preliminary list of militiamen who were killed, died of disease, were wounded or hurt or made prisoners of war and imprisoned in the United States.

ACKER, Abraham. 4th Lincoln, Private. Died, disease, November 1812.

ADAIR, John. 4th Lincoln, Private. Died, disease, November 18, 1812. Entered on Pension List.

ADAMS, David. 2nd Leeds, Private. Flanker. Wounded, September 21, 1812.

ADAMS, George. 1st Lincoln, *Lieutenant.* Wounded, Fort George, April 27, 1813. Entered on Pension List. Taken prisoner October 1813 and imprisoned. Paroled on December 22, 1813.

ADAMS, Samuel. 2nd Lincoln, Private. Killed in action at Chippewa, July 5, 1814. Entered on Pension List.

AEQUETTE, Pierre. Incorporated Militia, Private. Died, disease, May 31, 1813. Entered on Pension List.

AERHART, Simon. 1st Addington, Private. Returned as died on service.

ALEXANDER, Hugh. 3rd Lincoln, *Lieutenant.* Taken prisoner July 9, 1814, and removed to the United States. Returned March 18, 1815.

ALGEE, William. 1st Norfolk, Private. Flank Company. Returned as died in hospital at Fort Erie, December 1812.

ALLAIN, Charles. Returned as a prisoner of war held at Pittsfield, Massachusetts, in 1814.

ALLEN, Samuel. 1st Oxford, Teamster. Stabbed by a militiaman, September 27, 1812. Entered on Pension List.

ALWARD, (Allwood) Reuben. 1st Norfolk, Private. Wounded, loss of an eye, Fort Erie, November 28, 1812. Entered on Pension List.

ARQUIT, Pierre. 1st Glengarry, Private. Ruptured coming up the River St. Lawrence with a brigade of batteaux with troops and stores, October 22, 1812. Entered on Pension List.

AUGUSTINE, Abel. 1st Essex, Private. Died, disease, April 1, 1813. Entered on Pension List.

AVERY, Ebenezer. 2nd Leeds, Private. Wounded by an accident, Gananoque, January 26, 1813. Entered on Pension List.

BACCHUS, Ozias. Captain Cameron's Provincial Artillery, Gunner. Returned as missing after the action at Fort George, May 27, 1813.

BADICHON, Pierre. 2nd Essex, Private. Killed at the River Raisin, January 22, 1813.

BALDWIN, Nathan. 1st Middlesex, Private. Wounded at Lundy's Lane, July 25, 1814. Entered on Pension List.

BALM, Jacob. 2nd Lincoln, Sergeant. Died, disease, December 2, 1812. Entered on Pension List.

BARBER, Stephen. 2nd Lincoln, Private. Accidentally hurt, Queenston Heights, September 5, 1813. Leg fractured. Entered on Pension List.

BARNARD, Alexander. 1st Addington, Private. Returned as died on service.

BARNUM, Wheeler. 1st Norfolk, Private. Died, disease, March 16, 1813. Entered on Pension List.

BARTHOLEMEW, Henry. 1st York, Private. Died, disease, October 20, 1814. Entered on Pension List.

BARTON, William. 2nd Grenville, Private. Noted in a return of the Flank Companies that he died in 1813.

BARTOU, Edwin. 1st Middlesex, Private. Killed in action, Malcolm's Mills, 1814.

BASSELL, John. York. Killed in action, York, April 27, 1813.

BASTIDO, Joseph. 2nd Lincoln, Private. Killed at Chippewa, July 5, 1814. Entered on Pension List.

BATICHON, Pierre. 2nd Essex, Private. Killed at the River Raisin, January 21, 1813. Entered on Pension List.

BAXTER, John. 3rd Lincoln, *Captain.* Taken prisoner May 30, 1813, and removed to the United States. Returned March 10, 1815.

BAXTER, Nathan. 1st Leeds, Private. Wounded at Brockville, February 7, 1813. Entered on Pension List.

BEAMER, Levi. 2nd Norfolk, Private. Died, disease, October 24, 1812.

BEAUCHAMP, Pierre. 1st Essex, Private. Flank Company. Returned as killed in action at Chippewa, July 5, 1814.

BEAUPRIE, Charles. Provincial Marine, Seaman. Wounded by the enemy on Lake Erie, June 23, 1813, while in the launch of the *Queen Charlotte.* Entered on Pension List.

BELARD, Stephen. Incorporated Militia, Private. Wounded at Lundy's Lane, July 25, 1814. Entered on Pension List.

BELL, Nathaniel. 4th Lincoln, *Quarter Master*. Taken prisoner by the enemy, July 25, 1812. Wounded by the enemy at Schlosser while a prisoner of war, trying to effect his escape, July 26, 1814. Returned as a prisoner of war, held at Pittsfield, Massachusetts, in 1814. Entered on Pension List.

BENDER, John. Niagara Light Dragoons, Trumpeter. Taken prisoner May 28, 1813, at Twelve Mile Creek and removed to the United States.

BENDER, John. 2nd Lincoln, Private. Taken prisoner July 14, 1814, and removed to the United States. Returned July 28, 1814.

BENN, George. 1st Lennox, Private. Died, disease, December 31, 1813. Entered on Pension List.

BENNET, James. 1st Lincoln, Private. Died, disease, January 18, 1813. Entered on Pension List.

BENNET, John. Severely wounded in the leg at Fort Erie, November 1812. Severely wounded at Long Point, November 1813, and lost his other leg.

BERTRAND, John. Incorporated Militia, Bugler. Accidentally wounded on retreat from Fort Erie, October 8, 1814. Right arm amputated. Entered on Pension List.

BIGGERS, James. 5th Lincoln, Private. Taken prisoner July 12, 1813. Returned as a prisoner of war held at Pittsfield, Massachusetts, and having received aid between February 21 and June 24, 1814.

BISSELL, Gilbert. 2nd Grenville, Private. Joined the Incorporated Militia. Died at York, 1814.

BLANCHETTE, Lewis. 2nd Lincoln, Private. Killed in action at Chippewa, July 5, 1814. Entered on Pension List.

BLOOMFIELD (Blumfield), Thomas. 2nd Lincoln, Private. Killed in action at Chippewa, July 5, 1814.

BONDY, Laurente. 1st Essex, *Captain*. Killed at Fort Meigs, May 5, 1813. Entered on Pension List.

BONNET, John. 2nd Norfolk, Private. Wounded, Fort Erie, November 28, 1812. Leg amputated. Entered on Pension List.

BOOK, Joseph. 4th Lincoln, Private. Wounded near Twelve Mile Creek while on guard, July 24, 1814. Entered on Pension List.

BOOTH, Joshua. 1st Addington, *Captain*. Casualty (died) on duty, October 27, 1813. Entered on Pension List.

BORLAND, Andrew. 3rd York, Private. Wounded at York, April 27, 1813. Entered on Pension List.

BOSTWICK, Albia. 1st Grenville, Private. Flank Company. Returned as having died during the war.

BOUCK, David. 2nd Lincoln, Private. Returned as died between November 28 and December 31, 1812.

BOUTHELIER, Francois. 1st Essex, Private. Wounded at Mongwaga (sic), August 9, 1812. Entered on Pension List.

BOWEN, Henry. 1st Lennox, Teamster. Died, disease, February 8, 1813. Entered on Pension List.

BOWMAN, Adam. 2nd Lincoln, Private. Taken prisoner July 11, 1814, and removed to the United States. Returned as a prisoner of war, held at Pittsfield, Massachusetts, in 1814. Returned March 17, 1815.

BOWMAN, Abraham. 2nd Lincoln, *Lieutenant*. Wounded in the action at Chippewa, July 5, 1814. Taken prisoner July 11, 1814, and removed to the United States. Returned March 18, 1815.

BOYER, Martin. 1st Lincoln, Private. Died, disease, April 20, 1813. Entered on Pension List.

BRADT, John. 5th Lincoln, Ensign. Taken prisoner June 10, 1813, and removed to the United States.

BRIGHAM, Moses. 1st Middlesex, Private. Died, disease, August 15, 1814. Entered on Pension List.

BROOK, John. 2nd Lincoln, Ensign. Taken prisoner July 9, 1814, and removed to the United States. Returned March 18, 1815.

BROOKS, William. 2nd Lincoln, Private. Returned as died between November 28 and December 31, 1812.

BROWN, James. Norfolk, Private. Returned as wounded November 28, 1812, in action at Fort Erie.

BROWN, Isaac. 2nd York, Private. Died, disease, December 10, 1812. Entered on Pension List. In the return of 1819 it was stated that he died from the inclemency of the season and want of clothing.

BROWN, Neil. Loyal Kent Volunteers, Private. Wounded, Long Woods, March 4, 1814. Returned as unfit for service. Entered on Pension List. Died April 25, 1816.

BROWN, Robert. 1st Lennox, Private. Flank Company. Returned as died.

BROWN, William. 1st Lincoln, Private. Flank Company. Wounded at Queenston, October 13, 1812. Died of wounds.

BRYANT, John. Incorporated Militia, Corporal. Wounded, Fort Erie, August 12, 1814. Entered on Pension List.

BRYSON, Alexander. 2nd Lincoln Artillery Company, *2nd Lieutenant*. Returned as wounded at Frenchman's Creek, November 1812.

BUCHANNAN, William. 1st Essex, *Captain*. Died, disease, September 19, 1813. Entered on Pension List.

BUCHNER, Martin. 3rd Lincoln, Private. Flank Company. Died, disease June 30, 1813.

BUELL, William. 1st Leeds, Sergeant. Wounded, Ogdensburg, February 22, 1812. Shot through the left pelvis, coming out near the backbone; another ball went through the left arm. Entered on Pension List.

BUNDAGE, Nathan. Died of wounds received in the action at Ogdensburg, February 22, 1813.

BUNNEL, Jesse. Lincoln, Private. Taken prisoner July 9, 1814, and removed to the United States.

BURCH, John. 2nd Lincoln, *Captain*. Taken prisoner July 19, 1814, and removed to the United States. Returned March 18, 1815.

BURNHAM, Asa. 1st Northumberland, *Captain*. Noted as died in March 1813. It is not clear whether he was on actual service.

BURWELL, Mahlon. 1st Middlesex, *Lieutenant Colonel*. Taken prisoner November 30, 1814, and removed to the United States. Returned February 22, 1815.

BURWELL, Robert. 1st Middlesex, Private. Flank Company. Returned as wounded at Lundy's Lane, July 25, 1814. Entered on Pension List.

BUTLER, Francis. 1st Essex, Private. Flank Company. Returned as killed in action at Lundy's Lane, July 25, 1814.

BUTLER, Johnson. 4th Lincoln, *Lieutenant Colonel*. Died, disease, December 1, 1812. Entered on Pension List.

CABASIERE, Pierre. Incorporated Militia, Private. Died, disease, February 1815 while a prisoner of war. Entered on Pension List.

CAIN, Daniel. 1st Glengarry, Private. Wounded at Ogdensburg, February 22, 1813. Entered on Pension List.

CAIRNS (Carns), Peter C. 2nd Lincoln, Private. Taken prisoner July 9, 1814, and removed to the United States.

CAIRNS, Peter. Returned as a prisoner of war held at Pittsfield, Massachusetts, and having received aid between February 21 and June 24, 1814.

CAMERON, David. 1st Glengarry, Sergeant. Accident on duty, Cedars, June 7, 1814. Entered on Pension List.

CAMERON, William. 1st Lincoln, Private. Attached to Captain Powell's Artillery Company. Killed in action at Fort George, May 27, 1813.

CAMPBELL, James. 2nd York, Private. Wounded in the action at Queenston, October 13, 1812.

CAMPBELL, John. 1st Lincoln, Private. Accident on duty, Fort George, October 24, 1812. Entered on Pension List.

CAMPBELL, John. 5th Lincoln, Private. Stabbed by an Indian, Ancaster, November 1, 1814. Entered on Pension List.

CAMPBELL, John. 1st Lincoln, Private. Joined Captain Cameron's Artillery Company; wounded at Fort George May 27, 1813. Taken prisoner June 10, 1813. Returned as a prisoner of war, held at Pittsfield, Massachusetts, and having received aid between February 21 and June 24, 1814.

CAMPBELL, John. Incorporated, *Ensign*. Killed at Lundy's Lane, July 25, 1814.

CAMPBELL, William. 1st Glengarry, Teamster. Died, disease, March 1, 1813. Entered on Pension List.

CAMPBELL, George. 1st Lincoln, Private. Wounded, Fort George, May 27, 1813. Ball through leg and head. Entered on Pension List.

CANADA, C. 4th Lincoln, *Ensign*. Slightly wounded at Lundy's Lane July 25, 1814. (May be same as Ensign Charles Kennedy.)

CARPENTER, James. 5th Lincoln, Sergeant. Died, disease, January 26, 1813. Entered on Pension List.

CARROLL, John. 1st Oxford, *Captain*. Casualty, killed while a prisoner of the enemy, August 27, 1814. Entered on Pension List.

CARSCALLEN, Edward. 1st Hastings, Private. Died, disease, January 25, 1813. Entered on Pension List.

CARTHIER, Pierre. 2nd Essex, Private. Wounded at the River Raisin, January 22, 1813. Entered on Pension List.

CASSELMAN, John. Returned as a prisoner of war held at Pittsfield, Massachusetts, and having received aid between February 21 and June 24, 1814.

CHANDLER, Benjamin. 1st Norfolk, Private. Shot through the neck and killed November 13, 1814.

CHASE, George. Incorporated Militia, Private. Accident on duty, near York, July 1, 1813. Entered on Pension List.

CHISHOLM, William. Incorporated Militia, Private. Wounded, Lundy's Lane, July 25, 1814. Entered on Pension List.

CLAPP, Joseph. 1st Prince Edward, Private. Died on service at Kingston, November 23, 1812.

CLARK, William. 2nd Norfolk, Private. Died, disease, January 19, 1813.

CLARK, John. 1st Glengarry, Private. Returned as ruptured, January 20, 1813. Entered on Pension List.

CLARK, John. 2nd Lincoln, Private. Died, disease, December 4, 1812. Entered on Pension List.

CLEMENT, Jean Baptiste. 2nd Essex, Private. Flank Company. Returned as killed in action at the River Raisin, January 1813.

CLEMENT, Lewis. 2nd Lincoln, *Lieutenant.* Severely wounded at Chippewa, July 5, 1814. Entered on Pension List.

CLENDINNEN, Adam. 1st Norfolk, Private. Killed at Fort Erie, November 28, 1812. Entered on Pension List.

CLENDINNEN, Abraham. 1st Lincoln, Private. Died, disease, October 25, 1812. Entered on Pension List.

CLINTON, William. 5th Lincoln, Private. Taken prisoner June 21, 1813. Returned as a prisoner of war, held at Pittsfield, Massachusetts, and having received aid between February 21 and June 24, 1814.

CLOW, William. 1st Leeds, Private and Teamster. Died, disease, October 22, 1814. Entered on Pension List.

COGHELL, (Cockell), George, 1st Lincoln. Killed at Lundy's Lane, July 25, 1814. Entered on Pension List.

COHO, Nathan. 1st Lincoln, Private. Wounded near St. David's, July 22, 1814. Ball lodged in left shoulder. Entered on Pension List.

COLE, Abraham. 1st Lennox, Private. Died, disease, December 31, 1813. Entered on Pension List.

COLL, Daniel. Loyal Kent Volunteers, Private. Returned as taken prisoner and died.

COLL (Cull), John. Loyal Kent Volunteers, Private. Returned as wounded at Long Woods, March 4, 1814, and disabled in service. Entered on Pension List.

COLL (Cull), William. Loyal Kent Volunteers, Sergeant. Returned as wounded near St. David's, July 22, 1814. Entered on Pension List.

CONKLE, Abraham. 2nd Lincoln, Private. Severely wounded in the thigh at Chippewa, July 5, 1814

CONNELL, John. Incorporated Militia, Private. Wounded at Lundy's Lane, July 25, 1814. Right leg amputated. Entered on Pension List.

CONRAD, David. 2nd Norfolk, Private. Flank Company. Returned as severely wounded at Fort Erie, November 1812.

COOK, Charles. 2nd Lincoln, Private. Shot through the thigh at Fort Erie, November 28, 1812. Reported on January 1, 1813, as recovering very slowly.

COOK, Daniel. 1st (?) Lincoln, Teamster. Died, disease, February 15, 1815. Entered on Pension List.

COOK, Robert. 2nd York, Sergeant. Died, disease.

COON, John. 2nd Lincoln, Private. Died, disease, January 2, 1813. Entered on Pension List.

COPE, William. 1st Norfolk, Private. Died, disease, March 6, 1813. Entered on Pension List.

COPE, Henry. 2nd York, Private. Killed in action at Queenston, October 13, 1812.

CORBIN, Cyrenius. Incorporated Militia, Private. Died, disease, March 12, 1814. Entered on Pension List.

CORLIS, Swain P. 2nd Norfolk, Private. Severely wounded, Malcolm's Mills, November 6, 1814. Entered on Pension List.

CORNELIUS, Pr. (?) Taken prisoner June 1813 at the Sugar Loaf and removed to the United States until exchanged in 1814.

CORNELL, John. 1st Lennox, Private. Accident while on duty, Kingston, November 10, 1812. Entered on Pension List.

COTLAND, Richard. 1st Lincoln, Private. Killed in action at the Battle of Niagara (Fort George), 1813.

COUCENEAUX, Baptiste. 1st Essex, Private. Wounded, River Raisin, January 22, 1813. Ball entered right breast and was lodged there. Entered on Pension List.

COUGER, Gasham. 2nd Lincoln, Private. Returned as died between November 28 and December 31, 1812.

COUGHALL, George. 1st Lincoln, Private. Killed at Lundy's Lane July 25, 1814. He was in Captain Servos's Company. Left a widow and nine children.

COUCK, George. 2nd Lincoln, Teamster. Died, disease, December 4, 1812. Entered on Pension List.

COZENS, Joshua Y. 1st Stormont, *Captain*. Accident, returning from expedition to Salmon River, March 26, 1814. Shoulder dislocated. Entered on Pension List.

CRAWFORD, James. Private. Served as a volunteer with the Royal Naval squadron under Barclay. Wounded in the action on Lake Erie, September 10, 1813.

CRAWFORD, James. Loyal Kent Volunteers, Private. Wounded, at Fleming's, River Thames, July 9, 1814. The inspecting surgeon reported that Crawford suffered four wounds; one ball lodged in the body, two in the gluteus muscle, and a fourth cut across the left thigh. Entered on Pension List.

CRAWFORD, Joseph. 3rd York, Private. Died in hospital following the action at Queenston, October 13, 1812.

CRIER, Samuel. Disabled in the hand by a wound received in action at Chippewa, July 5, 1814.

CROSS, Daniel. 2nd Grenville, Private. Died October 21, 1812.

CROW, Jacob. Lincoln, Private. Taken prisoner July 9, 1814, and removed to the United States. Returned as a prisoner of war, held at Pittsfield, Massachusetts, in 1814.

CUDNEY, Caleb. 1st Lincoln, Private. Flank Company. Killed in action at Fort George April 27, 1813.

CURLES, Swain P. 2nd Norfolk, Private. Wounded at Malcolm's Mills, November 6, 1814. Several gunshot wounds in arm and stomach.

CURRY, James. 1st Grenville, Private. Flank Company. Returned as having died during the war.

CUSHMAN, Artimas William. Addington Dragoons, Private. Accident on duty, September 15, 1812. Entered on Pension List.

DARBY, Dudley. 1st Addington, Private. Died, disease, March 11, 1813. Entered on Pension List.

DAVID, Lewis. 2nd Lincoln, Private. Returned as died between November 28 and December 31, 1812.

DECHAMBER, John. 2nd Lincoln, Private. Taken prisoner July 11, 1814, and removed to the United States. Returned as a prisoner of war, held at Pittsfield, Massachusetts, in 1814. Returned March 14, 1815.

DECHAMBER, Martin. 2nd Lincoln, Sergeant. Taken prisoner July 11, 1814, and removed to the United States. Returned July 28, 1814.

DECOU, John. 2nd Lincoln, *Captain*. Taken prisoner May 29, 1813, and removed to the United States.

DeFORREST, John. 2nd Lincoln, Private. Taken prisoner July 11, 1814, and removed to the United States. Returned as a prisoner of war held at Pittsfield, Massachusetts, in 1814. Returned March 18, 1815.

DeLAMACE, Pierre. 3rd Lincoln, Private. Died while on actual service, 1813.

DELISLE, Jean Baptiste. 1st Essex, Private. Wounded near Fort Meigs, May 5, 1814. Entered on Pension List.

DENICK, Morris. 2nd Lincoln, Private. Wounded at Queenston, October 13, 1812.

DENNIS, Joseph. 3rd Lincoln, Private. Died, disease, January 1815. Entered on Pension List.

DERRICK, Morris. 2nd Lincoln, Private. Wounded at Queenston, October 13, 1812.

DESSEAUX, Joseph. 1st Essex, Private. Wounded at River Raisin, January 22, 1813. Entered on Pension List.

DETLOR, John. 3rd York, *Ensign*. Killed at York, April 27, 1813. Entered on Pension List.

DEVERAUX, John. 1st Lincoln, Sergeant. Died, disease, December 1, 1812.

DEVINE, Simon. 3rd York, Private. Died in hospital following the action at Queenston, October 13, 1812.

DEWAR, John. 2nd Glengarry, Sergeant. Accident, injury of the hip, June 30, 1814. Entered on Pension List.

DICKSON, Thomas. 2nd Lincoln, *Lieutenant Colonel*. Wounded at Chippewa, July 5, 1814.

DIMOND, Jacob. 1st Addington, Private. Returned as died on service.

DIXMAN, John. Incorporated Militia, Private. Taken prisoner July 28, 1813. Returned as a prisoner of war held at Pittsfield, Massachusetts, and having received aid between February 21 and June 24, 1814.

DOAN, Thomas. 2nd Lincoln, Private. Taken prisoner July 9, 1814, and removed to the United States. Returned July 30, 1814.

DOAN, Elijah. 1st Lincoln, Private. Taken prisoner July 25, 1814, and removed to the United States. Returned as a prisoner of war, held at Pittsfield, Massachusetts, in 1814. Returned March 18, 1815.

DOBY, James. 1st Lincoln, Private. Was a gunner in Captain Cameron's Artillery Company and served in the action at Fort George where he was wounded. Taken prisoner June 10, 1813. Returned as a prisoner of war, held at Pittsfield, Massachusetts, and having received aid between February 21 and June 24, 1814.

DONALDSON, Andrew. Captain Merritt's Troop, Private. Taken prisoner June 10, 1813. Returned as a prisoner of war, held at Pittsfield, Massachusetts, and having received aid between February 21 and June 24, 1814.

DRAKE, John. Incorporated Militia, Private. Taken prisoner July 28, 1813. Returned as a prisoner of war held at Pittsfield, Massachusetts, and having received aid between February 21 and June 24, 1814.

DRAKE, Richard. 2nd Norfolk, Sergeant. Wounded, Stoney Creek (Lake Erie), November 12, 1813. Entered on Pension List.

DUEL, Silas. Returned as a prisoner of war, held at Pittsfield, Massachusetts, and having received aid between February 21 and June 24, 1814.

DUFOUR, Jean Baptiste. 2nd Essex, Private. Flank Company. Returned as died on expedition to Fort Meigs, 1813.

DUQUETTE, Antoine. 2nd Lincoln, Private. Died of disease, November 1812.

EAMER, Peter. Stormont, *Lieutenant*. Ruptured by a fall, November 10, 1813. Entered on Pension List.

EATON, Ebenezer. Troop of Grenville Militia Cavalry, Private. Died, disease, March 6, 1813. Entered on Pension List.

EBERTS, Henry. 2nd Essex, Private. Flank Company. Returned as killed in action at Chippewa, July 5, 1814.

ELLIS, David. 1st Oxford, Private. Died, disease, October 27, 1813. Entered on Pension List.

ELSWORTH, George. 1st Northumberland, Private. Ruptured on board a bateau, April 16, 1814. Entered on Pension List.

EMPEY, William. Incorporated Militia, Private. Frostbitten on an expedition to Grass River on the United States side of the St. Lawrence, March 1, 1814. Entered on Pension List.

EMPEY, Philip. 1st Stormont, *Lieutenant*. Wounded, Ogdensburg, February 22, 1813. Right leg amputated. Entered on Pension List.

ENSINGER, Oman. 2nd Lincoln, Private. Returned as died between November 28 and December 31, 1812.

FALKNER, James. 1st Glengarry, Private. Accident at Fort Wellington, July 12, 1813. Fracture of the leg. Entered on Pension List.

FALLINGTON, Joshua. Returned as a prisoner of war, held at Pittsfield, Massachusetts, and having received aid between February 21 and June 24, 1814.

FARNUM, Archelaus. 2nd Leeds, Private. Wounded at Gananoque, September 21, 1812. Shot through the left arm. Entered on Pension List.

FARRINGTON, Samuel. 1st Prince Edward Regiment, Private. Died, disease, December 31, 1813. Entered on Pension List.

FIELDS, Nathan. 1st Kent, Private. Accident while on duty as one of the detachment who conducted the American General Winchester and other prisoners of war to Fort George, January 29, 1813. The knee-pan displaced. Entered on Pension List.

FIELDS, Daniel. Loyal Kent Volunteers, Private. Accident while on duty at Burlington Heights, January 4, 1814. Returned as unfit for service. Entered on Pension List.

FONGER, Philip. 1st Norfolk, Private. Returned as died in 1813. Left four orphan children.

FORBES, Adam. Incorporated Militia, Private. Died, disease, March 6, 1815. Entered on Pension List.

FOREMAN, Achilles. 2nd Leeds, Private. Severely wounded at Ogdensburg, February 22, 1813.

FORSYTH, James. 3rd Lincoln, Private. Served with 2nd Lincoln in 1814. Killed in action, Chippewa, July 5, 1814. Entered on Pension List.

FRASER, William. 1st Grenville, *Captain*. Died, disease, May 17, 1813. Entered on Pension List.

FRASER, Thomas. Incorporated Militia, *Captain*. Wounded, Lundy's Lane, July 25, 1814. Shot in the right arm. Entered on Pension List.

FREEL, David. 1st Leeds, Private. Flank Company. Returned as died on service.

FREY, Bernard. Captain. Killed, Fort George, November 21, 1812.

FULLER, Thadolphus(?). 2nd Grenville, Private. Died March 27, 1813.

FURRAY, John. 3rd Lincoln, Private. Taken prisoner June 16, 1813, and removed to the United States.

FURRAY, Lawrence. 3rd Lincoln, Private. Wounded at Black Rock, December 30, 1812. Recieved three wounds in the same action; one through the left arm, one through the body, and one through the right thigh. Entered on Pension List.

GALLIPOT, John. 2nd Lincoln, Private. Died of disease, November 1812.

GARLO, Peter. Returned as a prisoner of war held at Pittsfield, Massachusetts, and having received aid between February 21 and June 24, 1814.

GARVIN, Claude. 2nd Essex, *Ensign*. Wounded at Frenchtown January 22, 1813.

GENEREUX, Peter. 1st Essex, Corporal. Flank Company. Returned as died at Kingston, March, 1814.

GEORGE, James. 1st Lincoln, *Ensign*. Wounded at Stoney Creek, June 6, 1813. Entered on Pension List.

GILLET, Samuel. 3rd Lincoln, Private. Wounded at Black Rock, December 30, 1813.

GILLMAN, David. 2nd Grenville, Private. Flank Company. Killed in action February 22, 1813.

GIRTY, Thomas. 1st Essex, *Ensign*. Died, disease, September 18, 1812. Entered on Pension List.

GODDARD, Moses. Returned as a prisoner of war, held at Pittsfield, Massachusetts, and having received aid between February 21 and June 24, 1814.

GORDON, Aaron. Loyal Kent Volunteers, Private. Returned as died on service.

GORDON, James. 1st Essex, *Lieutenant*. Wounded at River Raisin, January 22, 1813. Entered on Pension List.

GORDON, John. 5th Lincoln, Private. Captain Hatt's, or First Flank, Company. Died of wounds following the action at Queenston Heights, October 1812.

GOULD, John. Returned as a prisoner of war, held at Pittsfield, Massachusetts, in 1814.

GRAHAM, Hamilton. Returned as a prisoner of war, held at Pittsfield, Massachusetts, in 1814.

GRAHAM, James. 3rd Lincoln, Private. Wounded at Black Rock, December 30, 1813. Entered on Pension List.

GRANT, Angus. 1st Glengarry, Private. Captain Duncan McDonell's Flank Company. Returned as having died on service.

GRANT, Robert. 2nd Lincoln, *Captain*. Taken prisoner July 23, 1814, and removed to the United States.

GRANT, William. 1st Glengarry, Private. Died, disease, February 18, 1813. Entered on Pension List.

GRASS, George. 1st Lincoln, Private. Wounded in the action at Fort George, May 27, 1813. Died in the United States while a prisoner of war.

GREEN, John. 5th Lincoln, Private. Captain Durand's 2nd Flank Company. Wounded at Queenston, October 13, 1812.

GREEN, Samuel. 2nd York, Private. Casualty, died, July 6, 1813. Entered on Pension List.

GRIFFEN, Jonathan. 4th Lincoln, Private. Died, disease, October 20, 1812.

GRIFFES, Bannero. 1st Lincoln, Private. Killed in action, Black Rock.

GROSS, George. 1st Lincoln, Private. Killed in action at Fort George, May 27, 1813. Entered on Pension List.

GROSS, Michael. 1st Lincoln, Private. Died, disease, December 17, 1812. Entered on Pension List.

HAGAR, Jonathan. 2nd Lincoln, Teamster. Died, disease, October 10, 1813. Entered on Pension List.

HAINER, Albert. Private. Died, disease, July 2, 1813.

HAINER, David. 1st Lincoln, Private. Died, disease, October 6, 1813. Entered on Pension List.

HAINER, George. 1st Lincoln, *Captain*. Died, disease, November 22, 1814. Entered on Pension List.

HAINER, Zachariah. 1st Lincoln, Private. Died, disease, February 2, 1813. Entered on Pension List.

HAMBLIN, Silas. 2nd Grenville, Private. Flank Company. Died, disease, February 8, 1813. Entered on Pension List.

HANNAN, William. 5th Lincoln, Private. Flank Company. Returned as died of wounds.

HARDISON, Benjamin. 3rd Lincoln, *Lieutenant*. Taken prisoner July 11, 1814, and removed to the United States. Returned March 18, 1815.

HARTNEY, Patrick. Volunteer with the 8th at York, April 27, 1813, wounded, barrack master at York. One ball passed through the right leg, one through the left, and a third entered the left thigh.

HASPLEHEM, George. Cameron's Provincial Artillery Company, Gunner. Returned as drowned at Queenston.

HATT, Richard. 5th Lincoln, *Major*. Severely wounded at Lundy's Lane July 25, 1814.

HAWEY, Stephen. 2nd Lincoln, Private. Severely wounded at Chippewa, July 4, 1814

HAZEL, Richard. 1st Essex, Private. Died, disease, October 10, 1812. Entered on Pension List.

HEAD, Jonathan. 1st Prince Edward, Private. Died on service, 1812.

HEBERT, Beela. 5th Lincoln, Private. Died, disease, November 1812. Entered on Pension List.

HEDENER, John. Taken prisoner June 1813 at the Sugar Loaf and removed to the United States until exchanged in 1814.

HENDERSHOT, John. 5th Lincoln, Private. Flank Company. Killed at the Lime Kiln near Queenston, September 18, 1812.

HERON, William. Private. Severely wounded in the action at Queenston, October 13, 1812.

HICKS, Joseph. 1st Prince Edward, Private. Died, disease, October 24, 1813. Entered on Pension List.

HICKSON, Daniel. 2nd Lincoln, Private. Returned as died between November 28 and December 31, 1812.

HILL, John. 2nd Lincoln, Private. Killed at Chippewa, July 5, 1814.

HODGKINS, Isaac. 2nd Lincoln, Private. Returned as died between November 28 and December 31, 1812.

HODGKINS, William. 3rd Lincoln, Private. Flank Company. Returned as died in 1814.

HODKINSON, Samuel. 1st Lincoln, Private. Wounded at Fort George, May 27, 1813. Entered on Pension List.

HOLLIDAY, John. Cameron's Provincial Artillery, Gunner. Returned as killed in an affray at Munn's Tavern.

HOLMES, Daniel. Loyal Kent Volunteers, Private. Wounded, Longwoods, March 4, 1814. Entered on Pension List.

HORTON, Samuel. 1st Norfolk, Private. Wounded, Fort Erie, November 28, 1812. Entered on Pension List.

HOVERLAND, John. Captain Alexander Hamilton's Troop of Horse, Private. Returned as died near Chippewa, 1812.

HULBERT, James. 1st Lincoln, Sergeant. Died, disease, May 4, 1813

HULL, Kiah. Incorporated Militia, Private. Died, disease, June 1813. Entered on Pension List.

HULL, Richard. Incorporated Militia, Private. Wounded, Fort Erie, August 12, 1814. Entered on Pension List.

HUMBERSTONE, Thomas. Incorporated Militia, *Lieutenant.* Taken prisoner and removed to the United States, where he was held as one of the "hostages."

HUMPHREY, Ezekiel. 3rd Lincoln, Sergeant. Flank Company. Returned as died in 1813.

HUNT, Edward. 2nd Lincoln, Private. Taken prisoner July 24, 1814, and removed to the United States. Returned November 12, 1814.

HURST, Isaac. Returned as a prisoner of war, held at Pittsfield, Massachusetts, in 1814.

HUTCHISON, George. Provincial Marine, Seaman. Wounded, Lake Erie, September 10, 1813. Entered on Pension List.

HUTT, John. 2nd Lincoln, Sergeant. Killed in action at Chippewa, July 5, 1814.

HUTTS, Anthony. Coloured Corps, Private. Returned as taken prisoner by the enemy and died while imprisoned.

JACKSON, John. Coloured Corps, Private. Died, disease, February 13, 1813. Entered on Pension List.

JARVIE, William. 3rd York, *Lieutenant.* Wounded and taken prisoner at York, April 27, 1813. Right hand disabled, musket ball passed through wrist. Entered on Pension List.

JARVIS, William M. 3rd York, *Lieutenant.* Wounded at York by the explosion of the magazine of the West Battery, April 27, 1813. Lost an eye. Entered on Pension List.

JOHNSON, Freeman. 1st Oxford, Sergeant. Died, disease, December 10, 1812. Entered on Pension List.

JOHNSTON, James. 4th Lincoln, Private. Died, disease, at Chippewa.

JOHNSTON, John. 4th Lincoln, Private. Died, disease, at Chippewa, November 12, 1812. Entered on Pension List.

JONES, John. 1st Lincoln, *Captain.* Died, disease, Burlington, Vermont, while a prisoner of war, December 24, 1814. Entered on Pension List.

KELLAN, Jacob. 1st Lennox, Private. Died at Kingston, 1812.

KELLY, John. 5th Lincoln, Private. Captain Hatt's Flank Company. Wounded between September 25 and October 24, 1812.

KENDRICK, Duke William. 3rd York, *Lieutenant.* Died, disease, January 1, 1813. Entered on Pension List.

KENNEDY, Andrew. 3rd York, Private. Wounded at Queenston, October 13, 1812. Leg amputated. Entered on Pension List.

KERBY, James. 2nd Lincoln, *Captain.* Wounded when a 24-pounder gun under his command burst at Fort Erie, December 2, 1812. Middle finger of his right hand disabled. Severe gunshot wound in his right shoulder, August 12, 1814. Entered on Pension List.

KERNS, Peter. 2nd Lincoln, Private. Taken prisoner June 10, 1813, and removed to the United States.

KERR, Robert. 5th Lincoln, Private. Wounded in the action at Queenston, October 13, 1812.

KILLMAN, Jacob. 2nd Lincoln, Sergeant. Taken prisoner July 22, 1814, and removed to the United States. Returned as a prisoner of war, held at Pittsfield, Massachusetts, in 1814. Returned March 18, 1815.

KING, George, 2nd York, *Lieutenant.* Died, disease, December, 1812. Entered on Pension List.

KIRKPATRICK, Robert. 2nd Lincoln, *Ensign.* Dangerously wounded at Chippewa, July 5, 1814. Entered on Pension List.

KNIGHT, Charles. 3rd Lincoln, Private. Taken prisoner July 12, 1813, and removed to the United States.

KNIGHT, John. Taken prisoner June 1813 at the Sugar Loaf and removed to the United States until exchanged in 1814. Returned as a prisoner of war, held at Pittsfield, Massachusetts, and having received aid between February 21 and June 24, 1814.

KYES, Asahel. 1st Leeds, Private. Died, disease, July 14, 1813. Entered on Pension List.

LAGUE, Jean Baptiste. Incorporated Militia, Private. Wounded at Lundy's Lane, July 25, 1814.

LAJAY, Joseph. Captain Fraser's Troop of Provincial Dragoons, Private. Returned as died in hospital, February 1815.

LAJEUNESS, Pierre. 2nd Essex, Private. Flank Company. Returned as died in service, 1812.

LAMPMAN, Peter Jr. 1st Lincoln, Private. Severely wounded at Fort George, May 27, 1813.

LA TOUR, Joseph. 1st Frontenac, Private. Died, disease, March 31, 1813. Entered on Pension List.

LANCASTER, William. 3rd York, Private. Died, disease, December 29, 1812. Entered on Pension List.

LANCE, Asa. Captain Brigham's Rifle Company, Private. Returned as deceased while on service.

LAUGHTON, John. Returned as a prisoner of war, held at Pittsfield, Massachusetts, in 1814.

LAURASON, Joseph. 5th Lincoln, Private. Wounded at Lundy's Lane July 25, 1814.

LAWE, George L. 1st Lincoln, *Captain*. Wounded at Fort George, May 1813. Taken prisoner and removed to the United States.

LAWE, George William. 1st Lincoln, Private. Killed in action, Battle of Niagara (Fort George), May 27, 1813.

LAWRENCE, George. Private. Taken prisoner at Fort George, May 27, 1813, and removed to the United States. Returned as a prisoner of war, held at Pittsfield, Massachusetts, and having received aid between February 21 and June 24, 1814.

LAYMAN, Tobias. Norfolk, Private. Returned as wounded, November 28, 1812, in the action at Fort Erie.

LeGREEN, Eustach. Incorporated Militia, Private. Wounded at Lundy's Lane, July 25, 1814.

LEE, Francis. 3rd York, Private. Wounded at Queenston, October 13, 1812. Two severe wounds. Entered on Pension List.

LEE, Peter. Coloured Corps, Private. Accident while on fatigue at Fort Niagara, March 10, 1814. Died, disease, January 1, 1817. Entered on Pension List.

LEMMON, William. 1st Grenville, Private. Fracture of left arm from fall from a blockhouse, Fort Wellington, June 5, 1813. Entered on Pension List.

LIMBURNER, (Lymburner) Alexander. 4th Lincoln, Private. Died, disease, August 13, 1814. Entered on Pension List.

LIVINGSTON, Robert. Indian Department, *Captain*. Wounded August 17, 1813, at the Cross Roads, near Fort George. Entered on Pension List.

LOGAN, Alexander. 5th Lincoln, Private. Taken prisoner June 16, 1813, at the Sugar Loaf and removed to the United States until exchanged in 1814.

LOGAN, Gabriel. 2nd Essex, Private. Flank Company. Returned as died.

LOGAN, James. Returned as a prisoner of war held at Pittsfield, Massachusetts, and having received aid between February 21 and June 24, 1814.

LONG, Joseph. Incorporated Militia, Private. Wounded at the Cross Roads near Fort George, September 19, 1813. Accidental discharge of a musket. Entered on Pension List.

LOTTRIDGE, John. 5th Lincoln, *Captain*. Died, disease, November 29, 1812. Entered on Pension List.

LOUKS, John. 1st Addington, Private. Returned as died on service.

LUNDY, Benjamin. 2nd Lincoln, Private. Killed by accident while off duty.

LUTZ, Jacob. Returned as a prisoner of war, held at Pittsfield, Massachusetts, in 1814.

LYKINGS, Archer. 5th Lincoln, Private. Died, disease, at Chippewa, December 1812.

MACKAY, Hector S. 2nd York, *Captain*. Slightly wounded at Lundy's Lane, July 25, 1814.

MADILEN, Stalia. Returned as a prisoner of war, held at Pittsfield, Massachusetts, and having received aid between February 21 and June 24, 1814.

MAJOR, John Pell. Niagara Light Dragoons, Cornet. Mortally wounded during the cutting out of the *Detroit*, October 9, 1812.

MAJOR, Thomas. 3rd York, Private. Captain Cameron's Company. Badly wounded at Queenston, October 13, 1812. Lost the calf of his leg. Entered on Pension List.

MALTIMORE, William. Incorporated Militia, Private. Shot in the leg at Lundy's Lane, July 25, 1814. Entered on Pension List.

MANUEL, Frederick. 1st Norfolk, Private. Flank Company. Returned as died, December 1812.

MARKLE, William. 5th Lincoln, Sergeant. Died at St. David's in January 1813.

MARKS, Cornelius. 1st Oxford, Sergeant. Died, disease, January 1, 1813. Entered on Pension List.

MARLET, George. 2nd York, Sergeant. Died, disease.

MARTEN (Martin), James. 3rd Lincoln, Private. Shot in the right arm, December 30, 1813, at Black Rock. Entered on Pension List.

MARTIN, John. Addington Dragoons, Private. Died, disease, December 4, 1814. Entered on Pension List.

MATHEWS, Christopher. 1st Durham, Private. Flank Company. Returned as died in hospital.

MATHEWS, John. 1st Norfolk, Private. Flank Company. Returned as severely wounded at Fort Erie. Entered on Pension List.

MAY, John. 1st Lincoln, *Lieutenant*. Died, disease, November 8, 1812. Entered on Pension List.

McAFEE, Dennis. 1st Lincoln, Private. Died, disease, December 3, 1812.

McBEAN (McBain), Farquar. 1st Glengarry, Private. Wounded at Ogdensburg, February 22, 1813. Wounded with seven shot in the right knee. Entered on Pension List.

McCARTHY, Adam. 2nd York. Private. Returned as having died during the war.

McCLEAN, Allan. 1st Kent, Private. Casualty, February 1, 1813.

McCLELLAN, Martin. 1st Lincoln, *Captain*. Killed at Fort George May 27, 1813.

McCOLLUM, Daniel. 4th Lincoln, Sergeant. Wounded at Lundy's Lane, July 25, 1814. Entered on Pension List.

McCOLLUM, Colin. 2nd Lincoln, Private. Died, disease, December 12, 1812. Entered on Pension List.

McCORMICK, William. 1st Essex, *Lieutenant*. Wounded at Frenchtown, January 22, 1813. Promoted *Captain*. Taken prisoner late 1813 or early 1814.

McDERMID, Donald. 1st Glengarry, *Lieutenant*. Wounded, Ogdensburg, February 22, 1813. Entered on Pension List.

McDONALD, Alexander. 2nd Lincoln, Private. Killed at Chippewa, July 5, 1814.

McDONALD (McDonell), Christopher (Christian). 2nd Lincoln, *Lieutenant*. Killed at Chippewa, July 5, 1814. Entered on Pension List.

McDONALD, David. Captain Merritt's Troop, Private. Taken prisoner June 10, 1813. Returned as a prisoner of war, held at Pittsfield, Massachusetts, and having received aid between February 21 and June 24, 1814.

McDONALD, Donald. 1st Glengarry, Private. Wounded at Ogdensburg, February 22, 1813. Entered on Pension List.

McDONALD, Lachlan. 1st Glengarry, Private. Hurt by accident on the retreat from Hoople's Creek, November 11, 1813. Entered on Pension List.

McDONELL, Angus. 2nd Glengarry, Private. Taken prisoner November 10, 1813, and removed to the United States. Escaped from Greenbush on February 26, 1814, and returned home.

McDONELL, Angus. 2nd Glengarry, Private. Died, disease, March 15, 1813. Entered on Pension List.

McDONELL, Archibald. 2nd Glengarry, Private. Taken prisoner November 10, 1813, and removed to the United States. Escaped from Greenbush on February 26, 1814, and returned home.

McDONELL, Donald. 1st Stormont, *Ensign*. Died, disease, March 20, 1813. Entered on Pension List.

McDONELL, John. 1st Stormont, *Captain*. Returned as hurt, February 22, 1814, contusion of the breast by the pole of a sleigh while returning from Four Corners. Entered on Pension List.

McDONELL, John. Incorporated Militia, *Captain*. Wounded at Lundy's Lane and lost left arm. Entered on Pension List.

McDONELL, John. 1st Glengarry, Private. Wounded in the action at Ogdensburg, February 22, 1813. Entered on Pension List.

McDONELL, Hugh. 2nd Glengarry, Private. Died, disease, February 28, 1813. Entered on Pension List.

McDOUGAL, Angus. Incorporated Militia, Sergeant. Wounded at Lundy's Lane, July 25, 1814. Entered on Pension List.

McDOUGALL, Daniel. Incorporated Militia, *Lieutenant*. Severely wounded (seven times) at Lundy's Lane, July 25, 1814. Entered on Pension List.

McDOUGAL, Donald. 2nd Glengarry, Teamster. Died, disease, February 1, 1813. Entered on Pension List.

McDOUGALL, Lauchlin. Loyal Kent Volunteers, Private. Wounded at Long Wood, March 4, 1814. A ball entered his abdomen and lodged there. Entered on Pension List.

McDOUGAL, Peter. Indian Department, Volunteer. Wounded in service at Lewistown, December 19, 1813. Entered on Pension List.

McGRATH, John. 1st Prince Edward, Private. Died, disease, April 30, 1814. Entered on Pension List.

McGRATH, John. Incorporated Militia, Private. Accidently wounded in the thigh, September 21, 1814, near Fort Erie and died three days later. Was returning from the batteries in front of Fort Erie when his detachment was fired on by one of the British picquets in reserve.

McGREGOR, James. Loyal Kent Volunteers, *Lieutenant.* Wounded July 9, 1814, on the Thames. A ball entered near his spine and was lodged near his hip joint. Entered on Pension List.

McGREGOR, John. Loyal Kent Volunteers, *Captain.* Severely wounded at Longwoods, March 4, 1814. Arm amputated. Entered on Pension List.

McGREGOR, John. 1st Glengarry, Private. Captain Duncan McDonell's Flank Company. Returned as having died of wounds.

McINTYRE, Angus. 3rd Lincoln, Private. Taken prisoner June 16, 1813. Returned as a prisoner of war, held at Pittsfield, Massachusetts, and having received aid between February 21 and June 24, 1814.

McINTYRE, John W. 5th Lincoln, *Adjutant.* Wounded, Queenston, October 13, 1812.

McINTYRE, William. 2nd Grenville, Flank Company. Died in 1813.

McKAY, Donald. 2nd Glengarry, *Captain.* Died, disease, May 4, 1813. Entered on Pension List.

McKEACHIE, John. 1st Dundas, Private. Hurt by accident at Fort Wellington, October 22, 1814. Lost an eye. Entered on Pension List.

McKEE, Peter. 5th Lincoln, Private. Wounded at Lundy's Lane, July 25, 1814.

McKENZIE, Roderick. 1st Glengarry, Private. Broke his leg while on duty at River Raisin, October 28, 1813. Entered on Pension List.

McKERLIE, William. Lincoln, *Ensign.* Taken prisoner July 22, 1814, and removed to the United States. It is not known in which regiment he was commissioned.

McKINNON, Charles. 2nd Glengarry, Private. Wounded during Wilkinson's advance, November 10, 1813. Entered on Pension List.

McLAUGHLAN, (?) He "received a severe wound in the head, by which he became deranged and sometimes outrageous and still continues."

McLAUGLIN (McGloughlan) Robert. Incorporated Militia, Private. Returned as killed.

McLEAN, Allan. 1st Kent, Private. Casualty, died, February 1, 1813. Entered on Pension List.

McLEAN, Archibald. 3rd York, *Lieutenant*. Wounded at Queenston, October 13, 1812.

MCLEAN, Donald. Volunteer. Killed at York, April 27, 1813.

McMARTIN, William. Returned as a prisoner of war, held at Pittsfield, Massachusetts, and having received aid between February 21 and June 24, 1814.

McMICHAEL, George. 1st Norfolk, Sergeant. Killed in action near Fort Erie, November 28, 1812.

McMULLEN, William. 1st Hastings, Private. Attached to the Addington Dragoons. Fractured his leg while on duty in conveying the military express bag, December 12, 1812. Entered on Pension List.

McNAUGHTON, Duncan. 1st Glengarry, Private. Captain Duncan McDonell's Flank Company. Returned as having died during the war.

McNAUGHTON, Robert. 1st Glengarry, Private. Hurt by accident while on duty, March 21, 1814. Entered on Pension List.

McPHERSON, Alexander. 1st Glengarry, Private. Hurt by accident while on duty at Fort Wellington, September 7, 1814. Entered on Pension List.

McPHERSON, Daniel. 1st Addington, Private. Died, disease, January 3, 1815. Entered on Pension List.

McPHERSON, John Sr. 1st Glengarry, Private. Captain Duncan McDonell's Flank Company. Returned as having died on service.

McPHIE, Angus. 2nd Glengarry, Private. Died, disease, March 15, 1813. Entered on Pension List.

MEEKS, Joseph. Returned as a prisoner of war, held at Pittsfield, Massachusetts, and having received aid between February 21 and June 24, 1814.

MELOCHE, Louis. 1st Essex, Private. Died, disease, May 18, 1813. Entered on Pension List.

MERKLEY, Christopher. 1st Durham, Teamster. Died, disease, March 15, 1814. Entered on Pension List.

MERRITT, William Hamilton. Niagara Light Dragoons, *Captain*. Taken prisoner at Lundy's Lane, July 25, 1814, and removed to the United States.

METTS, John. 1st Lennox, Private. Died at Kingston, 1812.

MILLARD, David. 2nd Lincoln, Private. Returned as died between November 28 and December 31, 1812.

MILLARD, Thomas. 2nd Lincoln, Private. Taken prisoner July 9, 1814, and removed to the United States. Returned as a prisoner of war, held at Pittsfield, Massachusetts, in 1814. Returned March 18, 1815.

MILLER, James. Provincial Marine, Acting Sailing Master. Died, disease, while a prisoner in captivity, October 9, 1814. Entered on Pension List.

MILLS, Solomon. 2nd York, Sergeant. Died, disease, July 5, 1814. Entered on Pension List.

MILLS, William. 1st Essex. *Captain*. Wounded at Frenchtown, January 22, 1813.

MITCHEL, John. Loyal Kent Volunteers, Private. Returned as wounded, Longwoods, March 4, 1814, and unfit for service. Entered on Pension List.

MITCHELL, William. Incorporated Militia, Private. Wounded at Fort Erie, August 12, 1814. Entered on Pension List.

MOONE, Edward. Provincial Dragoons. Returned as a prisoner of war, held at Pittsfield, Massachusetts, in 1814.

MOORE, James. 2nd Grenville, Private. Flank Company. Died January 22, 1813.

MONTANIER, Elijah. 3rd Lincoln, Private. Taken prisoner June 16, 1813. Returned as a prisoner of war, held at Pittsfield, Massachusetts, and having received aid between February 21 and June 24, 1814.

MONTRASS, Benjamin. Cameron's Provincial Artillery, Gunner. Taken prisoner after the retreat from Fort George.

MOREY, Samuel. 2nd Grenville, Private. Flank Company. Died January 16, 1813.

MOTT, Jeremiah. 1st Leeds, Private. Flank Company. Killed in action with the enemy.

MUDGE, Elijah. 1st Oxford, Private. Returned as hurt by accident, February 13, 1814. Entered on Pension List.

MULLET, James A. Incorporated Militia, Sergeant. Severely wounded in action at the Cross Roads, October 8, 1813. Entered on Pension List.

MUNRO, Finlay. 2nd Glengarry, Private. Wounded at Hooples Creek, November 10, 1813. Entered on Pension List.

MURPHY, John. Incorporated Militia, Private. Returned as a prisoner of war, held at Pittsfield, Massachusetts, and having received aid between February 21 and June 24, 1814.

MURRAY, Daniel. 3rd York, Private. Killed at York, April 27, 1813. Entered on Pension List.

NELLES, Henry. 4th Lincoln, *Captain*. Taken prisoner July 25, 1814 and removed to the United States.

NELLES, William. 5th Lincoln. Taken prisoner July 12, 1813. Returned as a prisoner of war, held at Pittsfield, Massachusetts, and having received aid between February 21 and June 24, 1814.

NELLES, William. 4th Lincoln, *Captain*. Slightly wounded at Lundy's Lane, July 25, 1814.

NEVILLS, Jacob. 2nd Lincoln, Sergeant. Taken prisoner July 22, 1814, and removed to the United States. Returned as a prisoner of war, held at Pittsfield, Massachusetts, in 1814. Returned March 17, 1815.

NEWKIRK, Benjamin. 1st Lincoln, Private. Died, disease, November 13, 1812. Entered on Pension List.

NUNN, Samuel. 4th Lincoln, Private. Died, disease, December 1, 1812.

O'REILLY, Daniel. 2nd York, *Lieutenant*. Taken prisoner July 22, 1814 and removed to the United States.

OVERFIELD, Emmanuel. 2nd York, *Lieutenant*. Severely wounded at Lundy's Lane, July 25, 1814.

OVERHATT, John Jr. 1st Lincoln, Private. Died, disease.

PALMER, John. Lincoln, Private. Taken prisoner July 22, 1814, and removed to the United States. Returned as a prisoner of war, held at Pittsfield, Massachusetts, in 1814.

PATTERSON, John. 1st Lennox, Private. Died, disease, December 12, 1812. Entered on Pension List.

PATTERSON, Leslie. 1st Middlesex, *Captain*. Taken prisoner May 20, 1814.

PEASE, Allanson B. 1st Middlesex, Private. Flank Company. Returned as died in service.

PEDRAIL, Francis. Returned as a prisoner of war, held at Pittsfield, Massachusetts, in 1814.

PEER, Stephen. 2nd Lincoln, Private. Wounded at Queenston, October 1812. Killed at Chippewa, July 5, 1814. Entered on Pension List.

PELTON, Phineas. Returned as a prisoner of war, held at Pittsfield, Massachusetts, and having received aid between February 21 and June 24, 1814.

PETERSON, William. 2nd Lincoln, Private and Teamster. Accident, May 3, 1813. Leg broken and amputated above the knee. Entered on Pension List.

PETIT, Uriah. 2nd Norfolk, Sergeant. Died, disease, January 1, 1813. Entered on Pension List.

PETRIE, Philip. 2nd Lincoln, Private. Wounded while on service.

PETRIE, Philip. Royal Provincial Artillery Drivers, Private. Hurt by the accidental explosion of a musket at Queenston, May 13, 1813. Entered on Pension List.

PETTIT, Isaac. 1st Prince Edward, Private. Died on service.

PEW, Samuel. 2nd Lincoln, Private. Died, disease, September 10, 1813. Entered on Pension List.

PLUMMERFELDT, John. 1st Lincoln, Private. Died, disease.

POWELL, Caleb. 1st Norfolk, Private. Wounded at Malcolm's Mills, November 6, 1814. Entered on Pension List.

POWER, William. 1st Lincoln, *Lieutenant*. Taken prisoner May 24, 1813, and removed to the United States.

PROSSER, Samuel. Incorporated Militia, Private. Wounded at Fort Erie, August 12, 1814. Entered on Pension List.

PULSE, David. 1st Addington, Private. Died, disease, June 14, 1813. Entered on Pension List.

QUICK, Alexander. 1st Essex, Private. Hurt in fall on the ice while on march to attack the enemy at River Raisin, January 22, 1813. Entered on Pension List.

QUICK, David. 1st Essex, Private. Wounded at River Raisin, January 22, 1813. Perhaps same as David Quick of the Kent Volunteers, returned as wounded and taken prisoner. Entered on Pension List.

RABBEE, Jean B. Provincial Artillery Drivers, Private. Casualty, March 20, 1813, kicked by a horse. Returned as killed during the war. Entered on Pension List.

RANDOLPH, Samuel. 2nd Grenville, Flank Company. Wounded, Prescott, October 24, 1812 (in one return date, given as October 4). Entered on Pension List.

REAUME, Paschal. 1st Essex, Private. Flank Company. Killed at River Raisin, January 21 or 22, 1813. Entered on Pension List.

REAUME, Michael. 2nd Essex, Private. Wounded at the River Raisin, January 22, 1813. He was shot through the right leg below the knee. Entered on Pension List.

REDDOCK, Adam. 1st Dundas, Teamster. Returned as a casualty, March 1, 1813. Leg amputated. Entered on Pension List.

RHEA, John. 2nd Lincoln, Sergeant. Killed in action at Chippewa, July 5, 1814.

RIBBLE, (Rible) Anthony. 2nd Lincoln, Private. Wounded at Chippewa, July 5, 1814. Ball passed through his lower body, coming out his right buttock. Entered on Pension List.

RICE, Joseph. 2nd Lincoln, Sergeant. Taken prisoner July 9, 1814, and removed to the United States. Returned as a prisoner of war, held at Pittsfield, Massachusetts, in 1814. Returned January 30, 1815.

RICHARDSON, James. Provincial Marine, *Lieutenant*. Wounded at Oswego, May 6, 1814. Entered on Pension List, but note made that he received an allowance from the Quarter Master General's Department.

RICHARSON, Robert. Provincial Artillery Drivers, *Lieutenant*. Severely wounded by a musket ball at Frenchtown, January 22, 1813.

RIFENBURG, George. Provincial Artillery Drivers, Private. Returned as killed during the war.

ROBERTS, William. 1st Essex, Private. Died May 10, 1813, as a result of wounds received at Fort Meigs, May 5, 1813. Entered on Pension List.

ROBINSON, James. 2nd Grenville, Flank Company. Wounded at Ogdensburg, February 22, 1813. Brother of Joseph B. Robinson.

ROBINSON, Joseph B. 2nd Grenville, Flank Company. Wounded at Ogdensburg, February 22, 1813. Entered on Pension List.

ROCK, John. 3rd Lincoln, Private. Died, disease, December 1, 1812. Entered on Pension List.

ROSE, Alexander. Incorporated Militia, *Lieutenant*. Hurt while on duty at Fort Wellington, July 26, 1813. Fell from a blockhouse and fractured his thigh. Entered on Pension List.

ROSE, Alexander. 1st Lincoln, Private. Wounded at Chippewa, July 5, 1814. Entered on Pension List.

ROSE, Michael (Hugh Rose?). 2nd York, *Ensign*. Taken prisoner July 3, 1814, and removed to the United States.

ROSS, Thomas. 1st Glengarry, Private. Wounded at Ogdensburg, February 22, 1813. Entered on Pension List.

ROW, Coleman. Provincial Marine, Seaman. Wounded in the action on Lake Erie, September 10, 1813. Entered on Pension List.

ROW, John. 2nd Lincoln, *Captain*. Killed at Chippewa, July 5, 1814.

RUTTAN, Henry. Incorporated Militia, *Lieutenant*. Severely wounded at Lundy's Lane, July 25, 1814. Shot through the upper body. Was still not recovered as of February 1816. Entered on Pension List.

RYAN, John. Royal Provincial Artillery Drivers, Private. Wounded at Lundy's Lane, July 25, 1814. Entered on Pension List.

RYCKMAN, Samuel. 2nd York, *Captain*. Severely wounded at Lundy's Lane, July 25, 1814.

RYERSON, George. 1st Norfolk, *Lieutenant*. Wounded at Frenchman's Creek, November 28, 1812. Shot through the mouth; the ball fractured the jaw and came out the neck. Entered on Pension List.

SABOUREN, Dominique. Returned as a prisoner of war, held at Pittsfield, Massachusetts, and having received aid between February 21 and June 24, 1814.

SAUNDERS, Mathias. 1st York, Private. Died of wounds received in action at York, April 27, 1813

SECORD, David. Returned as a prisoner of war, held at Pittsfield, Massachusetts, and having received aid between February 21 and June 24, 1814.

SECORD, James. 1st (probably should read 2nd) Lincoln, *Captain*. Wounded at Queenston, October 13, 1812. Entered on Pension List.

SEELEY, John. Incorporated Militia, Private. Wounded at Lundy's Lane, July 25, 1814. Arm amputated. Entered on Pension List.

SELLS, Anthony. 1st Oxford, Private. "Arm fractured in aiding and suppressing a Mutiny among a detachment of the said Militia," October 11, 1814. Entered on Pension List.

SERVIS, Thomas. 1st Stormont, Private. Wounded at Ogdensburg, February 22, 1813. Left leg amputated. Entered on Pension List.

SERVOS, John D. 1st Lincoln, *Captain*. Wounded at Black Rock and Buffalo, January 1, 1814. Entered on Pension List.

SERAM, Benjamin. 1st Middlesex, Sergeant. Flank Company. Returned as wounded in action with the enemy in Westminster.

SHANNON, Lanty. 2nd Lincoln, Private. Severely wounded at Chippewa, July 5, 1814.

SHAW, William. Loyal Kent Volunteers, Private. Returned as died of wounds, March 6, 1814.

SHEPARD, Joseph. 3rd York, Private. Captain Duncan Cameron's Company. Wounded in the explosion at York, April 27, 1813. Three left ribs broken and the left thigh "dreadfully mangled" and noted as still not healed in February 1816. Entered on Pension List.

SHUFELT, Casper. 3rd Lincoln, Private. Died on service, 1813.

SILVERTHORNE, Thomas. 1st Norfolk, Private. Wounded November 27, 1812. Entered on Pension List.

SIMONS, Titus Geer. 2nd York, *Major*. Dangerously wounded at Lundy's Lane and right arm disabled, July 25, 1814. Entered on Pension List.

SIMONS, John. 2nd York, *Adjutant*. Taken prisoner July 25, 1814, and removed to the United States.

SKELLY, Daniel. 3rd Lincoln, Private. Died on service.

SKINNER, Benjamin. 2nd Lincoln, Private. Returned as died between November 28 and December 31, 1812.

SKINNER, Colin. 2nd Lincoln, Private. Taken prisoner June 21, 1813. Returned as a prisoner of war, held at Pittsfield, Massachusetts, and having received aid between February 21 and June 24, 1814.

SKINNER, Hagai (Haggy). 2nd Lincoln, Private. Taken prisoner June 21, 1813. Returned as a prisoner of war, held at Pittsfield, Massachusetts, and having received aid between February 21 and June 24, 1814.

SKINNER, Timothy. 2nd Lincoln, Private. Killed in action at Chippewa, July 5, 1814.

SLY, John. 2nd Leeds, Private. Flank Company. Wounded, September 21, 1812.

SMALLMAN, George. 3rd York, Sergeant. Wounded at Queenston, October 13, 1812.

SMITH, Benjamin. 1st Prince Edward, Private. Died, disease, October 31, 1814. Entered on Pension List.

SMITH, Chancey. 1st Oxford, Private. Accidentally shot, died, November 5, 1814. Entered on Pension List.

SMITH, Gabriel. 2nd Lincoln, Private. Returned as died between November 28 and December 31, 1812.

SMITH, Jacob. 3rd York, Private. Ruptured while on fatigue duty by the rolling of a cask against the abdomen in the commissariat store at York, October 15, 1812. Entered on Pension List.

SMITH, John. Returned as a prisoner of war, held at Pittsfield, Massachusetts, in 1814.

SMITH, Mathias. 5th Lincoln, Private. Flank Company. Died at Chippewa, 1812.

SMITH, Stephen. 1st Leeds, Private and Teamster. Died, disease, February 24, 1813. Entered on Pension List.

SMITH, Thomas. 3rd York, Private. Killed in action at Queenston, October 13, 1812.

SMITH, Thomas. 2nd York, *Ensign* (or *Lieutenant*). Severely wounded and disabled at Lundy's Lane, July 25, 1814. Entered on Pension List.

SMYTH, John. Fraser's Troop of Provincial Light Dragoons, Private. Wounded at Chrysler's Farm, November 11, 1813. Wounded in the waist.

SNYDER, Jacob. Incorporated Militia, Private. Severely wounded at Lundy's Lane, July 25, 1814. "One ball passed through his body, one through his left hand, one ball injured his left side, another ball fractured his right shoulder and a fifth ball lodged in the cranium behind the right ear, which last wound impairs his understanding, especially at the change of weather." Entered on Pension List.

SPEARS, James. Loyal Kent Volunteers, Private. Returned as disabled in service.

SPOOR, Stephen. 5th Lincoln. Taken prisoner July 12, 1813. Returned as a prisoner of war, held at Pittsfield, Massachusetts, and having received aid between February 21 and June 24, 1814.

SPRINGER, Daniel. 1st Middlesex, *Captain*. Taken prisoner, seized from his home, bound and taken away in his sleigh, February 1, 1814, and imprisoned in Kentucky. Returned in time to lead his company at Lundy's Lane, July 25, 1814.

SPOONER, Nazareth. 1st Frontenac, Private. Died, disease, October 13, 1813. Entered on Pension List.

STEPHANS, Nicholas. 1st Lincoln, Private. Taken prisoner July 21, 1813, and removed to the United States.

STEPHENSON, Charles. 4th Lincoln, Private. Died, disease, November 8, 1812.

STEVENS, Michael. Returned as a prisoner of war held at Pittsfield, Massachusetts, and having received aid between February 21 and June 24, 1814.

STEWARD, Daniel. 1st Lincoln, Private. Wounded at Queenston, October 13, 1812. Entered on Pension List.

STEWART, Enoch. Militia Artillery, Private. Died, disease, March 19, 1813. Entered on Pension List.

STICKEL, John. 2nd Lincoln, Private. Died, disease, December 10, 1812. Entered on Pension List.

STOREY, Johnstone. 1st Essex, Sergeant. Died, disease, June 30, 1813.

STORKEY (Starkey), William. Incorporated Militia, Private. Taken prisoner June 16, 1813. Returned as a prisoner of war, held at Pittsfield, Massachusetts, and having received aid between February 21 and June 24, 1814.

STORMS, Henry. 1st Addington, Private. Died, disease, March 31, 1813. Entered on Pension List.

STOVEN, Martin. 1st Addington, Private. Returned as died on service.

STURGES, Daniel. 1st Lincoln, Private. Taken prisoner July 16, 1814, and removed to the United States. Returned as a prisoner of war, held at Pittsfield, Massachusetts, in 1814.

STURGIS, William. 5th Lincoln, Sergeant. Wounded at Lundy's Lane, July 25, 1814.

STREET, Timothy. 2nd York, Private. Noted as wounded and died.

STULL, Adam. 1st Lincoln, Sergeant. Wounded, Fort George, May 27, 1813. Entered on Pension List.

SUMMERS, George. Loyal Kent Volunteers, Private. Returned as died on service, July 9, 1814.

SWEARS, Peter. 2nd Lincoln, Private. Taken prisoner July 9, 1814, and removed to the United States. Returned July 30, 1814.

TALLAN, David. 2nd Lincoln, Private. Returned as died between November 28 and December 31, 1812.

TAYLOR, Robert. 2nd Lincoln, Private. Killed in action at Chippewa, July 5, 1814.

TEETER, Aaron. 4th Lincoln, Private. Accident while on the march to oppose the enemy, July 15, 1814. Entered on Pension List.

TEETER, Michael Jr. 4th Lincoln, Private. Died on service.

TERRY, John. Returned as a prisoner of war, held at Pittsfield, Massachusetts, and having received aid between February 21 and June 24, 1814.

THOMPKINS, George. 2nd Grenville, Private. Flank Company. Died January 4, 1813.

THOMPSON, David. 2nd Lincoln, *Adjutant*. Slightly wounded at Lundy's Lane, July 25, 1814.

THOMPSON, Edward. 3rd York, Private. Slightly wounded in the breast at Queenston, October 13, 1812.

THOMPSON, Frederick. 1st Lincoln, Private. Wounded at St. David's, July 18, 1814. Entered on Pension List.

THOMPSON, James. 2nd Lincoln, Private. Slightly wounded at Chippewa, July 4, 1814

THOMPSON, John. 2nd Lincoln, Private. Killed in action, Chippewa, July 5, 1814.

THORPE, Samuel T. 3rd Lincoln, Private. Taken prisoner June 16, 1813. Returned as a prisoner of war, held at Pittsfield, Massachusetts, and having received aid between February 21 and June 24, 1814.

TITUS, Gilbert. 2nd Leeds, Private. Flank Company. Wounded September 21, 1812.

TOLES, James. 2nd Lincoln, Private. Slightly wounded at Chippewa, July 5, 1814.

TOMKINS, Jeremiah. 1st Prince Edward, Private. Died, Kingston, December 27, 1812

TOWSLEY, Sikes. 1st Oxford, *Major*. Taken prisoner April 5, 1814, and removed to the United States. Exchanged and returned September 24, 1814.

TREANOR, David. 5th Lincoln, Private. Captain Durand's 2nd Flank Company. Wounded at Queenston, October 13, 1812. Died of wounds. Entered on Pension List.

TURNEY, George. 2nd Lincoln, *Captain*. Killed at Chippewa, July 5, 1814.

TYRER, John. 3rd York, Private. Severely wounded in both legs at Queenston, October 13, 1812.

VAIL, James. 1st Middlesex, Private. Flank Company. Returned as drowned near Fort Wellington, 1814.

VANATTA, Ambroise. 1st Lincoln, Private. Taken prisoner June 21, 1813. Returned as a prisoner of war, held at Pittsfield, Massachusetts, and having received aid between February 21 and June 24, 1814.

VAN CAMP, Jacob. 1st Grenville, Private. Flank Company. Noted as having died on service.

VANSICKEL, David. 5th Lincoln, Private. Died, disease, at Chippewa, December 1812.

VANSKINER, Peter. 1st Prince Edward, Private. Died on service.

VROOMAN, John. 2nd Lincoln, Private. Taken prisoner July 9, 1814, and removed to the United States. Returned July 30, 1814.

WALKER, Edward. Incorporated Militia, *Captain*. Killed at seige of Fort Erie, August 12, 1814.

WALKER, James. Coloured Corps, Private. Wounded at Fort George, May 27, 1813. Entered on Pension List.

WALKER, Isaac. 4th Lincoln, Private. Died, disease, November 4, 1812.

WARD, James. Captain Brigham's Rifle Company. Private. Returned as deceased while on service.

WARD, William. Loyal Kent Volunteers, Private. Returned as taken prisoner by the Americans.

WARNER, Zachariah. 2nd York, Private. Wounded, Lundy's Lane, July 25, 1814. Entered on Pension List.

WARREN, John 2nd Lincoln, *Ensign*. Taken prisoner July 22, 1814, and removed to the United States. Returned March 18, 1815.

WATERS, Hyel. 2nd Lincoln, Private. Returned as died between November 28 and December 31, 1812.

WATERS, John. 2nd Lincoln, Private. Flank Company. Returned as died while on duty in 1812.

WEIR, Samuel. 2nd Lincoln, Private. Wounded at Chippewa, July 5, 1814. Entered on Pension List.

WELLS, Jesse. Addington Dragoons, Private. Fracture of his arm while on duty, December 26, 1812. Entered on Pension List.

WHALEN, Patrick. 1st Lincoln, Private. Taken prisoner July 9, 1814, and removed to the United States. Returned as a prisoner of war, held at Pittsfield, Massachusetts, in 1814. Returned March 18, 1815.

WHEATON, Joseph. 1st Lincoln, Private. Wounded at St. David's, July 22, 1814. "A rifle ball passed through his left eye, which has deprived him of the use of it, and so injured his head, as to at times cause him very violent pain." Entered on Pension List.

WHITE, Nathaniel. 2nd Norfolk, *Captain*. Died on service, March 15, 1814.

WHITTEN, John. 1st Lincoln, Private. Wounded at St. David's, July 24, 1814. Lost an eye.

WIGLEY, Christopher. 1st Essex, Private. Died, disease, October 11, 1812.

WILKINSON, Jacob. 2nd Lincoln, Private. Killed in action at Chippewa, July 5, 1814.

WILLIAMS, John. 1st Lennox, Private. Flank Company. Returned as died.

WILLIAMS, Titus. 2nd Norfolk, *Lieutenant*. Taken prisoner by the enemy, May 25, 1813, and removed to the United States. Returned July 9, 1814.

WILSON, Gilman. 1st Middlesex, *Captain*. Taken prisoner May 20, 1814.

WILSON, John. Jr. 2nd Lincoln, Private. Taken prisoner July 9, 1814, and removed to the United States. Returned as a prisoner of war, held at Pittsfield, Massachusetts, in 1814. Returned March 18, 1815.

WILSON, Samuel. 1st Norfolk, Private. Flank Company. Returned as died in 1813.

WINTERBOTTOM, Samuel. Provincial Artillery Drivers, Private. Returned as killed during the war.

WINTERBOTTOM, Samuel. 1st Lincoln, Private. Served with Captain Cameron's Provincial Artillery Company and was taken prisoner May 28, 1813. Returned as a prisoner of war, held at Pittsfield, Massachusetts, and having received aid between February 21 and June 24, 1814. Returned as having rejoined the Artillery Company after exchange. (Perhaps same as above.)

WINTERMUTE, Abraham. 2nd Lincoln Artillery Company, Private. Returned as died on service, November 18, 1812.

WINTERMUTE, Philip. 3rd Lincoln, *Ensign*. Noted in a return of 1816 as "killed in action with the enemy in the late war."

WOLFROM, Philip. Captain Henry Davy's Company, Incorporated Militia, Private. Drowned at Kingston, August 23 (or 21), 1813.

WOOD, John. 1st Durham, Private. Flank Company. Died on service.

WOODRUFF, Henry. 1st Lincoln, Private. Taken prisoner July 11, 1814, and removed to the United States. Returned as a prisoner of war, held at Pittsfield, Massachusetts, in 1814. ·

WRIGHT, Charles. 1st Lincoln, Private. Attached to the volunteer artillery. Killed in action, Fort George, May 27, 1813.

WRIGHT, Peter. 2nd Lincoln, Private. Returned as died between November 28 and December 31, 1812.

WULFFE, Conrad. 1st Lincoln, Private. Attached to Captain Powell's Artillery Company. Returned as died on service.

WYCOFF, John. 2nd Norfolk, Private. Flank Company. Returned as killed in action at Fort Erie.

YEOMAN, Johnson. 3rd York, Private. Died on his return from Queenston, autumn of 1812. It is not stated if he had been wounded.

YOUNG, Charles. Provincial Marine, Seaman. Wounded in the action on Lake Erie. September 10, 1813. Entered on Pension List.

YOUNG, Harry. 1st Prince Edward, *Lieutenant*. Flank Company. Died at Kingston, December 1812.

YOUNG, Henry. 1st Lennox, Private. Died at Kingston, December 12, 1812.

ZULMER, George. Provincial Marine, Seaman. Wounded in the action on Lake Erie, September 10, 1813. Entered on Pension List.

BIBLIOGRAPHIC NOTE

THE records of the Upper Canadian Militia in Record Group 9 in the collection of the National Archives of Canada, Ottawa are the primary source for this handbook. The adjutant general's correspondence, militia returns, muster lists, and pay records present the researcher with a large, unwieldy, and often contradictory mass of information.

It would be impractical to note all the other sources of in formation used in this text. The register of volunteers has been primarily drawn from the nominal roll created in 1819–20 and found in RG 9, IB7. The officer's names recorded in the militia list were compiled and created by study of numerous documents scattered throughout Record Groups 8 and 9. Noting all the vagaries of spelling and dates of commission and appointment would have resulted in footnotes and explanatory notes as long as the book itself.

The list of casualties is based on the published list of those eligible to receive pensions and has been significantly augmented with references scattered throughout returns and muster lists. It is not complete, but it does give a truer picture of the situation. There are several men who are found in one register who should be found in another, but are not recorded there. This is because no reference to them was located in other accounts and in other contexts. This work must be viewed as an invitation for further research, not as the definitive work on the men and corps of 1812–15.

It must be emphasized that there are many discrepancies in the spelling of names, listing of appointments, and the submission of returns. In very many instances the numerical returns in the militia records reflect the last information submitted, which might well be one, two, or even three years out of date. What was called for was not necessarily what was reported. And beyond that, the reliability of each commanding officer in submitting the return must be considered on an individual basis.

The most reputable returns and dependable information about the militia concern pay. All claims submitted had to be endorsed by the regular officer in command and sworn by the militia commanding officer before a magistrate.

It is important to note that many of the surviving records, especially the collections of militia general and district orders, were assembled following the war and are not complete. Adjutant General Nathaniel Coffin collected what copies of orders he found in the files of the department and supplemented them with copies of orders required to authorize appointments, as a part of the process of establishing claims following the war. It would be fallacious to employ the volume of general orders to establish any sort of pattern for courts-martial and so on. The volumes can be used as an aid, but to use them in any other way is a distortion of the events and occurrences of the day.

The best and most complete records that have survived are those connected with claims. Paymaster Samuel Street of Niagara died before his accounts had been settled and the militia claims on the government had been satisfied, and as a result there is excellent documentation for this district. Those claims for pay and allowances (for example, for fuel, candles, bat and forage) for officers, though allowed, were not entertained or approved for months and in many cases years after incurred for the reason that they could not be met, as there was no specie to pay them with. As a result, these are also very well documented.

Other important sources include the Freer, Claus, Clark and McDonell Papers; Record Group 5, A1, Upper Canada Sundries; and Record Group 8, C series, British Military Records; all at the National Archives.

A number of the most significant documents in Record Group 8 have been reprinted by E. A. Cruikshank and Wm. Wood in their invaluable compilations, but there are still a great number of important letters and reports that have not been published and have not been adequately indexed or noted in the finding aids. A close examination of this record group proves very rewarding. While a number of the microfilm reels are available at the Archives of Ontario, its collection is incomplete.

The contemporary newspapers published in York (Toronto), Kingston and Lower Canada are essential sources, as are of course the statutes of the legislature. Much more work can be done on the occurrences of the wartime sittings.

Drawing on the existent pay records, I have assembled a list of some 11,000 men who served in one of the militia corps during the war. While one can establish with some confidence the rolls of those who served in most districts, the Eastern District must remain a mystery, with its astounding number of men with identical names, which difficulty is compounded by the idiosyncratic usage of Mc, Mac and M'— and, most notoriously, by the interchangeable use of McDonell and MacDonald. A further complication results from the practice in the Eastern, Johnstown and Midland Districts (and to a lesser extent in Newcastle) to note only the number of days served within a month or six-month period, which was a result of settling claims for pay months after service was rendered. Another difficulty in determining who was doing what and when is the result of many men serving outside their local units. For example, men from the 3rd Lincoln were mustered with the 2nd after the fall of Fort Erie in 1814 and the enemy's occupation of their townships.

The most comprehensive records for the areas west of Kingston commence in October 1812. For the most part, pay lists for the Niagara and the Home District for July and August, and in many instances September, 1812, have not survived.

Among the published works on the War of 1812, some of the most important are those of Ernest A. Cruikshank, whose knowledge of those times and numerous articles and collections of documents remain an essential resource. Like every other researcher, I only wish that many of his sources were available to us today. What was in those collections and notebooks he studied that he did not deem fit to include?

For the interested student, E. A. Cruikshank's documentary histories are inescapable and invaluable; so too is William Wood's *Select British Documents of the Canadian War of 1812* (Toronto: Champain Society, 1920).

L. Homfray Irvings, *Officers of the British Forces in Canada* (Welland: 1908), is a valuable work in that it is an invitation to build on what he had collated; but based on land records, it presents an incomplete list of the officers who did serve or were commissioned during the war.

Recently there have been a number of extremely good books published on specific aspects of the war and its participants; especially worthy of note are two works of D. E. Graves, *The Battle of Lundy's Lane* (Baltimore, Maryland: 1993) and *Red Coats and Grey Jackets* (Toronto: Dundurn Press, 1994).

G. F. Stanley's *War of 1812, Land Operations* (Toronto: MacMillan, 1983) is an important and lively account of the war on the land across the continent, but awaits the companion volume(s) still in preparation on the war on the Lakes.

The *Dictionary of Canadian Biography* is the right arm of anyone studying Canadian history. The references are always succinct and to the point. The only complaint a researcher can have is of the men who were not included, but should have had some recognition, in this definitive account of the men and women who played crucial roles in shaping our past.